"With *The Perfect Loaf* Maurizio Leo has given all bread-heads, whether newbies or experienced bakers, the ideal gift. In his organized and engaging writing style, Maurizio has demystified the process and science of sourdough baking so that anyone can make, and even improve upon, their loaves."

—PETER REINHART, author of *The Bread Baker's Apprentice* and host of *Pizza Quest*

"Maurizio Leo's book has everything anyone would want to know about the art and science of bread baking, written beautifully and clearly for the first-time baker and the long-obsessed. This book is an encyclopedic and approachable addition to the canon from an anchor of the bread baking community."

—JENNIFER LATHAM, author of *Baking Bread with Kids*

"Maurizio has distilled a lifetime of knowledge into a perfectly complete bible for every bread baker. This thorough guide to baking the best bread you've ever tasted is a must-have for anyone who loves bread."

—DAN RICHER, author of *The Joy of Pizza*

"There is no book written specifically for home bakers that surpasses this one. Maurizio presents each topic, however small, with precision and clarity, and meticulously elucidates even the most complex subjects. Maurizio has written a classic, and his book will have enduring relevance."

—JEFFREY HAMELMAN, baker and author of *Bread: A Baker's Book of Techniques and Recipes*

"For those looking to make professional-quality bread and perfect every element of baking bread at home, *The Perfect Loaf* will guide you there by giving you not just recipes but also the tools to think like a baker."

—BRYAN FORD, author of *New World Sourdough*

"For the home and professional baker, Maurizio's deep dive into the craft of sourdough is an incredible addition to our arsenal of grain greatness, an ideal marriage of science and sensibility. He reminds us of what brings us to the table and what we remember and yearn for once we step away from it. Perfect indeed."

—CHRIS BIANCO, author of *Bianco* and chef/owner of Pizzeria Bianco

WITHDRAWN

THE
PERFECT
LOAF

For Luca and Avi

THE PERFECT LOAF

The Craft and
Science of
Sourdough
Breads, Sweets,
and More

Maurizio Leo

Photographs by Aubrie Pick

CLARKSON POTTER/PUBLISHERS
NEW YORK

CONTENTS

INTRODUCTION

IT'S EARLY MORNING IN MY HOME KITCHEN and, as usual, I'm at the counter with my red grain mill loaded with wheat berries. I ready the hand-operated gristmill to produce fresh, fragrant flour for today's dough as sunlight streams in through the windows. I smell the aromas of fresh flour and sourdough starter and feel a familiar mix of anticipation and early morning energy. This ritual kicks off a day structured around fermentation, mixes, folds, and shapes. An opportunity to connect my hands with a tangible output, a pathway for creativity and expression. In today's world of notifications and keyboards and screens, the simple act of dunking my hands into a bowl containing only sourdough, salt, flour, and water—squishing and squeezing to combine the elementary ingredients—is utterly satisfying. A primordial contentment.

Made from three simple ingredients, bread doesn't need to be complicated—they certainly didn't have a digital thermometer in ancient Rome. The beauty of baking bread is it's a craft that can be as deep and complicated as you want it to be. It can be as simple as mixing that handful of ingredients in a bowl, letting it ferment, and then baking it when ready. But it can be complex, too: Just talk to any longtime baker about their starter maintenance or levain builds and you'll likely uncover a topic of great passion and intricacy.

As your baking experience increases, your proficiency and knowledge of every facet of the process grow deeper. Over time, even the seemingly smallest details, like what temperature your starter is kept at in the kitchen, or the angle at which you hold your bench knife to preshape dough, can become exciting areas of focus, opportunities for growth, or a chance to test something new. The entire act of baking becomes a playground, a place to satisfy a curiosity or express your creativity, all leading to the enjoyment you feel as you nourish yourself and others. And no matter your experience or your level of rigor, the resulting bread will almost always be delightful.

But what exactly is "the perfect loaf"? If you talk to ten different bakers, each will furnish a different story. Each will pause in thought, then proceed to talk about the crust, the crumb, the aroma, the flavor—a laundry list of distinctive qualities that attempt to pin down the loaf they are searching for, the loaf that might finally come out of the oven the next bake. For me, it's the loaf that is light in hand with an open interior, a crunchy crust baked dark and menacing that shows all the colors between dark mahogany and light brown. It's bread with just enough sourness from the natural fermentation to make your mouth water, with enough wholesomeness from whole grains to let you know this food is nourishing and honest. This list with these adjectives is constantly unfolding as my skill set evolves and expands, as experiments are performed and lessons learned—an endless pursuit of perfection that begins anew with every mix of flour and water.

In truth, I don't think there is such a thing as a perfect loaf, but rather, it's in the work toward that goal where the reward for baking truly lies: The small steps along the winding path, the valuable additions and revelations uncovered—that's where we discover the joy in the smallest of details. The baker's journey is replete with these moments of satisfaction: each time we get our hands dirty mixing flour and water, when we're presented with a light and airy dough that's just asking to be shaped, and that moment we pull loaves from the oven that have us gasp in contentment. Sure, there will be missteps along the way, loaves that didn't rise how we wanted (or even at all), ones that tasted uninspiring, others with a dull and inert crust. But in every mix, every shape, every bake, there's a lesson to be learned. And with each lesson, we're a step further along our path. The joy is in the process, the discovery, endless exploration, and constant improvement. The result of our toil with fermentation, flour, hydration levels, and doughs of all kinds is the contentment seen on the faces of those with whom we share our bread.

Ultimately, baking sourdough bread is your own personal journey toward the bread you want to bake and enjoy, and this book is the result of my attempt to help you get there.

ABOUT ME, THE OBSESSED SOURDOUGH BAKER

I GREW UP AMID SACKS OF FLOUR, CANS OF tomatoes, artichokes, and black olives, flour on the bench and in the air, the sounds of a giant mixing arm diving, spinning, and churning pizza dough. As a kid in my dad's Italian restaurant, everything was something to explore, to taste, to take apart, a chance to learn something new. I was always surrounded by food made by hand, whether it was in our restaurant or at home with my mom and grandmother, making pasta from scratch or polenta "like we had in Italy." This early exposure to the joys of cooking and baking stuck with me, even though I ended up going on to get a master's degree in computer science. My engineering degree was in the complete opposite direction from cooking and baking, but it was a place for me to explore and tinker in a different way, appealing to my love of precision, algorithms (they're recipes, after all), and experimentation.

After nearly a decade of being a software engineer, I serendipitously found my way into baking sourdough bread after reading Chad Robertson's *Tartine Bread*. His story and description of naturally leavened bread—sourdough, a breathing and living thing—captivated my scientific side and my appreciation for dedicating yourself to a time-honored craft. My baking was further influenced by experts such as Dave Miller (for his use of sourdough, freshly milled flour, and whole grains), Jeffrey Hamelman (whose sheer breadth of baking knowledge and willingness to teach others are inspiring), and Ken Forkish (for writing a pragmatic book for the home baker who is filled with questions and scientific curiosities). These bakers helped evolve my idea of what it means to make real, honest bread. Many of the techniques I use now grew from what I learned from these bakers, and it's safe to say my baking wouldn't be where it is today without their instruction and inspiration—to them (and many others) I owe my thanks.

In 2012, I launched The Perfect Loaf, my website dedicated to naturally leavened bread. I created the website to document my sourdough baking experiments and to help others learn from my discoveries in the home kitchen. The site has given me the opportunity to connect with many inspiring bakers from around the world, learning from their styles of baking and sharing mine—sourdough bread baking never ceases to be an area for study, discovery, and even debate. The bread-baking community is a special lot made up of people from all walks of life, a generous and caring bunch who've discovered this craft in one way or another, and found themselves equally as gripped as I am.

Since creating my first sourdough starter more than a decade ago, the world of science in that little jar has kept me fascinated with baking sourdough bread. It's been a way for me to engage my scientific side and reconnect with my roots in food. I've been baking sourdough ever since, in an ever-increasing quantity, and these days so much so that I might as well be running a bakery from my home.

This book is the culmination of all my sourdough trials, experiments, classes, research, and countless interactions with bakers at all levels over the past decade. My hope is that after you read it you will approach sourdough baking with the same unending curiosity and eagerness I do—there are endless avenues for exploration, learning, and satisfaction when baking sourdough from home. This book will help you find your way down the path of breadmaking and jump-start the discovery of your own style of sourdough bread. And regardless of just how winding or crooked your path is, it doesn't hurt that the result of each experiment is a loaf of incredibly delicious and nutritious bread.

HOW TO USE THIS BOOK

I WROTE THIS BOOK AS A GUIDE TO TEACHING you how to think like a baker, not follow a recipe. While there are plenty of fantastic recipes in here, this book is also about learning to adopt the sourdough baker's mindset, to sharpen your senses, and to build your own baker's intuition. This means learning to interpret the signs of your starter and "read the dough," assessing its consistency and how it's progressing as it ferments each day. Though these recipes and techniques have been meticulously tested, there's rarely a time when the conditions in your kitchen are exactly like mine, so learning to adapt is key. I'll explain every fundamental part of the process in immense detail, anticipating and answering any question you might have and addressing the potential issues you may encounter. (My time with my website over the past decade, and the many questions I answer there daily, has certainly taught me the needs of home bread bakers—beginners or not.)

Many of the recipes in this book are brand new, of course, but I've also selected some of the fan favorites from the past ten-plus years at *The Perfect Loaf*—the classics, if you will. Together, this compilation of recipes represents a comprehensive survey of sourdough baking in an array of forms and difficulty levels. The recipes cover a whole range of sourdough creations—from classic loaves and pizzas to more unexpected offerings, like drop biscuits, bagels, and even sweets like cinnamon rolls and doughnuts. (Note that the recipes in the Free-Form Loaves and Pan Loaves chapters are roughly listed from easy to advanced methods.) Each recipe was chosen not only for how delicious the result is, but also to teach you a different facet of sourdough baking, like a mini lesson. For example, a recipe may teach you how to adjust the sourness in your bread, how to effectively mix in enrichments (dairy, egg, and sugar), or how to time your starter, levain, and dough so your bread is ready to bake when you are. Armed with this solid foundation, many recipes to flex your burgeoning skills, and countless tips, you'll learn not only to bake beautiful bread, but also to make the necessary adjustments along the way with confidence, relishing in both the process and the result. Throughout, you'll also find QR codes that link to helpful instructional videos if you are a more visual learner—simply scan with the camera app on your phone (no special app needed) and follow the link.

This book is uniquely organized to speak to both beginners and seasoned bakers alike, so you can choose your own way to experience it, dipping into the depths you're comfortable with or most excited about. No matter your baking experience, this book offers a place for you to dig in, stoke your curiosity, hopefully learn something new, and in the end, bake some delicious sourdough bread.

If You're a Total Beginner

If you have never baked sourdough bread or are intimidated by the whole thing, don't be. The breadmaking process may initially seem very long and complicated, but mostly the dough is left to rise unattended, with you stepping in from time to time to guide it along the way. Once you have a few loaves of bread under your belt, your confidence will grow alongside your proficiency, and what was once unknown and intimidating will be not that big of a deal. And again, the amount of detail and guidance I'll provide will never leave you feeling lost. At each step I'll describe and show how the dough should look, feel, and even smell—all to help you hone your senses and begin building your baker's intuition.

For beginners or those who need a refresher, dive right into Welcome to Your First Sourdough Loaf (page 24). This section takes you from making a sourdough starter from scratch to a finished sourdough loaf with ease, and should dispel any intimidation factor. Just pick up a few bags of flour and some tools, make a starter with my foolproof technique, and about a week and a half later you will enjoy your very first sourdough loaf.

This first recipe for a simple sourdough is written tutorial-style, heavily annotated so you'll feel like you're sitting in a baking class with me, where I walk you through each and every step. I recommend sticking with this basic recipe for a few bakes to get a feel for the process and how to handle the dough. The temptation to quickly skip to another recipe is great, but resist if you can; sticking to the same recipe will quickly build your baking proficiency and make subsequent bakes that much easier. At the end of the recipe, you'll find ways to level up for next time and a troubleshooting guide if you need it.

Riff and practice with this loaf as long as you like. Once you're ready to know more, you can try all the great recipes in the book—an endless baking playground to explore. And to level up your sourdough baking, check out the in-depth Technique section (page 58)—to dig into each step of the process in more detail—and Sourdough Science 101 (page 132) to learn more about maximizing fermentation, dialing in a dough's hydration, the impact dough temperature has on bread flavor and texture, and more. Beginners may find these sections intimidating at first glance, but think of them as a reference, full of FAQs and troubleshooting tips, for when inevitable questions come up and extra guidance is needed.

If You're a Seasoned Bread Baker

I hope this book brings a few more insights into your baking and helps you become a better, more intuitive baker, just as I have learned from the generosity of many others. If you're already a bread baker, then you know how inviting and encouraging the bread-baking community is—and I'm hoping this book, in perhaps some small way, contributes to the craft that's captivated us all.

To begin, you might first head to the Technique section and Sourdough Science 101, which provide a comprehensive and detailed look at my approach to sourdough baking as well as the fascinating science that helps guide us in the kitchen. Then, check out a few of the recipes that sound challenging and interesting to you. Many of the recipes in this book provide an opportunity to play and experiment, and you'll find a How to Tinker section at the end with ideas to take things further. If you're looking for immediate baking satisfaction, might I suggest the Rustico (page 195) or Naturally Leavened Brioche (page 283)? Rustico is one of my all-time favorite recipes for its nuanced depth of flavor and heightened textural contrast between a crispy crust and tender crumb—it's sure to delight. The brioche is a challenging yet elegant loaf that showcases the strength of gluten and the power of natural fermentation.

BAKER'S INTUITION

Mastery of any task requires repetition and feedback, and, unfortunately, sourdough bread baking has a relatively long feedback loop. Little notes throughout the book point out key things to observe and a little science to help inform and build up your baker's intuition. Over the years, I've found that some of my biggest baking advancements come from the moments when I've stepped back to assess the dough with a clear perspective and asked questions about why the dough looked and felt a certain way. It's through the accumulation of these small moments that I've built up an intuitive sense for how fermentation is progressing, how the dough strength has evolved, and even how my direct interaction with the dough has impacted the process.

I

ESSENTIAL INGREDIENTS AND TOOLS

Ingredients

TO ME, ONE OF THE MOST SPECTACULAR THINGS about baking sourdough bread is the fact that you need only water, flour, salt, and your starter. That's it. Just four things to make a voluminous bread with a crunchy crust and tender interior that also happens to be incredibly flavorful and nutritious. The following list of essential ingredients is short because to make wonderful sourdough bread, you don't need all that much.

Flour

Flour is arguably the most important ingredient in baking. As the single largest component in most bread recipes, it should be given the same careful consideration a chef gives to choosing a star ingredient in a recipe. At this moment, we're in a lucky position: Small, local mills are springing up all over, and ordering flour and grain online couldn't be easier. For a home baker keen on experimentation, this means almost limitless combinations of flour varieties, each with its own flavor profile, baking properties, and nutritional characteristics. It's certainly an exciting time to be a baker.

In this section, I'll look at the flours used most often in this book and offer some practical advice on buying, using, and storing flour in the home kitchen.

Note: The recipes and processes in this book are from the perspective of a baker in the United States, where flour is typically stronger (i.e., with a higher protein percentage) than the varieties found in other parts of the world. With stronger flour, an increased dough hydration is typically needed for the best eating quality. Many of the recipes call for holding back a portion of the water to help you adjust the hydration as necessary to suit the flour in your area.

FLOUR USED IN THIS BOOK

When it comes to flour, I tend to gravitate toward using organic flour for the health aspect of it, though not always so—but I avoid bleached flour. Flour can be a complicated topic, as there are no agreed-upon standards throughout the world, with each country having its own classification system. If you don't have access to a flour listed in a recipe in this book, refer to What If I Don't Have the Flour Called for in a Recipe? on page 18 for substitutions.

Here's a list of a few flour brands that will work well in the recipes and that are readily available:

- King Arthur Baking Company

- Bob's Red Mill

- Arrowhead Mills

In addition to these common flour options, I'd encourage you to look in your area for local growers and millers, who often have flour specifically designed for breadmaking in addition to heritage varieties of wheat, spelt, rye, and other grains. Ultimately, finding your preferred flour for breadmaking takes trial and error and is highly specific for the type of bread you're looking to make in your kitchen. I recommend ordering a 5-pound bag from a few places and giving them a try! The following list is only a handful of the wonderful growers and millers out there, but here are a few of my favorites across the United States:

- Central Milling (for Artisan Baker's Craft Plus and Type-85, two of my most used flours)

- Giusto's Vita-Gran (for Artisan Unbleached Malted Bread Flour)

- Cairnspring Mills (excellent high-extraction flour of all types)

- Barton Springs Mill (a wonderful mix of heritage grains)

- Hayden Flour Mills (beautiful Sonora wheat)

Next, let's look at a few classes of flour you'll find throughout this book.

White Flour (~11.5% Protein)

I sometimes like to refer to this category as "medium-protein bread flour" to signify that it falls somewhere between high-protein and low-protein flours, since the protein level is key here. (See Bread Flour vs. High-Protein White Flour, opposite, for more on the sometimes confusing labeling conventions.) I prefer a medium protein level for loaves with a delicate and tender crumb, but one that still has ample volume. Generally, all-purpose flour falls into this bucket, though the term "all-purpose" can encompass a very wide range of flour specifications (especially the protein percentages, which can vary wildly from brand to brand) as the flour is meant to address a wide range of baking needs (quick bread, cookies, pies, biscuits, etc.). Therefore, I do find that flour specifically designed for breadmaking, such as Central Milling Artisan Baker's Craft—which can handle longer fermentation times, kneading, and more bread-specific processes—can produce better results than a general all-purpose flour. However, if you're using an all-purpose flour, readily available brands that work well for this flour class include King Arthur Baking Company, Bob's Red Mill, and Arrowhead Mills.

Whole Wheat Flour

Whole wheat flour in this book refers to flour that is made from 100% of the whole wheat berry. The protein percentage of whole wheat is higher than all-purpose, typically 13% to 14% protein and can be even higher, because the flour uses the entire wheat berry, including the bran portion, which is high in protein. In general, you'll find recipes that have higher percentages of whole wheat also require a higher dough hydration (as the bran and germ particles that are present absorb significantly more water). The resulting bread will usually have a tighter, more compact crumb, but with dramatically increased flavor and nutrition.

High-Protein White Flour (~12.7% to 14% Protein)

High-protein white flour is typically around 13% protein and is sometimes labeled "bread flour." I use high-protein white flour to:

- Lay a strong structural foundation, especially when a dough needs additional strength to support a large quantity of inclusions (like nuts and dried fruit) or a high percentage of enrichments (like butter in a brioche)

- Handle longer fermentation times

- Give the resulting product a little extra chew (like with Bagels, page 367)

WHY WHEAT?

Wheat has properties that have led it to be the prominent grain used in breadmaking. Wheat is unique due to its viscoelastic nature—that is, when mixed with water and formed into a dough, it's able to stretch and expand without tearing (extensible), while at the same time it's shapeable and formable (elastic). Gluten, a storage protein and important component of wheat, is mostly composed of two specific types of protein, gliadin and glutenin. Malleable gliadin gives the dough its ability to expand, while glutenin is responsible for elasticity and strength. Together, these two make up the viscoelastic nature of a wheat-based dough. This provides bakers with an airtight medium in which carbon dioxide gas can be trapped as fermentation progresses, and with a dough that can still be formed into any desired shape.

Assuming all else is in place, the higher protein content typically results in a taller rise with a more open interior.

Generally, I prefer to use as little high-protein white flour as possible in my baking. Depending on the recipe, I find using too much high-protein white flour can result in bread with excessive chew and a gummy texture; this is especially true for lean doughs (doughs without enrichments).

Type-85 Flour

Type-85 flour is flour that is somewhere between white (which has very little bran and germ) and whole wheat (which has all of its bran and germ). I love using Type-85 flour in my baking because it hits the sweet spot: There's ample flavor and nutrition from the increased bran and germ, but it still retains many of the characteristics of white flour, producing light and airy loaves with a delicate texture. In the end, this can result in a loaf with a tall rise, open interior, and fantastic flavor.

If you can't find Type-85 flour, you can get close in crumb color by mixing 65% white flour (~11.5% protein) with 35% whole wheat. As always, the dough might need a slight adjustment to the hydration. If you often find yourself baking recipes in this book calling for Type-85, I encourage you to try sourcing some (see Resources, page 424) so you can see—and taste—how this flour performs.

Additionally, this flour is sometimes referred to as "high extraction flour" because it has a higher extraction percentage than white flour. At the most basic level, the extraction percentage represents how much mineral content there is in the flour, which also corresponds to the ash content. Specifically, the higher the extraction, the higher the ash percentage, and therefore, the closer you get to whole-grain flour.

Whole Spelt Flour

Spelt flour ranks up there as one of my favorite grains to work with—and you'll see it used often throughout this book. I always use it in its whole-grain form (sifted spelt, or "white spelt," is also available) to get increased nutritional benefits and flavor. And it is incredibly flavorful! Spelt is considered an "ancient grain" and is a subspecies of the common wheat we use today. I find it is typically sensitive to overhydration and if pushed too far, can result in a dough that's sticky and hard to handle. Additionally, spelt usually contributes increased extensibility when mixed into a dough, allowing the dough to stretch significantly before offering resistance.

Whole Rye Flour

All the rye flour used in this book is whole-grain rye flour, which is 100% of the rye berry milled into flour. Rye has different gluten properties than wheat and won't form the same viscoelastic dough when mixed—the dough will be sticky and lack wheat's gas-trapping properties. Rye is incredibly flavorful, though, and I love using it even in small percentages because I find in addition to contributing an earthy flavor, it brings increased crust color.

BREAD FLOUR VS. HIGH-PROTEIN WHITE FLOUR

In the United States, some millers label their high-protein white flour "bread flour," while other millers use this term for *any* of their flours specifically designed for breadmaking. This means that you may find bags of flour labeled "bread flour" that are not what I would consider high protein (~12.7% to 14%). Therefore, it's important to double-check the label (or search online) for the protein level. When I call for high-protein white flour in the recipes throughout this book, I'll label it precisely that: "high-protein white flour." This includes the widely available King Arthur Baking Bread Flour, which is around 12.7% protein.

Water

If your water is safe to drink, it will work well for baking bread. I use water straight from my tap when mixing. Be sure to adjust the water temperature as necessary to help you meet the desired dough temperature of the recipes in this book (see Water Temperature Is Key, page 135). To have cool water at the ready, I keep a large carafe of water in my refrigerator. For warm water, I either pull warm water from the tap or heat water in the microwave.

Salt

Salt is added in such a small percentage for most wheat doughs (typically between 1.8% and 2% to the total flour weight) that it's hard to imagine how such a minuscule addition can have such a large impact. But it has several effects: It enlivens the flavor of the other ingredients it accompanies, tempers fermentation, has a tightening effect on the dough, lengthens mixing time, and helps preserve color and flavor by reducing oxidation. Salt is a powerful tool that bakers use to control excessive gas production (which can lead to a compromised dough structure) and to help avoid a weak, sticky dough.

For baking, I prefer to use fine-grained sea salt. Kosher salt can also be used, but be sure to weigh it (as with all other ingredients), as some grinds are very coarse and others are very fine, which can lead to errors if measured by volume. I also avoid table salt with iodine. (See Mixing in Salt, page 81, for more on adding salt during mixing.)

The recipes in this book have carefully tested salt levels that are kept as low as possible. In some cases, increasing the salt can be beneficial to balance the flavor profile or accentuate the flavor of other ingredients. Generally, I keep the salt in wheat bread doughs around 1.8%, with some pastry and sweets around 2% or higher, as needed, to complement any enrichments.

Sugar

Sugar, of course, adds sweetness to any baked good but it also helps bring color to the crust due to increased caramelization during baking. Like salt, sugar is hygroscopic, meaning it pulls and holds water from its surroundings. Because yeast cells need water for metabolic activity, adding sugar leads to a reduction in fermentation activity when included at higher percentages (like in enriched doughs).

I prefer using superfine sugar (also called caster sugar) because it absorbs quickly and easily into a dough, with minimal impact on its structure. It is finer than white granulated sugar, which you can also use. Just be sure not to use powdered (aka confectioners') sugar, which contains cornstarch and won't work.

TESTING NEW FLOUR

When you buy a new flour that you've never used before, it's a good idea to give it a test to understand its characteristics in action and to give you a baseline for when you eventually bake with it. The easiest way is to use some to refresh your sourdough starter. Since you refresh your starter one or two times a day, every day, your muscle memory is attuned to its consistency and viscosity. If you change up the flour you use for refreshments, you'll immediately be able to tell whether the flour needs more or less water to mix it to the same consistency. Apply the results of your test to your baking: If your starter mixes up stiffer than usual, expect to increase the water in the recipe, and vice versa.

Malt

Malt is made by first sprouting grain (such as wheat or barley), halting the germination process at just the right time by heating it, then milling the sprouted grain into a fine powder. The temperature at which the grain is heated determines whether the grain is diastatic (lower temperature) or nondiastatic (hotter).

- Diastatic malt: With its functional enzymes (most important, amylase), diastatic malt can aid fermentation by converting more of the starch in flour to sugar (maltose). This provides more fuel for the fermentation in a dough. The additional sugar also helps the crust further caramelize, contributing color and flavor to the final loaf.

- Nondiastatic malt: This has undergone high heating temperatures, deactivating all its enzymatic activity (thus, it will not affect fermentation). One common form of nondiastatic malt is barley malt syrup. It is high in maltose (sugar) and is used to add a nutty/malty flavor to dough, as with Bagels (page 367), or to enhance crust color.

When raw wheat berries are milled, the resulting flour will have some level of active amylase. This means the flour already has the components necessary for converting its starches to maltose—sugar available for fermentation by the yeasts and bacteria in sourdough—but in some cases, the amylase activity in the flour is not at high enough levels to make quality bread. To correct this, the miller might increase the enzymatic activity of the flour by adding diastatic malt powder, resulting in flour with sufficient enzymatic activity to fuel strong fermentation.

WHEN TO USE DIASTATIC MALT

With most white flour that's available today, you likely won't need to add diastatic malt because it already contains it (look for "malted barley flour" or "barley flour" in the ingredient list). But in some cases, adding some malt might help take your loaf from good to great. (Typically, I don't add diastatic malt to my recipes containing large percentages of whole wheat flour or with freshly milled flour because these flours usually have plenty of enzymatic activity.) Use diastatic malt if a recipe calls for a large percentage of white flour that doesn't already contain malt and if any, or all, of the following apply:

- Fermentation appears sluggish.

- The recipe has long fermentation times (e.g., an overnight proof).

- Crust color is lacking (and you're sure it wasn't because of steaming, baking temperature, or overproofing issues).

Ultimately, the best way to determine if your flour needs malt is to run an experiment! Try a small bake with a small percentage of malt added to the mix and see how your loaves turn out.

When adding diastatic malt powder to a bread dough, I mix it with the flour in the recipe (including before beginning an autolyse, if there is one). Start by adding a low percentage to the dough, usually 0.25% of the total flour weight, and increase this percentage very slowly, as needed, through testing. *Be cautious. Do not add too much diastatic malt to your recipes; start at a low percentage and work up as necessary.* Generally, I find the range between 0.25% and 1% to total flour weight acceptable. If too much diastatic malt is added, excessive starch is broken down during fermentation and the resulting bread can have an overly reddish hue to the crust and an unpleasantly gummy interior.

WHEN TO USE NONDIASTATIC MALT

Nondiastatic malt, which has no enzymatic activity, adds only maltose (sugar) for enhanced flavor and crust color. Some recipes, such as sourdough Bagels (page 367), explicitly call for nondiastatic malt to achieve a particular flavor profile and crust color.

FRESHLY MILLED FLOUR

An entire series of books could be written on baking with freshly milled flour. This section is simply a guide on how to get started, with a few helpful tips. Many of the recipes in this book can be modified to include freshly milled flour and, in fact, I do so often. These days, for increased flavor and nutrition, many of my bakes incorporate some percentage of freshly milled flour.

What is freshly milled flour?

I call flour "fresh" when it's been milled within a few days of mixing. I'm not sure there's a technical designation for how soon flour needs to be milled to be labeled as fresh, but I generally think of it as within the past week or sooner. As a home baker who works with smaller dough batches, I typically mill my flour on demand, as in the day before, so I can use the flour to create my levain and then mix the next day (if the recipe calls for an overnight pre-ferment).

How does it act differently in the breadmaking process, and how do I swap it into recipes?

Generally, I find most freshly milled flour requires an increase in total dough hydration compared to aged flour. Of course, if the flour is whole grain, you have the added bran and germ particles that absorb significant water, but even if the fresh flour has been sifted to remove some, or all, of these bits, I find increasing the hydration is necessary to achieve proper dough consistency. Additionally, in terms of mixing and dough

strength, I find freshly milled flour usually benefits from longer mix times to ensure proper gluten development. The reason is twofold: First, dough with freshly milled flour typically requires increased hydration levels, which usually necessitates more strengthening to ensure proper dough consistency and structure. Second, because fresh flour has had little oxidation time (compared to aged flour), which helps gluten develop, mixing for a longer time can help produce a stronger and more elastic dough. Typically, I'll extend mixing by a few minutes in a mixer or several more by hand.

Throughout the book, look to any portion of whole-grain flour in a recipe as a place for swapping in—one to one—freshly milled for some of the aged flour. Try to match the fresh flour to an aged flour equivalent in the recipe as closely as possible. For example, if the freshly milled flour has been heavily sifted, it might be appropriate to use it when white flour is called for. Additionally, some millers will sift their fresh flour somewhere between white and whole grain and call it "high extraction." If you're buying freshly milled flour from a miller, ask them how to best use their flour; I'm sure they'll be happy to help!

How does it contribute to the texture and flavor of the final bread?

One of the reasons I love using freshly milled flour is the increased flavor and delightful aroma. The benefit of fresh flour is apparent right from the moment you begin milling: The flour has a beautiful creamy color and an amplified nutty, sometimes grassy, aroma. If you've only worked with aged flour, you'll immediately experience the difference—perhaps this is a slight exaggeration, but I almost equate it to having been able to see only in black and white and then suddenly being able to see color. The ingredient you once worked with day in, and day out, suddenly takes on a new dimension.

As far as texture, generally I find bread made with freshly milled flour has a tighter crumb, especially when the fresh flour is not sifted (i.e., it's 100% whole grain). But the tightness does not imply the crumb is tough or chewy; in fact, when properly hydrated, a loaf with freshly milled flour will have a delightfully soft texture. And what these loaves may lack in terms of volume, they make up for in flavor, aroma, and nutrition.

Can I buy freshly milled flour?

Many mills across the United States now mill fresh flour to order, and even if it's not milled the day it ships, it's still fresh enough that you will taste and smell the difference.

How do I mill it myself?

I reach for either my electric KoMo Classic or Mockmill home grain mill. These electric mills can mill small quantities of fine flour in minutes at the press of a button. Alternatively, I use my hand-operated GrainMaker 116 mill that's capable of milling extremely fine flour at the expense of time and a little hard work. I prefer milling flour early in the morning or the day before mixing to let the flour cool before use so it doesn't adversely affect the final dough temperature. In most cases, I use the finest setting and I use the fresh flour within a few days for the best crumb and crust color, texture, and flavor.

How long does it stay fresh? Can you mill it in batches and store it?

For the home baker, I find it convenient to mill the flour fresh the day before or the day of mixing. This way, you're using the flour when flavor and aroma are at their maximum, before the flour begins to oxidize. While oxidation is what makes aged flour stronger and more elastic when mixed into a dough, I find using flour soon after milling produces the best flavor and aroma in the final loaf of bread. If you want to mill flour fresh and store it, I would keep it somewhere cool (or in the refrigerator) and use it within a few weeks of milling. Be aware that if you store the flour exposed to the air in the refrigerator or freezer, it may absorb the flavor and aroma of other foods.

Should you sift freshly milled flour?

These days, when I'm milling fresh flour, I rarely sift it—that is, remove parts of the larger bran and germ particles to produce "whiter" flour. My feeling is, if I'm going to mill flour on demand, I might as well use it at 100% whole grain! However, sifting is an option if you'd like to get a lighter loaf with more volume. To sift, you'll need a flour sieve (a dedicated flour-sifting screen or the finest mesh sieve you have). Pour your fresh flour into the sifting screen or sieve and shake while the screen traps the larger bran and germ particles. The finer the screen, the more bran and germ you'll sift out, and the resulting flour will be whiter and ever closer to a proper white flour. See How to Tinker (page 222) for a way to reincorporate the sifted particles back into a dough.

Where do I buy the wheat berries and how do I store them?

For where to buy, see Resources (page 424). To keep my whole berries fresher for longer, I often store them in the freezer in a sealed, nonporous container (like a freezer bag or plastic container), where they will keep nearly indefinitely. Milling berries straight from the freezer also helps offset the heating effect of the milling.

WHAT IF I DON'T HAVE THE FLOUR CALLED FOR IN A RECIPE?

If you don't have a flour called for in a recipe, try to find the closest match, using the cheat sheet below to help. For example, if you don't have a high-protein white flour, most all-purpose flour will be strong enough to stand in its place; just check the protein level (King Arthur Baking All-Purpose is a good example of a flour that can stand in for the high-protein white flour called for in this book, though King Arthur Baking Bread Flour would be the ideal choice of the two).

While it's fine (and, frankly, expected!) to swap flour in a recipe to some degree, if you try to swap too much of the flour, you'll ultimately change the fundamental intention and goal of the bread formula. Not only will the hydration need adjustment, but the pre-fermented flour percentage and process may need adjustment as well. If you stick to the swaps in the chart below and heed the Notes, the recipes in this book should generally be fine when you switch out one flour for another.

IF YOU DON'T HAVE THIS FLOUR	USE THIS	NOTE
High-protein white flour (~12.7% to 14% protein)	White flour (~11.5% protein) or all-purpose flour	Will likely need to decrease hydration and slightly increase dough strengthening time (during mixing or stretches and folds in bulk fermentation)
Whole spelt flour	Whole wheat flour	May need to slightly increase hydration
Whole rye flour	Whole wheat flour	Except for Roggenvollkornbrot, page 288, which must be 100% whole rye
Type-85 flour	65% white flour (~11.5% protein) and 35% whole wheat	May need to adjust hydration (up or down depending on dough consistency)
Pastry flour	All-purpose flour	May need to slightly increase hydration
Type 00 flour	White flour (~11.5% protein) or all-purpose flour	If using Caputo brand flour, may need to slightly decrease hydration

FEW TOOLS ARE STRICTLY REQUIRED TO BAKE great bread at home. Aside from the right ingredients, a mixing bowl, an oven, and a kitchen scale, everything else is nice but optional. However, having a few of the right tools can make baking easier—and more consistent. Consistency is a challenge for all bakers, and frankly, it's part of the reason baking is so enjoyable (at least to me!). Not only must ingredients be accurately measured, but baking conditions—namely temperature and humidity—are always changing in the kitchen, requiring the baker to be aware of their environment, how their starter is that day, and how the dough behaves in each step of the breadmaking process. These are the key tools to get you there:

The Must-Have Tools

Kitchen Scale

An absolute must, the single tool that is not optional. Weighing your ingredients, as opposed to measuring by volume, is far more accurate, and this is the first tool I recommend any baker purchase. Measuring flour (and salt!) by volume using measuring cups is incredibly inaccurate, as flour can be scooped and compacted into a measuring cup differently from day to day. By using a scale, we can be 100 percent confident we know exactly how much flour is measured out. Consistency aside, measuring by weight is also cleaner and faster. You don't have to scoop flour from a container, level it off, and repeat countless times to fill your mixing bowl.

Instant-Read Thermometer

An indispensable tool to help you reliably measure dough temperature—and handy for measuring your ambient kitchen temperature, too. (See Temperature, page 135, for more on why dough temperature throughout the process is so important that you might as well consider it an ingredient.) A thermometer is also useful for determining when a loaf of bread has finished baking, and although over time you'll grow less reliant on the thermometer, when you're starting out, a quick poke with one helps. I like to use a Thermoworks Thermapen.

Proofing Bowls, Baskets, and Bannetons

Bowls and baskets provide structure to your dough while it proofs. There are many options, and even a simple kitchen mixing bowl lined with a tight-woven towel (such as a flour sack towel) will work well.

There are also specialty bread proofing baskets, called bannetons or brotforms, made from wicker, cane, wood pulp, and other materials. These baskets come in a wide variety of shapes and sizes: oval ones for baking a bâtard shape, round ones for boules, and other specialty shapes. Some baskets, like cane bannetons, will leave a pattern on the dough after proofing, whereas others, such as wicker baskets lined with canvas, will not. Ultimately, the basket choice is yours.

In this book, I use a few basket types and sizes to proof dough. However, for most of my recipes, I'd recommend starting with two 10-inch round proofing baskets or two 10-inch oval proofing baskets.

ROUND LOAVES

- 8-inch round (500g to 650g dough)
- 10-inch round (700g to 1,000g dough)
- 12-inch round (1,100g to 1,300g dough)

OVAL LOAVES

- 10-inch-long oval (600g to 900g dough)
- 14-inch-long oval (950g to 2,000g dough)

When choosing the right basket for your dough, keep the dough consistency and recipe in mind:

- **Highly hydrated dough:** A dough such as this that lacks structure can be expected to spread during proofing. Using a large basket with too much space will allow the dough to spread outward, ultimately reducing loaf volume. In this case, I'd choose a smaller basket to give the weak dough extra structure—or failing that, ensure that the dough is shaped tightly enough to prevent spreading.

- **100% whole-grain and highly hydrated dough:** For this I often use a basket on the smaller side, knowing the dough won't have as much rise (typical for whole grain) and it will benefit from extra structural support to prevent spreading during proofing.

- **Stronger dough made from mostly white flour:** Here I might choose a basket that has extra room on the sides, such as my 14-inch-long oval basket. This gives the dough room to relax and spread during proofing, adding to loaf volume.

Mixing Bowls

I like to stock a few 5-quart stainless steel bowls for mixing bread dough. Stainless steel helps prevent dough from sticking, plus it's easy to clean, extremely tough, and nonreactive. I also like to have a few smaller, 3- or 4-quart stainless steel bowls on hand to hold seed soakers and freshly milled flour, or for any other small mixing tasks.

Bowl Scraper

A sturdy, yet flexible, curved plastic or silicone bowl scraper will help you remove dough from your mixing bowl, mixer bowl, bulk fermentation bowl, and your hands. These scrapers usually come with a flat side and a curved side, where the curve is useful for scooping the inside of a mixing bowl, and the flat edge can be used to scrape a counter or even divide dough if you don't have a bench knife.

Bread Lame or Sharp Knife

A proper bread lame, which is typically a razor blade attached to a handle, or a sharp knife is used to score (cut) the dough just before baking.

Bench Knife or Bench Scraper

A bench knife is a rectangular plastic or metal blade (sometimes with a wood or plastic handle) used to cut and divide dough, transfer dough from one surface to another, and preshape and shape dough on the

HOW TO SEASON A CANE BANNETON

Much like a brand-new cast-iron skillet, a cane banneton needs to be seasoned before its first use. This initial seasoning helps to ensure the dough won't stick to the sides. Using a handheld mister, spray the new banneton with an even, fine mist of water over its entire interior surface. Then, sift an even layer of white flour over the inside. Tap out any excess flour. The flour should stick to the basket in a single, thin layer. Let the basket thoroughly dry before using. After this first seasoning, all that's required before placing dough in it for proofing is a light dusting of flour inside to ensure it remains nonstick.

counter. I also like to use my bench knife to scrape up stray flour and ingredients. The bench knife differs from the bench scraper only in that it's typically metal, more rigid, and sharper.

Dutch Oven or Combo Cooker

A 3.2-quart combo cooker or 5-quart (or larger) Dutch oven can be used to bake your bread dough in the oven. I prefer using the Lodge 3.2-quart cast-iron combo cooker for baking round loaves, but any Dutch oven will work well as long as the lid creates a tight seal to trap steam when baking. Choose a pot that is ovenproof up to temperatures of around 475°F (246°C). All of my pots are cast-iron (some with and some without an enameled interior—either is okay), but I'd imagine even a stainless steel pot would work just fine. Regardless of the material, be sure none of the pots have any parts that will melt at high temperature, such as rubber or plastic handles or knobs. Note that if you have a Le Creuset Dutch oven with a plastic knob, it might not be safe to use at high temperatures, but a metal knob can be bought and swapped in.

Challenger Breadware makes a cast-iron pan that's specifically designed to act like a Dutch oven or combo cooker, but it's larger and intended for breadmaking. This pan is large enough to fit a 1,000-gram oval loaf. Other specialty bread pans and pots are also available; see Resources (page 424).

Wire Cooling Racks

A wire cooling rack allows air to circulate around the loaf after baking and helps prevent the crust from becoming soggy. I have many of these racks, but I recommend buying two 18 × 13-inch ones so you can cool multiple loaves simultaneously.

Parchment Paper

Not all parchment is created equal. Some brands of paper tend to stick when baked at high temperatures. (I have the best luck with brands of brown parchment.)

Pullman Pan

Named after the size and shape of a pan used on old railway cars, Pullman pans are great for not only sourdough loaves but also quick breads like Banana Bread 2.0 (page 418). I love Pullman pans because they have straight sides for thin, neat slices. A Pullman pan also has a lid that slides on to create a loaf with a minimal crust and four straight sides as in Soft White Sandwich Bread (page 269).

For all the recipes in this book that call for a 9 × 4 × 4-inch Pullman pan, I use one from USA Pan that is coated with a natural, nonstick silicone liner. If yours doesn't have a nonstick liner, be sure to liberally grease the interior or use parchment paper, as instructed in the recipe, to ensure your loaf removes cleanly.

If you don't have a Pullman pan, a standard loaf pan (9 × 5 inches) will work in its place.

DOUGH PROOFER

As I've mentioned before, the stability of dough temperature is very important. A small countertop dough proofer, which has controls for consistent temperature settings, helps eliminate wild temperature swings to keep your starter and dough warm, ensuring active, lively fermentation. A proofer isn't strictly necessary (your dough will eventually reach sufficient fermentation activity given enough time), but in my baking, I've found it to be such a useful tool it's hard to imagine not using one in my kitchen.

A dough proofer can be an off-the-shelf device such as a Brød & Taylor Folding Proofer, or it can be something you've constructed yourself at home. You can create your own using a cooler with a tight-sealing lid and a plant seedling mat with a thermostat laid on the bottom to control the internal temperature.

Alternatively, you can also keep your starter and dough somewhere insulated to prevent temperature fluctuations (see Starter Maintenance, page 59).

Additional Tools

Pizza Peel

A pizza peel is such a handy tool in the kitchen I'm not sure how I'd bake without one. I use it not only for transferring pizza dough to the oven, but also for transferring bread dough. I prefer a wood peel, but a metal one will also work. If you don't have a pizza peel, an inverted baking sheet or a large cutting board can be used in its place.

Baker's Couche

Also called baker's linen, a couche is made from linen and is a large rectangular piece of cloth. Shaped dough is placed on a floured couche and the couche is then pleated or folded to support the dough as it's proofing. It's essentially a proofing basket that can be morphed into any desired shape. It's used to proof baguettes (see Demi Baguettes, page 251), but can also be used to proof other shapes, like large ciabattas, large ovals, or any same-day dough that needs proofing support. A couche should never be washed; just scrape off any dried dough and excess flour and store it somewhere dry to prevent mold growth. A large, clean kitchen towel can be used in the same way in a pinch.

Small Silicone or Plastic Spatula

I use this to stir a starter when refreshing it and for any other spreading task in the kitchen. I like one that has a pointy end that tapers to a rounder side so I can scrape the straight sides of a jar or the round sides of a bowl with equal effectiveness.

Reusable Bowl Covers

These come in different sizes and are either plastic covers with elastic at the opening or silicone discs that seal to the top of bowls. They're useful for covering bowls of dough, seed soakers, or anything you wish to keep from drying out. You can also simply use large proofing bags (see below).

Large Proofing Bags

These large reusable plastic bags (10 × 24 inches) easily fit over proofing baskets (even the larger 14-inch-long oval baskets and 12-inch round baskets) or a half sheet pan (when proofing rolls, pretzels, and many other things). If kept clean, these bags can be reused.

Glass Storage Jars

I'm a big fan of using glass jars to hold my starter, seeds, and soakers, and for many other baking tasks. I love Weck jars for my starter (see What Container Is Best for My Starter?, page 33).

Baking Stone or Steel

A thick baking stone or baking steel is a wonderful addition to any home kitchen, not just for baking bread but also for baking pizza or flatbread (see Baking Directly on a Surface, page 124). A baking steel is very efficient at conducting heat and is virtually unbreakable, but it can be heavy and requires occasional seasoning (like you would season cast-iron). While I don't place my Dutch oven or combo cooker directly on a stone or steel surface when baking bread, a surface can help provide insulation between any bottom heating element and the pot—a good solution if the bottoms of your loaves are getting burned. If you have a bottom heating element, place the surface on a rack at the lowest slot and bake on a rack above it.

Mechanical Mixers

None of the recipes in this book strictly requires a mechanical mixer, but a mixer can make incorporating and strengthening a dough easier—especially when the dough is enriched with butter, sugar, or egg. I use a 7-quart professional-line KitchenAid for mixing enriched doughs such as Soft Dinner Rolls (page 333). It also works well for Focaccia (page 304) and Sourdough Pizza Dough (page 294). A professional-line mixer is not mandatory, but its powerful motor and larger capacity can help when scaling up recipes. For recipes in this book calling for a KitchenAid, I typically use the mixer on two speeds: low speed (usually labeled "Stir") for incorporating ingredients and medium speed (labeled "2") for strengthening the dough.

Standard Loaf Pans

These pans are the typical loaf pans with slightly tapered sides that measure 9 × 5 inches. The advantage to using these pans is that you end up with more of a bloom in the top crust as the loaf is allowed to expand more. Additionally, I find loaves bake slightly faster in these pans than in Pullman pans.

II

WELCOME TO YOUR FIRST SOURDOUGH LOAF

Baking sourdough bread can seem daunting at first. Not only do you have to create and care for a living thing—your sourdough starter—but you also must work through a long breadmaking process with many moving parts. I urge you to see past all this: The process is incredibly forgiving, and in almost all cases, the loaf you pull from the oven will be satisfying, nourishing, and delightful. Here's my best advice for beginning bakers.

BE MINDFUL

First and foremost, it's helpful to keep an attentive mind. Pay attention to your sourdough starter—how it looks, feels, smells, and even tastes—through its refreshment intervals. Pay attention to the dough as you're mixing—does it feel elastic, strong, and smooth? Or is it slack and weak, requiring more mixing and development (i.e., kneading)? It's helpful to period-ically pause for a moment during the breadmaking process, step back, and ask yourself questions, look at the dough, and note how it's developing. It's through careful observation that you will build up your baking intuition and develop an innate understanding of the entire process.

STICK TO THE SAME RECIPE FOR A WHILE

Start with Simple Sourdough (page 40) in this section and stay there for as many bakes as you can. Because baking is a long process (although much of it is hands-off) with many variables, it can take a few iterations before you learn to connect how a single change in the ingredients or process affects the eventual out-come. By sticking to the same recipe you'll ensure many of the core variables are consistent. This way, you can learn to read the dough, how it should look and feel at each step of the process without any of the other parameters—such as flour, hydration, or durations—changing.

BE CURIOUS AND EXPERIMENT

Explore every facet of baking and ask questions. Many of us remember the dreaded science fair each year in middle school. We were given time and resources to explore any area we'd like, to first form a hypothesis, then run some experiments, collect data, and finally draw a conclusion. While I remember many of my classmates not having fun during these mandatory multimonth assignments, I loved everything about them. I looked forward to my chance to indulge my curiosities, to explore, play, and learn.

I like to take this same approach with baking bread. Often in my kitchen I've had an idea for doing something a different way or wondering if something I've read was really the way it was described. What better way to verify something than to run a little test? If you're curious whether a certain flour compo-sition for a levain might lead to a sourer or milder loaf of bread (hypothesis), run a side-by-side "test bake" and see for yourself (experiment). Compare the two loaves at the end (collect data) and see which is closer to what you were after (conclusion).

HAVE FUN!

It's easy to get bogged down in numbers and methods and results—at the end of it all, your loaf of delicious sourdough bread is meant to nourish and be enjoyed. Sourdough bread baking is incredibly forgiving, and in almost all cases, the result will be a loaf of bread you can be proud of because you made it with your own hands.

What Is Sourdough?

SOURDOUGH IS BREAD CREATED THROUGH A natural fermentation process that involves suitable bacteria and wild yeasts present in the environment and on the grain. Generally, bacteria are primarily responsible for producing organic acids (lactic acid and acetic acid), which acidify the dough, gradually lowering the pH (a scale used to specify how acidic or basic a solution is, with lower numbers being more acidic). This acidity contributes to the flavor, texture, and storage qualities of sourdough bread. The wild yeasts are the primary provider of carbon dioxide gas and ethanol during fermentation. This gas is trapped in the dough's airtight gluten matrix that is developed during kneading, which causes the dough to rise, creating a final loaf of bread with a light and airy texture. The delicate dance of these microorganisms is evidence of nature's well-orchestrated hand in helping humanity create one of the oldest forms of fermented foods.

SOURDOUGH VS. NATURALLY LEAVENED

All the bread recipes in this book are called "naturally leavened" because they are 100 percent leavened by a sourdough starter with naturally occurring bacteria and wild yeasts (no commercial yeast is used). In some nonbread recipes, like Flaky Drop Biscuits (page 382 and Sunday Morning Pancakes (page 410), you'll find sourdough starter included alongside another leavening agent such as baking soda or baking powder. With these recipes, sourdough starter is added simply for flavor, not as the primary means of leavening, so of course these recipes would not be considered "naturally leavened." In the baking world, there's a bit of a gray area with the term "sourdough" because some bakers use it to describe bread or baked goods that contain any amount of sourdough starter (even a small amount) but rely on other leaveners (such as commercial yeast, baking powder, baking soda, etc.) to help with leavening. For me and my baking, when I label bread as "sourdough bread" or "naturally leavened bread," it uses only sourdough as the means of leavening.

Overview of the Breadmaking Process

THIS IS A BRIEF OVERVIEW OF THE STYLE OF sourdough breadmaking I follow: eight steps to delicious bread. While it might seem like eight steps is long and complicated, most of this time is hands-off. Your sourdough does its thing, only requiring you to be the shepherd, dropping in from time to time to guide the dough toward your desired destination. There's no need for you to micromanage every movement and every step, just set the path for your dough to follow, and while it might meander to and fro, do your best to keep it on the path. In the end, sometimes it doesn't quite reach the destination in the way you had intended, and that's okay—it's part of the learning process and part of your transformation into an experienced sourdough bread baker.

The following breadmaking process is the core of my sourdough baking, and whether you're making a hearth-style loaf (a loaf that's baked free-form on a baking surface and not in a loaf pan), a pan loaf, or an enriched dough (dough with added sugar, egg, and/or dairy), many—but not always all—of the steps will be used.

See the Technique section (page 58) for detailed information on each of these steps, but first let's take a quick look at each.

1 ☰ LEVAIN (PAGE 71)

A type of pre-ferment, a levain is an offshoot of your continually maintained sourdough starter. Made from fresh flour, water, and some ripe starter, it's meant to be used in a single bake and is responsible for making the dough rise and adding flavor through fermentation.

2 ☰ AUTOLYSE (PAGE 79)

Pronounced "auto-lease," this optional step at the beginning of the breadmaking process is one in which only the flour and water are combined and set aside to rest. It can make mixing and strengthening a dough easier while also adding increased dough extensibility (the ability to extend or stretch without tearing).

3 ☰ MIX (PAGE 77)

Mixing is the physical act of combining the ingredients, followed by dough strengthening, as in kneading with a technique such as slap and fold (this is also called developing the dough). The ingredients might include a dough that has optionally undergone an autolyse (step 2) but will also include more water, salt, the levain, and any other inclusions (seeds, fruit, etc.) or enrichments (butter, oil, sugar, etc.).

4 ☰ BULK FERMENTATION (PAGE 88)

The dough enters bulk fermentation (aka its first rise) when the pre-ferment kicks off the fermentation process, generating acidity (and other flavor compounds) and leavening the dough. You will periodically perform sets of "stretches and folds" to contribute to dough strength. This step culminates with a dough that is sufficiently strengthened and well risen and has substantial yeast and bacteria populations.

5 ☰ DIVIDE, PRESHAPE, AND BENCH REST (PAGE 96)

If there are multiple loaves to make, the dough is first divided into smaller pieces. The dough is usually preshaped into a form that will facilitate the final shaping to come. After preshaping, it's left to rest (aka bench rest) so the dough can relax, which helps prevent tearing during final shaping.

6 ☰ SHAPE (PAGE 99)

The preshaped pieces of dough are shaped into their final form, whether it's a pan loaf, bâtard (oval), boule (round), or other shape. The shaped dough is placed in a basket, bowl, on a couche (a large piece of canvas or kitchen towel), or in a pan for proofing.

7 ☰ PROOF (PAGE 110)

The dough proofs (aka its second rise) when fermentation continues, further flavoring the dough and making it rise. Recipes in this book call for either a room-temperature proof (usually 1 to 4 hours) or a cold proof (typically overnight).

8 ☰ BAKE (PAGE 122)

Once the dough is sufficiently proofed, it's scored (cut) to promote controlled expansion in the oven, then baked in a steamy environment to encourage maximal volume and a golden crust.

What Is a Pre-ferment?

It's either your sourdough starter or a levain, which is essentially a bit of flour and water fermented ahead of time that's used to seed the larger dough and begin fermentation.

Anatomy of the Perfect Loaf

I'm going to say this up front: I'm not entirely sure "the perfect loaf" truly exists. I chose the name for my website (and this book) because it's more about the constant practice and work toward that ideal that keeps us bakers transfixed. Of course, there's always satisfaction for us in every bread we pull from the oven, even if the loaf doesn't quite hit the mark. But the truth is, the perfect loaf is entirely subjective and quite ephemeral. What I find to be an exquisite bake one day may just be great the next—and that's okay! We all have a sensorial image for the type of bread we're looking for, whether it's a mash-up of childhood food memories, a bread style you're obsessed with, or even more simply, a loaf you want to eat every day from here on out.

Because of bread's subjectiveness, it's hard to make blanket statements about what makes bread great, but this anatomical breakdown of one of my loaves is what I look for in my baking. While some of these things may not resonate with you, I find it's useful to point out these characteristics—especially to new bakers— because it helps one appreciate the nuance, detail, and myriad characteristics in a great loaf of bread if you know where to look. It helps us all assess the bread coming out of the oven, and this assessment isn't meant to pressure or criticize, but rather, it's a chance for you to delve deeper into the details of each loaf. The end goal is to help guide you on your path to quantifying, and finding, your perfect loaf.

OVERALL

- The loaf is light in hand, indicating it is properly fermented.

- The score (cut) is defined with a clean edge.

- The loaf has an overall nice rise and clean structure, a gentle top-slope from side to side.

- The bottom of the loaf is flat against the surface and the sides gently round upward (you don't want the loaf to look like the letter U—an indication of underproofing).

- The mouth should water when the first bite is taken; the flavors of the grain variety are prominent; and the aroma has a captivating grain bouquet.

CRUST

- A sheen across the entire crust; crackles when gently squeezed

- A range of colors from deep mahogany to light brown in the area where the score lifts the crust

- Depending on the bread, either thin and crispy, or thick and substantial

- Small microblisters on loaves that are proofed overnight at a cold temperature

- A malty and nutty flavor, with hints of molasses, as I prefer to bake my loaves darker

CRUMB

- Evenly open across the loaf interior: The alveoli (holes) shouldn't be excessively large in areas and tight in others

- Soft and tender; a beautiful creamy hue with shine

- Ample, but not overwhelming, sourness and an overall complex flavor; a balanced mix of smooth dairy- and vinegar-like sourness

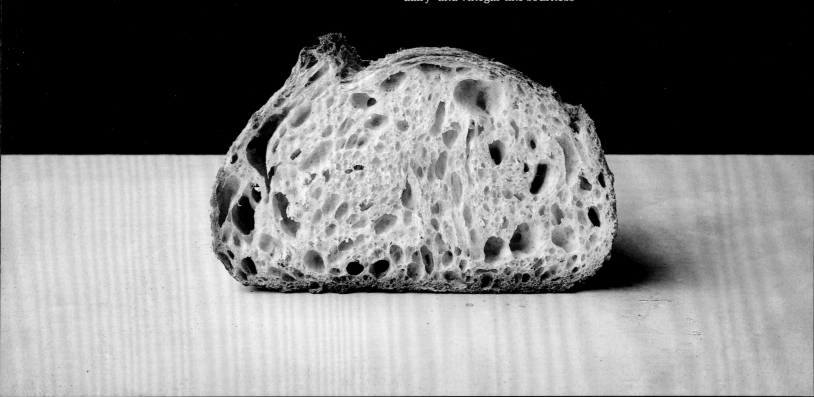

Create Your Sourdough Starter

BEFORE YOU BAKE YOUR FIRST LOAF OF SOUR-
dough bread, you're going to need a sourdough starter of course. Here's what you need to know.

What Is It?

A sourdough starter is a mixture of flour and water that hosts a stable blend of beneficial bacteria and wild yeasts. This mixture is continually maintained with regular refreshments (or feedings) and is used to leaven and flavor new dough. The starter is the basis for natural fermentation, and learning how to best care for and use one is the key to successful sourdough bread baking.

What Happens When You Create a Starter?

When you create a starter, you're providing the right environment (climate and food) for beneficial microbes (bacteria and wild yeasts) to move in and begin fermentation. The bacteria and wild yeasts use the fresh flour as food and produce the following as by-products:

1. Acids and other compounds that add flavor

2. Carbon dioxide gas that leavens the bread dough

As your starter ferments the flour, at some point (about 12 hours for the process described in this book) more fresh flour needs to be added so the microbes have a continued food source. You first discard a large portion of the "spent" food, which includes by-products such as acids, alcohols, and other compounds, to ensure that the microbes can thrive in a healthy environment.

Then the portion that's left is "refreshed," or fed, with additional fresh flour and water and the cycle continues anew. This cycle is a sort of microevolution where the fittest microbes (in the evolutionary sense) survive and continue to flourish—natural selection at work in your kitchen. The microbes that continue to flourish in your starter form the backbone of your baking. The unique mix of yeasts and lactic acid bacteria changes from starter to starter, which is one reason why sourdough bread tastes different from baker to baker. In a sense, a sourdough starter is like a well-worn pair of jeans or natural leather gloves: Over time it begins to take on the characteristics of its owner and their environment.

How to Create Your Own Starter from Scratch

Strong fermentation—and by necessity, the health of your sourdough starter—is the foundation of healthy and delicious sourdough bread. To get connected with the process and routine right from the beginning, I encourage new bakers to create their own starter from scratch. (However, if you prefer not to make one, there are online options available; or ask your favorite baker if they'll give you some of theirs!) The starter creation process kick-starts you into quickly learning how to refresh: how to read the fermentation cues during each daily refreshment cycle as well as how to get into the good habit of working refreshing into your daily routine. And really, creating a starter is very easy! With the right ingredients, a few key tips, and some things to watch out for, you can have your own sourdough starter bubbling away on your counter in 7 to 10 days—all with just one or two 5-minute mixes each day.

WHAT YOU NEED TO GET STARTED

INGREDIENTS

- Two 5-pound bags of white flour (~11.5% protein) or unbleached all-purpose flour

- One 5-pound bag of whole rye flour (recommended for best results) or whole wheat flour

- Drinking water (warming it to 80°F/26°C, ideally)

TOOLS

- Kitchen scale

- Small silicone spatula

- One glass jar, 750 milliliters (28.7 fl oz) or 1 liter (35.9 fl oz)

  NOTE: Some bakers prefer to use a second jar when they refresh their starter—meaning, they put the necessary amount of discard, fresh flour, and water in a new, clean jar each time they refresh, which helps keep the container cleaner and can feel more streamlined for some.

WHAT CONTAINER IS BEST FOR MY STARTER?

I've tried many, many types of jars over the years, and while it may seem like a small thing, the vessel you use to keep your starter can have a big impact on its maintenance. If you refresh your starter once or twice a day for the next year, this means you'll have hundreds of interactions with the tools needed for each refreshment. What follows is a list of the things I look for in my ideal jars (though of course this doesn't mean the jars in your kitchen won't work well, too).

- I prefer glass over plastic because I tend to use as little plastic as possible and have personal reservations about an acidic solution sitting in plastic for extended periods.

- The jar should be just big enough to hold the starter when it rises to its max height. (A 750-milliliter/28.7 fl oz or 1-liter/35.9 fl oz jar is needed for the quantities listed in this book.) If the jar is too wide, your starter will spread in a thin layer at the bottom, making it susceptible to temperature fluctuations and making it harder to visually inspect its ripening progress.

- Choose a jar without nooks and crannies where dried flour can accumulate and make cleaning more difficult.

In the end, the best jars I've found are Weck canning jars. They have slightly tapered sides (making it easy to get your hand inside) with only a small edge at the top. They are readily available and are extremely tough. I also like the glass lid, which can just rest on the top of the jar (when not clamped down), thus allowing any excessive gas buildup to escape. Ball, Pyrex, mason jars, and other glass or ceramic jars will also work well.

- Keep it warm, ideally 80° to 86°F (26° to 30°C) or as close as you can get. Find a warm spot in your kitchen, like on top of the refrigerator, near another appliance that's turned on most of the day, or even inside your turned-off oven but with the light inside turned on. It can also help to periodically take the temperature of your starter with an instant-read thermometer or keep a small ambient thermometer nearby; these will help you get a feel for your kitchen temperature during the day (which we might otherwise not pay attention to!).

- Don't get discouraged if you see a lapse in activity on Days 3 and 4; this is normal. Keep with the process of discarding and carrying some starter over, adding fresh flour and water, and letting it sit until the next refreshment time.

- Don't skip using whole rye flour, as the added minerals and nutrients help kick-start the process. If you don't have access to whole rye flour, a high-quality whole wheat flour will work well in its place.

CREATION PROCESS

DAY	# OF REFRESHMENTS PER DAY	INGREDIENTS
1	n/a	100g rye flour 125g water
2 and 3	1	75g carryover 50g rye flour 50g white flour 115g water
4, 5, and 6	2	20g carryover 30g rye flour 70g white flour 115g water
7 and onward	2	20g carryover 30g rye flour 70g white flour 100g water

Day 1

1. Turn on your scale and place your clean, empty jar on top and write down its weight (you will use this later to determine how much to discard each day).

2. With your jar still on the scale, tare (zero out) the scale.

3. Add 100g rye flour and 125g warm water (80°F/26°C) and mix well. To gauge the amount of rise, I find it helpful to place a rubber band around the jar at the height of the mixture after stirring.

4. Cover and store in a warm place (80°-86°F/ 26°-30°C is ideal) for 24 hours. I like to lay the jar's lid on top so no air gets in, but gasses inside can still escape; if your jar has a threaded lid, it's okay to screw it on.

Day 2

On Day 2, you might see a burst of fermentation activity (which might also have an "off" aroma). This activity is usually not the result of the mature symbiosis of bacteria and yeasts we're looking for. Whether you see this burst of activity or not, at this point, your starter is not yet ready to bake with. This initial surge will typically disappear by Day 3 or 4. Stick to the schedule and it will come back, but be more stable!

1. Discard the contents of your jar down to the recorded weight of the empty jar plus 75g (so you have 75g of the mixture left in the jar).

2. Add 50g rye flour, 50g white flour, and 115g warm water and mix well.

3. Cover and store the mixture in the same warm spot for 24 hours.

Day 3

In the morning, you may start to see more activity, or you may see none. Regardless, don't fret, stick to the schedule. Remember, if it's cold in your kitchen, warm your mixing water to 80°F (26°C) to help.

1. Discard the contents of your jar down to the recorded weight of the empty jar plus 75g (so you have 75g of the mixture left in the jar).

2. Add 50g rye flour, 50g white flour, and 115g water and mix well.

3. Cover and store the mixture in the same warm spot for 24 hours.

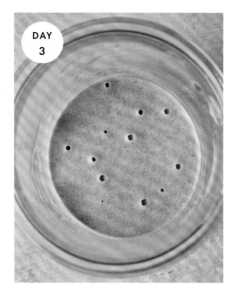

Day 4

In the morning, you should start to see (more) signs of fermentation activity if you haven't already. There will be bubbles scattered on the sides and top, and the level of the mixture may have risen and fallen a little (evidenced by streaks on the sides of the jar). With Day 4, you'll start refreshing your mixture twice a day for the rest of the creation process.

Refresh the mixture in the same way as on Day 3 (discarding, adding flour and water, and stirring). Let it rest for 12 hours.

After this 12-hour rest, discard down the contents to 75g and refresh again with the same ratio of ingredients. Let the new mixture rest overnight.

Days 5 and 6

For Days 5 and 6, continue to discard down the contents of the jar and then refresh with the same ratio of ingredients as Day 4, twice a day, as fermentation activity increases more and more.

Day 7 and Onward

In the morning on Day 7, discard what's in the jar down to 20g of the mixture. To this, add 30g rye flour, 70g white flour, and 100g water. Mix well, cover, and let rest for 12 hours. In the evening (after about 12 hours), discard the jar contents down to 20g, add the same ratio of ingredients as earlier in the day, and let rest overnight.

WHEN IS MY STARTER READY TO USE?

At this point, you should see consistent signs of fermentation (or ripeness) every day. This consistency indicates you have a stable balance of bacteria and yeasts in your starter and it's strong enough to be used for your first bake.

Every 12 hours between refreshments, look out for these *signs of ripeness*:

- There are bubbles on the surface and at the sides.

- The consistency has loosened since first mixing and it will be very easy to stir.

- It has a pleasantly sour aroma (but not excessively pungent).

- It has risen to some degree (the amount of rise is highly dependent on the flour you use and your starter's hydration; in general, I like to see at least a 30 percent increase in volume).

If your starter is still struggling to show these signs of consistent and predictable fermentation activity, keep refreshing with the same ratio of ingredients for another day, or several more, until things pick up. This process can sometimes take longer, depending on the flour used and the environment (especially if it's cool in your kitchen). Be patient and stick to the schedule!

Once your starter is showing consistent signs of fermentation each day, you can choose to (1) drop down to one refreshment per day, (2) stick to two per day as I do, or (3) place your starter in storage from time to time if you need a break from baking. See Starter Maintenance (page 59) and Storing Your Starter (page 69) for more.

DO I HAVE TO REFRESH MY STARTER TWICE A DAY . . . FOREVER?

Many equate having a sourdough starter with having a pet, and I think this is mostly true. Much like a dog, the starter sort of enters your life as another thing to care for. A starter, however, only requires maybe 5 to 10 minutes a day for refreshments, and I find this small investment each day is well worth the return: an endless supply of delicious baked goods! Your starter is an organism that will live indefinitely if it's cared for; and for times when you want to go stretches without baking, you can always put it into short- or long-term storage (see Storing Your Starter, page 69). I still use the same starter I created over a decade ago, and while I'm somewhat attached to the goopy mess that it is, if it ever came down to it, I could create a new one in a week without too much trouble. I've heard it said that if you want to become a better person, get a dog. Well, I think the same is true for a sourdough starter.

RIPENESS

As you can see during each refreshment cycle, your starter goes from freshly mixed to increasingly more fermented as it sits. In the rest of the book, I use the word "ripe" to designate when my starter has fermented for some number of hours and is ready to either mix into a dough, make a levain, or, if I'm not baking, be given a refreshment. This point in the refreshment cycle is also referred to as a starter's "peak," but the concept is the same: The starter is at a strong stage with high populations of bacteria and yeasts. There's no single point in time or clear-cut indicator letting you know when a starter is ready for use, but rather, it's a collection of sights, smells, and consistency changes that all need to be considered. In the end, the key is to use your starter after it's left to ferment for several hours (which, for the process and schedule outlined in this book, is around 12 hours) until it's ripe. Many new bakers tend to use their starter too early; in most conditions, if you're unsure, it's better to use a starter that's slightly overripe than under.

ALL ABOUT SOURDOUGH STARTER DISCARD

What's up with the discard? Why do we have to throw out parts of the starter?

When you start baking sourdough at home, you may be shocked by how much sourdough starter is wasted every time you refresh your starter. The first thing to keep in mind is that this isn't waste at all: The beneficial bacterial and wild yeasts are using the fresh flour to survive. Discarding is an essential part of the starter refreshment process because it's the time when you get rid of the by-products of fermentation: acids, alcohols, and other compounds. If left in your mixture, the culture would eventually become overly acidic, weaken, and if left long enough, cease to live. By discarding and adding fresh flour and water, we're ensuring the microbes in our starter are fed and have a healthy environment.

When can I start using sourdough starter discard in recipes like pancakes and waffles?

I would advise against using your starter discard until it is showing consistent signs of ripeness each day. This consistency usually comes 7 to 10 days after beginning the process of creating a sourdough starter. Because suitable lactic acid bacteria fermentation hasn't yet properly taken hold of your starter, using discard at this early stage might mean using bacteria we're not looking to cultivate in the end (i.e., not beneficial bacteria)—and there likely won't be any flavor advantage to it anyway.

Saving and Using Discard

- Create a starter cache in the refrigerator: Once your starter is strong and consistent, each day you discard, add it to this jar instead of the trash, cover it, and return it to the refrigerator where it will keep for up to 7 days. Draw from this cache of saved starter when you want to make a discard recipe (see suggestions below).

- Clearing the cache: I like to clear it out every weekend whether I've used it completely or not. I don't recommend using this saved starter to make bread, as it is likely overly acidic (which is great for flavor, but not balanced in terms of yeast and bacteria populations for making bread).

- Discard recipes: Use your discard to make any of the following recipes, which use the starter primarily for flavor rather than leavening:

Skillet Corn Bread (page 381)

Sunday Morning Pancakes (page 410)

Buttermilk Waffles (page 412)

Sourdough Scones (page 415)

Flaky Drop Biscuits (page 382)

Sourdough Starter Crackers (page 384)

Crêpes (page 416)

Banana Bread 2.0 (page 418)

Peach and Blueberry Crostata (page 421)

Cherry-Almond Biscotti (page 422)

SOURDOUGH STARTER TROUBLESHOOTING

Oh no, I forgot to feed my starter.

It happens—don't worry about it. Give your starter a refreshment when you realize you missed one, and then give it another when you would usually refresh it (e.g., that next evening or morning). Unless you missed many, many days in a row, your starter will spring back and be just fine. If you had planned to make a levain that day and your starter has a very acidic aroma and is the consistency of water, you might want to hold off on baking until a timely feeding of fresh flour and water can mellow it out.

Nothing is happening Days 3 through 5. Did I kill it? What do I do?

It's not dead. Sometimes it takes longer to see fermentation activity at this phase—it's normal. Try the following:

- Keep your starter warm (80°F/26°C is ideal) and use warm water (85°F/29°C) for the refreshments. It can also help to wrap your container in a few layers of kitchen towels to keep it warm (or use the oven with the light turned on periodically as a makeshift proofer—just be sure it doesn't get *too* hot in there).

- Use whole-grain rye flour if you're not doing so already.

- Switch back to one refreshment per day for a few days, then once you see consistent fermentation activity, switch back to two refreshments per day. Sometimes in the beginning, if we discard too much too often, we reduce bacteria and yeast populations too frequently, never allowing them to get a foothold.

- Try using bottled spring water from the market for your refreshments until your starter is established.

My starter doesn't double in height (or collapse). What's wrong with it?

It is not necessary for your starter to double in height for it to function properly. The rise height is highly dependent on the flour and starter hydration. Consider, for example, a starter that's refreshed with 100% whole wheat flour versus one that uses 100% high-protein white flour—the latter will rise significantly higher. The most important thing is to spot consistent signs of fermentation each day.

I fed my starter the wrong amount of flour or water.

Don't worry about small deviations! If you find the mixture is too stiff or too loose compared to how it usually feels, add a little more flour or water to adjust the consistency.

How do I know if my starter has gone bad?

If your starter is fed consistently and is kept warm it's very resilient. If no mold is present, it should survive just about anything. If you see activity that's outside of "normal" for your starter, try giving it timely refreshments (one or two times a day) for a few days until it gets back on track. If you do this for 2 weeks and it refuses to spring back with consistent signs of fermentation, I'd create a new one.

I think I see mold.

If you don't see signs of typical food spoilage (pink colors, fuzzy white, anything green), then your starter should be fine. If you do see off colors, create a new one from scratch. Also, use your nose as a guide (see next paragraph).

My starter has a strange smell.

When creating a new starter, you might find it has a strange smell on Day 1 or 2, but this is normal and expected—proceed with the process as directed. If your starter is already established, it can be common, depending on the beneficial bacteria that are flourishing in your starter, for it to develop a strong "musty" smell. I often have this with my own starter when it's refreshed with a high percentage of whole-grain flour, especially freshly milled. But if it smells *very* off, like spoiled milk or molded fruit, then I strongly suggest starting over.

There's a thin layer of clear liquid on my starter.

This is common and could be a sign your starter simply needs more frequent refreshments. This thin layer, sometimes called hooch, is the alcoholic by-product of fermentation. Pour off the layer of liquid (or mix it back in) and refresh your starter a little more often. Depending on the temperature, the amount of ripe starter left in the jar after discarding (i.e., the carryover percentage), and the flour used, this might mean once a day, twice a day, or in some cases, three times a day. See Starter Maintenance (page 59) for tips.

I need to take a break from this sourdough life. What do I do with my starter?

Your starter can survive for weeks when refreshed and then stored in the refrigerator. I generally don't like to go past 2 weeks in the refrigerator without a refreshment, but I've done 3 weeks without harm. Check out page 69 for more on storage options.

I left my starter in the refrigerator for a long, long time. It looks fine. Can I use it?

Absolutely. As long as you don't see signs of mold, let it warm to room temperature. Then give it a refreshment as you normally would. Give it a few more refreshments and keep it at room temperature for a few days and you should see fermentation activity return. If you do not, you can continue to refresh this starter and hope it comes back—or create a new one.

Tutorial
SIMPLE SOURDOUGH

Here is your first loaf of naturally leavened bread:
a mild-flavored bread with satisfying fermentation and
wheat flavors, and a deeply colored, crunchy crust

THIS IS WHERE IT ALL BEGINS: At this point, you've gone through the process of creating your own sourdough starter and perhaps you've picked up a few tools, too. You've probably been talking about baking bread with your friends, family—some of whom now want you to stop talking so much about bread already. I get it, I've been there. This straightforward recipe is the perfect spot to begin: It's a forgiving hydration, uses only a single type of flour, and it doesn't require any extensive kneading. But that doesn't mean the loaf isn't going to be incredibly flavorful, any less healthy, or one bit less satisfying—it's going to be awesome.

Compared with the recipes that begin on page 143, this one is written in a longer, tutorial style, with very detailed explanations along the way. The idea is that you'll feel like you're sitting in a beginner's bread baking class with me—I'll be right there with you at each step of the process. The tutorial also includes a suggested schedule to help you map out your baking days.

If you're new to baking bread, I recommend baking this recipe a few times before you move on to other recipes to get a feel for the process and how the dough progresses through its various stages on its way to the oven. The benefit of sticking to this beginning recipe is that after you bake it a few times you'll feel more comfortable with the steps, worrying less about the process itself and focusing more on managing fermentation and the dough, guiding it as it evolves through the day.

First Things First

STARTER: Do you have a ripe starter set to go? If not, go to How to Create Your Own Starter from Scratch (page 32) and come back when it's ready! If you have a starter, be sure to begin the levain-making process (step 1 in the recipe, page 44) at night when you'd normally refresh (feed) your ripe starter. It's okay if your starter is a little over-ripe (it may have a sour aroma, loose consistency, and might have fallen—which is fine).

TIMING: Heads up that this recipe will be made over the course of 3 days. Don't worry: A lot of that time will be hands-off, with the dough doing its thing while you do yours. I recommend starting by making the levain with your ripe starter Friday night so you have Saturday morning to mix and can peek in on the dough as it's evolving throughout the day. Plus, then you'll have fresh bread to enjoy all Sunday. I list sample times of day for each step in this recipe; you can follow them exactly or shift them earlier or later to suit your schedule.

READ THE RECIPE: It will help to read through the recipe in its entirety and watch the instructional QR code videos before you start!

Have these on hand:

INGREDIENTS

- 1,100g (plus a little more to help with shaping) white flour (~11.5% protein) or all-purpose flour

- 20g salt (I use fine sea salt)

EQUIPMENT

- Kitchen scale

- One large mixing bowl

- One bowl scraper or silicone spatula

- Instant-read thermometer

- Bench knife (bench scraper)

- Two medium mixing bowls or two proofing baskets

- Two large plastic bags (to hold proofing dough in bowl/basket)

- Razor blade (baker's lame), sharp knife, or scissors

- 4- to 5-quart (or larger) Dutch oven or 3.2-quart combo cooker

- Notebook or notes app on your phone

Simple Sourdough from start to finish

BAKING TIMELINE

1 Levain

    12 hours (overnight)

2 Autolyse

    30 minutes

3 Mix

4 Bulk Fermentation

    4 hours

5 Divide, Preshape, Bench Rest

    35 minutes

6 Shape

7 Proof

    18 hours (overnight)

8 Bake

    50 minutes in the oven

TOTAL

35 hours and 25 minutes

VITALS

Total dough weight	1,900g
Pre-fermented flour	9.1%
Levain	22.0%
Hydration	69.1%
Yield	Two 950g loaves

TOTAL FORMULA

INGREDIENT	BAKER'S %	WEIGHT
White flour (~11.5% protein)	100.0%	1,100g
Water 1 (levain and autolyse)	63.6%	700g
Water 2 (mix)	5.5%	60g
Fine sea salt	1.8%	20g
Ripe sourdough starter, 100% hydration	1.8%	20g

Each recipe will have a **BAKING TIMELINE** that serves as a snapshot of how long the overall recipe will take, plus the specific durations of the various steps in the baking process.

The **VITALS** table is essentially a snapshot of what to expect for each recipe; it tells you how much the recipe makes (both total dough weight as well as the number of loaves, rolls, or buns), how much levain is in the dough, the hydration percentage (to give you a sense for how stiff or loose the dough will be, where a higher percentage typically means a looser dough, depending on the flour), and any other notes. You'll see in the Yield row that this recipe makes two loaves of bread; to make just one loaf, divide all the ingredients, even the levain, in half.

The **TOTAL FORMULA** table outlines all the ingredients you'll need to bake this bread. It shows the baker's percentages and weights of each ingredient and includes the flour needed for the levain, any seed soakers, and other inclusions like nuts or fruit. For example, in this recipe you'll need a total of 1,100g of flour, which is 100% of the flour in the recipe—meaning all the flour in this bread is white flour. When the recipe has a mix of flours, you will see a separate row for each type of flour with its percentage and weight (and if you add up all the flour percentages, you'll always have 100%).

You might notice that most recipes in this book have two rows for water. The first water (Water 1), which is always a much larger quantity, is the majority of the water in the recipe and is used to make the levain and mix the optional autolyse or start the final dough mix. The second water (Water 2) is held in reserve and used, if needed, to adjust the consistency of the dough during final dough mixing. (See Adding Water in Phases, page 142, for more detail.)

If these tables look confusing to you now, don't worry, I'll tell you exactly what ingredient you'll need at each step of the process. Once you get the hang of reading these tables, you'll be able to understand any bread recipe very quickly—it's a concise way to show the relationship between all ingredients through baker's percentages. For an in-depth look at the percentages and tables used in recipes throughout this book, refer to Baker's Percentages (page 129).

The **BAKING STEPS** are where we finally get our bowls out and our hands in some flour and water. You'll notice that the recipe includes a few smaller tables that are set in the margin next to the baking steps. Each of these shows the specific ingredients that are needed for the step you are about to do. For example, the Levain table shows which ingredients from the Total Formula table are going to be used to make the levain. Similarly, you'll see tables for Autolyse (if there is one) and Final Dough. Each step has not only the approximate duration, but also a specific timeline as a general guideline, only if needed. Your timing may of course differ based on how your dough is progressing or when you'd like to start the recipe.

Taking Notes

Throughout this book I talk about taking notes when baking, and I've found it to be one of the greatest things I've done to advance my baking. The notes you take don't have to be super extensive, just enough to help you remember temperatures, what things you changed, what you should try changing next time, and how the bread turned out. I like to use a notebook or a notes app on my phone to quickly jot down key details (mixing time, final dough temperature, bulk times, and proof times) during each bake. See Resources (page 424) for a baking notes template you can use in your kitchen.

INGREDIENT	BAKER'S %	WEIGHT
White flour (~11.5% protein)	100.0%	100g
Water 1 (levain)	100.0%	100g
Ripe sourdough starter, 100% hydration	20.0%	20g

1. Levain

- **Time:** 9:30 p.m. (the night before mixing)
- **Duration:** 12 hours at warm room temperature: 74°–76°F (23°–24°C)

A levain is a mixture of flour, water, and some ripe sourdough starter that is left to ferment for several hours ahead of mixing the dough. Like a starter, it's a "pre-ferment," meaning it will leaven your dough (make it rise) and be responsible for the flavors produced during fermentation. Unlike your perpetually maintained starter, all of it gets used up in a recipe. A levain gives us the chance to change the flavor, performance, and timing characteristics of our pre-ferment without having to adjust our starter. In this case, we have a 12-hour levain made from all white flour that will ripen overnight. (For more information, see the Levain chapter, page 71.)

- **ADJUST THE WATER TEMPERATURE:** Warm or cool the water to 78°F (25°C).

For most of the recipes in this book, the desired temperature for the levain is 78°F (25°C). It's helpful to get your levain to this temperature in order to stick to the recipe's intention and schedule. To easily adjust the water temperature, weigh out some of the called-for water in a measuring cup, take its temperature, and then add either warm or cool water as needed to get it close to 78°F (25°C).

- **MIX THE LEVAIN:** In a medium jar, thoroughly mix the levain ingredients until incorporated. This is a liquid levain, which is typically equal parts water and flour (see Liquid Levain, page 75, for more information), and will feel quite loose after it's mixed.

- **LET THE LEVAIN RIPEN:** Loosely cover the jar and store it in a warm place, around 74° to 76°F (23° to 24°C), for about 12 hours.

Now that you've taken some of your starter to make this levain, *it's time to refresh your starter* by giving it fresh flour and water to keep your culture going. (See Starter Maintenance, page 59, for more information.)

INGREDIENT	WEIGHT
White flour (~11.5% protein)	1,000g
Water 1 (autolyse)	600g

2. Autolyse

- **Time:** 9 a.m. (start 30 minutes before your levain is expected to be ready)
- **Duration:** 30 minutes at warm room temperature: 74°–76°F (23°–24°C)
- **Desired dough temperature (DDT):** 78°F (25°C)

Not every recipe calls for an autolyse, but it's a very simple process (mix flour and water; let sit) that can help reduce the overall mixing time and, depending on the flour, help achieve a light and open interior in your bread. (See Autolyse, page 79, for more detail.)

- **ADJUST THE AUTOLYSE WATER TEMPERATURE:** Heat or cool the water so the temperature of the mixed dough meets the DDT for this recipe.

Since this is the largest volume of water used in the recipe, it will have the biggest impact on the final dough temperature. Thus, it's important to adjust the water temperature before mixing it with the flour. Getting the dough near the desired dough temperature (DDT) means it will follow the recipe timetable more closely and will ultimately result in bread with the intended flavor and texture. Use the following quick calculation (example included) to get the water temperature needed to hit the DDT for this recipe:

$$\text{Water temperature} = (\text{DDT} \times 4) - \left(\begin{array}{l} \text{flour temperature} \\ + \text{ levain temperature} \\ + \text{ ambient temperature} \\ + \text{ friction factor} \end{array} \right)$$

$$= (78 \times 4) - (72 + 78 + 72 + 0)$$
$$= 312 - 222$$
$$= 90°F \ (32°C)$$

Use your thermometer to get the flour and levain temperatures; note that the flour temperature is usually the ambient temperature of your kitchen (72°F/22°C). The friction factor is 0 for this recipe because we're mixing by hand (see What Is Friction Factor?, page 139). The formula tells us we need to warm our mixing water to 90°F (32°C) to hit the target DDT post-mixing. (For more on how to use this calculation and the importance of dough temperature, see Temperature, page 135.)

● **MIX THE AUTOLYSE:** Place the water and flour in a large bowl and use wet hands to mix until no dry bits remain; the dough will still be shaggy and loose. Use a bowl scraper to scrape down the sides of the bowl to keep all the dough in one area at the bottom.

● **LET THE DOUGH REST:** Cover the bowl and place it near your levain for 30 minutes.

3. Mix

▪ **Time:** 9:30 a.m.
▪ **Desired dough temperature (DDT):** 78°F (25°C)

● **CHECK THE LIQUID LEVAIN:** By now your levain should show signs of readiness: It should have risen at least moderately in its container; have bubbles on the top and at the sides, a loose consistency, and a sour aroma; and if you use a wet finger to gently pull back the top of the levain, it will feel very soft, look bubbly, and may collapse a bit. If you don't see these signs, let it ferment 1 hour more and check again. Conversely, if you think it looks like your levain may have overfermented a little—perhaps it's sour smelling, very bubbly, and broken down—that's okay, too. Just use it and keep an eye on the dough during bulk fermentation, as it might need to be divided a little earlier (I'll discuss the signs to look for when dividing).

● **ADJUST THE WATER TEMPERATURE:** Take the temperature of the dough and compare it to the DDT for this recipe: If it's higher, use cold water for the remaining water; if it's lower, use warm water.

INGREDIENT	WEIGHT
Water 2 (mix)	60g
Fine sea salt	20g
Levain	220g

Mixing dough by hand in bowl

● **MIX THE DOUGH:** To the autolyse, add about half of the water (30g), the salt, and ripe levain (A). Using wet hands, squeeze the ingredients into the dough, then mix thoroughly until everything is incorporated into a single shaggy mass. The hydration of this dough is moderate: It should feel firm yet sticky, but not be soupy or runny. If it feels very wet and slack, don't add the remaining water (if it's extremely runny and won't come together, add a little flour, and mix it into the dough to firm it up). Otherwise, add the rest of the water and continue to mix until the dough comes together and all the water is absorbed.

One important aspect in the breadmaking process is adjusting the amount of water used. From our perspective as bakers, flour is an ever-changing ingredient that almost always requires some hydration adjustment. Also note that you're going to use all the levain in this recipe, but depending on how vigilant you are about scraping out your levain jar, you might end up with a little less than the 220g amount called for—and that's okay. Just scrape out as much as possible.

● **STRENGTHEN THE DOUGH:** Wet one hand and grab one edge of the dough, lift, and stretch it over to the other side (B). Rotate the bowl a little and repeat the stretching and folding action. Continue this folding for 4 to 6 minutes. The dough should start to smooth out, have edges that are more defined, be a little stronger (elastic), and begin to hold its shape (C). Leave the dough in the bowl or transfer it to another container for bulk fermentation.

I find that beginning bakers tend to understrengthen their dough the first several times they bake; you might want to continue folding for a minute or two longer than you think the dough requires! (And no, you can't overstrengthen the dough.) Also, don't worry if the dough doesn't smooth out completely; it will be strengthened further during bulk fermentation.

● **MEASURE THE TEMPERATURE OF THE DOUGH:** Compare it to the DDT and record it as the final dough temperature. Cover the dough.

If the measured temperature is several degrees above or below the 78°F (25°C) DDT, your bread will still turn out great—but do take note and adjust the mixing water temperature next time. When proceeding with the rest of the recipe, be flexible with bulk fermentation, adjusting the duration as needed. If your dough temp is lower than the DDT, expect the bulk fermentation to take longer. Conversely, if your DDT is higher, you might have to divide earlier. (See When to End Bulk Fermentation, page 92, for more information.)

4. Bulk fermentation

- **Time:** 10 a.m. to 2 p.m.
- **Duration:** About 4 hours at warm room temperature: 74°–76°F (23°–24°C)
- **Folds:** 3 sets of stretches and folds at 30-minute intervals

Bulk fermentation is the critical step in the breadmaking process in which the bacteria and yeasts in your sourdough will begin to acidify and leaven the dough. During this period, you will also perform a series of stretches and folds, which help to further strengthen the dough.

● **SET TIMER AND MAKE A NOTE:** Write down the current time as the start of bulk fermentation, set a timer for 30 minutes, and let the dough rest. At this time, I also find it good to set an alarm (usually on my phone) for 4 hours so I know when bulk fermentation should be finished. (I do this because on more occasions than I'd like to admit, I've forgotten about the dough!)

● **STRETCH AND FOLD:** When your timer goes off, give the dough one set of stretches and folds. To do this, wet your hands and grab one side of the dough (D) and lift it up and over to the other side (E). Rotate the bowl 180 degrees and repeat. Then, rotate the bowl a quarter turn, and stretch and fold that side. Rotate the bowl 180 degrees again and finish with a stretch and fold on the last side. The dough should be folded up neatly (F). Cover the bowl and repeat these folds every 30 minutes for a total of 3 sets of stretches and folds.

Vigorous stretching and folding

Notice that with the first set of stretches and folds, the dough is still shaggy and not smooth; it stretches out easily without too much resistance. Before you do subsequent sets of stretches and folds, take notice of how the dough transforms through the entire bulk fermentation, slowly rising in the container and going from shaggy and slack (extensible) to increasingly smoother and stronger (elastic). Use the number of stretches and folds in the recipe as a guide, but you can stop giving the dough these sets when it starts holding its shape more in the container (it won't relax outward to fill the bowl so quickly) and it has less of a flat surface and more of a curved, domed look. The dough will also feel stronger and start to show definition: Stretches will be harder to perform as the dough becomes more elastic and feels thicker, more substantial.

● **LET THE DOUGH REST:** After the last set, cover the bowl and let the dough rest for the remainder of bulk fermentation, about 2 hours 30 minutes more, depending on the temperature.

5. Divide and preshape

▪ **Time:** 2 p.m.

● **CHECK THE DOUGH:** At the end of bulk fermentation, the dough will have risen perceptibly in the container, perhaps around a 30 percent volume increase. It may have some bubbles on top and at the sides, and it should look smooth and less shaggy. Look to the edge of the dough where it meets the container; the edge should be slightly domed, indicating some strength and rise. If you wet a hand and gently tug on the dough, you'll feel elasticity: The dough will be stronger and resist stretching out. Another good test is to jostle the container a bit; the dough should jiggle and wobble, indicating it's risen and aerated. If you don't see dough that's airy, strong, and "alive," leave it for another 15 minutes in bulk fermentation and check again.

Look at the photo below of my dough just before dividing (G). You'll see smoothness, bubbles, and domed edges. If you jiggle the container, you'll see the dough

  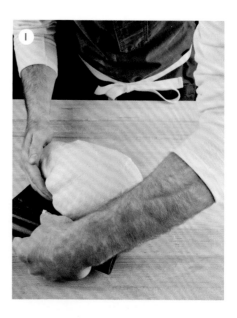

wobbles a bit, showing signs of life and strength. This dough is ready to be divided. If the dough still looks shaggy and dense, and isn't billowy, give it another 15 minutes to ferment longer. On the other hand, an uncommon, but possible, scenario is that the dough has risen excessively, feels very loose and sticky, and has lots of bubbles on top, indicating it might have fermented a little too long (don't worry, things will still work out just fine, but do take note of this and adjust next time). If this is the case, proceed with dividing the dough, but be extra gentle when handling it since the dough will be more fragile.

● **DIVIDE THE DOUGH:** Place a small bowl of water next to your work surface to keep your hands wet during dividing and preshaping. Using a bowl scraper, gently scrape the dough onto a clean work surface. Dampen your hand and use your bench knife to divide the dough directly in half (H).

Dividing and preshaping

I like to use a wet hand to divide and preshape my dough, but some bakers prefer using a dusting of flour (see Dividing, page 96, for my rationale). Both achieve the same goal: making your hands and tools nonstick. Choose whichever method you think you'll be comfortable with. If your dough looks wetter, shaggier, and generally more unruly than what you see in the photos, you might want to go with flour because it will help dry the dough a bit and make it easier to manage.

● **PRESHAPE THE DOUGH:** Hold a bench knife or bowl scraper in your dominant hand and wet your other hand. To preshape, use the bench knife to push the dough against the work surface, creating tension. As you use the knife to push the dough along the work surface, use your other hand to help guide the dough around into a round shape (I). Your free hand also ensures that the dough doesn't stick to the bench knife by holding it in place at the end of each rounding motion.

Preshaping helps gather the divided pieces of dough into organized shapes for easier final shaping. At the end of preshaping, you want the dough to be tight enough so that it holds its shape on the work surface. The dough should be gathered up into a taut round with defined, rounded edges, not spread out into a thin layer. If you find your dough is excessively sticky, wet your hand and assertively use it and your bench knife to tighten up the dough.

● **LET THE DOUGH REST:** Let the rounds rest for 35 minutes, uncovered.

This period, also called the bench rest, gives the dough time to relax outward, making it easier to shape without tearing. Periodically observe the dough during this bench rest.

▪ Is it stuck in a tight round without any spreading? Try giving it another 10 minutes to relax further and check again.

▪ Is it spreading out quickly, approaching more of a pancake shape than staying taut and collected? If so, perform a second preshape, rounding and tightening with your bench knife, as directed above, to give it more strength. Then, let it rest an additional 15 minutes and check again. Next time, add another set or two of stretches and folds during bulk fermentation to give the dough more strength.

6. Shape

▦ **Time:** 2:50 p.m.

● **PREPARE THE PROOFING BASKETS:** Line two proofing baskets or medium bowls with clean kitchen towels. Dust lightly and evenly with white flour.

● **SHAPE THE DOUGH:** This dough lends itself nicely to being shaped as a boule (a round shape). To shape as a bâtard, see page 102 for details.

▦ After the dough has bench rested for 35 minutes, it should have relaxed outward and reduced in height.

▦ Lightly flour your work surface, the top of both resting rounds, and your hands.

▦ Using a bench knife, scoop up and flip over one round so the top, floured side is now facing down. After flipping, if the dough is very compact and tight, use both hands to gently stretch it outward in all directions to form a slightly larger round.

▦ Using both hands, grab the bottom edge closest to you and fold it up to the middle, pressing gently so it sticks (J).

▦ Gently tug outward on the bottom two corners (K). Take the right side and fold it up over to the middle (L); repeat for the left side so it folds up and slightly overlaps the just-folded right side in the middle (M).

▦ Take the top and fold it down over the entire round so it touches the work surface (N). The dough will slightly flip down and over (O) when doing this, and the result will be a folded-up shape with the seam facing down.

▦ Shape both hands into little cups and cup them around the far side of the dough. Keeping the seam-side down, gently drag the dough toward you with your pinky fingers dragging against the work surface (P). The dry surface will ever so slightly hang on to the dough, thus forming a taut outer skin.

▦ Next, rotate the dough by using both hands to slightly push away the dough while at the same time rotating it slightly. Use both hands to again drag the dough toward you, creating tension with your hands and pinky fingers.

▦ Repeat rotating and dragging until there's an even, smooth, and taut surface on the outside of the dough, but not so much that it tears. It should hold itself in a round shape on the work surface (Q). Repeat the shaping process with the second piece of dough.

▦ When both are shaped, use a floured hand and the bench knife to scoop up one piece of dough and flip it over into a prepared proofing basket so that the seam (bottom) is facing up. Repeat with the second piece of dough. If there are major seams in the shaped dough, pinch them closed. Place each basket inside a reusable plastic bag and seal.

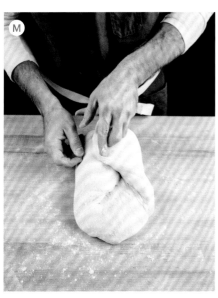

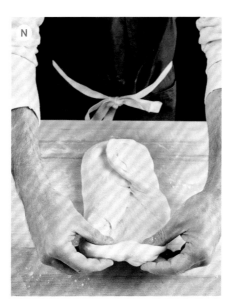

Shaping
a boule,
slack dough

7. Proof

- ▪ **Time:** 3 p.m. to 9 a.m. (overnight)
- ▪ **Duration:** About 18 hours in a home refrigerator: 39°F (4°C)

- ● **LET THE DOUGH PROOF:** Place the baskets in the refrigerator to proof overnight.

While not all the bread I make is proofed overnight in a cold refrigerator (also called retarding), I prefer the method in this recipe for a few reasons: First, it's convenient. Baking the next day means a break in the process, and the dough will hold well in the refrigerator until the next afternoon, evening, or night. Second, a cold proof brings increased flavor complexity through continued fermentation. While you won't see a significant rise in the dough when you pull it out to bake the next day, rest assured that fermentation continued during this cold proof.

8. Bake

- ▪ **Time:** 9 a.m. (or later in the day, as desired)
- ▪ **Duration:** 50 minutes in the oven

This dough can be baked first thing in the morning, in the afternoon, or even in the evening. The longer you extend the cold proof, the less rise you'll see in your loaves, and they may have an increased sour flavor.

- ● **CHOOSE YOUR STEAMING METHOD:** For this recipe, we'll be using a Dutch oven or combo cooker.

When baking bread, steam helps the loaf achieve a caramelized, deeply colored crust. Additionally, steam promotes a clean score and ear (the little piece of dough that peels up as the loaf bakes) and ekes out a bit more rise. Steaming in a home oven can be a little challenging, as that is not what the oven was designed for, but there are a few workarounds (see Baking with Steam in a Home Oven, page 123). For this recipe, the easiest and most effective approach is to bake your bread in a sealed Dutch oven or combo cooker inside your oven. As the dough bakes in this sealed environment, the vapor released from the dough is trapped, creating a steamy microenvironment that helps prevent the crust on the dough from hardening and setting too rapidly, giving it time to rise and expand in a controlled manner.

- ● **PREPARE THE OVEN FOR BAKING:** Place an oven rack in the bottom third of the oven (usually one up from the bottom slot) with no rack above it. Place the Dutch oven pot (or the shallow side of a combo cooker) on the oven rack and place the lid next to it. Preheat the oven to 450°F (230°C) for 30 minutes.

- ● **PREPARE THE DOUGH FOR BAKING:** When the oven has finished preheating, take one of the proofing baskets out of the refrigerator, uncover, and put a piece of parchment paper over the basket. Place a pizza peel or inverted baking sheet on top of the parchment and, using both hands, flip everything over (R). Gently remove the basket; your dough should now be resting on the parchment paper on the pizza peel (S).

If you find your dough sticks excessively to your proofing basket towels, dust a little more flour into the basket next time. This can also be a sign that your dough is not shaped tightly enough to develop a smooth, strong skin on the outside. Next time, shape the dough a little tighter and with even tension (see Shape with even tension, page 99).

● **SCORE THE DOUGH:** Using a baker's lame (a razor blade attached to a handle), bare razor blade, sharp knife, or scissors, score the dough (T). Be sure to slice into the dough at least 1 inch deep, and use confident, clean motions to make the cuts. It's okay if you use the blade to cut into the same line again to ensure it's deep enough—the cut should look like it's gone in below the outer skin and the dough beneath will show bubbles. For a boule, I like to cut a box shape in the center with a little X in the middle. An even simpler, but no less beautiful, score is a straightforward, large X on top.

Scoring dough

When bread dough is baked, the radiant heat of the oven increases fermentation activity rapidly to generate more gas, gasses already trapped in the viscoelastic dough expand, and dissolved gasses in the dough are forced out of solution. All of this causes the dough to rise high and expand in the oven. If left on its own, eventually the taut exterior skin (which we created during shaping) would burst uncontrollably, potentially causing the loaf to bulge and tear. To avoid this, we score—cut—the dough in order to guide the loaf into rising where we want it to. This relieves some of the pressure built up during baking, allowing gasses to escape and the dough to open. But scoring is also a way to have a little fun and be creative—a way for each baker to leave their own signature on the loaf they're baking. (See Decorative Scoring, page 120, for more instruction and inspiration.) You'll also see here that the chilled dough (from cold proofing) is pretty easy to score.

Baking in a Dutch oven

● **BAKE THE DOUGH:** Using ovensafe gloves, carefully remove the Dutch oven pot from your oven and place it on a heat-resistant surface near your scored dough. Then, lift the pizza peel and drag the parchment paper holding the scored dough into the preheated pot. It's okay for the parchment paper to bake with the dough in the

oven. Return the pot to the oven and cover with the lid. Bake for 20 minutes. Vent the pot of steam: Uncover the pot and remove the lid from the oven. Continue to bake for 30 to 35 minutes more. When done, the loaf should have an internal temperature around 206°F (96°C), and the crust should be a deep mahogany color and produce a satisfying crunch when gently squeezed with gloves on.

● **FINISH AND COOL:** Place the baked loaf on a wire cooling rack. Return the pot to the oven and preheat again for 15 minutes. Remove the second loaf from the refrigerator and repeat the scoring and baking process. Let the loaves cool on a wire rack for 1 to 2 hours before slicing.

> Hold that bread knife! I know, I know, warm bread directly from the oven is incredibly tempting, and having to wait while it's sitting there cooling, filling the kitchen with an incredible aroma, is torture. By letting the loaf completely cool, however, we avoid slicing into bread with a gummy interior, and we'll enjoy the bread when it's most flavorful. As just-baked bread cools from the oven, the starches need time to cool and set; once this happens, the flavor of the loaf will shine through.

POST-LOAF RECAP

You did it! You successfully baked your first sourdough loaves. How did it go? If the loaf didn't end up the way you expected, don't worry: This is a learning experience, and I'm sure the bread still tasted great! See the Troubleshooting section on page 56 for help on any not-so-perfect loaves. This recipe is a great starting point and if you're a beginner, I recommend making it several times to hone the process. Once you're ready, see How to Tinker (below) for variations that will help you continue to build your skills.

There's endless tinkering you can do, but there's a lot more book to explore! From here, dig into the in-depth information on techniques (page 58), and the science (page 132) to get a deeper understanding of all things sourdough. And of course, there are tons of recipes (starting on page 143). Explore, be curious, experiment, and happy baking!

HOW TO TINKER

TRY DIFFERENT FLOUR TYPES

You can easily replace up to 15% of the flour in this recipe with another variety. That is, leave out 165g of the called-for white flour and replace it with whole wheat, spelt, Khorasan, durum, rye, or emmer.

ADD NUTS OR DRIED FRUIT INCLUSIONS

Try adding up to 150g of chopped toasted walnuts or pecans or dried fruit. Add the nuts or fruit to the top of the dough during bulk fermentation, just before the first set of stretches and folds. Spread the nuts in a thin layer on top of the dough in the container and, with wet hands, fold them into the dough while performing stretches and folds. Perform the additional sets of stretches and folds as directed and continue with the rest of the recipe. (See How and When to Add Inclusions, page 86, for more detail.)

BAKE THIS RECIPE ALL IN A SINGLE DAY

Instead of retarding (proofing at a cold temperature) the dough overnight in the refrigerator, switch to baking this dough the same day. Proceed with the recipe all the way up to the point where you would normally put the covered dough into the refrigerator to proof. Instead, let the dough proof on the counter for 1 to 3 hours, temperature depending. For me, this dough is ready to bake after about a 2-hour proof at my typical kitchen temperature (74°F/23°C). The best way to tell if this dough is ready to bake is to use the Poke Test (page 116).

Here is a guide to the ten most common issues that beginner bread bakers have with their loaves—and most important, how to solve them.

My loaf is really gummy and dense inside.

This could be the result of underproofing, underbaking, or slicing the loaf too early. First, be sure to use your sourdough starter when it's ripe to create your levain, and use your levain when it's ripe to mix into your dough—using your pre-ferment early can lead to underproofing. If your levain doesn't show signs of ripeness (bubbles on top and at the sides, a sour aroma, and a loose consistency), give it another 30 minutes to 1 hour to ferment, then check again. From there, be sure you let the dough sufficiently ferment in bulk fermentation until you see the signs listed in the recipe (smooth texture, domed edges, increased strength) to avoid underproofing. Finally, don't slice your loaf too soon after baking, as it needs time to fully set.

My loaf is flat and sad.

Usually, a loaf that fails to rise in the oven is the result of overhydration (too much water in the dough), insufficient dough strength (not enough kneading during mixing and/or insufficient stretches and folds during bulk fermentation), or overproofing (dough left too long in bulk fermentation and/or its final proof). Overhydration and insufficient dough strength are related: If the dough has too much water added, it will require additional strengthening so it holds its shape and rises tall in the oven. Next time, try reducing the water in the recipe (leaving out the reserved water will bring strength to the dough) and add in one or two more sets of stretches and folds during bulk fermentation. If your loaf has lots and lots of little holes in the interior and sometimes small holes with one large hole up top between the crust and crumb, it's likely it overproofed. Next time, note the final dough temperature after mixing, and if it's higher than the DDT, consider reducing the bulk fermentation time by 15 to 30 minutes.

My loaf has scattered massive holes in it.

Underproofed dough can have excessive oven spring (the amount the dough rises during baking) and an interior with dense spots and large, scattered holes. You're looking for an interior that has plentiful holes that are even, medium-sized, and uniformly distributed. Be sure to give the dough sufficient time in bulk fermentation: It should not be divided until it's well risen, smooth, and showing signs of strength (domed edges and a resistance to stretching outward). Since this recipe was proofed overnight in the refrigerator, it can be hard to tell in the morning if it's had enough fermentation time at room temperature. At the end of proofing, you want to look for dough that's puffy and smooth, and if you poke it, it should leave an indentation and feel very soft (see the Poke Test, page 116, for more information). Finally, if your loaf has evenly distributed holes with no dense spots (meaning it's well proofed), but there's a single large cavern somewhere, that's usually a result of improper shaping. Next time, be assertive with shaping and impart even tension across the entire piece of dough.

My loaf is very burned (or excessively thick) on the bottom.

Baking in a Dutch oven or combo cooker has a tendency to slightly burn the bottom if the pot is too hot and the dough is baked for too long. Try preheating your pot for less time or at a lower temperature, or (carefully) remove your loaf from the pot after it has fully set and bake directly on the oven rack for the last 10 minutes. See My Bottom Crust Is Always Burned (page 126) for more tips on avoiding a burned bottom crust.

The score didn't pop like yours—no ear! (Or it cracked in a weird place.)

This can be due to overproofing, understrengthened dough, insufficient shaping and/or score depth, insufficient steam in the oven, or too much top heat from your oven.

- It's overproofed: If the interior has lots of little holes but it's slightly gummy, try reducing the bulk fermentation time by 30 minutes or reduce the time the dough is in the refrigerator. See the Proofing chapter (page 110) for more detail.

- Be sure your dough is strong and shaped tightly enough to hold its shape after shaping.

- Score (cut) in deep enough. With most doughs, I like to cut about 1 inch deep with the blade. See the Scoring chapter (page 118) for more detail.

- If you're baking in a pot with a sealed lid, it's likely not a steaming issue. Otherwise, see Baking with Steam in a Home Oven (page 123).

- If your oven is too hot near the top of your dough, it will prematurely harden before opening fully. Move the oven rack holding your dough down one or two slots.

My bread is doughy and raw or wet and sticky in the middle.

This can be due to underproofed dough, underbaked dough, a dough that's overhydrated, or cutting the finished loaf too early. Be sure to bake the loaf completely; it should have a well-colored crust, crackle when gently squeezed, and register an internal temperature around 204°F (95°C). After baking, let the loaf cool on a wire rack for at least 1 to 2 hours, until cool to the touch, before slicing.

The crust is pale and isn't crusty enough. (Or it's too crusty—it's hard to bite through!)

For ample crust color, be sure the oven has sufficient steam during the first 20 minutes of baking (if you're baking in a sealed pot, this shouldn't be an issue). The thickness of the crust is generally related to how hot and how long the dough is baked. If it's too thin, try reducing the temperature of the oven in the second

half of the bake (after steaming) by 25°F (20°C) and lengthen the bake until fully baked through. Conversely, if it's too thick, try baking for a reduced time (with potentially a higher heat). Additionally, in some cases, to achieve a thinner crust, it can help to introduce more steam into your baking vessel by adding an ice cube (which helps create a shinier crust, too). See My Crust Is Always Dull (page 126) for more details.

My bread doesn't taste sour enough.

This first recipe won't have a super-sour flavor due to the levain parameters, flour choice, temperatures, and other factors. If you want to dig into how to make your sourdough bread more sour, check out Tinkering with Sourness (page 234) and Extra-Sour Sourdough (page 237) for tips.

I never even made it to the end because everything became a sticky mess.

Your dough is likely overhydrated. Remember, the recipes in this book are general guidelines, meant to get you very close, but they ultimately will need some adjustments based on your climate and flour. Next time, don't add the reserved water (Water 2).

The bread keeps disappearing too fast!

Bake more bread! Really, though, once you bake that first loaf, I almost guarantee you're going to be baking fresh sourdough bread on the regular from here on out. Get ready to become the person who always brings bread to any and all gatherings (and everyone will love you for it).

III

TECHNIQUE

Sourdough Starter

Sourdough Starter Science

The bacteria (primarily lactic acid bacteria, aka LAB) and wild yeasts that coexist in a sourdough starter come from the environment and from the grain used in both its creation and maintenance. Over time, various strains of each come and go as a sort of microevolution unfolds through the starter's continued maintenance. During this process, new strains are introduced from both the environment and the added flour, but only the fittest (in an evolutionary sense) remain in the culture. In essence, you're selecting a subset of bacteria and wild yeasts that best adapt and thrive in the environment you've created and continue to maintain.

A well-maintained sourdough starter is typically composed of lactic acid bacteria and wild yeasts in a ratio of about 100 to 1, respectively. The lactic acid bacteria in a starter are primarily responsible for acidifying the dough through the production of organic acids, while the wild yeasts are primarily responsible for the leavening of the dough through the production of carbon dioxide.

Starter Maintenance

Consistent maintenance is key and will ensure your culture can leaven and acidify your dough with the same effectiveness each time. It is important to keep these essential elements as consistent as possible with each refreshment:

- The hydration (how much water is in your starter with respect to flour)

- The temperature of your starter

- How often you refresh (or feed) the starter, which determines how acidic the culture becomes

- The type of flour used

The reality is that a sourdough starter is downright hearty and resilient. If you forget to refresh it for a day, it'll be just fine. If you run out of your usual flour, use another one you have in your pantry. Aside from massive temperature swings (yeasts begin to suffer at around 120°F/48°C, and I don't like to go above 85°F/29°C) or extreme neglect, it's likely that with a little attention and care, your starter will recover.

See also Create Your Sourdough Starter (page 32) and Sourdough Starter Troubleshooting (page 38).

KEEPING A STARTER HEALTHY

Here are three principles I follow to keep my sourdough starter strong and healthy:

1. **Refresh it often:** Refresh it at least once a day. However, since I bake so often, I typically refresh my starter twice a day in 12-hour intervals.

2. **Keep it warm:** Find a warm spot in your kitchen to keep fermentation activity high (I like to keep mine around 74°F/23°C to 76°F/24°C). If it's cold in your kitchen, warm the mixing water you use for refreshments.

3. **Be observant:** Check in with your starter periodically during the day to see how it's progressing. Take note of its appearance, aroma, and consistency. These observations will help you gauge its fermentation progress during a refreshment cycle and learn how to adjust as necessary. Over time, you won't need to check in with it quite so often, but in the beginning, it helps establish an observational baseline.

LEVAIN ≈ STARTER

There are a few key differences (see Levain vs. Starter, page 72), but a sourdough starter and a levain are essentially the same thing: They are both pre-ferments, meaning a mixture of flour and water that's seeded with a small bit of ongoing culture and left to ferment. As both a starter and a levain ripen they each show the same signs (increased rise, bubbles, a progressively sourer aroma) as they move from "just mixed" through "ripe" and eventually to "overripe," and the descriptions of the stages for a starter can apply interchangeably to a levain.

12 HOURS

REFRESH RIPE STARTER

TO BAKE

MAKE LEVAIN

Sourdough Starter Fermentation Life Cycle

As with many steps in the breadmaking process, it's tough to set clear-cut boundaries for the various stages of a sourdough starter's refreshment cycle. Each cycle is a continuum that begins with a just-mixed concoction of flour and water and a little bit of your ongoing culture. From there, it transforms as the bacteria and yeasts metabolize the sugars present in the flour, acidifying and leavening the starter mixture.

Let's look at the photographs on the next page for some characteristics of a starter at various stages in its refreshment cycle. The starter shown is composed of 70% white flour and 30% whole rye flour at 100% hydration, which is what my typical starter makeup looks like; see How to Maintain Your Starter, page 62. (Note that the starter in How to Create Your Own Starter from Scratch, page 32, calls for slightly different flour and water ratios to help spur spontaneous fermentation.)

REFRESH STARTER OR MAKE LEVAIN

JUST MIXED ⟶ YOUNG ⟶ RIPE ⟶ OVERRIPE

ACIDITY ↓ PH ↑

ACIDITY ↑ PH ↓

AROMA: *Fresh, like fresh flour*
TASTE: *Mild, grassy, little to no sourness*
ACIDITY: *Low (assuming small inoculation percentage)*
VISUAL: *Shaggy, clumped, concentrated at the bottom of the jar*
CONSISTENCY: *Pliable (depending on hydration and flour used)*

AROMA: *Lightly sour and sweet*
TASTE: *Minimal sourness, slightly sweet*
ACIDITY: *Minimal*
VISUAL: *Risen, some scattered bubbles at the side and top but not excessively bubbly*
CONSISTENCY: *Pliable, starting to loosen but still showing some viscosity*

AROMA: *Sour but not overbearing, perhaps like a mild cheese*
TASTE: *Sour but not excessively sharp*
ACIDITY: *Mild*
VISUAL: *Risen, many bubbles at sides and top*
CONSISTENCY: *Lower viscosity, loose, fluid, if top of mixture is touched it may collapse, easy to stir*

Time for the starter to be used in a recipe and/ or given a refreshment!

AROMA: *Like vinegar, nearing fingernail polish*
TASTE: *High sourness, mild vinegar*
ACIDITY: *High*
VISUAL: *Bubbly, frothy, possibly collapsed in jar*
CONSISTENCY: *Lowest viscosity, high fluidity, very loose, thin*

Getting to Know Your Starter

Once you have an established sourdough starter showing consistent signs of fermentation each day, the next step is getting to know how it progresses through its fermentation refreshment cycle. Because your starter is a living, evolving thing, it'll change in response to your maintenance and its environment. Check in on your starter a few times during the day to observe how it changes from one refreshment to the next.

- Take note of how its texture changes from shaggy and lifeless to smooth, bubbly, and well risen.

- Its aroma is another indicator of its transformation: It will progress from aromas of fresh flour, straw, and even a little sweetness to increased pungency, taking on sour notes like mild vinegar.

- Be aware of the seasons and the temperature of your kitchen. If it's a warm summer day, your starter will ripen faster and may require a refreshment earlier to ensure it doesn't become overripe and overly acidic. Conversely, if it's cooler, it may mean extending the time between refreshments to ensure sufficient fermentation has taken place.

The goal is to be observant and respond to how your starter is fermenting each day, performing the necessary adjustments in time, temperature, and/or ingredient ratios. See How to Maintain Your Starter (page 62) for techniques on how to adjust your starter to sync its ripening with your schedule.

SOURDOUGH STARTER

Using a Starter's Rise Height as a Gauge for Ripeness

In my experience, the amount of rise in a starter isn't as important as other signs of fermentation (such as aroma, presence of bubbles, and its consistency) when gauging its level of ripeness. Take, for example, a starter consisting of 100% high-protein white flour compared to a starter consisting of 100% rye flour; these two starters will display completely different rise characteristics (the former rising much higher than the latter). Further, depending on the flour used, the hydration percentage of the starter also will greatly affect its rise height. For example, a 60% hydration (stiff consistency) starter made from 100% whole wheat will not rise as high as a 100% hydration starter with 100% white flour.

It is important to see some rise in your starter, regardless of the flour used. Rise indicates carbon dioxide production, which means you have a healthy yeast population. So, while I find rise height not to be the best single indicator for ripeness, it's one data point among several under consideration.

Using a Starter Before or After It's Ripe

Since there's no single point when a starter is perfectly ripe, it's often the case that you use your starter a little early or a little late—and this is okay. However, I find I make better bread (flavor, texture, and overall eating quality) if I err on the side of using my starter when it's very ripe, rather than underripe. Using your starter when it's at its strongest and has the highest populations of bacteria and yeasts will directly translate into a strong levain, which means strong fermentation in a final dough. Using your starter in an underripe state slows the fermentation timeline and ultimately may result in underproofed bread if not corrected later in the baking process.

There's a limit, though. Avoid using your starter when it's excessively acidic, meaning it's extremely overripe. This is

Use a ripe sourdough starter to create a levain, and similarly, use a ripe levain to mix into a dough.

usually the case when a starter is left for hours after it needs a refreshment. The texture will be very broken down (sometimes "watery") and have a sharp nail polish–esque aroma. Using a highly acidic starter at this stage may result in increased fermentation activity and a dough that's unstable. In this case, I prefer delaying my baking plans, giving my starter a timely refreshment or two, and then proceeding with baking the next day.

How to Maintain Your Starter

There are many ways to maintain a sourdough starter and there's no single right way. It's more about finding what works for you as a baker and how you can maintain your starter to fit your baking schedule. The following are the key factors that affect starter maintenance, and for each I describe what works best for me to keep my starter healthy and vigorous. Whether you want to bake bread just about every day as I do, or whether you want to make bread once a month, this section should give you the understanding and tools necessary to maintain your starter on your terms.

TEMPERATURE

Choose any spot in your kitchen with a relatively stable temperature—preferably on the warm side but anywhere between 68°F (20°C) and 86°F (30°C) is ideal. If your kitchen is cool, you can warm the mixing water to offset the cool ambient temperature and expect additional fermentation time to ripen after each refreshment. (Conversely, if your kitchen is hot, use cooler mixing water.) You may also choose a well-insulated container for your starter or place your starter jar inside another closed container to create an insulated buffer of air to further stabilize its temperature. (Personally, I prefer to keep my starter around 74° to 76°F (23° to 24°C) in a small home proofing box. In the summer, if temperatures in the kitchen rise, I'll either take my starter out and keep it in my cool pantry or continue to keep it in the proofer but turn the proofer off.)

FLOUR

Over the years I've experimented with using just about every flour that's passed through my kitchen to refresh my sourdough starter, from all-purpose to bread flour to whole spelt. In the end, I've found that just about any flour will work. However, my preference is a mix of white flour and whole rye. This mixture provides my starter the best of all worlds: a boost to fermentation activity thanks to the nutrient-rich whole rye flour, and a mild acidity, tall rise, and sufficient gas-trapping ability from the white flour. Also, white flour's ability to trap a lot of gas helps make spotting the signs of ripeness easier.

Typically, I use 30% whole rye and 70% white flour at 100% hydration. See What Sourdough Starter Ratios Work Best? (page 65) for more detail.

TIME

For optimal results, I find it best to refresh a starter at least once a day if it's kept out of the refrigerator. If a starter is left for too long without a refreshment, it becomes overly acidic as the organic acids in the culture begin to build up from continued fermentation. If the acidity reaches high enough levels, the microbial population in the starter suffers due to an increasingly inhospitable environment.

For my starter and baking schedule, I refresh twice a day: once in the morning and once in the evening. This schedule is convenient because I have two points in the day when I can make a levain for baking or use my starter directly in a mix.

If you find yourself baking only once a week, you can switch to refreshing your starter once a day. Make sure to reduce the starter carryover percentage to reduce fermentation activity and lengthen its fermentation cycle (see Inoculation Percentage, page 65). To store your starter for longer periods of inactivity, see Storing Your Starter (page 69).

HYDRATION

I prefer to keep a "liquid starter" at 100% hydration; that is, equal quantities of flour and water (though it could range anywhere from 90% to 120% hydration). It's loose and easy to mix with a spatula in a jar, which makes for quick, low-effort refreshments.

Many bakers prefer to keep a "stiff starter," which is typically around 50% to 65% water to total flour. The consistency is exactly what it sounds like: It's stiff and requires kneading with your hands or in a small mixer. One benefit is it seems to handle warmer ambient temperatures without becoming overly acidic, and it has a larger window of ripeness and usability.

A liquid or stiff starter will work for all the recipes in this book (in my experience, the levain has a larger impact on the final dough characteristics than the starter). Each recipe begins with making a levain, and they assume a 100% hydration starter to make this levain. If you maintain a stiff starter, you may need to add more water when making a levain in this book. For recipes that use starter discard directly without making a levain, you may need to add more liquid to achieve the intended consistency.

STARTER REFRESHMENT PROCESS

1. Using a spatula, discard most of your ripe sourdough starter (you can save the discard in a discard cache or use it to make something delicious straightaway; see Saving and Using Discard, page 37). Wipe the edges of the jar and the spatula clean.

2. Place your jar with the starter that remains (aka the carryover) on your scale and tare to zero.

3. Add fresh flour and water according to the quantities in your refreshment practice.

4. Stir vigorously until no dry bits of flour remain.

5. Place a lid loosely on the jar and let it ferment until ripe.

THE
SOURDOUGH
STARTER
GEOGRAPHY
MYTH

It's widely believed that sourdough starters—and their blend of bacteria and yeasts—are unique to their geographical location. A prime example is the famed San Francisco sourdough: Some people believe a starter from that city has a unique microbial composition that will lead to specific bread qualities. Contrary to this widespread belief, it has been shown that geographic location does not determine the microbial composition of a starter. Rather, it's more important factors—such as the flour used for refreshments, its maintenance temperature, and the refreshment process itself—that determine the microbial composition.

INOCULATION PERCENTAGE (CARRYOVER PERCENTAGE OR SEED)

The inoculation percentage is the amount of ripe (or mature) sourdough starter either carried over between refreshments or used to create a levain. This percentage is calculated the same way as all other ingredients using a baker's percentage (see Baker's Percentages, page 129), and it's relative to the total flour. It's called "inoculation" because you're essentially *inoculating*, or introducing, a small bit (but a large population) of bacteria and yeasts into a mixture of fresh flour and water. That small bit will eventually turn the entire mixture into a larger, bubbling culture as the bacteria and yeasts multiply.

Use the inoculation percentage to regulate the ripening timeline for your starter—in fact, the inoculation percentage is the most important variable I modify to synchronize my starter with my daily schedule because it's effective and easy to control. Simply put, the more starter carryover used in your refreshment, the faster it will ferment. Is your starter sluggish because it's cool in your kitchen and you need to refresh it earlier? Or do you need to make a levain earlier than usual and need to be sure your starter is ripe when you need it? Leave more starter in the jar at the next refreshment to speed up its ripening. And the opposite is also true: If you need to slow or delay ripening, leave less in the jar during the next refreshment.

The inoculation percentage can vary anywhere from 15% to 100%. For the temperature at which my starter is typically maintained (74° to 76°F/23° to 24°C), my starter carryover is generally around 20% for a 12-hour refreshment cycle. In the warmer months of the year, I might drop this percentage if I find my starter is ripening too quickly, and in the cooler months, I might bump this up. See Adjusting Your Starter Through the Seasons (page 66) for more.

What Sourdough Starter Ratios Work Best?

There's no set ratio of starter ingredients that works best for all bakers in all conditions; it comes down to personal preference. A sourdough culture will adapt to what it's given, and in turn its flavor and performance characteristics will change. Over the years, I've settled on the following makeup for my starter, where the ratio may change slightly through the seasons as the temperature changes.

How I refresh my starter twice daily when kept at 74° to 76°F (23° to 24°C):

INGREDIENT	BAKER'S %	WEIGHT
Flour	100% (70% white flour + 30% whole rye)	100g (70g white flour + 30g whole rye)
Water	100.0%	100g
Inoculation (ripe sourdough carryover)	20%	20g

It's important to know that ultimately your starter ratios might be a little different than mine—and that's okay! My 20% inoculation might need to be 15% or even 25% for your starter and your climate for 12-hour

SMALLER INOCULATION = MORE FLAVORFUL STARTER

You may think that carrying over more ripe starter will mean a more sour, more flavorful result, but that's not necessarily the case! By carrying over only a small percentage, the pH of the mixture will start higher (less acidic) when fresh flour and water are added. A high pH allows bacteria to function more efficiently and for longer, which over the next 12-hour period can result in a starter with a more sour profile (flavor!).

refreshments. The key takeaway is that the carryover percentage is the best tool for adjusting your starter's refreshment timeline.

For example, if you bake bread only once a week on the weekend, or you simply want less maintenance during the week, it might make more sense for you to refresh your starter once a day. In this case, I would change the ratios for the refreshment to slow down fermentation so the starter can last longer and not get overly ripe by the next refreshment. So if the carryover percentage was 20% for 12 hours, try dropping it down to 10% and see if the starter is overripe after a full 24 hours. If it is overripe, reduce even more, perhaps to 5%, and adjust further as necessary.

Since I almost always make a levain when baking, the starter maintenance becomes a little less important compared to the levain (assuming the starter is strong and heathy). The levain works as a sort of equalizer or buffer, giving the bacteria and yeast populations from your starter a chance to grow and increase metabolic activity in the best conditions. It's also an opportunity for us to skew the balance between the bacteria and yeasts to change the performance characteristics and to set the stage for your desired bread flavor.

Adjusting Your Starter Through the Seasons

As you refresh your starter daily, you'll grow accustomed to spotting the signs of reduced or increased fermentation activity, especially as the seasons and temperatures change throughout the year. As summer and warm weather approach, I'll notice that the starter feels looser and less viscous, a little more watery, with more bubbles and a sourer aroma. At this point,

I reduce the amount of starter I leave in my jar to decrease fermentation activity and keep my starter on my desired timeline. I'm also likely to back off on the whole grain percentage in my starter. As cold weather arrives, the opposite signs start to creep in and I begin to move in the opposite direction, leaving more and more starter in my jar at each refreshment and perhaps creeping my whole grain percentage back up. This cycle in starter maintenance continues through the year and becomes a sort of instinctual response to the ebb and flow of the seasons.

KEEPING A STARTER WHEN IT'S WARM

↓ Inoculation percentage
↓ Whole grain percentage
↓ Hydration

A warmer climate increases fermentation activity, so you may reduce the inoculation and whole grain percentages to help rein it in. If temperatures rise above 78°F (25°C), I might drop my inoculation down to a very small percentage, perhaps 5% or even lower, depending on the temperature. (You might be shocked to see my starter when it's maintained in the hot summer of the Southwest; my jar will be nearly empty with only smears of starter left in the jar.)

In extreme cases, when your starter ripens too fast even with a very small inoculation percentage, it might help to reduce the hydration of your starter. too. In my experience, a stiff starter seems to cope better with warmer temperatures because it can hang out in a ripened state for longer (see Hydration, page 140) without becoming overly acidic.

HOW TO AFFECT STARTER FERMENTATION ACTIVITY

To increase activity:
↑ Temperature
↑ Whole grain percentage
↑ Hydration percentage
↑ Inoculation percentage

To decrease activity, decrease any or all of the above.

KEEPING A STARTER WHEN IT'S COOL

↑ Inoculation percentage
↑ Whole grain percentage

A cooler climate slows fermentation, so it can be helpful to increase the starter carryover and whole grain percentages for each refreshment. This boosts the populations of bacteria and yeasts carried over to the new mixture, speeding up the fermentation process. In addition, a higher inoculation percentage will drop the pH in the starter (making it more acidic), helping to increase yeast activity and gas production. In cooler temperatures, my typical inoculation percentage (20%) could go up to 30% or higher, and I may increase the whole grain percentage from 30% to 50%, depending on the temperature.

How to Synchronize Your Starter with Making a Levain

All the recipes in this book call for making a levain from a starter either the night before (for a 12-hour levain) or in the morning on the day of mixing (for a 3- or 5-hour levain). But what if your starter refreshment schedule doesn't perfectly align with when you need to make your levain?

YOUR STARTER WILL RIPEN TOO EARLY

- If it's within 2 or 3 hours of when you want to make the levain, just let your starter sit until you need it. (It's okay if it's overripe.)

- If it ripens 3 or more hours earlier (meaning it will be very overripe), make an Intermediate Levain (see page 74).

- The night before, when you refresh your starter, decrease your inoculation percentage so it ripens more slowly. A reduced inoculation percentage will delay ripening.

YOUR STARTER WILL RIPEN TOO LATE

- Just wait until your starter is ripe to make your levain! (You'll get better results with a starter that's ripe versus underripe.)

- The night before, when you refresh your starter, increase your inoculation percentage slightly so it ripens more quickly. The higher the inoculation percentage, the faster it ripens.

Maintaining a Smaller Starter

Depending on your baking needs, you might want to maintain a smaller starter to reduce the amount of flour used for refreshments. I keep a larger starter (about 200g) because I bake just about every day, often in larger quantities.

The following refreshment ratios are the smallest I'd feel comfortable maintaining while still being able to mix a dough at a moment's notice. Sure, it's possible to go even smaller, but the following will provide you with about 50g of starter ready to create a levain for many of the recipes in this book (and if you need more, you can scale up your starter by simply adding more water, flour, and ripe sourdough according to Baker's Percentages, page 129). Note that the smaller your starter becomes, the harder it is to see the signs of fermentation each day.

For about 50g of starter, refreshed twice a day:

INGREDIENT	BAKER'S %	WEIGHT
Flour	100.0%	25g white flour (~11.5% protein)
Water	100.0%	25g
Sourdough (carryover)	20.0%	5g

Yes, 5g of carryover sourdough is small! Your jar will look nearly empty, but it is still 20% of the total fresh flour added, which will ensure it has the same fermentation runway as a larger starter with the same inoculation percentage.

If you want to maintain a smaller starter *and* bake less frequently, I recommend the following for about 100g of starter, refreshed once a day:

INGREDIENT	BAKER'S %	WEIGHT
Flour	100.0%	50g white flour (~11.5% protein)
Water	100.0%	50g
Sourdough (carryover)	10.0%	5g

Overall, these changes have the effect of slowing fermentation to increase the time between refreshments so your starter doesn't become overly acidic.

Storing Your Starter

Sometimes, you need a little time away from your sourdough starter, whether it's because of a long trip you're taking, you're busy with work, or you want to take a break from baking for a while—life happens! It turns out, there are several techniques for storing your starter that are easy and very effective.

Since we're dealing with a living thing that also happens to be food, in a way, the usual things you'd think of work well: refrigeration and dehydration. In a starter, cold temperatures drastically slow the fermentation activity, and reducing the hydration deprives them of a necessary component for metabolic activity—water. When placing your starter in the refrigerator for short-term storage, also reducing the hydration, even just 20%, seems to help it handle the cooler temperatures better and spring back faster. When those components return to normal—temperatures rise, or water is reintroduced—they'll spring back to life. With a few timely refreshments thereafter, your starter will be ready for baking.

A SLIGHT PAUSE: SLOW YOUR STARTER

↓ Hydration

↓ Inoculation percentage

To slow your starter for a day or two because you need to adjust its ripening time, or you simply need to skip a refreshment:

1. Mix your starter to a stiffer consistency (e.g., reduce 100% hydration to 70%).

2. Reduce the ripe starter carryover amount (e.g., reduce 20% carryover to 10%, or lower).

3. Store the starter at room temperature as usual.

4. When you want to return to a 12-hour refreshment cycle, the next time your starter is ripe, swap back to your old refreshment regimen.

SHORT-TERM STORAGE: REFRIGERATE

↓ Hydration

↓ Temperature (i.e., refrigerate it)

To take a break from baking for up to two weeks:

1. To a clean jar with a lid, add 20g ripe starter along with 100g all-purpose flour. Add 80g room-temperature water (which will yield a slightly stiffer consistency) and mix until no dry flour remains.

2. Cover and let sit on the counter for 1 to 2 hours to allow fermentation to get going. Place in the refrigerator for up to 2 weeks.

3. To revive, let the starter sit at room temperature 1 to 2 hours to warm up. Stir the contents so everything is reincorporated (it may or may not have bubbles at this point; that's okay).

4. Proceed with your normal starter feeding (discard out, add fresh flour and water) and place the jar in a warm spot until it's ripe (see When Is My Starter Ready to Use? on page 36) and needs a refreshment. For my starter sitting at 74° to 76°F (23° to 24°C), this is usually around 12 hours later. Give the starter two or three more regular refreshments, then it's ready to be used for baking.

LONG-TERM STORAGE: DEHYDRATE

↓ Hydration

To take a break from baking for many weeks, months, or even longer (or to create a backup starter, see page 70):

1. To a large bowl, add a large dollop (somewhere around 30g to 50g should do) of your ripe sourdough starter. Add 150g of flour (any white flour will work). Use a spatula to mix everything until it's mostly incorporated. After mixing, you'll see large clumps throughout.

2. Using your hands, pinch through the mixture repeatedly, seeking out any large clumps and breaking them up into smaller and smaller clumps. Continue doing this for several minutes. If at any point the mixture feels damp or wet, add a little more flour to dry it out.

3. Once the mixture feels completely dry, let it sit out exposed to air for 1 to 2 hours.

4. Transfer the contents to a small jar and seal shut for storage. Keep the jar sealed and in a dry area in your pantry away from light and moisture for up to 1 year, or even longer.

5. To revive your starter, add the entire contents of the jar to a mixing bowl or large jar and add 50g fresh flour and enough water (100g to 200g) to make mixing easy—it should mix up to a smooth paste. Let the mixture ferment for 12 to 24 hours at warm room temperature (74° to 76°F/23° to 24°C).

6. Once you see fermentation activity in the mixture, and it looks like it needs a refreshment, continue with your typical refreshment schedule.

Tips for Long-Term Storage

- The key to this method is your starter must be completely, utterly dry—if there's any moisture present, it's possible the mixture will mold over time.

- Find a small jar that forms a good seal to prevent any moisture from creeping in. (I like to use Weck jars with their rubber gasket and clips in place for this; see Resources, page 424.)

- You can spread the contents across two or three jars if you'd like to keep a few backups or give some away to friends.

A BACKUP STARTER: PREPARING FOR THE WORST

When working with sourdough, you're intimately involved with the schedule and routine of your starter—each day it requires a little attention. As a home baker, you will probably only maintain a single culture, which means you're placing all your eggs in one basket. But what happens if you drop your starter jar on the floor or accidentally use the entire thing in your dough, which you realize only when your bread is in the oven? One does not simply open a brand-new jar of sourdough starter. For this reason I always prepare for the worst by drying some of my starter (see Long-Term Storage: Dehydrate, above) and keeping it stored somewhere dry in my cool pantry. If anything happens, I can be back to baking in just a few days.

A LEVAIN (PRONOUNCED LUH-VOHN), ALSO called a leaven, is made from a small portion of sourdough starter, and as you might guess from its name, it's responsible for leavening your dough (making it rise). It's a pre-ferment, which essentially means it's flour that is fermented ahead of mixing into a dough (and unlike your starter, the entirety of the levain you make gets used). A levain helps you ensure your dough will start fermentation with strong populations of beneficial bacteria and wild yeasts, and it also lets you adjust the ratio between the two (see Tinkering with Sourness, page 234). When mixed into the main dough, the levain seeds it with the beginnings of fermentation. These microbes are responsible for leavening the dough, giving it exceptional storage qualities, and for much of the flavor in the final loaf of bread (thanks to the by-products of natural fermentation).

Why Make a Levain?

If you have a well-maintained sourdough starter, making a levain is not strictly mandatory (you can always just use your starter!). However, I learned to bake sourdough bread using a levain for each bake, and over the years I've found just how helpful it is for home bakers to get in the routine of making one for a particular bake. A levain serves a few purposes:

1. **It can be used to alter the flavor, texture, and potential volume of the final loaf without having to modify your sourdough starter.** Think of it as a custom-made starter for each recipe you embark on. A levain can skew the flavor profile of the bread toward more sour or less sour by altering its "build parameters": the flour used, the inoculation or seed percentage (the amount of ripe starter used to make the levain), the time it takes to ripen, and its temperature. I also like that it helps make my recipes consistent for other bakers: Since people maintain (and sometimes neglect!) their starters in all sorts of ways, building a levain means we're all starting on the same page.

2. **It can be used to scale up the pre-ferment to cover recipe requirements.** If your recipe calls for a large amount of pre-ferment, a levain allows you to scale up the pre-ferment in a single step to cover the recipe's requirements. Some bakers prefer to keep a much smaller starter (see Maintaining a Smaller Starter, page 67), so a levain helps bridge the gap between a small, continually maintained starter and a recipe's pre-ferment requirement.

3. **Because a levain is mixed in a separate small jar, you won't accidentally use all your starter—and possibly forget to refresh it.** This is perhaps a minor concern for some, but I do prefer to keep my pre-ferment for the day's bake separate. Right after I use my ripe starter to make a levain, I refresh my starter and put it away for the rest of the day.

Starter
Refreshment
Cycle
(see page 61)

Ripening 3/5/12 hours

MAKE LEVAIN WITH
RIPE STARTER
+ fresh flour
+ water

RIPE LEVAIN
MIXED INTO
DOUGH

Levain vs. Starter: What's the Difference?

A sourdough starter and a levain are, at their core, the same thing: They are both pre-ferments.

However, there are a few key differences. In this book, I use the term "starter" to refer to my continually maintained sourdough culture. Some might call this their chef, *lievito madre*, mother culture, mum, mother dough, and so on. My starter is never used completely in a bake because then I wouldn't have any left to continue its propagation. It's on a continuous cycle of ripening where it's refreshed and left to ferment for some time until ripe again, at which point it can be used to mix into a dough, or create a new levain, or can be refreshed to continue the cycle.

A levain, on the other hand, is created with some portion of a ripe sourdough starter, left to ferment for a period, then used in its entirety in the dough mixed that day. Since it's a branching from a sourdough starter and created for a single use, it can be used to adjust fermentation characteristics (e.g., increased or decreased sourness).

SOURDOUGH STARTER	LEVAIN (LEAVEN)
A pre-ferment	A pre-ferment
Ongoing culture, refreshed regularly	Used once for a single bake
Usually refreshed with the same flour and kept at approximately the same temperature	Can be any flour combination and the temperature can change
Mostly consistent characteristics (acidity/flavor profile) because it's maintained in a consistent manner	Can be used to change the flavor and texture of a single batch of dough

Can I Just Use My Sourdough Starter Instead of Making a Levain?

All the recipes in this book use a dedicated levain for the reasons already discussed (to adjust the flavor profile, modify the timeline of the bake, and scale up the pre-ferment), but if you've forgotten to make a levain and *really* want to bake, just use your ripe starter! It will mean a different flavor profile if the levain is a drastically different build (different flour, hydration, and temperature), but it's better than not baking at all. Just be sure you don't use your entire sourdough starter in the bake—as always, save a little to keep your culture going.

What Flour Should I Use for My Levain?

Any fermentable flour can be used for making a levain, from white to whole wheat to grains such as spelt, einkorn, or Khorasan. I have a set of go-to flour choices, depending on my desired outcome for the levain, and each brings different properties to the levain, the final dough, and subsequently, the finished loaf of bread. Note that the resulting loaf of bread will not taste like the levain itself; it is simply the seed to start fermentation.

Generally, I prefer my levain to be made up of at least 50% whole grains. Pairing whole-grain flour with sifted white flour leads to a balanced levain with ample flavor and leavening power. Adding whole-grain flour allows the levain to take on more acid before bacterial activity drops, which means an overall increase in organic acids and other flavor compounds. The 50% white flour balances out the whole wheat, keeping it milder by preventing the acidity from increasing too dramatically. Of course, you can go to either end of the spectrum as well: a 100% white flour levain (like the one in Soft White Sandwich Bread, page 269) leads to greatly reduced acidity, while a 100% whole-grain levain (like the one in 100% Whole Wheat, page 219) brings more acidity and flavor complexity.

When Is a Levain Ready to Use?

Like a sourdough starter, a levain ferments (or *ripens*) over time. At either end of this continuum, you have a mixture that isn't ideal for use in making bread. At the start, there are insufficient bacteria and yeast populations, and it's essentially raw flour and water with a small seed of ripe sourdough starter. At the other end of the continuum, you have a mixture that's very acidic, broken down, and loose, as fermentation has gone on for too long. There are no concrete times for this process because the duration will be highly dependent on the starter inoculation percentage (the amount of ripe starter added to the mixture), its final dough temperature after mixing it together (and the temperature at which it's maintained), and the flour used. Regardless of whether the timeline is 3 hours or 20 hours, every levain still travels along this continuum, passing through these states as fermentation progresses.

First, let's step back and look at what's happening during the life of your levain. At the onset, a measure of flour and water is *seeded* with a percentage of a ripe sourdough starter—commonly called the seed percentage or inoculation percentage. Once this is mixed, fermentation begins: The beneficial bacteria and wild yeasts start to metabolize the new food source (the sugars in the flour), increase their numbers, and produce the by-products of fermentation (organic acids, gasses, etc.). As fermentation progresses, your levain mixture will begin passing from "just mixed" to "young" to "ripe" to "overripe."

A levain (and a sourdough starter, for that matter) can be used at many points in the ripening continuum: from a few hours after mixing all the way to when the levain is extremely ripe, or even overripe. The point at which you opt to use the levain is a personal choice and has implications for the rest of the bake. My preference is to use my levain when it's just ripe; it will have bubbles on top and at the sides, a looser consistency, and a sour aroma. Remember, this ripening timeline is a continuum with no discrete points along the path and with no best time for using your levain. Like knowing when to use your starter, it's more about learning to read the signs for ripeness and what the effect will be if you use it a little on the young side or a little on the overripe side. And if you're a little off in one direction or the other, don't worry about it, you can always adjust down the line by reducing or lengthening bulk fermentation, the proof, and other baking parameters.

For a description and look at each stage when a levain is ripening, flip to page 61, where this is shown for a sourdough starter. Many of the characteristics—aroma, taste, visuals, and consistency—will generally be very similar (assuming the two have the same hydration percentage).

Can You Use a Levain Before or After It's Ripe?

Ideally, you use a levain at the right time (when it's ripe), but it is also very forgiving! If you use your levain early, expect the fermentation activity to be sluggish because of the reduced populations of bacteria and yeasts. As you assess the dough's progress during bulk fermentation, you may need to delay the divide time. Conversely, a riper levain will have increased fermentation activity and might require an earlier divide. At the far end, if you find your levain is drastically overripe—it has a sharp sour aroma bordering on nail polish and a thin, broken-down consistency like runny pancake batter—then create an intermediate levain (see next paragraph).

Spotting the signs of levain ripeness and learning to adjust later in the breadmaking process will come as you bake more and gain experience. In general, you're going to find much better results with an overripe levain than an underripe one, so if you're not totally confident about your skills in reading the signs of ripeness, err on the side of overripeness!

Remember to always create your levain from a ripe sourdough starter to begin with strong bacteria and yeast cell populations.

Intermediate Levain

Sometimes if I can't get to using my levain when scheduled and it becomes very overripe and extremely acidic, I'll mellow it out with what's called an intermediate levain build. A convenient approach is to make a fast 3- to 4-hour levain at the same hydration with an inoculation percentage of 100% (see Baker's Percentages, page 129).

For example:

INGREDIENT	ORIGINAL LEVAIN (NOW OVERRIPE)	INTERMEDIATE LEVAIN (NEW 3-HOUR BUILD)
Flour	100g (100%)	100g (100%)
Water	100g (100%)	100g (100%)
Sourdough starter or previous levain	10g (10%) sourdough starter	100g (100%) overripe levain

Using some of the overripe levain, at 100% to total flour in the new levain, will mean faster ripening to quickly get you back to baking. Be sure the total quantity of the new levain will cover your requirements and keep it warm, around 78°F (25°C), to ensure it's ready in 3 to 4 hours.

Levain + Dough Temperature

In the same way a dough is mixed to a desired dough temperature (DDT)—see Final vs. Desired Dough Temperature (page 81) for more—a levain is also mixed to an ideal final temperature to adhere to a timeline and promote a particular balance of bacterial activity versus yeast activity. In general, the levain builds in this book will target 78°F (25°C), with only a few exceptions (such as Roggenvollkornbrot, page 288).

Levain Hydration

Regardless of whether you maintain a liquid starter (usually around 100% hydration and above) or a stiff starter (usually 50% to 65% hydration), you can always use your existing starter to make any of the levains in this book. It's not necessary to "convert" your starter to a different hydration, just be mindful of the hydration: All the levain builds and recipes in this book assume you are working with a 100% hydration sourdough starter, so if you maintain a stiff starter, you might need to add extra water to the newly created levain or dough mix.

My Three Levain Types

There are many ways to make a levain, but in my baking, and as used throughout this book, I turn to three main classes: a liquid levain, a stiff levain, and a sweet levain. Each type has a benefit and specific purpose; let's look at each.

☰ LIQUID LEVAIN

Many recipes in this book use a liquid levain, that is, one that's around 100% water to total flour. I find a liquid levain to be a well-rounded approach to creating a pre-ferment and it's what I turn to most often: It's mild (if used at the right time) in both aroma and acidity, it can help bring added extensibility to the dough (which helps if the dough is composed of a high percentage of strong white flour), it's easy to mix, and it's easy to assess fermentation progress.

☰ STIFF LEVAIN

Some recipes in this book call for a stiff levain (e.g., Miche, page 209), which is anywhere between 50% and 65% hydration and mixes up to a firm consistency. The following are some beneficial properties of a stiff levain. (Note that this does not mean a stiff levain is superior to a liquid levain; it's just a different approach to making a pre-ferment with a certain set of characteristics.)

- **Additional dough strength:** A stiff levain adds a noticeable measure of elasticity to a dough due to its lower water content. I find this added strength useful for whole-grain loaves, especially those with high percentages of freshly milled flour.

- **Wider usage window:** A stiff levain reduces bacterial activity, which results in less acidification. This helps prevent a levain from quickly becoming overly acidic. Because of this, I find a stiff levain to be more flexible, especially for days when it's warmer than expected or to help with deviations in my schedule. In my experience, a stiff levain has a usage window of at least 3 hours if fermented overnight, and 1 to 2 hours if fermented the same day.

- **Different flavor by changing acid balance:** With a stiff levain, I use a high percentage of whole-grain flour (usually 100%). This flour choice, coupled with a decrease in hydration in the levain, emphasizes a more up-front flavor profile. This is in part due to the increase in substances in whole wheat flour that are used by bacteria to generate acetic acid. Further, whole-grain flour can take on more acid before the pH drops enough to reduce bacterial activity.

SWEET LEVAIN (SWEET STARTER)

Some recipes in this book (Naturally Leavened Brioche, page 283, or Naan, page 319, for example) rely on what's commonly called a sweet starter, or sweet levain. I first learned of this levain preparation from Ian Lowe, an inspiring baker at Apiece bakery in Australia. The levain has roots in Italian panettone production (which uses sugar in the first dough, or *primo impasto*). To make a sweet levain, add sugar, usually 20% to 25% of the total flour in the levain, to the levain mix itself. Adding sugar suppresses bacterial growth, which skews the flavor profile of the final baked good toward minimal sourness. With less bacterial growth, the yeasts are left to flourish, which increases their leavening power and results in a final product that rises higher and has a lighter texture.

I use the sweet levain approach sparingly and only where it makes sense. After all, we're making naturally leavened bread and we do want some acidity and sourness—this creates flavorful bread! But in some cases, such as with enriched dough (like Italian Doughnuts, page 399), a sweet levain is an incredibly effective way to reduce overall acidity.

Just as is the case with other levain types, be sure to use the sweet levain when it's ripe. It will have a sweet aroma, be extremely bubbly, and usually display significant rise (be sure to use a large container when making it to avoid overflow).

WHAT IF THE LEVAIN COMES UP SHORT OF THE WEIGHTS LISTED IN THE RECIPES?

Depending on how vigilant you are about scraping your spatulas, jars, and lids, you might find the levain you make comes up a few grams short of the weights listed in the formulas. This is okay and expected. In almost every case, this is not a problem, just proceed with the recipe as outlined. If you come up excessively short, perhaps 20g or more, use your sourdough starter (if it's ripe at that time) to fill in the gap or extend your bulk fermentation time to give the dough a little more time to ferment.

MIXING IS AN IMPORTANT AND OFTEN OVER-looked step in the breadmaking process. It's more than simply incorporating all the ingredients in a bowl and strengthening the dough: It's a multistep process that I like to think of in phases. While some aspects of this mixing process can be shifted around between the phases, it's helpful to have a system in place for successful and consistent mixing, as it sets the stage for the entire breadmaking process. There are key elements to get right—like weighing ingredients accurately, incorporating them sufficiently, developing the dough to the right level, and more—and in the end, you'll have a dough that's easier to work with, has strong fermentation activity, and is on track for a successful bake.

What's Happening During Mixing?

Mixing begins with adding water to flour. The starches (those damaged during milling) and proteins present in the grain absorb the water, and enzymatic activity begins. For breadmaking, the dough must be viscoelastic—as in a material that acts somewhat like a liquid and a solid at the same time. Two proteins in flour play a pivotal role in this: gliadin and glutenin.

Gliadin proteins contribute to a dough's viscosity and are responsible for a dough's inherent extensibility (enabling the dough to deform and stretch without breaking). Glutenin proteins are responsible for a dough's elasticity (or strength, the tendency for it to spring back when stretched). When hydrated, these two proteins combine to form gluten. Initially, gluten appears as scattered clumps throughout the dough, but through mixing, these clumps begin to elongate and bind together (gluten cross-linking), forming a larger, more continuous matrix.

Think of this gluten network—sometimes called the gluten matrix—as a three-dimensional web with scattered connections, and in between these connections, most importantly, are the starches found in the flour and the tiny air pockets introduced during mixing. The starches comprise a large portion of the nutrition in bread, help create a workable dough, and contribute to the final loaf's structure. The small air pockets introduced during mixing are spots where gasses produced during fermentation congregate and fill, creating the holes we see in the crumb of a final loaf of baked bread.

Another important process that takes place during mixing is dough oxidation. Oxidation gets a bad rap most of the time, but with bread dough, it's a critical process for developing a strong gluten network.

1	2	3	4
Incorporate the flour and water	Autolyse (optional)	Strengthen (develop) the dough	Add major enrichments and inclusions (optional)

As dough is exposed to air during mixing, the oxidation increases gluten cross-linking, which creates a more tightly knit gluten web. This web can then more effectively hold on to the gasses created during fermentation and enable the dough to hold its shape when formed into a loaf. A stronger dough is easier to handle during preshaping and shaping, has increased loaf volume, an open interior structure, and most important, an overall increased eating quality.

While it's possible to take mixing too far and overoxidize bread dough (which can strip carotenoid pigments and lead to loss of flavor and color), in my experience this is almost impossible to do in the home kitchen and not a major concern. For most home bakers who mix by hand, it's essentially impossible to overoxidize your dough because of the gentle nature of this mixing. In fact, I've found that most home bakers tend to *understrengthen* their dough far more often than anything. In the end, don't be afraid of mixing your dough sufficiently; it's very hard to overoxidize unless you're mixing in a professional mechanical mixer for excessively long mix times—times that are much longer than my recommendations in this book.

The Four Phases of Mixing

After you have a few bakes under your belt, these steps become second nature and you won't give the process another thought. But in the beginning, it is helpful to break them out for further inspection to get a handle on what's added when, and to point out a few things to look out for.

1 INCORPORATE THE FLOUR AND WATER

- **What's added in this step:** flour, water
- **Focus on:** adjusting water temperature as necessary

Now that your ingredients are all measured out and prepared, it's time to get your hands (or mixer) working with the flour and water. During this incorporation phase, you start by combining the water and flour in a mixing bowl or mixer, mixing at low speed. If you're mixing by hand, it's naturally at a slow speed, but in a mechanical mixer, it's best to perform incorporation at low speed ("Stir" on a KitchenAid). In this stage, you're not looking to aggressively develop the gluten in the dough; you only want the flour and water combined and the flour fully hydrated—significant gluten development will happen later. At this point, you should have already adjusted the water temperature so the dough will meet the recipe's desired dough temperature (DDT). See Water Temperature Is Key, page 135, for tips.

If I'm using a mechanical mixer, I like to add some of the mixing water before adding flour to the mixing bowl to help prevent dry bits of flour from accumulating at the bottom. If I'm mixing by hand, I wet my hands in the process to help keep my hands nonstick while incorporating the ingredients.

To perform the mixing, I use my wet hands to pinch through the dough from side to side, then fold it over itself and repeat. I'll continue this pinching and folding motion on the dough until everything comes together and I have a single, shaggy mass with no dry bits of flour.

WEIGHING INGREDIENTS

Before mixing can take place, you need to measure, or scale, your flour, salt, and any other ingredients going into the dough mix for the day. I like to do as much of this as possible at the beginning—analogous to the chef's mise en place. Preparing everything in advance reduces stress later in mixing, and it helps ensure you don't forget to add any ingredients (like salt!).

When scaling ingredients into the same bowl, it's helpful to scoop each ingredient into a neat pile in a defined region in your mixing bowl. This way, if you accidentally add too much of something, you can scoop some off its pile without disturbing other ingredients. Alternatively, you can always measure new additions in a small container first, then dump that into the main mixing bowl.

2 AUTOLYSE (OPTIONAL)

- What's added in this step: nothing
- Focus on: keeping the dough covered and warm

The autolyse ("auto-lease") technique is the act of leaving the combined flour and water to rest for a period of time. An autolyse can help reduce mixing time, increase dough extensibility, and help preserve flavor. The technique was invented by Professor Raymond Calvel, a baker, teacher, and the author of *The Taste of Bread.* By utilizing this short autolyse period, Calvel found it was possible to reduce a dough's mixing time but still have sufficient elasticity. When water is first mixed with flour during the autolyse period, gluten bonds begin forming without the need for physical strengthening (kneading), resulting in an elastic and strong dough that leads to more volume and gas-trapping capability. With water now present, enzymes in the flour also begin to function. Specifically, the protease enzyme works to break down protein bonds, slackening the dough, resulting in a dough with a more extensible feeling overall. Note that salt is *not* added to the dough during an autolyse, because it inhibits enzymatic activity and has a tightening effect on the dough, thus working against the purpose of an autolyse.

In addition to reducing the need for extended mix times, an autolyse can also help increase a dough's extensibility. Having sufficient extensibility is an important characteristic for bread dough as it allows the dough to expand and fill with the gaseous byproducts of fermentation, which ultimately means a lighter loaf with increased volume.

From a home baker's perspective, in many cases I prefer using the autolyse technique because it helps me reduce the amount of time I spend physically kneading the dough for sufficient development.

How to Autolyse

To autolyse, mix the flour called for in a recipe with some or all of the mixing water. Then cover the bowl and keep it at warm room temperature until it's time to add the reserved water, salt, and pre-ferment.

Two things to keep in mind during an autolyse:

1. **Keep the dough covered** during this time to prevent it from drying out.

2. **Keep the dough warm** if it's cold in your kitchen. If it is cold, you've likely already warmed the mixing water, but depending on the length of the autolyse, you'll still want to keep the dough somewhat warm (for me, typically around 74° to 76°F/23° to 24°C). The warm temperature will also encourage enzymatic activity in the dough, which will ensure the autolyse is doing its job.

Autolyse Timing

The duration of the autolyse ultimately depends on the flour and recipe at hand. I tend to use quarter-hour increments for my autolyse times: 15, 30, 45, or 60 minutes. In this book you'll see the most common autolyse time is 30 minutes, which typically yields a dough that is stronger and smoother, and has sufficient extensibility. It's okay if you go a little under or a little over the specified autolyse times, but going too far in either direction could result in a dough that needs correction later in the process. For example, reducing the autolyse time significantly will likely require a longer dough strengthening time or added sets of stretches and folds during bulk fermentation.

Should I include my pre-ferment (levain) in my autolyse?

An important thing to remember when doing an autolyse is once you add your pre-ferment, fermentation begins. So, if you were to perform an autolyse with a levain added, the entire time the dough is resting it will also be fermenting. Additionally, this is fermentation time without any added salt, which means fermentation will proceed at an extremely rapid pace. Therefore, if you do a long autolyse with levain added, you risk overproofing your dough.

I rarely include my pre-ferment in my autolyse; however, in some cases it might be necessary. If you have a liquid pre-ferment (usually 100% hydration or higher) and your dough hydration is low, you might need the water that's in the pre-ferment to facilitate mixing.

When should I autolyse?

- If a dough has a *high percentage of aged whole wheat flour*, an autolyse can help soften the dough and increase extensibility, which can result in a more open and lighter interior.

- If the dough is composed of a *high percentage of high-protein flour*, an autolyse can help reduce the elasticity of the dough, allowing it to expand and fill with gasses more readily.

- *When mixing by hand*, even a short (10- to 20-minute) autolyse can help reduce the mixing time needed to sufficiently strengthen a dough.

When should I *not* autolyse?

- I prefer not to autolyse doughs made up of a *large percentage of freshly milled flour* because it can result in a dough that's weaker (due to compounds present in freshly milled flour, which interfere with gluten cross-linking) and, assuming all else is equal, a dough that's stickier and harder to work with.

- When a formula has a *large percentage of spelt flour*, it inherently contributes to overall extensibility (compared to modern wheat, spelt has a significantly higher gliadin to glutenin ratio, which means it's already quite extensible).

- You want to simplify your mixing schedule.

What if I don't have time or forget to do the autolyse called for in a recipe?

It's fine to skip the autolyse entirely, knowing you might have to strengthen the dough for longer to reach the same level of development as called for in the recipe.

Can I autolyse my dough overnight to save time in the morning?

When performing an autolyse, it's possible to go too far and let the dough rest for too long, which can result in an overly extensible dough that's hard to develop. If you are short on time and can't fit the autolyse into your schedule, skip it.

ADDING WATER WHEN MIXING

Many of the recipes in this book call for holding back some of the mixing water in reserve, often called bassinage or double hydration. The formulas will usually show two water additions, Water 1 and Water 2. Why? Because once water is added to your dough, that's it, there's no taking it out if the dough feels too wet or slack. In many cases, the dough will probably be fine as it progresses through the rest of the process, but to be sure and safe, hold some water (Water 2) out of the initial steps of mixing, and slowly add it into the dough in later stages, a splash at a time, assessing the dough's consistency and how it's strengthening. See Adding Water in Phases, page 142, for more detail.

- **What's added in this step:** reserved water, levain, salt, and any sugar, honey, eggs, milk, or diastatic malt
- **Focus on:** adjusting dough consistency by adding or holding back reserved water; strengthening the dough to a sufficient level for the recipe

Mixing a dough (kneading by hand or with a mechanical mixer) strengthens and further organizes the three-dimensional gluten network, which boosts the dough's structural quality and ability to trap gas. However, all the necessary dough development doesn't have to take place here at the beginning of the breadmaking process. In fact, many no-knead recipes—as the name suggests—opt for no strengthening of the dough at this point and instead call for stretches and folds later during bulk fermentation. Generally, I prefer some strengthening up front during this phase of mixing, which, depending on the dough, will result in fewer sets of stretches and folds during bulk fermentation, potentially leading to a loaf with a more open interior.

What should my dough look and feel like when I'm finished mixing?

Regardless of whether you mix your dough by hand or with a mechanical mixer, for the best final texture, structure, and eating quality of the loaf, it's always important that your dough (and the gluten network therein) be sufficiently strengthened by the time the dough is divided. In general, by the end of strengthening, I look for a dough that is smoother and more elastic (strong), and has moderately defined edges—what I consider "medium (improved) development." This dough will then finish gaining strength later in the process during bulk fermentation with multiple sets of stretches and folds. (The number of sets depends on the dough's consistency and strength coming out of mixing, with a stronger dough requiring fewer sets.)

Heavily enriched doughs, such as Naturally Leavened Brioche (page 283), should be fully, or near fully, strengthened (intensive mix) and pass the Windowpane Test (page 83). Stretches and folds can still be performed on enriched doughs to help further strengthen and adjust consistency later in the process (as I call for in the brioche recipe).

If you're just getting started with baking, it's helpful to remember to take a step back and assess the dough's consistency during this strengthening phase. Periodically pause and ask: How has the dough changed from the beginning of mixing and strengthening? Does it feel slack and weak or is it strong, smooth, and elastic? Does it look like it can handle all the reserved water, or should I omit the rest? These little pauses will help you build up your baker's intuition (see page 9), slowly internalizing how the dough feels in that moment so you can later draw a connection between that dough and how it transforms through bulk fermentation, into shaping, and out of the oven.

Mixing in Salt

Some bakers prefer adding salt at the beginning of mixing, others somewhere in the middle, and finally, some prefer adding it at the very end with any reserved water to help it dissolve. Over the years, I've changed the times at which I've added salt, but for a home baker, I've found it makes little difference. Generally, and you'll see this throughout this book, my preference is to add salt up front during strengthening, whether I'm mixing by hand or with a mechanical mixer.

FINAL VS. DESIRED DOUGH TEMPERATURE

Throughout this book you'll see mention of the desired dough temperature (DDT) and final dough temperature (FDT). The recipes in this book will list a DDT at the Autolyse and/or Mix step—think of it like your target, ideal temperature for the dough so it adheres to the intended fermentation timeline and produces the best end result. After mixing is finished, you'll measure the dough temperature and record the FDT, which is the actual temperature of the dough you ended up with. It's useful to compare the FDT with the DDT and see how large the difference might be, knowing that a FDT that is higher will mean a dough that might need to be divided earlier. Conversely, a FDT that's lower than the DDT might mean a dough that needs more time in bulk fermentation.

DOUGH STRENGTHENING METHODS

In each recipe in this book, I will indicate whether I prefer mixing and strengthening the dough by hand, with a mixer, or either. But generally, you can mix any of the recipes by hand or with a mixer and still arrive at the same result.

When I started baking sourdough bread, I didn't have a mixer; in fact, it wouldn't be until several years later that I purchased one. And to this day, as a home baker, I still mix most of my doughs by hand. It's mainly because mixing small batches is easy and effective by hand, but also because I enjoy it! There's a tactile joy in engaging the senses and getting my hands in the flour and water, sloshing things around, folding, pinching, and strengthening. Some days, it feels like mixing my bread dough is my only respite from the hustle of life, a few minutes when I can focus and enjoy a connection to creating something with my hands. Ultimately, the choice between mixing by hand or with a mixer is yours, and you can make wonderful bread either way.

Some doughs, such as those with enrichments—that is, dough with added egg, butter, oil, or sugar—or those that are highly hydrated (such as focaccia) do benefit from having a mechanical mixer more efficiently develop the gluten. If you don't have a mixer, you can still mix all the recipes in this book by hand, but it will require more time to get the dough to sufficient strength.

By Hand

At this point, the flour and water should already be incorporated in your mixing bowl, pinched and squeezed together with no dry bits of flour remaining. It may be coming out of autolyse, too, if the recipe called for one. Before strengthening the dough, we'll typically add the ripe pre-ferment (levain or starter), salt, some of the reserved water, and potentially some enrichments. Let's look at a few ways to strengthen the dough.

Mixing dough by hand in bowl

IN THE BOWL

- Easy

- Keeps surfaces clean

To strengthen the dough in the bowl, I like to use one hand to stretch the far side of the dough up and over itself and then push it away from me down into the bowl. Rotate the bowl and perform this action again. I'll continue this stretch, fold, and push several times in a row with scattered sessions of pinching and squeezing.

The total duration for mixing by hand in the bowl will vary based on the dough recipe, with higher hydration doughs needing more time, and stiffer doughs, or doughs with a high percentage of high-protein flour, needing less. At the end of this strengthening, typically somewhere between 2 and 8 minutes, the dough should still be a little shaggy and rough, but much smoother and cohesive—right around an improved mix (medium development). The dough will likely need sets of stretches and folds (see Using Stretching and Folding to Further Strengthen the Dough, page 89) during bulk fermentation to finish strengthening.

THE SLAP AND FOLD TECHNIQUE (AKA FRENCH FOLD)

- Effective and efficient in a short amount of time

- Works well with highly hydrated doughs

- Results in a well-aerated dough

I first heard of this effective kneading technique many years ago from the baker and writer Richard Bertinet. Through a series of slaps, stretches, and folds, the dough is efficiently strengthened and air is incorporated into the dough. While this method is incredibly efficient, it's marginally messier than folding the dough in the mixing bowl. To keep things clean, use wet hands and keep a plastic scraper nearby to occasionally pause and scrape the counter clean. With this technique, your hands will always be close together with thumbs and index fingers pointing toward each other like two crab claws. (See photographs on page 84.)

Mixing dough with slaps and folds

THE WINDOWPANE TEST

The windowpane test is a simple way to determine the level to which the gluten has been developed in a dough. To perform the test, tear off a small bit of your just-mixed dough with wet hands. Then, begin to spread the dough out gently, pulling with your fingers as the dough stretches and spreads apart. If the dough tears quickly and easily, your dough is understrengthened (short mix). If the dough spreads apart and stays connected, forming a thin membrane—or windowpane—that is translucent, the gluten in the dough has been fully developed (intensive mix). In between those two extremes is a dough that's at medium strengthening (improved mix). I use the windowpane test primarily when mixing enriched doughs (it's sufficiently mixed and ready for enrichments when the windowpane stays intact).

1. Scrape the dough out of the mixing bowl onto a clean work surface.

2. Using damp hands, pick up the sides of the dough near the top farthest from your body, then slap the bottom to the counter. While keeping your hands in place, stretch the dough toward yourself as the bottom part clings to the counter and elongates.

3. Then, in a swift motion, move your hands to fold the dough up and over away from your body.

4. Drop the top of the dough so it falls above the bottom of the dough on the counter.

5. Next, use both hands (always in that same crab claw arrangement) to pick the dough up at the left or right side and repeat. By grabbing the dough at the side, we're effectively rotating the dough a quarter turn each time, working a different area of it.

6. Continue slapping and folding in this manner until the dough starts to smooth out and feel stronger—it will begin to hold itself in a taut cylinder shape on the work surface. Moisten your hands as necessary to keep them from sticking and tearing the dough.

Help! My dough is ripping or breaking apart when doing slap and fold.

When performing slap and fold vigorously, you might find the dough tears and rips periodically—this is okay. Think about how much tearing and ripping happens to the dough when it's in a mixer! When I see tearing, I attribute it to overworking the same area of the dough and like to flip the dough over to work the underside. Upon doing so, the dough will break apart, but keep slapping and folding until it comes back together, then continue with development. Keep your hands slightly wet during this whole process to reduce sticking to your fingers, which can also cause the dough to tear.

With a Mechanical Mixer

While I tend to mix most of my doughs by hand, using a mechanical mixer is an effective and efficient means of dough strengthening. Nowadays, there are several mechanical mixers that are large (but not too large) and work well in the home kitchen. When I first started baking bread, these were all but impossible to find, but now you can find high-quality spiral dough mixers that can mix upward of 8 kilograms of dough and still fit under a kitchen cabinet. (See Resources, page 424.) Some bakers might feel there's a loss of quality when using a mechanical mixer, but in my experience, my bread is just as flavorful and nutritious whether I'm mixing by hand or with a machine.

When it comes to enriched doughs, I always use a mechanical mixer (usually my home KitchenAid) because they are very effective at incorporating fat, sugar, and dairy. With these doughs, it's important to strengthen them until they pass, or nearly pass, the Windowpane Test (see page 83) before adding large quantities of fat and sugar (which inhibit gluten development).

I mix and strengthen dough in a mixer the same way I mix by hand. The pre-ferment, salt, and optional enrichments are added to the flour and water in the mixer bowl, and I turn the mixer to low speed for 2 to 3 minutes to incorporate. After this time, I'll turn the mixer up to medium speed to begin gluten development, usually for 3 to 6 minutes, until the dough begins to show signs of elasticity and smoothness. Occasionally, at this stage I'll let the dough rest in the mixing bowl for 5 to 10 minutes to allow it to relax and begin to smooth further. After the optional rest, I'll continue to mix on medium speed for another 2 to 4 minutes to continue strengthening the dough as necessary, adding any reserved water slowly as the mixer is running to adjust the consistency of the dough. Finally, for those recipes requiring a high percentage of fat (usually butter), once the dough has been intensively developed, I'll begin adding the butter with the mixer on low speed until it has all been absorbed into the dough.

What if I don't have a mechanical mixer for an enriched dough?

Thoroughly incorporating soft butter into a dough by hand can be challenging. Here are a few tips:

- You might need to warm your mixing water a little more to meet the desired dough temperature (DDT), because you won't have a mixer heating the dough as it mixes.

- Use the slap and fold technique (see page 83) to efficiently strengthen the dough in the beginning, then add one pat of butter at a time by smearing it onto the dough and folding it in. Continue to slap and fold until all the butter is incorporated and the dough becomes smooth, elastic (strong), and slightly shiny.

4 ADDING MAJOR ENRICHMENTS AND INCLUSIONS (OPTIONAL)

- **What's added in this step:** butter, high percentages of sugar, oil, some seeds, nuts, and dried fruit

Enrichments: Butter, Sugar, Eggs

I prefer using a mechanical mixer, such as a KitchenAid, when mixing enriched doughs. However, while laborious, it is possible to mix them entirely by hand instead of using a mixer. When doing so, hold back some (or all) of the sugar and all the butter to facilitate more effective strengthening by hand. Use the slap and fold technique (see page 83) to efficiently strengthen the dough and plan for more time when mixing by hand: If a recipe calls for 5 minutes in the mixer, you might need to triple, or more, the time.

The order in which these enrichments are added is important and can impact total mix time, because many of them inhibit gluten development. Add them in this order:

1. **Oil:** Depending on the amount of oil in the recipe, it can be added early in mixing for small quantities, or later in mixing for larger quantities. When adding larger quantities in a mechanical mixer, I like to slowly drizzle the oil into the mixer as its running to help it incorporate into the dough.

2. **Sugar:** Sugar behaves almost like a liquid when added to a dough during mixing and can inhibit gluten development. If the recipe has a high percentage of sugar to total flour weight, around 10%, I prefer holding back half or all the sugar, adding it near the end of mixing (just before adding butter, if called for).

3. **Butter:** Like any fat, butter can prevent dough development as fat coats gluten proteins, preventing them from forming an organized network. Add butter at the very end of mixing once the dough has been sufficiently strengthened (usually to intensive mix). Make sure the butter is at room temperature: Cold butter will not easily incorporate, clumping together and endlessly mixing around in the mixer bowl. Conversely, if the butter has melted, it might result in a greasy dough. Butter is at perfect room temperature when your finger easily presses into it with little resistance.

Inclusions: Dried Fruit, Nuts, Cracked Grains, and More

Adding extra ingredients to a bread dough—often called inclusions or mix-ins—is an endless playground of possibility. I tend to stick to simple and balanced flavors when deciding what to mix in, but I also take inspiration from the season. I prefer to keep the inclusions sparse, adding just enough so their flavor and texture are evident but still balanced with the grain and natural fermentation flavors.

How and When to Add Inclusions

If the inclusions are small and soft, like currants, adding them at the start or midway through mixing your dough will work well. The benefit to adding an inclusion early is you can see its effect on the dough firsthand: Will it absorb moisture and require adding additional water to the dough? Or is it moist and will release water into the dough? On the other hand, adding in inclusions early also exposes them to the stresses of mixing, which might break them apart into smaller pieces.

If the inclusions are large, sharp, or fragile, like walnuts, I prefer adding them during the first or second set of stretches and folds during bulk fermentation. Adding large inclusions later in the process reduces their impact on the gluten network of the dough, which allows us to develop the gluten and strengthen the dough more effectively during mixing.

To add inclusions during bulk fermentation with minimal impact on dough structure, I spread one-quarter of the ingredients evenly over the surface of the dough in the bulk fermentation container. Then, I perform my stretches and folds as described in Using Stretching and Folding to Further Strengthen the Dough on page 89, spreading another one-quarter of the ingredients each time a clean piece of dough is exposed, sprinkling any remaining inclusions over the top after the last set.

INCLUSIONS
AT A GLANCE

INGREDIENT	PREPARATION
Nuts · walnuts, pecans, almonds, pistachios, pine nuts, hazelnuts, etc.	Generally, nuts are hygroscopic (tending to absorb water) and will pull moisture from a dough; add additional water to compensate. Toast nuts at 350°F (175°C) on a sheet pan until fragrant for increased flavor. If large, coarsely chop into smaller pieces.
Dried fruit · figs, apricots, cherries, raisins, cranberries, etc.	If large, coarsely chop into smaller pieces. If very dry, soak in some of the dough's mixing water for several hours (or overnight) to soften.
Seeds · flaxseed, sunflower, sesame, poppy seed, pumpkin, chia, etc.	Cold water soaker needed: Combine the seeds and at least equal parts water (taken from the total dough mixing water), cover, and let soak overnight. In this book, the soakers are not drained of excess water before adding to a dough unless otherwise indicated.
Cracked grains · wheat, spelt, rye, Khorasan, einkorn, barley, rice, etc.	Hot water soaker needed: Combine the cracked grains and at least equal parts boiling water (taken from the total dough mixing water), cover, and let soak overnight. If you have a home grain mill, you can crack your own grain on a very coarse setting, or you can buy it precracked.
Oily or briny add-ins · olives, sun-dried tomatoes, etc.	Ingredients in brine should be thoroughly rinsed and dried completely. Ingredients in oil can optionally be rinsed; add during the first set of stretches and folds in bulk fermentation because oil can interfere with gluten development.

Bulk Fermentation

BULK FERMENTATION, OR FIRST RISE, BEGINS when mixing finishes and continues until the dough is divided. This is a critical period in the breadmaking process when the dough begins fermenting in a single, large mass. During this time, organic acids, carbon dioxide, and other compounds are produced. These compounds bring desirable flavors, storage qualities, and improved texture, while carbon dioxide ensures a light and airy loaf of bread.

Choosing a Bulk Fermentation Container

When I started baking, I went through at least five different containers before I found one that's still my favorite after all these years: a large ceramic serving bowl from Heath Ceramics in San Francisco. I love this bowl (which is 4½ inches tall and 10 inches in diameter) because it fits 2 kilograms of bulk fermenting dough, has thick sides that help keep the dough temperature mostly stable, and, because it's ceramic, is basically nonstick. This bowl is my personal favorite, but find one that works for you. This is what you should look for:

- **Size:** Find a container with ample headspace but not one too large for the size of dough you often work with. If a container is too large, the dough may spread significantly into a thin layer, reducing fermentation effectiveness. For 2 kilograms of dough (many of the recipes in this book make 1,800 grams), a container that holds 4 to 5 quarts is just right. For larger batches, an 11-quart (14 × 12 × 5½-inch) tub can hold between 2 and 8 kilograms.

- **Material:** Tough plastic, ceramic, nonreactive metal (like stainless steel), and glass are great because they are mostly nonstick when it comes to dough, whereas a rough-textured container will be disastrous, as it hangs on to every bit of dough.

- **Thickness and insulating properties:** Either thick or thin containers will work well, just be mindful of how each might affect the dough temperature. Thick-walled or insulating containers will keep the dough's temperature constant, even in the presence of changing external temperatures. Conversely, thin or thermodynamically neutral containers will keep the dough closer to ambient temperatures.

Finally, you can always choose not to transfer your dough out of the mixing bowl and just keep it there from mixing to dividing. (I prefer moving my dough from the bowl I use to mix, which is a very wide, thin stainless steel one, to a tighter ceramic bowl with thick walls.)

Using Stretching and Folding to Further Strengthen the Dough

As I mentioned in Dough Strengthening Methods (page 82), during mixing I prefer to develop the gluten in most doughs to, or a little less than, an "improved mix" (moderate development; note that enriched doughs and sweet applications are an exception). This means the dough requires more strengthening during bulk fermentation for optimal gas retention and volume. This additional dough development is achieved through stretching and folding.

Stretching and folding accomplishes four primary goals:

1. Further strengthens the dough

2. Helps to equalize dough temperature

3. Gives you a chance to check in on the dough's progress

4. Traps a small amount of additional air into the dough

There are numerous ways to accomplish the stretching and folding. Some methods call for dumping the dough out onto the counter to strengthen it. I prefer to do stretching and folding right in the bulk fermentation container because it is easy to handle most dough sizes, keeps surfaces clean, and is very effective.

In this method, we literally stretch the dough out and fold it over itself, helping to further organize and develop the gluten matrix. The stretches and folds are done in sets that are spaced apart by a time interval dependent on the dough's consistency; for most of the recipes in this book, it's around 30 minutes. For each set, I take one of two approaches: a vigorous set or a gentle set. If the dough is understrengthened (weak, slack, and shaggy), it gets a vigorous set to impart significant strength. If the dough is stronger (has defined edges and is holding itself together in the container), it gets a gentle set. It's even okay to skip a set, or stop performing sets altogether, if the dough looks and feels sufficiently strong (i.e., it hasn't relaxed out after the last set, has very clearly defined edges, and is hard to stretch).

Let's look at what a vigorous and gentle set of stretching and folding entails.

VIGOROUS STRETCHING AND FOLDING

Place a small bowl of water near your bulk fermentation container to wet your hands, making them nonstick. Using wet hands, use your fingers to scoop down into the container on the north side and grab the dough Ⓐ (see page 90). Stretch it up until resistance is felt Ⓑ. Finish by folding it over to the south side of the container Ⓒ. Then, rotate the container 180 degrees to do the other side. Next, rotate the bowl a quarter turn and stretch and fold that side. Rotate the bowl 180 degrees again and finish with a stretch and fold on the last side. Doing the stretching and folding on opposing sides like this—that is north first, then south, not north then east—helps keep the dough tight in the center and leaves it in a long rectangle, making the final two folds—east and west—easier to perform. Finally, after all four sets, I

Vigorous stretching and folding

like to pick up the dough with two hands at the center and let the ends fold down and under to keep the dough in a neat package at the bottom of the container, which is essentially a gentle stretch and fold.

GENTLE STRETCHING AND FOLDING

Place a small bowl of water near your bulk fermentation container to wet your hands, making them nonstick. Using wet hands, reach down into the container at the center of the dough D . Lift the center of the dough up and slightly toward your body E , allowing the far side to fall and fold under your hands and the center of the dough. Then, rotate the bowl 180 degrees and

Gentle stretching and folding

perform the lifting action at the center. The dough should now resemble a long rectangle in the container. Rotate the bowl a quarter turn and perform the same lifting and folding, then rotate 180 degrees and repeat on the remaining side of the dough. The dough should end gathered up in the middle of the container in a square shape F .

Regardless of how vigorous the motions, after performing a set, I find it helpful to leave the dough in a smooth, neat package in the container. Leaving the dough so there's a single, smooth surface on the top will help you visibly inspect the dough's strength, making it easier to determine when to perform another set, or whether to end bulk fermentation and divide the dough.

VIGOROUS

GENTLE

How long do you wait between sets of stretches and folds?

Before performing a set of stretches and folds, it's important that the dough has sufficiently relaxed outward. Consider for a moment a dough that was stretched and folded 30 minutes earlier, but that when you go to give it another set, it's still gathered up in the center of your bowl, looking strong with defined edges. If you tried to give this strong dough a stretch and a fold, you'd be fighting the dough, forcing it to comply and potentially tearing it. Instead of forcing the issue, give the dough more time to rest (check again after another 30 minutes) to let the gluten relax and become extensible again, and then perform another set (if at all).

In most cases, I like to wait around 30 minutes between sets. This time seems to be a good starting point for most doughs to relax and spread out in the bulk fermentation container—which is precisely when you want to give it another set. However, if you've minimally mixed (around a short mix) and the dough is understrengthened, you might only need 15 minutes of rest between sets (as seen in My Best Sourdough, page 257). In this case, you can perform a few early sets spaced out by 15 minutes, then increase the interval as the dough strengthens and starts showing a reluctance to spread back out in the container.

How many sets of stretches and folds are needed, and when should I stop?

Ultimately, the number of sets of stretches and folds will depend on the dough composition (flour choices, hydration, etc.) and its strength level after mixing. The purpose of these sets is to move your dough along the development continuum toward a dough that's sufficiently strong for optimal structure and volume. Some doughs—like highly hydrated recipes—need more help to get there; others—like low-hydration recipes—are strong enough and need less help. You should also consider what else will be happening to your dough after bulk fermentation:

- Are you preshaping tightly? If so, fewer sets are needed.

- Do you intend to shape the dough lightly or with a heavier hand? Light shaping could mean the dough needs additional sets, and strong shaping could mean fewer.

- Is the dough going to be retarded in the refrigerator overnight? If so, fewer sets can be given, as the cold temperature brings strength to a dough.

For the type of bread I typically bake—and the majority of the recipes in this book—I start with a baseline of three sets of stretches and folds during bulk

DOUGH STRENGTH

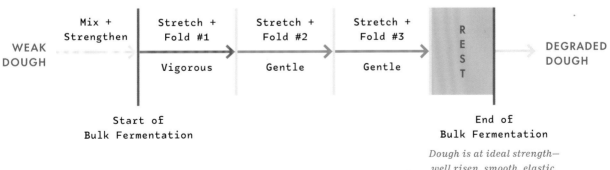

Dough is at ideal strength—well risen, smooth, elastic, and with a domed edge—and is ready to divide and shape.

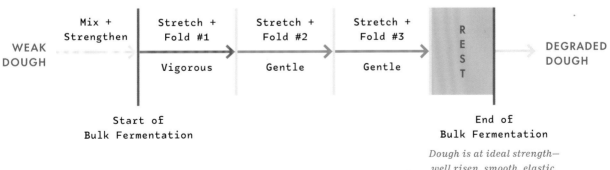

fermentation. If the dough comes out of mixing on the weak side, I'll increase that number, and if it's stronger, I'll reduce the number of sets as appropriate. I like to stop giving the dough sets when I see significant signs of strength: The dough becomes thicker and more elastic, has cleanly defined edges, and most important, starts to resist relaxing outward in the bulk fermentation container after its typical 30-minute rest.

If you're unsure whether your dough should have another set, give it one! In my experience, most beginning bakers tend to understrengthen their dough.

As shown in the diagram on page 91, I see the dough as always moving from left to right, starting as a shaggy, weak mess while mixing and, as it's strengthened, moving closer to its ideal dough strength. Vigorous sets of stretches and folds move the dough farther along the continuum, whereas gentle sets not so much. The dough will also continue to strengthen during its rest—the period after you've stopped giving it stretches and folds but before dividing. Eventually, your dough reaches a point where it's strong enough and has had sufficient fermentation time, the point at which it can then be divided and preshaped.

Note that what's not shown in the diagram, and is very hard to quantify, is how the dough strengthens organically as a result of fermentation. To a degree, organic acid production as a by-product of fermentation has a tightening and strengthening effect on the gluten network, which helps the dough strengthen without any mechanical input at all.

When to End Bulk Fermentation

After you finish your last set of stretches and folds, you let the dough rest for the remainder of bulk fermentation. But how long do you leave the dough to rest? Frankly, it can be difficult to determine the exact point at which to end this process. It's a critical step in breadmaking, and nailing that perfect point is hard to consistently get right. But in this section, I'll help you spot the signs and learn to use your baker's intuition to make the right judgment call.

The key to determining when to end bulk fermentation is to catch your dough when it has enough strength so it can be handled during the rest of the

process and still hold its shape, and it's fermented enough to be well aerated (billowy) and flavorful. It's most important to use your senses and your intuition to help answer when to divide. Of course, the recipes throughout this book will give you a time frame for when a dough should be ready, but it's always helpful to step back and assess how the dough is progressing that day and adjust the schedule as needed.

Here's how to determine your dough's readiness (see the photograph on page 95):

- **Look for a risen dough with domed edges:** The dough should have risen in the container, it should be billowy, and it should jiggle when you gently shake the container. In my experience, the *amount* of rise (which depends on the hydration and flour composition of the dough) is less important than the fact that it has risen and looks "alive" and well aerated. Assuming the dough is not extremely highly hydrated, it should not be flat in the bulk fermentation container, and the edges where the dough meets the sides of the container should be domed (rounded).

- **Feel for a stronger dough:** Just like it does during sets of stretches and folds, the dough's texture should have evolved from shaggy toward smooth and elastic with defined edges and clear lines. Tugging on the dough should show resistance to stretching outward, a sign of elasticity.

- **Use your intuition:** Take the dough composition (flour, hydration, pre-ferment) into account and use this to help you get a gut feel for when to divide the dough (this will come with baking experience). Example: You may need an earlier divide due to increased fermentation activity if your levain was overripe.

- **Use dough temperature as a guide:** Temperature is one of the most (if not *the* most) important factors in setting the timeline for bulk fermentation. If the final dough temperature (the temperature of the dough measured after mixing) comes in below the desired dough temperature for a recipe, expect to extend bulk fermentation. Conversely, if the final dough temperature comes in even a few degrees higher, expect to divide earlier.

Don't worry if this seems intimidating now. In the recipes throughout this book, I'll give times and further descriptions on when to end bulk fermentation and divide your dough.

Bulk Retarding

In addition to retarding shaped dough for proofing (called a shape retard), you can also bulk retard it, where the dough is placed—in a single, large mass before dividing—into the refrigerator for bulk fermentation. Bulk retarding is a useful technique in which the dough is bulk fermented at a warm temperature for some period and then placed into the refrigerator, usually overnight. This technique has a few advantages:

- You can split the work over two days.

- It helps build additional flavor.

- Handling cold dough from the refrigerator is easier.

The downside to bulk retarding is that it can be tricky to time. The dough needs to have had sufficient time at a warm temperature to ensure fermentation is off to a good start, but not so much that it overproofs in the refrigerator. Remember, a large mass of dough will take longer to cool, during which time fermentation will continue.

I find a good starting point is to retard the dough in bulk after 2 to 2½ hours at a warm temperature—assuming the final dough temperature is not excessively outside the range of 76° to 78°F (24° to 25°C). You want to see some fermentation activity in the dough: a little puffiness, some smoothness, and generally a sign that fermentation is off to a good start. If you put it in the refrigerator too early, the dough will take excessively long to sufficiently ferment the next day, and I've found it may never reach the same overall potential. This technique does take practice, and the best method for improving your efficiency with it is to be observant, mindful, and to take notes from bake to bake.

I use this technique in several recipes in this book, most notably with my Demi Baguettes (page 251) and Ciabatta Rolls (page 341). With baguettes, it's useful to bulk retard the dough so it's shaped, proofed, and baked all on the second day. I find bulk retarding tends to result in a slightly thicker crust from the exposure to the cold in the refrigerator. For ciabatta, it's mostly for scheduling, but in addition, dividing and handling a very highly hydrated dough like ciabatta are easier when it's cold and firm.

Note that the dough can't just be thrown into the refrigerator at any time without a second thought, especially doughs at the end of bulk fermentation. Take for instance a 2,000-gram batch of dough comfortably fermenting at a final dough temp of 78°F (25°C) in a thick-sided ceramic bowl, just about ready to be divided. Remember that it takes significant time for the dough mass to cool down enough to slow fermentation. So if you stuck it in the refrigerator then, it would keep fermenting for a period of time—too much time at this point in the process. All that extra fermentation would mean the dough would eventually overferment.

Do I have to then let my dough warm up before dividing?

I usually let the dough warm for a few minutes out of the refrigerator (typically around 15 minutes or so) until it can be divided and preshaped without extreme force, but not so much that it warms completely to room temperature. One of the benefits of retarding in bulk is that dividing and preshaping a dough from the cold refrigerator are easier, and in some cases (like with Ciabatta Rolls on page 341), the cold temperature is used precisely for this purpose.

STAGES OF BULK FERMENTATION

Let's look in more detail at a single dough as it progresses through bulk fermentation. Note that the characteristics discussed here are for a dough that's not excessively over- or underhydrated. This is a set of benchmarks for most of the recipes in this book unless stated otherwise.

Stage 1:
Right out of mixing

- Several stretch-and-fold sets yet to come

- Texture ranges anywhere from shaggy to somewhat smooth, depending on the level of strengthening

- For doughs that are mixed by hand, the dough will still show a lack of defined edges and have a shaggy, ragged appearance

Stage 2:
Early in bulk fermentation

- After one set of stretches and folds

- Dough gains some strength, but still has a shagginess to it and will require more time and/or stretching and folding

- Where the edges of the dough meet the bowl, notice how they are flat and parallel with the ground—this shows lack of strength

JUST
RIGHT

Stage 3:
Time to divide

- Nearing the end of bulk fermentation and well fermented

- The dough has risen, may have bubbles on the top and the sides, and looks inflated

- When you gently shake the container, the dough will jiggle

- The texture will be much smoother rather than shaggy

- If you wet your hand and tug on the dough, it's more elastic, resisting stretching outward

- Notice how the edges of the dough dome downward toward the bowl, indicating the dough has expanded with gasses and is strong enough to contain them

Stage 4:
Bulk gone too far

- A dough that's potentially overfermented

- It will have a sticky surface, be excessively gassy (risen and aerated), and feel more extensible than elastic

- At this stage, the dough is more fragile and will need to be handled with a lighter hand

- If you're using a clear container, or when you scrape your dough out to the work surface, you'll likely see many little bubbles trapped at the bottom and sides of the dough, looking almost like frothed, bubbly milk

Dividing, Preshaping, and Bench Rest

THE NEXT PHASES OF THE BREADMAKING process transform our bulk-fermented dough into smaller pieces by first dividing the dough. Then, these small pieces are preshaped to help facilitate final shaping. Finally, the pieces are left to bench rest to help relax the gluten and make final shaping possible.

Dividing

When dividing and preshaping, I always use a wet hand and wet bench knife instead of dusting the dough with flour. Using water at this stage eliminates the chance of incorporating excessive raw flour into the dough (which can show up as raw spots in the final bread), and I find it's a little cleaner—less flour on the floor! If you'd prefer to use a light dusting of flour—and many bakers choose this method—use only as much flour as necessary to prevent sticking.

HOW TO DIVIDE YOUR DOUGH

1. Fill a small bowl with water and place it on the work surface. There's no need to wet the work surface to prevent sticking at this stage because you will use the bench knife to scrape the surface as you move the dough around, ensuring it never has the chance to stick.

2. Remove the dough from the bulk container: Tip the container on its side and use your bowl scraper to help loosen the dough at the top of the container, working your way down as it spills onto the work surface. If you're worried about the dough sticking to the work surface, lightly flour the top of the dough or the surface before tipping the dough out. Scraping the dough from the container is a gentle process; avoid cutting or degassing the dough as much as possible during this time—just give it assistance in oozing out of the container into a mound.

3. Lightly wet your free hand and bench knife. Divide the dough by cutting directly down into it and scraping away a piece. If you're making only two loaves, you will divide the mass in half, but if you're making additional loaves, weigh each cut piece and adjust by adding or removing small bits of dough to get to the desired loaf weight.

Preshaping

Preshaping happens right after the dough has been divided. You gather each piece of dough into a form that closely resembles its final shape. While it isn't a mandatory step, it is one I find helpful to set the stage for easier—and more consistent—final shaping.

The reason preshaping is optional is that in some cases it might not be necessary or even desired. Certain bread types, such as ciabatta, don't require a preshape because the pieces are cut from the bulk mass, weighed, and then simply placed on a couche or baking sheet to proof. Additionally, dough strength must also be assessed: If the dough is very strong, it might be appropriate to skip right to final shaping.

Dividing and preshaping

HOW TO PRESHAPE YOUR DOUGH

Before you begin preshaping, look at your dough on the work surface. Depending on how you scraped it out of your bulk container it might look like two long rectangles. Coercing that dough into two taut rounds will take practice; going from long rectangle to tight round can be challenging. With your bench knife, compress the rectangle by dragging the knife against the dough on the short side of the rectangle to compact it a little. Once it's squished up into more of a square shape, quickly remove the knife from the dough, using your free hand to help hold the dough in place. Then, begin with the steps below.

1. Hold your bench knife at a shallow angle (15 to 20 degrees) to the work surface for a gentler preshape. (To preshape tighter, increase the angle.)

2. With wet hands and a slightly wet bench knife, push the dough with the bench knife as you tuck the dough under itself with your free hand. It's a gentle push with a slight rounding motion, then a slight tuck under with your free hand to create tension in the dough while at the same time removing the bench knife from under the dough. Repeat this push with the knife, tuck with the free hand, and quick removal of the knife, over and over until the dough is symmetrical, smooth, and taut.

3. Let it rest on the work surface, uncovered, for the bench rest.

PRESHAPING SLACK, STICKY DOUGHS

Here are some tips for working with slack, sticky doughs:

- Pop the bulk fermentation container into the refrigerator, uncovered, for 30 minutes to 1 hour to firm up the dough and make shaping easier.

- Leave the bulk fermentation container uncovered for 5 to 10 minutes to allow the surface to dry slightly, reducing stickiness.

- Perform two preshapes separated by a short rest. This will bring additional strength to the dough, and the second preshape should be easier to perform.

- If you're still having trouble and the dough is an unwieldy shape, you can also do a light shaping: Lightly flour the top of the dough, then flip it onto your work surface, floured-side down. Fold the bottom third of the dough up to the center, then fold in the left and right sides. Fold the top flap down and press gently to stick. Flip the round over and gently gather it up into a round shape.

- In some cases, a dough that's extremely sticky, slack, and weak might be either overhydrated or understrengthened. Next time, reduce the water in the recipe to better match the flour you're using, knead the dough for longer to give it more strength, or increase the number of stretches and folds by one or two sets during bulk fermentation.

Bench Rest

After all the dough is preshaped, it's left to rest for what's commonly called the bench rest. During this time, the dough will relax outward as the gluten relaxes, facilitating final shaping. The duration of this bench rest depends on how tightly the dough was preshaped: the tighter the preshape, the longer the bench rest required to sufficiently relax. Generally, I let my dough bench rest between 25 and 45 minutes, depending on the dough and how tightly it was preshaped.

I don't cover the dough during the bench rest; I find a little air exposure during this time helps make shaping easier because the exterior of the dough dries just enough to make it less sticky. However, if your kitchen has a strong draft or the air conditioner is running, cover each piece of preshaped dough with an inverted large mixing bowl, a greased piece of plastic, or a damp kitchen towel to prevent a crust from forming on the dough.

WHAT BENCH ARE WE TALKING ABOUT?

Bakers sometimes refer to their work surface as a bench or workbench (for home bakers, this might simply be their kitchen counter). The term "bench flour" refers to flour that's used on the work surface when preshaping or shaping. Similarly, a "bench rest" refers to the time the dough rests on the work surface, waiting for final shaping.

Shaping

ALL THE BREADMAKING STEPS UP TO THIS point—mixing, strengthening, bulk fermentation, and preshaping—have been performed, in part, to strengthen the dough to facilitate shaping. The dough needs to have an inherent level of gluten development to be able to trap the gaseous by-products of fermentation. Through shaping, we leverage this development to mostly fix the dough into a final form that holds all the way to baking.

There's a correlation between how fermented the dough is and how gently you must handle it in this phase. If the dough is very well fermented at shaping time, it is likely in a more delicate state, requiring gentle handling during preshaping and shaping. When I have a dough that's coming out of bulk fermentation feeling sticky or tacky and looking fragile with many bubbles, I prefer to proceed with gentle shaping to prevent excessive degassing. And the opposite can also be true: A dough that's divided earlier and feels strong and elastic can usually handle more intensive shaping.

The resulting shape of the final loaf of bread is more than aesthetics; it also affects the overall characteristic of the bread and the eating experience. For instance, take a batch of the dough from Demi Baguettes (page 251) and instead of shaping it into thin, tapered cylinders, shape it into larger, round boules. Even with the same base dough, the boules will have less crust surface area and a thicker crust than the baguettes. A completely different bread.

Finally, I like to think of shaping as a point when your creativity can run free. If you take two different bakers and have them work the same dough, the result will likely be bread with drastically different forms and even different eating qualities.

Shaping in Detail

Shape with even tension: Tension is created when you drag the dough against the work surface as you shape it. The dough will slightly stick to the surface and pull taut as it is pushed and pulled by your hands. With proper movement and force, an outer "skin" will form on the dough, which is what keeps the dough in shape all the way until it is scored and baked. It's important to shape with even tension across the entire piece of dough, which will ensure consistent expansion in the oven. Think of the outer skin of the dough as the eventual crust of the loaf. You want this skin to be evenly taut during shaping because areas that are tighter won't expand as easily as those shaped more loosely. Uneven tension will result in a lopsided loaf or one with areas that bulge and others that stay contracted.

Determine the outside of the final loaf and avoid working in excess flour: Shaping is typically performed with a dusting of raw flour to help keep the dough, your hands, and the work surface nonstick. It's important to avoid working excessive raw flour into the dough at this stage as this will show up in the product as gummy areas or cavernous holes. When looking at your piece of dough to shape, mentally designate a side of it as the "inside" of the final loaf of bread. If you've preshaped your dough, the future "inside" will usually be the bottom of the preshaped piece of dough, because the rested round will be flipped over and shaped. With the inside now designated, try not to get any raw bench flour on that area of the dough.

- **Create a flour gutter:** When I'm shaping, I like to lightly dust my work surface off to the side of my active working area. Usually this is to both the left and right, in what I call the gutter. As you're actively shaping, you can quickly run your hands in the gutter to pick up a light dusting of flour to keep them nonstick. After I shape a piece of dough, I dust a little more flour into the gutter as necessary.

MY SHAPING WORKFLOW

Depending on the dough, my typical shaping flow looks something like this:

1. Lightly dust the bare work surface (in my case, my wooden shaping board) and my hands with flour. Dust a little flour to the left and right of my work area as a flour gutter to run my hands in if they start to stick to the dough.

2. Lightly dust the top of the preshaped round (what will be the "outside" of the final loaf) with flour.

3. Using my bench knife in my dominant hand and my other (floured) hand, gently scoop up the preshaped round and flip it over onto the floured work surface. Now the "outside" of the final loaf that was dusted with flour is down on the floured work surface—two very thin layers of flour preventing it from sticking while I shape. The "inside" of the final loaf is now exposed and facing up (which is the area you want to avoid working in raw flour).

4. With floured hands, shape the dough, all the while being mindful of not introducing excessive raw flour into the "inside" of the dough.

5. At the end of the process, the dough should be neatly shaped with sufficient, and even, tension on its surface; it should hold its shape on the work surface. The "outside" of the final loaf should now be facing up—and it might have flour on it from this process, and that's fine because it's the outside of the final bread.

6. Transfer the dough to a prepared proofing basket with a lightly floured hand and a bench knife slid underneath the dough to help scoop it up, flip it over, and drop it gently into the basket, seam-side up.

7. If you feel like it might not have been shaped tightly enough, pinch the seams closed with your fingers to ensure they stay put or do a "stitch" for a bâtard: Pick up a few spots along the sides of the dough and cross them over each other, pressing lightly to seal, as you work along the long length of the dough, from one side to the other.

SHOULD I DEGAS MY DOUGH?

I generally do not degas my dough, but at the end of bulk fermentation, if your dough is extremely well aerated, potentially with large, visible bubbles, it might be helpful. Degassing is simply patting or pressing the dough to help redistribute large alveoli—bubbles—that are filled with the gasses during fermentation, essentially popping the large ones and making them form smaller, more even bubbles throughout. Degassing can also help if you're making a pan loaf destined for toast or sandwiches, when you want a tighter, more even crumb. For the most part, I rely on my shaping methods described in this book to help even out the dough, as they are just intensive enough to ensure no large bubbles make it into the final loaf of bread.

To lightly degas your dough, after flipping your preshaped round over and just before shaping, use a floured flat hand (like a paddle) to gently tap the dough repeatedly from top to bottom. This can be performed after you fold the sides of your dough in during the first steps of shaping, shortly after you flip your preshaped round over and are about to shape.

HELP! MY DOUGH IS REALLY STICKY!

A common question I receive from readers goes something like this: "My dough is so much stickier than the way your dough looks. Why is mine so hard to shape?" And similarly: "How come you don't need as much flour on your work surface as I do?" In almost every case, the issue here is your dough is likely not strong enough or it's overhydrated, which are related. If your dough is not sufficiently strengthened (see Strengthen the Dough, page 81), meaning the gluten network is not adequately developed, your dough won't be as smooth, cohesive, and elastic. It's also possible, though not as common, that your dough is under- or overproofed.

These tips can help:

- Move quickly and confidently, which prevents the dough from sticking.

- Rely more on your bench knife, as it tends to stick less.

- Use as much bench flour as needed to ensure the dough doesn't stick to your hands or work surface.

TO PREVENT THE PROBLEM

Repeat the same recipe, keeping everything the same, except this time, do one or a combination of the following (in order of my preference):

- Slightly reduce the hydration of the dough (in many recipes this can be done by omitting the Water 2 listed in the ingredients, which is held in reserve).

- Knead the dough longer (slap and fold is a good technique; see page 83).

- Add one or two more sets of stretches and folds during bulk fermentation.

- Be sure to bulk ferment your dough to the correct point: If you cut bulk fermentation time too short, the dough will be shaggy and hard to handle. If you bulk ferment too long, the dough will be sticky and degraded.

Before You Start: Make Your Dough and Work Surface Nonstick

There's a sense of freedom when you take a baking class or bake in a bakery: You can throw flour on the work surface and dough without a second thought—the shackles are off, it's a bakery, it's expected that flour is everywhere. The reality is, I'm far too neat for this at home. And while I do throw and dust my fair share, I try to keep it contained on my work surface, more of a light dusting than an explosive puff. But there's an important reason why you see bakers throwing flour: It takes to the air and evenly coats wherever it's thrown. Instead of clumps of flour scattered here and there, which might find their way as pockets of raw flour in the end loaf of bread, the even dusting creates a thin and even nonstick layer.

I find a balance at home: I throw or dust just enough flour to coat a small target area, but I don't do a handful—just a pinch. This takes some practice, and much like a chef might practice sprinkling salt to ensure even coverage, we bakers can practice in the same way.

I use two methods: dusting from above and throwing from a distance.

☰ METHOD: DUSTING

Grab a pinch of white flour with your fingers, then hold your hand over your target area and, starting from the left or right side of the area, quickly move your hand back and forth while releasing a small amount of flour as your hand crosses to the other side of the target area. The goal is to release a small amount of flour with each back-and-forth motion of your hand, so the flour takes flight as it's dropping toward your target.

☰ METHOD: THROWING

To do a light dusting, grab a small bit of flour in your hand and move it quickly toward your work area. Release the flour from your hand 6 inches or so from the target and let the flour glide in the air to evenly coat your target.

Shaping a Bâtard

A bâtard—an oval—is without a doubt my favorite way to shape a hearth loaf. I love the visual appeal of a long loaf with a single or double slash that opens high and wide. But in addition to aesthetics, a bâtard tends to slice better in the way I like to eat bread: It has narrow, tall slices (compared to a round boule), which makes it perfect for larger sandwiches.

The following shaping methods start with a piece of dough that's mostly in a round shape and has been sufficiently dusted with flour, then flipped over onto a floured work surface. Note that while I almost always preshape my bread dough (see page 96), it's not mandatory—if your dough is strong and in a mostly gathered-up, orderly state, it's possible to skip preshaping and go right into shaping with one of the methods below.

☰ SHAPING A BÂTARD, STRONG DOUGH

This is my preferred way to shape a bâtard. It does take practice, and it can be difficult if your dough isn't sufficiently strengthened going into shaping. With this method, you want a dough that's smooth and elastic; if the dough is excessively extensible or very slack, it can be hard to roll and push to produce sufficient tension in the end. What I like about this method is its simplicity, but it's also a gentle method that yields a loaf that has a uniformly open interior.

When shaping in this way, I like to imagine I'm rolling the dough and tucking just its *outside* skin, keeping the inside of the cylinder intact without squishing it excessively (for more dough strength, roll and tuck more aggressively).

1. Reposition the dough (floured-side now down) in front of you to ensure it's a mostly even round. You can quickly pick up the sides, top, or bottom and drag it in or out to try and get the shape into a relatively balanced round.

2. Take the left or right side of the round and fold it over into the middle, pressing lightly to stick.

3. Take the other side and fold it over and into the middle, overlapping the other side that was just folded.

4. With both hands, take the top of the dough and fold it down just a bit to start a small cylinder at the top of the rectangular piece of folded dough now in front of you.

5. With both hands, begin rolling the dough down the rectangle. Gently push the cylinder forward into itself with your thumbs, creating a roll. Continue rolling the dough down, pushing it at each revolution to tighten the cylinder.

6. Once you've rolled up the dough completely, the seam will be on the bottom. At this point I like to pinch the sides closed, but this is optional (if pinched, the dough will have round ends; if not, it will have a blunter shape). Finally, transfer the shaped bâtard to a proofing basket, seam-side up.

Shaping a bâtard, strong dough

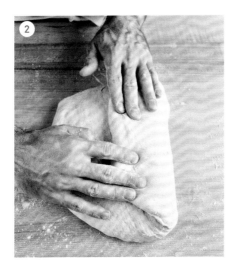

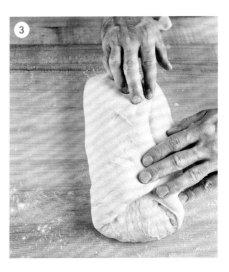

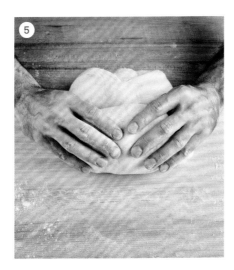

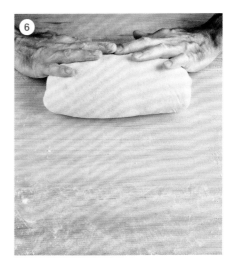

SHAPING A BÂTARD, SLACK DOUGH

When you're dealing with a dough that's extremely extensible and slack, it is important to add structure and strength to it to ensure it does not spread excessively during proofing—or even during baking. It helps to keep your hands moving and to quickly shape the dough with swift and confident motions. If the dough rests on the work surface or your hands for longer than necessary, it tends to stick. As always, if the dough is sticking excessively, use a little more flour on your hands and work surface.

Shaping a bâtard, slack dough

This method of shaping is based on the technique used at Tartine Bakery in San Francisco. Many have called it "stitching," and for good reason: The motion you make produces a series of stitches on the dough, from top to bottom. I keep this method on the simple side with minimal steps. With each stitch, the dough gains a buttress that helps keep it tight and in shape, without excessively degassing it.

1. Fold a small piece of the bottom of the dough up to about the bottom third.

2. Fold the left and right sides of the round up and toward the middle, with a small overlap in the middle.

3. Fold the top flap of the round down to about the top third. You'll now have a relaxed letter shape.

4. Starting at the top of the letter, gently grab the top left and right corners of the dough. Then, stretch each piece down a little and over the other so it forms an X shape—a stitch—at the top of the letter.

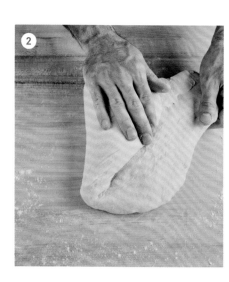

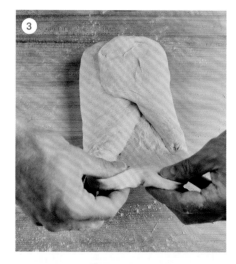

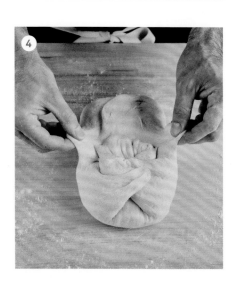

5. Repeat this stitch two or three more times, working down to the bottom of the dough. It's important to grab only the smallest bit of dough at each side to pull and stitch over. Your dough should now look like a tighter cylinder in front of you, with the long sides to your left and right.

6. Roll this long cylinder down very gently from top to bottom. You shouldn't have to perform many revolutions of this roll; you're almost just gently folding it over itself, so the top meets the bottom. Let the dough rest on the counter for a few minutes to seal, then transfer to a proofing basket seam-side up.

Shaping a Boule

In my eyes, a loaf baked as a boule—a round shape—has a certain rustic charm that's uniquely appealing. I find I prefer shaping certain types of bread into boules, such as porridge loaves (like the oat porridge loaf on page 229) and recipes that include a high percentage of inclusions. Boules tend to have an interior structure that's a little tighter than a bâtard or other shape, but that tightness contributes positively to the overall eating experience. A prime example of this would be a miche (see page 209), which is a large round loaf that typically has a slightly tighter crumb structure.

There are many ways to shape a boule, some more involved than others, but the methods presented here are my go-to ways to shape various types of dough. The following shaping methods start with a piece of dough that's mostly in a round shape and has been sufficiently dusted with flour, then flipped over onto a floured work surface.

ADD TOPPINGS TO YOUR BREAD DOUGH

Adding toppings to the exterior of bread not only increases the health benefits, but also adds character and visual appeal—which is, of course, the first step to eating. My favorite toppings are oats (finely cut instant oats are best), sesame seeds (both black and white), flaxseeds, and even pumpkin seeds. Because the toppings toast as they are exposed to the heat of the oven while the bread is baking, there's no need to prepare them in any way. But by the same token, toppings can burn, so sugary items like dried fruit are not typically used.

My preferred method of coating the exterior of my dough with toppings is to sprinkle them on a sheet pan or clean kitchen towel placed near where I'm shaping my dough. After shaping the dough, I gently pick it up, seam-side up, and transfer it right into the middle of the toppings. I then tip the dough to pick up the toppings: rocked left and right if it's a bâtard or around in a circle if it's a boule. The toppings should stick in a thin layer on the exterior. Finally, transfer the coated dough to its prepared proofing basket to proof.

Sometimes when working with a low-hydration dough, it can be difficult to get the toppings to stick because of the dry exterior. In this case, dampen a kitchen towel and lay it out next to where your toppings have been spread. After shaping the dough, quickly and gently tip or roll the shaped dough on the damp towel to moisten it (just the part of the dough where you want the toppings to stick), then dip the dough into the toppings.

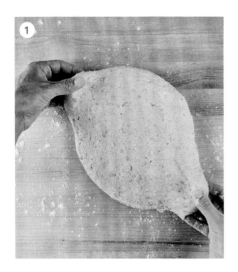

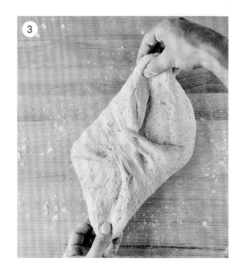

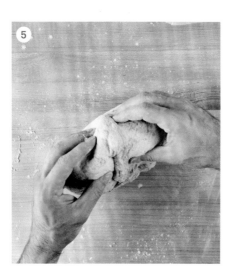

SHAPING A BOULE, STRONG DOUGH

When a dough is smooth and elastic, sufficient shaping requires only a light hand and a few key movements. I like to perform what I call a "gather up" technique to simply pick up several points along the circumference of the preshaped round and fold them over to about two-thirds of the way to the other side.

Shaping a boule, strong dough

1. In each hand, take opposing points along the outside round of dough.

2. Gently tug these points up and over, one after another, toward the middle of the round. You'll now have two sections of dough pulled and overlapping in the middle.

3. Choose two other opposing points along the outside of the round and repeat this folding.

4. Repeat this crossing with two fresh points along the round for a total of 3 to 5 times, as necessary, to keep the dough in a round shape with mostly even tension.

5. Flip the gathered-up dough over so the seams are now down on the work surface.

6. Using both hands, push and drag the entire mass of dough on the work surface to just tighten the exterior skin on the dough slightly. Let the dough rest, seam-side down, on the work surface for a few minutes to ensure the bottom seams seal before transferring to the proofing basket, seam-side up.

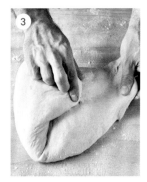
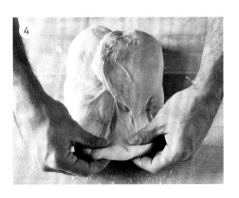

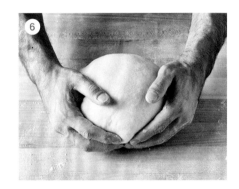

SHAPING A BOULE, SLACK DOUGH

When shaping a slack, soft dough, additional folds help set the stage for adding extra tension. With this approach, the dough is first folded to resemble a letter shape, then flipped over and pushed and/or pulled to continue to increase the tension on the outside skin of the dough.

1. Fold a small piece of the bottom of the dough up to about the bottom third and gently press to stick.

2. Gently tug outward on the bottom two corners of the dough.

3. Fold the left and right sides of the round over and toward the middle, with a small overlap. Gently press to stick.

4. Take the top and fold it down over the entire round so it touches the work surface.

5. The dough will slightly flip down and over when doing this, and the result will be a folded-up shape with the seam facing down.

6. Using both hands, cup them around the side of the dough farthest from you so your pinky fingers are pressed against the work surface. Slowly drag the dough toward your body. You will feel the dough begin to tighten and pinch slightly between your pinky fingers and the work surface. Rotate the dough and repeat until you have a uniformly round dough that's evenly taut across the surface. Let the dough rest, seam-side down, on the work surface for a few minutes to ensure the bottom seams seal before transferring to the proofing basket, seam-side up.

Shaping
a boule,
slack dough

Shaping a Pan Loaf

I absolutely love sourdough pan loaves. Baking in a pan confines the dough, but in a way also liberates the baker—the structure of the pan affords us a chance to work with a super-high hydration, add in loads of mix-ins, and push dough enrichments higher than you might otherwise.

When shaping a pan loaf I use an approach similar to the one I use for shaping a strong dough into a bâtard shape. The difference with a pan loaf is that you want the dough to be slightly degassed to create a tighter interior (which is perfect for toast and sandwiches).

To begin, I lightly grease my Pullman pan with a neutral oil or butter—even if my pan is nonstick (you can also use a parchment paper sling; see below). Then I place the pan in front of me on the work surface to give me a visual guide on how wide to shape my dough for it to fit comfortably in the pan. It's okay to shape a little shorter than the pan; the dough will spread during proofing and eventually fill the pan's length.

As usual, work with a floured work surface and flour the top of the pre-shaped, and relaxed, round of dough. Flip the preshaped round over so the floured side is down.

Shaping a pan loaf

1. With lightly floured hands, fold both the right and left sides of the round in toward the middle, stopping so the resulting length of the dough is just shy of the sides of your pan. You will have a long rectangle in front of you.

2. If your dough feels very gassed up, lightly tap from the top of the rectangle down to the bottom to help expel some of the excess gas. Next, using both hands, grab the dough farthest from you and fold it down a little—this is the start of a series of rolls and tucks downward toward your body.

3. Now that a small bit at the top has been folded down, use both hands to continue rolling the dough downward toward your body. With each revolution, use your two thumbs to push the new roll away from you, tucking the dough slightly into itself. Each roll and push will impart additional tension in the dough.

4. Once the entire rectangle is rolled, you'll have a cylinder in front of you with a smooth, taut surface that is just shy of the length of the Pullman pan. Using both hands, or one hand and a bench knife, scoop the dough into the pan, seam-side down. While it's nice to have a level surface to the dough after you place it in the pan—so it rises nice and tall with a gentle curve—avoid pushing the sides of the dough down into the pan, which will cause dense spots at the sides of the loaf when it's baked.

USING A PARCHMENT PAPER SLING

One challenging aspect of shaping pan loaves can be the act of transferring the shaped dough to the pan (this is especially true if using a long pan, such as a 13-inch-long Pullman pan). To make this transfer easy, cut a piece of parchment so the short side is the length of the bottom of the pan and the long side is long enough for the parchment to drape over the sides, creating a makeshift dough sling. After you've shaped your dough into a long cylinder shorter than your pan, scoop it up with your bench knife and drop it right in the middle of the parchment paper. Then grab the ends of the paper to pick up the tube of dough and gently drop it right into your pan. Bake the dough with the parchment paper.

Shaping Small Rounds, Buns, and Rolls (Including Pizza Dough Balls)

Shaping dough for buns and rolls requires a different approach than that for a large, free-form hearth-style loaf. The dough for these smaller breads is typically much softer as it often includes enrichments—butter, sugar, or eggs—making it important to achieve a tight exterior on the dough so the rounds hold their shape all the way to bake time. Additionally, the tight exterior needs to be uniform to prevent bulging or an uneven rise. If you find your dough is excessively sticky or soft, see Help! My Dough Is Really Sticky! (page 101) for tips.

The following methods work for shaping buns and rolls but are also a useful way to tightly preshape balls of Sourdough Pizza Dough (page 294), English Muffins (page 358), and other small rounds. Each shaping method is tailored to the type of dough.

SOFT DOUGH: USE A BENCH KNIFE

When a dough is very sticky, soft, or well fermented, using the bench knife in one hand with the other hand lightly floured is a great approach. The bench knife is mostly nonstick, which reduces the chances for the dough to snag on your hands. Using the bench knife in one hand and at a shallow angle to the work surface, push the small piece of dough so it drags slightly on the surface, creating tension in the outside skin of the dough. Simultaneously, use your other hand to encourage the edge where the dough meets the surface to curl and tuck under. You can do this in a straight pushing motion, or while following a curved arch, much like you would do when preshaping a large free-form loaf. Transfer the dough using your bench knife to a prepared baking sheet for proofing.

Shaping small rounds, soft dough, bench knife method

STIFF DOUGH: PINCH IT

I use this method when the dough is on the stiffer side, elastic, and not excessively sticky, which is typically the case for my pizza dough or any low- to moderate-hydration doughs. Pick up a piece of divided dough and place it in the palm of one of your hands. With the other hand, make a ring shape with your thumb and index or middle finger and use that to grab the edges of the dough, bringing them up to pinch closed at the top. Rotate the dough in your palm and continue to pinch with this ring shape, pinching the sides of the dough and pulling it up to the top. After a few rotations, you'll end up with a ball of dough in your palm that has a sealed top. Place this top seam down on a baking sheet for proofing.

Shaping small rounds, stiff dough, pinching method

Proofing

PROOFING, ALSO CALLED THE SECOND RISE, final rise, or final fermentation, is the time after shaping when the dough is left to continue to ferment to build up additional acidity and gain volume. Like many steps in the breadmaking process, proofing is a continuum, beginning right after dough shaping and finishing when you finally score the dough and move it to the oven to bake.

There are two general methods of proofing. The first results in a *same-day bake* in which the dough is left out on the counter at room temperature (or placed in a warm dough proofer), then generally baked within 1½ to 3 hours. The second method is *retarding*, where the shaped dough is placed in the refrigerator for a number of hours (usually overnight), then baked after this time period—either cold from the refrigerator or after having been left to come up to room temperature to continue to ferment (I almost always bake straight from the refrigerator). In both instances, the proof duration is subject to adjustment based on the dough temperature (generally, the warmer the temperature, the shorter the proof).

Much like determining when to finish bulk fermentation, finding the optimal end point to a proof can be challenging. The fact is, there is no single, clear indicator; it's more of a set of factors and indicators that need to be holistically assessed. This includes the percentage of pre-ferment, the hydration of the dough, the total duration of bulk fermentation and the dough's state going into proofing, how long the dough has been proofing, and *especially* how the dough looks and feels. But don't be intimidated. In this section I'll walk you through exactly what to look for and what to think about to help you decide when your dough is fully proofed and ready to be baked.

I attended a professional-level baking course a few years back taught by baker Jeffrey Hamelman, and his words have stuck with me: When attempting to determine whether your dough is ready for the oven, think and act like a doctor. You need to use your hands and senses to try to determine what's happening below the surface, what's happening on the inside. And of all your senses, touch will be the greatest tool in your arsenal (see Poke Test, page 116, for more).

Examining the Right Level of Proof

The three classifications on page 112—underproofed, just right, and overproofed—are snapshots of the same dough baked at three different points on the proofing continuum. Just like determining when to finish bulk fermentation, there's no single, precise point when it's best to end proofing—it's more a window of time that extends a little before and a little after the optimum. The goal is to try and bake within that window using your senses, instinct, and experience. With time and ever-growing baking experience, your ability to diagnose the dough and find the right time to bake will increase, reducing the chances for under- or overproofed bread. However, there will still be times when you're just a little off—even to this day I can still miss the mark despite my best intentions. Regardless, the bread is perfectly edible and delicious—plus, it's a learning experience, a way to add another data point to your baking knowledge.

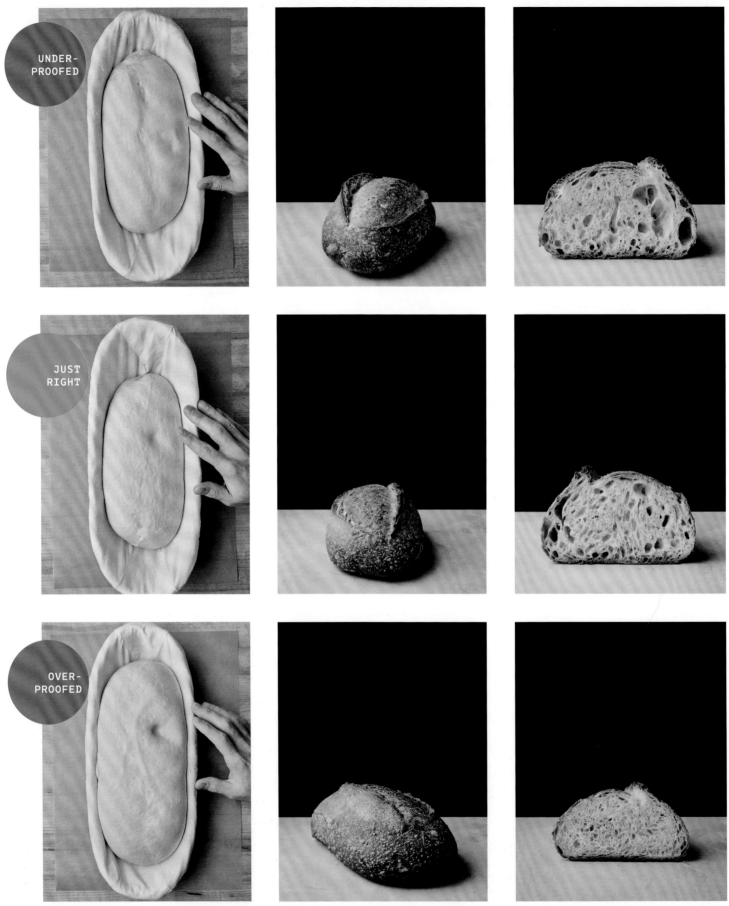

UNDER-PROOFED

JUST RIGHT

OVER-PROOFED

112

UNDERPROOFED

Before baking: The dough looks compact and tight with a few bubbles yet smooth. Dough at this underproofed state usually feels dense when gently poked and, if proofed at room temperature, will fail the Poke Test (page 116) and the indentation will spring back quickly.

After baking: The loaf exhibits excessive rise in the oven, often with unexpected fissures on the crust (despite scoring) and the bottom usually bows upward in a U shape. Sometimes these loaves will also have very large "ears" (see page 121) from scoring, as the excessive oven spring causes the crust to peel back dramatically.

Cut open: The bread has a crumb that's mostly dense but with scattered large holes. The eating experience is bland and one-dimensional with a texture that is usually gummy and dense.

JUST RIGHT

Before baking: This dough looks smooth and has volume to it. It looks and feels airy and "alive." If the dough is proofed at room temperature, it will slowly spring back when gently poked, perhaps not completely filling in the indentation. This is a good indication the dough has relaxed and fermented enough to expand optimally in the oven.

After baking: The loaf exhibits moderate rise with controlled expansion along the cuts from scoring—no fissures and no excessive peeling back along the score line(s).

Cut open: The bread has an even crumb, meaning the alveoli (holes) are uniformly distributed across the loaf with no massive holes or dense spots. The eating experience is a loaf with ample flavor, no gumminess, and a light and tender texture.

OVERPROOFED

Before baking: This dough looks very relaxed, excessively risen, and might have large bubbles showing, with the dough looking thin in areas. If proofed at room temperature, when it's gently poked the indentation will sit and never spring back. The dough feels exhausted and excessively weak.

After baking: The loaf has minimal oven spring if slightly overproofed, or a complete collapse if pushed too far. Any score on the surface fuses back together and never pulls up and off the surrounding crust.

Cut open: The bread has a dense crumb with many scattered, small holes. The eating experience might be one that's very flavorful given the extra acidity built up in the dough, but the texture will be heavy.

Proofing Stages at a Glance

Let's take a look at the diagram below. If we assign numbers to the level a dough is proofed, they would start at 0%, when the dough has just finished being shaped, and run to 100%, when the dough is fully proofed (and really, it would go beyond this all the way to overproofing, when the dough is so broken down that you'd have little to no rise left when it's baked in the oven). Generally, you do not want to bake the dough when it's fully proofed because in doing so, you'd bake a loaf that has little life left, minimal rise, no "ear" (see page 121), and a denser interior. I like to think about baking a dough when it's roughly 80% to 85% proofed. This way, there's still some life for the dough to give as the heat from the oven increases fermentation activity to produce additional gasses until the microbes are exhausted. In addition, and perhaps more important, the expansion of gasses already present in the dough also causes the dough to further rise in the oven.

Proofing Methods

An important note: The following results for each style of proofing and baking are most applicable to the recipes and processes found in this book. For instance, my recipes with a same-day bake generally have milder flavor profiles compared to those retarded (proofed at cold temperature) overnight. However, one can achieve that mild flavor with an overnight retard, too, as these characteristics are of course highly dependent on the ingredients and overall process (starter maintenance, final dough temperature, mixing times, and more) as well. The following will provide you with a way to adjust your baking to make the recipes your own.

≡ SAME-DAY BAKE

- Shorter timeline
- At room temperature (no refrigerator space required)
- Mild-flavored loaf with up-front grain flavor
- Thinner crust (generally)

Many of the recipes in this book rely on a same-day proof for scheduling reasons, and there's an undeniable charm in the flavor and texture of bread that's baked the same day without a long, cold proof. With recipes like Country Italian (page 241) or Soft White Sandwich Bread (page 269), I opt for a same-day bake to ensure mild fermentation flavors in order to place more emphasis on the flavor of the grain itself. In addition, I find the crust takes on a desirably brittle texture that readily crunches and cracks while eating.

End of shaping (0% proofed) — PROOF TIME

(Underproofed)
As proofing progresses, dough will relax, rise, and smooth.

Time to bake (85% proofed)

Fully proofed (100%)

(Overproofed)

DOUGH IS:
Strong, tight, some aeration

IF BAKED NOW:
Erratic rise in oven, ruptures, bottom shaped like a U, dense with scattered large holes, massive oven spring

DOUGH IS:
Soft, well risen, airy, smooth

IF BAKED NOW:
Controlled rise, no erratic ruptures, evenly open, well-fermented interior, clean score with "ear"

DOUGH IS:
Weak, overrisen, excessively bubbly, relaxed too far in the basket

IF BAKED NOW:
Reduced rise, tighter interior, lack of "ear" as score doesn't open as dramatically

RETARDING
(IN THE REFRIGERATOR)

- Longer timeline (convenient scheduling for home bakers)

- More depth of flavor from increased fermentation time

- Easier scoring

- More substantial crust (generally)

- Potential crust blistering

One of my greatest motivations for retarding is the flavor gain. The lengthy cold fermentation (below 46°C/8°C) time allows the bacteria and yeast to continue to function for a time, building up more acidity in the dough, which directly translates to deeper fermentation flavors in the final loaf. In addition, biochemical processes by enzymes found in the flour are also given time to do their work and contribute to flavor. This overall depth of flavor, and sometimes up-front sourness, might not be desired for every bread or baked good, in which case a same-day bake is more appropriate. For example, with enriched doughs or strictly sweet doughs (like Hot Cross Buns, page 388), it might be best to skip any retard and bake the dough the same day, if possible.

The process also produces a loaf with a slightly more substantial crust. The exposure to the cold seems to thicken the crust when the loaf is eventually baked. This can be a desirable trait for many free-form hearth-style loaves, but for bread like Demi Baguettes (page 251), rolls, or buns, I prefer to bulk retard the dough or simply bake them the same day. The dehydrating effect of the refrigerator also leads to more blistering (see Blistering, page 117), which I like for added texture and visual appeal.

A final benefit to retarding is that it helps make scoring (page 118) easier. Since the dough is typically baked straight from the refrigerator (more on this soon), it's still cold and firm, which makes scoring with a blade vastly easier.

For recipes that are supposed to be retarded, can I bake them the same day instead?

Absolutely. Instead of an overnight proof in the refrigerator, proof the dough on the counter instead. Generally, it'll take anywhere from 1½ to 3 hours to proof, temperature depending (warmer means less time). Use the Poke Test (page 116) to determine when the dough is ready for baking.

How long can I retard my dough in the refrigerator?

With many of the recipes in this book, there's at least several hours of leeway on either side of the proofing time outlined in each recipe. This is because a typical home refrigerator is quite cold at around 39° to 40°F (3°C to 4°C) and reduces fermentation activity significantly. However, there's no single answer to this question because it really depends on the state of your dough when it goes into the refrigerator to proof. Take, for example, a dough that was pushed very far in bulk fermentation, perhaps even farther than it should have gone, and has resulted in a dough that's very gassy and a little on the weak side structurally—a dough that clearly needed to be divided earlier. This dough would not last quite as long in proof as a dough that bulk fermented for less time, regardless of whether the proof was performed in the refrigerator or on the counter.

So, I like to say you can usually push the retard time with most doughs, especially recipes in this book, but expect that you'll be moving the dough ever closer to overproofing—fermentation is continuing after all, even if at a slower pace. In the end, this means the longer the dough is in the refrigerator, the less rise and the more sour the flavor of the final loaf of bread.

Can I bake straight from the refrigerator, or do I need to let the dough warm up first?

Yes, you can absolutely bake straight from the refrigerator; there's no need to let the dough warm to room temperature first. In fact, I'd say nearly all my baking is done right from the refrigerator. The only instance

THE POKE TEST

Poke test

If you've baked a loaf of bread, you have no doubt stumbled on the term "poke test" at some point. Many bakers use and advocate for this technique to help determine when a dough is sufficiently proofed and ready for baking.

The test is simple: Using a wet or lightly floured finger, give the surface of the proofing dough a few quick pokes. If the indentation

- springs back and fills back in quickly, the dough likely needs more proofing time.

- very slowly springs back, perhaps not quite filling in the indentation, *this is optimal* and signifies a dough that's relaxed and has risen sufficiently; it's ready to be baked.

- stays depressed and never springs back at all, it might be overproofed or getting close, so bake ASAP.

While I consider the poke test to be mostly accurate, it's not a foolproof test, and there are several other factors that require additional inspection. For instance, consider a dough that's been retarded in the refrigerator: It will be very cold and firm coming out, meaning it has a different plasticity versus a dough that's proofed at room temperature. Or take a highly hydrated whole wheat dough: This dough won't be as elastic and airy as an all-white-flour dough at low hydration, so it might fail the poke test but still be ready to be baked. Finally, if the gluten in the dough isn't developed sufficiently (which is a common problem for beginning bakers), the dough will simply not be strong enough to display the signs we look for with the poke test. (For more on dough strengthening, see page 81.)

So if the poke test isn't foolproof, why use it? As I've mentioned, poking in general is a good thing! It's another data point, another way to discern how the dough is progressing and add to your baker's intuition.

Often beginners tend to bake their dough before it's sufficiently proofed, resulting in excessive rise and a dense crumb with scattered large holes.

116

when it would be wise to let the dough warm is if you find the dough is still underproofed in the refrigerator. If this is the case, remove it from the refrigerator and let it warm up and continue to proof at room temperature until it's ready (use the Poke Test, page 116). Keep in mind that warmer dough is a little more challenging to score.

Why does my dough keep overproofing when I retard?

Keep in mind when you retard your dough it takes time for your dough to cool down to the temperature of your refrigerator. If your dough is in a thick basket and then sealed in a bag with warm room-temperature air, it's going to take many minutes for your home refrigerator to cool it to where fermentation is slowed. During this time, your dough will continue to ferment, possibly going further than you expect or desire. To remedy this, you can shorten bulk fermentation, reduce the bench rest time, skip any room-temperature proof time before placing the dough in the refrigerator, shorten the final proof time, or a combination of these.

Why doesn't my dough rise when proofed in the refrigerator, and how can I tell if it's under- or overproofed?

A common question I receive is from bakers who place their dough to proof in the refrigerator overnight only to find it looks almost the same in the morning with little rise and no obvious signs of change. While many strains of yeast (the primary CO_2 generators) continue to function at the low temperatures—39° to 40°F (3° to 4°C)—in a home refrigerator, many will not. Generally, this is almost always okay! It's fine if the dough isn't super puffy coming out of the cold. However, the dough should not feel very dense, tight, or lifeless, which indicates it might be underproofed. An easy correction to this is to place the covered proofing basket on the counter and let it come up to room temperature for additional warm-temperature proof time. Next time extend bulk fermentation or leave the shaped loaves out on the counter for additional room-temperature proof time before retarding—even just 15 to 20 minutes will help. If the dough feels very weak, is excessively airy with lots of bubbles (which may have a thin membrane), and has spread significantly, this might be an indication it has overproofed. Next time, reduce bulk fermentation time by about 15 minutes or reduce the time the dough is in the refrigerator.

BLISTERING

Though considered a defect by some, I enjoy a moderate amount of blistering on my crust. For me, the blisters, which look like the crust has popped out a bit, add a little extra crispness and crunch with each bite. Blisters form more readily when any or all of these factors exist: the dough has strong fermentation, is made up of mostly white flour, is a higher hydration and/or is not exceedingly strong, is slightly dehydrated from retarding in the refrigerator overnight, and is in an oven extremely well steamed at the onset of baking (see Why Is Steam Necessary When Baking Bread? on page 123).

Scoring

SUCCESSFUL SHAPING RESULTS IN DOUGH that has a smooth, taut outer skin. Think of this skin like the rubber of a water balloon: It's stretchy (extensible) but strong (elastic), able to expand and yet contain the dynamic lattice of bubbles expanding, compacting, and coalescing in a loaf's interior. But this outer skin has limits; it can only stretch and expand so much before it reaches its viscoelastic extents. When dough is placed in the oven for baking, the sudden intense heat causes fermentation activity to dramatically increase and gasses to expand, prompting the dough to dramatically rise and expand in a short period. Scoring—which is simply intentionally slicing into the taut skin of the dough with a sharp implement—by the baker helps direct and relieve the pressure built up inside a piece of dough as it bakes.

If the dough isn't cut, or scored, the loaf will rise until it eventually ruptures in one, or multiple, undetermined areas. While this style of breaking is appropriate for some types of bread (rye in particular), for most hearth-style loaves, the dough is scored to create a weak spot or spots where the baker can direct and control the expansion.

These areas are usually cut with either a razor blade held directly in the hand (not my preference) or a specialized tool called a baker's lame (pronounced lahm), which is a razor blade attached to a handle (usually plastic). The handle of the lame is specifically designed so you can change the razor blade once it dulls. There are many ways to perform these cuts, ranging from simple slashes to complex patterns. The important thing when scoring is to always ensure the cuts are performed evenly over the surface of the

IMPLEMENT	PRODUCES	ANGLE	USEFUL FOR	EXAMPLE
Curved razor blade	A cut that peels back and lifts open to form an "ear"	Hold the blade at a shallow angle to the dough to encourage more of the peeling back effect	Offset or double parallel score (as with baguettes)	My Best Sourdough (page 257)
Straight razor blade, sharp knife, or scalpel	A cut that splays open	Hold the blade at a straight-on (90-degree) angle to promote splaying open, but can also be used at a shallow angle to promote lifting	Intricate scoring designs (see Decorative Scoring, page 120)	Miche (page 209)
Scissors	A jagged cut (like a zigzag)	Best to hold the scissors at a shallow angle	To avoid snagging doughs that have chunky toppings	

dough to encourage even rise and expansion across the entire loaf. If one side is scored more deeply than the other, the result might be a lopsided loaf where the side with fewer cuts rises higher or bulges outward.

Scoring also serves an aesthetic purpose in addition to a practical one: It's another point in the breadmaking process where a baker can add their creative mark. The dough is a blank canvas for expression, a place to add visual appeal—we eat first with our eyes, after all.

Scoring Tools

Anything that is sharp enough to cleanly cut the dough can serve as a scoring implement: A razor blade (probably the most common choice among bakers), a knife, scissors, or even a surgical scalpel will all work. Each of these implements is better suited to a particular outcome (see chart, opposite).

I use both a straight and a curved razor blade for almost all my bakes. Regardless of your choice of tool, it's important that it remain sharp. Razor blades are a cheap and effective tool, but they can quickly dull. If you notice your blade beginning to snag on the dough when scoring, rotate it to use a different edge or replace it with a new one.

How to Score Your Dough

Before scoring, it's important to pause for a moment and assess your proofed dough. I like to run through a quick mental checklist:

1. Was the dough retarded (cold-proofed)? If it was, and it's still cold, it can usually handle a deeper score than if the dough was proofed at a warmer temperature, perhaps a 1½-inch cut as opposed to a 1-inch depth, depending on the dough.

2. How does the dough look? Are there large visible bubbles on the dough's surface in the basket? Does it look stretched and very gassed up? If so, it is likely very well fermented and will require a score that's gentler and shallower (just below the dough's outer skin).

3. How does the dough feel? Related to #2, does the dough feel weak and very gassed up? If so, a gentler score will be better suited for this well-proofed dough. Conversely, does the dough feel strong and taut? If so, it likely will need a deeper score.

Next, choose a scoring implement that is most appropriate—both structurally and aesthetically—for the loaf at hand. Using the answers to my mental checklist, I'll then consider whether to score deeply or shallower. Holding the lame at the end of the handle, as far away from the blade as possible, I cut into the dough in a fluid and confident motion. If the scoring design requires more cuts, continue cutting in the same fashion. Moving the blade in a smooth cutting action will ensure it doesn't snag on the dough. This takes practice, so when starting out it's okay to move more slowly, with more control. If you find your cuts do not go sufficiently deep, it's fine to use the blade to go over the cut area a second time, cutting in deeper.

Scoring

DECORATIVE SCORING

While I tend to score my loaves with a single long slash, a series of slashes, or sometimes my favorite box top, occasionally I like to get a little fancy. Baking bread doesn't have to be all formulas and process-driven rigor, after all. And there are so many places for creativity in the breadmaking process, places for inspiration to guide your hand and create something unique. I do find that intricate scoring is more easily performed on dough that's firm and slightly cold to the touch. The cold dough slices cleanly with fewer snags and is more accepting of many cuts before excessive spreading.

Additionally, when doing decorative scoring, and for the best contrast, it helps to have a slightly thicker coating of white flour on the dough. Right before scoring, use a small fine-mesh sieve to dust white flour evenly over the surface of the dough. Gently use your hand to smooth out the flour.

Here are some simple scoring patterns to try. They all can be done with either a straight or curved blade, but the slashes, spiral, and circle top patterns work best with the shallow scoring you get from a curved blade.

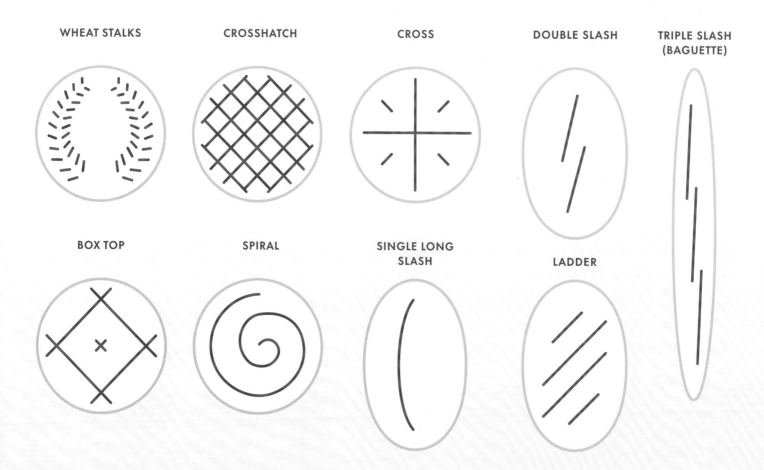

WHEAT STALKS   CROSSHATCH   CROSS   DOUBLE SLASH   TRIPLE SLASH (BAGUETTE)

BOX TOP   SPIRAL   SINGLE LONG SLASH   LADDER

SCORING TROUBLESHOOTING

My crust never lifts off to form an ear and instead seals back together.

This could be due to a number of factors, including:

- **Overproofed dough:** Dough that's overproofed won't have enough "life" left in it to spring dramatically in the oven.

- **Insufficient dough strength (or overhydration):** If your dough is weak from insufficient strength in mixing and/or bulk fermentation, or it's overhydrated (which manifests similarly as understrengthened dough), it will lack the structural integrity to rise tall in the oven. Reduce your dough hydration, give it more kneading time up front, or increase the number of sets of stretches and folds in bulk fermentation to give it more strength.

- **Insufficient steam in the oven:** Steam helps keep the outer skin of your dough moist and pliable (see Baking with Steam in a Home Oven, page 123), giving your loaf time to rise up and open along the score. If your oven lacks sufficient steam, the crust could harden off before it has a chance to separate, resulting in a singular crust with no separation.

- **Insufficient score depth:** Be sure to cut in far enough to slice through the outer, tough skin that forms on the outside of your dough. You'll know you're in past this point when you look at the cut: The outer skin is usually the section of the dough that has little to no visible holes, almost like a balloon's rubber skin.

- **Excessive top heat in the oven:** If your oven has an exposed heating element at the top near the crust, too much downward heat for too long can stunt loaf expansion prematurely (the crust hardens before the ear has a chance to peel back). Move your oven rack down a slot or two, farther away from the heating element.

My crust lifts too high and the ear is enormous.

Your dough is likely underproofed and could have used more time in bulk fermentation or proof.

My loaf deflated when I scored.

This is almost always due to overproofed dough. Remember, the more proofed your dough, the gentler your scoring must be.

My loaves with long single slashes have large, cavernous holes in the crumb.

A loaf with a single long slash increases the chance for large holes in the crumb directly underneath the slash. Be sure to shape the dough with even tension along the length of the loaf, degas the dough gently if it feels excessively airy, or increase the number of slashes next time.

WHAT IS AN "EAR"?

When all the steps in the baking process are executed just right, your loaf will have a beautiful and controlled rise in the oven. Along the edges of where you've scored into the dough, a ridge will form on one side, or sometimes both sides. The ridge, and the accompanying area that's below, peel away from the rest of the loaf and is sometimes called an "ear" by bakers.

Baking

BAKING IS THE CULMINATION OF THE ENTIRE breadmaking process, when we finally get to see the results of all the steps we've performed to transform flour, water, and any other ingredients into a living, dynamic system. The heat of the oven forces the dough into a state of rapid transformation: The microbes in the dough accelerate their fermentation activity and gasses expand, causing the dough to rise dramatically (which is called "oven spring"), and the proteins and starches physically change, transforming the dough from soft and extensible to sturdy and elastic. Most of the resulting bread's volume will be attained during this time.

The radiant heat of the oven works its way from the outside to the center of the loaf. As this heat migrates throughout the baking dough, it causes the release of water vapor through the surface layers that have become permeable due to heat exposure. Once baking has progressed sufficiently, the outer layers eventually dehydrate to form a crisp and crunchy crust, while the interior crumb remains moist and tender. Additionally, through the Maillard reaction (see page 273), sugars in the dough react with amino acids to give the crust its golden-brown color, aroma, and flavor.

During baking, it's important to provide the right environment to encourage optimal oven spring and sufficient crust coloring. In the home kitchen, you can do this by baking your dough in a sealed Dutch oven or combo cooker or by using steaming pans at the beginning of baking. The trapped or introduced steam, respectively, helps keep the outer layers of the dough supple and expandable, resulting in a loaf that rises tall with a well-colored and shiny crust.

When Is My Bread Done Baking?

Baking is finished when the crust is well colored and the center of the dough has reached a suitable temperature for a stabilized structure that prevents collapse, at least 194°F (90°C). The crust color of the final loaf of bread is linked to the temperature of the oven: the hotter the temperature, the darker the crust. The thickness of the crust is directly linked to the total bake time for the dough: the longer the bake time, the thicker the crust.

Throughout this book, many recipes indicate you should bake a loaf until the interior reaches around 206° to 208°F (96° to 97°C), which is a good range for many loaves. Enriched doughs (that is, dough with egg, butter, or sugar) are typically considered fully baked when the internal temperature is around 195°F (90°C), but sometimes higher. The recipes in this book will indicate an approximate internal temperature and visual cues to look for when the dough is fully baked. If you live at a very high altitude, your free-form hearth-style loaf may never reach 206°F (96°C); it might cap out around 200°F (93°C)—but it doesn't mean your loaf isn't fully baked. To check if the loaf is finished baking, pull it from the oven and use a combination of the following cues to make a determination:

- The crust should be well colored over the entire loaf. Look for a deep mahogany-colored crust with no pale and pliable spots hiding at the sides or bottom (light areas inside where the crust has peeled back from scoring are okay).

- If you gently squeeze the crust, it should produce a satisfying crunch and crackle. If the crust feels soft and pliable, it's not finished baking (unless you're baking a crust that should be soft, of course).

- The loaf should sound hollow and expansive if you tap or knock on the bottom. If it sounds dense and muted, give it more time in the oven.

Why Is Steam Necessary When Baking Bread?

If you've baked a loaf of bread before, you're likely familiar with the fact that baking bread dough benefits from steam in the oven at the start. This steam helps bread dough retain its viscoelastic properties—the ability of the dough to stretch and expand during baking. Water vapor introduced into the oven (or trapped inside in the case of a sealed pot) gathers on the outside of the baking dough, delaying its drying and setting its structure. This delay allows oven spring to continue for a longer period. In the end, the result is a loaf that has increased volume versus a flatter loaf baked in a dry oven.

Steam can also help create a shiny crust with increased browning. The water vapor settling on the exterior of the baking dough is absorbed into the starches heating in the oven; these starches swell and eventually pop and liquefy, forming a friable and glossy shell. Because steam keeps the surface of the dough cooler for longer, the crust has a chance to caramelize for longer (i.e., more browning) before going too far and burning. Plus, the cooler exterior means it won't harden and dehydrate before the interior of the loaf is fully baked through.

However, it's not mandatory that your oven be steamed to bake sourdough bread. Without steaming, your loaf will still rise in the oven if properly strengthened and fermented; it just may have a duller and thicker crust and slightly reduced volume—still delicious, though!

Baking with Steam in a Home Oven

Professional bakers typically work with steam-injected ovens, which saturate the oven chamber with a blast of steam at the push of a button. There are some home ovens on the market with this capability, although for most of us, a conventional electric or gas oven is what we must work with. But fret not, steaming your oven is a relatively easy task with a little planning and preparation, and in my experience, any conventional home oven will work fine. In fact, armed with a Dutch oven or combo cooker, you can bake bread in any oven that can heat to at least 425°F (220°C).

While there are many ways you can create a steamed environment in which to bake your dough, in the end it's going to come down to your preference. I find the easiest way to start is to use a large Dutch oven or a combo cooker. Baking your bread dough in a sealed pot has the advantage of trapping water vapor escaping your dough while it bakes, providing just the right environment for ample crust color, loaf volume, and enjoyable texture.

Before You Bake: Get Ready

When it comes to baking, I like to do as cooks do and set up a mise en place for my oven with everything I'll need within reach. I place my Dutch oven in the oven and start preheating. Next, I put my ovenproof gloves next to the oven and a heat-resistant mat on my counter. Then, out comes my lame (see page 20) and parchment paper. Before taking my dough from the refrigerator, I quickly run through the steps in my head as if I'm rehearsing a script, from preheating the Dutch oven to taking out my dough and scoring it, to finally getting the dough into the oven. Having all my tools out, ready, and my plan in place, I can begin. Running through the steps quickly before beginning sets the stage for less stress and a smoother process.

BAKING IN A DUTCH OVEN OR CAST-IRON COMBO COOKER

See page 21 for how to choose the right Dutch oven or combo cooker.

- **Pros:** Easy (just load the dough and cover the pot); creates excellent steam; combo cookers are inexpensive

- **Cons:** Can create a thicker crust; can slightly overbake the bottom crust; pans are heavy and cumbersome; loaf shape is restricted by pot shape (i.e., a round Dutch oven can't be used for bâtards)

Arrange the oven rack in the center position. Place the pot on the rack with the lid next to it. Preheat the oven to the temperature listed in the recipe (typically, 450°F/230°C). Place a piece of parchment paper on top of the proofing basket (and the dough). Set a pizza peel or inverted baking sheet on top of the parchment and, using both hands, flip everything over. Gently remove the basket and score the dough. Using oven-proof gloves, carefully remove the bottom of the pot from the oven and place it on a heat-resistant surface near your scored dough. Then, lift the pizza peel and drag the parchment paper holding the dough into the preheated pot. Place it in the oven and cover with the lid. Bake for the time listed in the recipe. Uncover the pot, remove the lid from the oven, and continue to bake for the remaining time in the recipe. If baking a second loaf, preheat the pot again for 15 minutes before repeating.

Baking in a Dutch oven

NOTES

- If your crust has gotten a little overbaked, see the tips for remedying that in Crust Troubleshooting (page 126).

- Yes, you can bake multiple loaves at a time with two pots side by side in the oven (and you can preheat the pots with their lids on so you have room).

- No, you do not need to put the Dutch oven or combo cooker on a baking surface (a baking stone or baking steel). In fact, I've found using one can burn the crust.

BAKING DIRECTLY ON A SURFACE

- **Pros:** Creates excellent steam; can accommodate almost any dough shape; can bake multiple loaves at once

- **Cons:** Requires a baking surface in the oven; can slightly overbake the bottom crust; is a slightly more complex process with loading and pouring in ice; a little hectic

Another common method for baking bread in a home oven is to have one or more pans placed at the bottom of the oven that continually generate steam during the first part of baking. I started experimenting with this technique early on in my home baking once I began baking larger loaves and breads with unique shapes (Fougasse, page 313, or Bagels, page 367) that didn't work with my Dutch oven or combo cooker. This steaming technique requires the use of a baking surface, such as a baking stone or baking steel, placed on an oven rack in the bottom third of the oven. It also calls for a roasting pan that can optionally be filled with culinary-grade lava rocks (or ceramic briquettes) or left empty. The lava rocks help increase the surface area in the pan, which expedites steam generation when ice is thrown in (see Resources, page 424). I also like using ice instead of room-temperature or boiling water, because it doesn't spill or splash, which means it's much easier and safer to handle.

The baking surface placed in your oven can be anything that is safe for food and retains and transfers heat effectively. Typical baking stones (such as the ones used for making pizza) are great and will work fine. A baking steel, which is simply a slab of steel, is another great choice. Compared to a baking stone, a baking steel conducts heat more efficiently. In my experience, either one works just as well to bake bread, but I find the baking steel wins when it comes to both pizza *and* bread. Do note that the baking steel can sometimes be a little *too* effective and, if preheated at too high of a temperature for too long, can overbake the bottom of your loaves (see Crust Troubleshooting, page 126, for ways to mitigate this).

Baking directly on a surface

Need extra steam? Use towels, too

If you find your loaves have a dull crust (perhaps your oven is particularly prone to venting steam) or you are baking bread that benefits from a little extra steam, such as Demi Baguettes (page 251), use this method to add more. Prepare another pan with rolled-up kitchen towels, in addition to the roasting pan where ice is added. The rolled-up towels, which are soaked with boiling water, provide a constant source of steam for the first 20 minutes of the bake, since they slowly release into the oven (whereas the lava rocks provide a solid blast that quickly dissipates). When preparing the oven for baking, prepare the roasting pan (with optional lava rocks) as described below, but also boil a cup or two of water. Pour the boiling water over the rolled-up towels in the second roasting pan and slide it into the bottom of the oven before scoring the dough. Remove this pan along with the other roasting pan when the oven is vented after 20 minutes.

Convection setting

I do not turn on convection (fan assist) when baking hearth-style loaves (that is, loaves baked free-form directly on a baking surface). Why? Because I don't want the fan blowing away the steam I worked hard to create. The exceptions are baked goods like German-Style Soft Pretzels (page 375), Cinnamon Babka (page 405), and Bagels (page 367), where the convection helps promote even browning and rapidly increases the temperature of whatever I'm baking. The recipes in this book will clearly state whether the oven should have convection turned on. If it's not stated, then convection is not used. If your oven does not have convection, you can instead increase the oven temperature by approximately 25°F (20°C).

1. Place a baking stone or steel on an oven rack in the bottom third of the oven and an empty roasting pan (with optional culinary-grade lava rocks in the pan and another pan of water-soaked towels to increase steam) at the very bottom of the oven. Fill a cup with ice and set it next to the oven.

2. Transfer the dough from your proofing baskets to a parchment-lined inverted baking sheet, a large thin cutting board, or a pizza peel. Score the dough. Slide the dough with the parchment paper directly onto the baking surface in the oven.

3. Carefully pour the cup of ice into the roasting pan. Shut the oven door and let the dough bake with steam for 20 minutes. After 20 minutes, carefully open the oven door to vent the steam and remove the roasting pans. Continue to bake according to the recipe.

CRUST TROUBLESHOOTING

My bottom crust is always burned.

I find the problem of a burned and overly thick bottom crust presents itself much more in certain home ovens. Generally, if you find the bottom of your bread becomes overly thick, dark, or on the verge of burned, your bread is getting too much bottom heat from your oven, the baking surface, or the baking vessel. This can be a common problem when baking in a Dutch oven or combo cooker.

The following solutions, either alone or in combination, should help:

- **Reduce the oven temperature:** Try reducing the oven temperature by 25°F (20°C) when preheating and baking. If the problem persists, try reducing the preheating time as well. This is especially true with a baking steel, which is much more effective at conducting heat and benefits from a cooler temperature (great for pizza, not so great for some breads!).

- **Insulate:** Some ovens have an exposed bottom heating element. To insulate, place a baking stone or baking sheet on a rack in the bottom slot of the oven between the heating element and the baking dough. Additionally, if you use parchment paper to drag your dough into the baking vessel or onto the baking surface, double up and use two pieces to add a little more insulation.

- **Raise the baking surface:** Raise the oven rack holding the baking surface up one slot in your oven to give it more distance from the bottom heating element.

- **If baking in a Dutch oven, remove the bread from the pot early:** Once the crust on the loaf has fully set, usually in the last third of the bake time, carefully remove the loaf from the vessel and finish baking directly on the oven rack.

- **Add coarse cornmeal:** Dust the bottom of your dough with coarse cornmeal before flipping it out to parchment paper to help insulate the dough.

My crust is always dull.

There might be insufficient steam. If you're using a Dutch oven, after you place the dough inside, grab an ice cube and put it next to the dough (not on top) in the space between the side of the dough and the edge of the pot. Cover with the lid. The additional steam from the melting ice cube will supersaturate the interior of the pot and result in a loaf that's extra shiny (and likely thinner, too). If you're baking directly on a baking surface, try using more ice thrown into the roasting pan to produce more steam, or throw another round of ice into the roasting pan 5 to 10 minutes into the first part of baking. Also, see how to level up your steaming with Need Extra Steam? (page 125).

Another possible cause could be overproofed dough. If your dough is left to ferment for an excessively long time, there may not be enough fermentable sugars left to caramelize during baking.

My crust is very thick. How do I make it thinner?

You might be baking too long. The longer the dough is exposed to the heat of the oven, the more dehydration and heat penetration the dough will be subjected to. Try reducing your bake time by increasing the temperature of the oven slightly to expedite baking.

Another cause may be that you have insufficient steam. See page 125.

My crust ruptures and splits unexpectedly.

This could be due to underproofed dough, lack of steam, or insufficient scoring. Check the following: Examining the Right Level of Proof (page 110) for help on diagnosing underproofed dough, Baking with Steam in a Home Oven (page 123) for steaming tips and techniques, and How to Score Your Dough (page 119) for help with scoring.

ALL THE BREAD FORMULAS IN THIS BOOK use a common method to represent formulas called baker's percentages (or baker's math or formula percentage). Using baker's percentages provides several advantages:

- It allows us to easily scale a formula up or down to make more or less bread while still maintaining the same ratio of ingredients.

- It provides an easy way to quickly adjust the hydration percentage in response to changing flour (flour is not a static ingredient!).

- It's a common baker's language and a convenient way to share formulas with other bakers.

- All ingredients are weighed so you only work with a single unit of measure.

The key part to understand about using baker's percentages is that *all the flour used in a formula will always add up to 100%*. The flour is the main ingredient to which all other ingredients are compared—the other ingredients are expressed as a percentage of the total flour weight.

When you first start baking and see formulas and percentages, they might not carry much significance to you. However, as your baking experience grows, you begin to attach an instinctive association with an ingredient's percentage and what it means in a bread formula. An analogy might be the outside temperature: When you see an outside temperature of 95°F (35°C), you *know* it's a hot day outside. Similarly, with baker's percentages, a certain percentage of an ingredient might convey a sense of the dough's texture or overall flavor.

Hydration Percentage

Baker's percentages give the baker an immediate sense for the impact of each ingredient, and this most acutely seen through the hydration percentag The hydration percentage is the weight of the tota water (no other liquid) in the recipe with respect t the weight of the total flour in the recipe (again, wit baker's math, everything is related to the total flou weight). This percentage gives you the ratio of wate to flour, and that, taken into consideration with th flour blend (the types and quantities of each used will convey a sense for how the dough will feel whei mixing, folding, and shaping. For example, a dougl with mostly white flour at 55% hydration (like Bagels page 367) will be very stiff and strong compared to the same dough at 85% hydration, which will be soft and slack. (See Hydration, page 140, for more detail.)

To calculate the hydration percentage, you take the total water weight in a recipe and divide it by the total flour weight. To take Simple Sourdough (page 40) as an example, here is how the hydration percentage is calculated:

$$\text{Hydration \%} = \frac{\text{total water weight}}{\text{total flour weight}} \times 100$$

$$= \frac{760\text{g}}{1,100\text{g}} \times 100$$

$$= 69.1\%$$

Serving and Storing Bread

One of the wonderful things about sourdough bread is its natural ability to stay fresh and keep from spoiling long after baking. During the necessary lengthy fermentation time, the lactic acid bacteria acidify the dough, and this acidification not only results in remarkable flavor but is responsible for helping delay staling and spoilage. Generally, I find my loaves last between 6 and 9 days on the counter or in a breadbox. But even with these natural preservatives, bread drying and staling are inevitable.

When serving and storing the bread you worked so hard to create, remember a few things:

1. **Wait to slice until your bread fully cools!** This is incredibly important. Typically, you should wait 1 to 2 hours after baking, but with some breads (like Miche, page 209, and Roggenvollkornbrot, page 288) you might need to leave it longer to fully set. I know, the commonly held belief is that warm bread right from the oven is the best there can be, but the truth is, waiting for the bread to cool allows for fullest flavor development. When a loaf is cut too early, it can result in a gummy and sticky interior. There are exceptions to this, of course, most notably Soft Dinner Rolls (page 333).

2. **Never place your baked bread in the refrigerator.** Counterintuitively, it causes bread to stale faster than when it's kept at room temperature.

3. **Store bread cut-side down.** Let the crust do its job. Slice a free-form loaf vertically right through the middle to make two halves. Cut more slices from the middle of each half and, when finished, place the halves cut-side down on the cutting board, keeping the interior crumb surrounded by the cutting board and crust. My bread typically lasts one to two days this way, before I transfer it to a breadbox.

4. **Use a breadbox.** A breadbox is a purpose-built container designed to trap just enough moisture inside to keep bread from drying out, but not so much that it becomes soggy. My bread lasts about a week in one of these.

5. **Reusable bags or wraps.** More options to keep your bread from drying include reusable beeswax wrap, paper bags (which allow some moisture loss but not all), clean kitchen towels, and in some cases, a plastic bag. I find storing hearth-style loaves in a plastic zip-top bag tends to make them soften excessively, but for some baked goods, like German-Style Soft Pretzels (page 375) or any of the buns in this book, this is the best option.

How to Freeze Bread

For long-term storage, the freezer is the ideal spot. Bread can be stored there for up to 6 months.

☰ FREEZING SLICES

Freezing individual slices of bread is a convenient way to have slices that are almost like freshly baked bread at a moment's notice. Once your loaf is thoroughly cooled (ideally overnight), slice the whole bread. Place the slices in a zip-top freezer bag in layers where each layer's slices are rotated 90 degrees from the one below. Press out as much air as possible and place the bag in the freezer. When you want some bread, take one or two slices out and reheat directly in the toaster (many toasters have a "frozen" setting that first thaws the slice and then toasts it). The plastic freezer bag can be reused many times.

FREEZING A WHOLE LOAF

Many of the recipes in this book make two loaves at a time, so the freezer is a great option for that second loaf. Once the loaf is fully cooled (ideally overnight), wrap it in plastic wrap. Place the wrapped loaf in a zip-top freezer bag, press out as much air as possible, and freeze. When you want to eat the bread, take it out to thaw in the refrigerator for a few days or on the counter overnight.

Keeping Your Baking Tools and Kitchen Clean

If you're not a regular baker, bread or otherwise, you may be worried about the potential mess this new-found hobby will bring to your kitchen (flour, flour, flour everywhere!). Here's how to keep things as tidy as possible.

FLOUR

I keep the white flour I use for dusting when shaping in a proofing basket and leave it covered. After dusting the work surface and shaping is finished, use your bench scraper to collect all the flour. Then scoop the flour into a fine-mesh sieve held over the flour basket. Sift out any large bits of dough, let the clean flour fall back into the basket, and toss the sifted bits into the compost. This shouldn't be done with dough containing anything other than water, flour, and salt (i.e., no enriched doughs); in that case, simply discard the cleaned-up dough and flour.

DOUGH ON BOWLS AND OTHER TOOLS

Immediately after mixing, I like to fi mixing bowl with warm, soapy wat ing it straightaway with a sponge. easier, be sure to do this before the dries. Use sponges with an even su sive scrubbing side (dough gets e with no hope of removal) to clean b

PROOFING BASKETS

Moisture is the proofing basket's g thick layer of flour and prolonged n itably invite mold. After removing baking, let your baskets dry thoroug near my warm oven or in a sunny sp use a dry, stiff-bristled brush to gent from the baskets. The goal is not to away; it's okay if a little dry flour is as that contributes to its nonstick p baskets and cane bannetons should When dry, stack your baskets in a pa for storage.

COTTON OR CANVAS LINERS

I like to use liners in my proofing bas sons: They're much easier to clean themselves, and replacing a liner i than replacing a basket. If you're baki inclusions, such as figs or cranberries juice, a liner will also keep your bask the liners many times until they look a washing. Then, I'll wash them gent a little Castile soap, rinse thoroughly, a

COUCHE

As with proofing baskets, a linen cou baker's linen) should never be washed- or in a washing machine. After using it shake and brush out excess flour (I a and hang it somewhere with airflow to

Pre-fermented Flour Percentage

The pre-fermented flour (PFF) percentage of a formula is the percentage of the total flour that is fermented ahead of mixing a dough recipe (and in this book, this is your levain). This percentage can vary depending on the recipe, but typical numbers are between 1% and 50%. This is a large span, and sometimes numbers can even be outside of this range, but ultimately the PFF percentage comes down to the formula and process at hand. Generally, lower percentages mean longer fermentation times and the opposite is true for higher percentages. For recipes in this book, you'll typically find the PFF percentage at the lower end, around 6% to 10%, which suits the bulk fermentation (3½ to 4½ hours) and proof times (1 to 3 hours at room temperature or overnight).

Like the hydration percentage, the PFF percentage gives the baker a sense of what the resulting bread might be like, and eventually you'll begin to draw a connection between the percentage and how the dough will act during the breadmaking process. Of course, there are other important factors to consider, such as flour variety, temperature, and process, but the PFF percentage gives you a good bird's-eye view of the fermentation schedule.

To continue with the Simple Sourdough (page 40) example, the following is how the PPF percentage is calculated:

$$PFF\ \% = \frac{\text{pre-fermented flour weight}}{\text{total flour weight}} \times 100$$

$$= \frac{100g}{1,100g} \times 100$$

$$= 9.1\%$$

NOTES ON PERCENTAGES

Some bakers include *all* the liquids in a recipe—water, oil, eggs, etc.—in their hydration percentages to convey a sense of the dough's consistency. However, in this book, the hydration percentage only includes the water because other liquids won't affect the dough's consistency in the same way as plain water. Because of this, the hydration percentage listed for enriched doughs won't be as instructive as it is for lean doughs.

You may also wonder why the flour and water used in the sourdough starter are not included in the total weight of flour and water in the formulas in this book. Here's why: The amount of starter used is relatively small since each recipe makes a dedicated levain. So for simplicity, I do not count the starter's flour and water in the total flour and water percentages. This means that while technically the percentages of the ingredients are very slightly off from the values listed, they're close enough to ensure that you bake a fantastic loaf of bread—which is the goal of this book in the end, after all.

Levain Percentage

Both the PFF percentage and the levain percentage are essentially a view into the same component of a bake: the amount of pre-ferment in the formula. I've included both percentages because some bakers prefer to look at the levain percentage. This is the weight of the pre-ferment related only to the weight of the remaining flour used in the dough (as in, the total flour weight minus the pre-ferment flour weight).

For example, in Simple Sourdough (page 40), the PFF percentage is 9.1% as shown in the previous section. By contrast, the levain percentage for this recipe is 22%.

$$\text{Levain \%} = \frac{\text{total levain weight}}{\text{total flour weight} - \text{total levain flour weight}} \times 100$$

$$= \frac{220\text{g}}{1,000\text{g}} \times 100$$

$$= 22.0\%$$

Scaling a Recipe Up or Down

TO SIMPLY HALVE OR DOUBLE THE RECIPE

Many of the recipes in this book make two fresh loaves of bread.

- **To halve a recipe (e.g., make a single loaf):** Simply divide all the ingredients in the recipe by two, including the levain.

- **To double a recipe (e.g., make 4 loaves):** Do the opposite; multiply all the ingredients by two (double them), including the levain.

TO SCALE A RECIPE TO ANY DOUGH YIELD

When armed with a bread formula and its corresponding baker's percentages, it's easy to adjust the yield (i.e., how much dough you're making) up or down. While it's straightforward math and easy to do by hand, for ease of use and simplicity, I prefer using spreadsheets to do this. See The Perfect Loaf website, where you can download my baker's percentages spreadsheets for scaling recipes, adjusting percentages, and more.

SOURDOUGH SCIENCE 101

Fermentation

PART OF THE NEVER-ENDING FASCINATION I have with sourdough bread is how in each bake there's a science experiment going on right before your eyes. Sourdough baking utilizes a sourdough starter—a stable community of wild yeasts and beneficial bacteria—that's alive and mixed into seemingly lifeless flour. Over the course of many hours, it transforms the ingredients into a digestible and delicious loaf of bread. To ancient bakers, this must have seemed like a magical process, a transmutation that was key to the survival of many cultures throughout history. While they certainly couldn't inspect things under a microscope, in more recent times we've been able to discover what's really happening as our starter works and fermentation progresses.

What's Happening During Sourdough Fermentation?

As I mentioned, a sourdough starter is made up of a stable community of lactic acid bacteria and wild yeasts. The lactic acid bacteria and yeasts live in balance within a dough system, working in harmony and keeping other microorganisms out. The acid produced by the bacteria and the ethanol (alcohol) produced by the yeasts make the dough environment inhospitable to other microbes (including unwanted pathogens). Remarkably, suitable bacteria can tolerate ethanol, and suitable yeasts are able to proliferate in a high-acid environment. While the lactic acid bacteria and yeasts do get along and work well together, they each work in different conditions: The lactic acid bacteria

prefer a higher pH (less acidic) environment, whereas yeasts are mostly okay when the pH begins to drop as the dough acidifies.

To provide the "food" for the bacteria and wild yeasts to do their fermentation work, the right type of sugars need to be present in the dough. From the moment water is added to flour, enzymes (most notably amylase) naturally present in the flour work to transform the complex sugars (starch) found in the grain into something the bacteria and yeasts can metabolize. Bacteria and yeasts require simple sugars—glucose, sucrose, fructose, and maltose—and enzymes act as facilitators, working to transform the complex sugars into these simple sugars that can be used during fermentation.

In addition to producing a lofty and great-tasting loaf of bread, the effects of sourdough fermentation have other benefits. The acidity in the dough staves off staling and mold formation, allowing the bread to last a week or longer at room temperature. Also, acidification in the final loaf coupled with the enzymatic activity through the entire breadmaking process results in bread that is softer, has improved digestibility of gluten, and has an increased bioavailability of the nutrients present in the flour.

It seems nature designed the perfect symbiosis between these lactic acid bacteria and wild yeasts, and in turn, humans have done their part by influencing the selection of these microorganisms through generations of sourdough starter refreshments.

Why Are pH Levels So Important in Sourdough Baking?

On the pH scale, which indexes how strongly acidic or alkaline a solution is, the lower the value, the more acidic. How acidic the dough is through the fermentation refreshment cycle is important because it impacts not only the structure of the dough itself but the balance of bacteria and yeasts. The wild yeasts most common in sourdough starters are mostly unaffected as the dough acidifies from the production of acids by lactic acid bacteria. However, lactic acid bacteria prefer a less acidic environment and are adversely affected as acids accumulate through the process.

Knowing that pH is a regulating factor for bacterial growth and function, we can modify this variable to either encourage or discourage bacterial activity, which in turn, can directly affect the texture and flavor of your bread. For instance, by increasing the percentage of whole-grain flour in a recipe, we increase the "buffering capacity" of the dough. The buffering capacity is a measure of the resistance to change in pH even when acids or bases are added. Therefore, a higher buffering capacity helps keep the pH higher (less acidic) for longer before bacterial activity is reduced. This allows for more total accumulated acidity in the final loaf of bread, potentially resulting in a sourer-tasting loaf. And as mentioned previously, the higher acid content of sourdough bread also improves its keeping qualities and results in a softer texture.

P.S.

If you're not interested in the science behind fermentation, that's okay! You don't have to know about pH, enzymes, buffering capacities, or any of the many things that go on behind the scenes when baking a loaf of bread. Though the science behind sourdough fermentation can help inform our decisions in the kitchen, and we can use high-level concepts as levers for improving our bread baking, it's not necessary for baking great sourdough bread at home.

Temperature

WHEN I FIRST STARTED BAKING BREAD, I DIDN'T quite appreciate just how important temperature is in the breadmaking process. My bread quality fluctuated throughout the year as the seasons changed, and with them, the temperature in my kitchen. Consequently, the temperature of my sourdough starter, and the dough I was mixing that day, were in flux. Since temperature affects the rate of fermentation in a dough and the flavor profile, I'd create wonderful bread one week, only to be disappointed the next.

Once I started paying attention to the temperature of my starter, dough, and kitchen, I saw some of the biggest improvements in my baking. Not only was my starter more vigorous, but my bread was also well fermented and more flavorful. The structure improved: I achieved taller loaves with better texture. (In developing this sensitivity to temperature, I like to think that sourdough bakers can also add "weather forecaster" to our hobbies.)

Temperature greatly impacts fermentation and the growth of the bacteria and yeasts that make up our sourdough cultures. This means temperature is the baker's greatest tool for controlling how fast a dough ferments, which ultimately dictates the day's baking schedule. Assuming all else is equal:

- Warmer dough = a shorter bulk fermentation and proof

- Cooler dough = a longer bulk fermentation or proof to sufficiently ferment the dough

Each recipe in the book lists an ideal temperature for your final dough—aka desired dough temperature (DDT). For many of the recipes and processes, that target is 78°F (25°C) for a healthy balance of strong yeast and bacterial activity. For doughs with higher percentages of whole grains, I like to drop this to 74° to 75°F (23° to 24°C) to help avoid overproofing.

Water Temperature Is Key

If you consider all the ingredients that go into making bread, each contributes in some way to the final dough temperature, but the easiest temperature for us to control is that of the mixing water. Water is one of the largest ingredients and therefore has significant impact on dough temperature. So altering the water temperature by warming (on the stove or in the microwave) or cooling (using the refrigerator or ice) before mixing helps us hit the desired dough temperature.

KNOWING THE RIGHT TEMPERATURE

How do we know how warm or cool the water should be each time we bake?

First, always pay attention to the weather and the temperature in your kitchen. These two factors have the biggest impact on the final dough temperature, and you should always adjust accordingly (for example, if it's summer and hot in your kitchen, you may need to use cooler water).

Next, if you've been taking notes during your baking (which will help you spot seasonal temperature trends), you might be able to reference these and have a feel for what your mixing water temperature should be.

Finally, to be the most exact, see How to Calculate the Mixing Water Temperature (page 138), especially if you are baking somewhere new, or temperatures have changed dramatically from the last time you baked, or you need a way to get a rough temperature without any previous notes. After a while, you will develop an instinct for whether you need to heat or cool the mixing water and will only need to perform this calculation occasionally.

MAINTAINING DOUGH TEMPERATURE DURING BULK FERMENTATION AND PROOF

For home bakers working with smaller batches of dough—which are more easily affected by temperature fluctuations—it's challenging to retain dough temperature during the lengthy process of baking naturally leavened bread. In the frigid lows of winter and the sweltering peak heat of the summer, temperature stability is at its most challenging. Here are a few techniques to help keep dough temperature stable.

Treat temperature as an ingredient.

In winter

- Use warmer water for mixing to be sure you hit the desired dough temperature (DDT) for a recipe. If it's very cold, it might be useful to overshoot the DDT by a few degrees to offset the dough cooling during bulk fermentation.

- Set the dough in the oven with the light on. The oven is a sealed chamber designed to retain heat. I like to place my starter or bulk fermentation container in the turned-off oven with a small thermometer on top of the dough container. Then I'll turn on the internal oven light—which has significant warming capability—to warm the chamber, toggling it on and off as necessary to maintain the desired temperature. Keep an eye on the temperature to ensure the oven doesn't get too hot (over about 85°F/29°C, which can happen in some ovens!) and attach a note to the outside of the oven telling others not to turn it on.

- Use the microwave with a bowl of hot water. Like the oven, the microwave is a mostly sealed and insulated chamber that does well to maintain temperature. Place your starter or dough tub inside along with a bowl of boiled water.

- Use a dough proofer (see page 21). It's specialized equipment, but a dough proofer is personally my favorite option.

In summer

- Use cooler water for mixing.

- During bulk fermentation, before the first set of stretches and folds, place the dough (covered, in its container) in the refrigerator. It's an effective way to drastically alter a final dough temperature. Be sure to check on the dough so it doesn't get too cold!

AUTOLYSE AND WATER TEMPERATURE

Some recipes call for an autolyse (page 79), which is when the flour and water are first combined and left to rest for several minutes or for hours. In the case of a long autolyse, if it's very cold or warm in your kitchen, the dough temperature may be affected during this rest period. For example, if the recipe calls for a 1-hour autolyse and a desired dough temperature of 78°F (25°C), and it's very cold in the kitchen, you might want to overshoot and heat the water to 80°F (26°C), expecting that the dough will cool a few degrees while it's resting. The key is to be aware of the dough during this rest period and try to keep it close to the desired dough temperature.

Temperature FAQs

What if the recipe calls for cold ingredients, like milk?

Several recipes in this book call for cold ingredients, such as milk and eggs, straight from the refrigerator. These ingredients will obviously cool the final dough temperature at the end of mixing, but it usually works out that the cold ingredients and the heating action from the mechanical mixer when mixing offset one another. If it's very cold in your kitchen, or you're expecting your final dough temperature to come in under the desired dough temperature, you can always warm the milk, or other liquid, in the microwave or on the stove.

What's an easy way to warm my mixing water?

Many bakers like to use warm tap water, but I find it's easier to measure out all the water needed for the dough mix and heat it in the microwave (I use a glass pitcher). Either way works!

What if I keep my flour in the refrigerator or freezer?

It's helpful to keep whole-grain flour well sealed in the freezer to extend its life. If you do so, measure out the flour you need for the entire recipe the night before when you make the levain and leave it on the counter to warm to room temperature overnight. Alternatively, if you use the flour straight from the freezer, you'll have to warm the mixing water to compensate (and the formula in How to Calculate the Mixing Water Temperature on page 138 will help).

Can I use my oven's bread proofing function?

Absolutely. However, be mindful that some of these ovens have a proof temperature that is around 100°F (35°C), which is far too hot to proof your dough. As I mentioned earlier, I prefer not to exceed 85°F (29°C) in most cases.

What's an easy way to find the ambient temperature in my kitchen?

Use your instant-read probe thermometer! With something like the Thermapen, simply open the probe and stick it up in the air; it'll tell you the ambient temperature instantly.

CHEAT SHEET FOR FIXING DOUGH TEMPERATURE

If the Dough Is Too Warm

- Place the covered dough in its bulk fermentation container into the refrigerator for 15 to 30 minutes, depending on how high the temperature is over the DDT. After this time, take the dough's temperature and remove it from the refrigerator if cooled sufficiently.

- Alternatively, shorten the bulk fermentation and divide the dough earlier.

If the Dough Is Too Cool

- Place the dough in a turned-off oven with the oven light on (or in a warm dough proofer; see page 21). Be sure not to excessively heat the dough (I don't like to go over 85°F/29°C).

- Alternatively, lengthen the bulk fermentation and divide the dough later.

HOW TO CALCULATE THE MIXING WATER TEMPERATURE

To help determine the mixing water temperature, a simple calculation can be performed. This quick calculation considers the various temperatures that factor into a dough mix: the flour, levain, ambient, and the friction factor if using a mechanical mixer (see What Is Friction Factor?, opposite). This calculation is not an end-all calculation; it glosses over many things (such as the mass of the ingredients: a larger amount of water will have more impact when heated if the flour and levain are small by comparison), but it's a great rough starting point. It's also very handy if you're baking somewhere away from home and need a guidepost from which to start. I also find it helpful to take note of the temperature of your mixing water and the final dough temperature, which will help you dial in future bakes.

$$\text{Mixing water temp} = (\text{desired dough temp} \times 4) - \left(\begin{array}{l} \text{flour temp} \\ + \text{ levain temp} \\ + \text{ ambient temp} \\ + \text{ friction factor} \end{array} \right)$$

Let's Look at an Example

A recipe's desired dough temperature is 78°F (25°C), which is common in this book. We'll assume the flour temperature is the same as the ambient temperature of your kitchen, and for this example, we'll say 72°F (22°C) for both. For the levain temperature (which you can quickly measure with an instant-read thermometer), we'll go with 78°F (25°C) since that's what I typically call for in recipes throughout this book. Finally, the friction factor will be 0 since we are mixing the dough by hand.

$$\begin{aligned} \text{Mixing water temp} &= (78 \times 4) - (72 + 78 + 72 + 0) \\ &= 312 - 222 \\ &= 90°F \ (32°C) \end{aligned}$$

The result of plugging in the numbers and running the quick calculation is 90°F (32°C)—the temperature to which we need to warm our water in order to reach the desired dough temperature of 78°F (25°C).

INPUT	TEMPERATURE
Flour temperature	72°F (22°C)
Pre-ferment (levain or starter) temperature	78°F (25°C)
Ambient temperature	72°F (22°C)
Friction factor temperature	0°F (0°C)
Desired dough temperature (DDT)	78°F (25°C)

Help! I Hate Math. What Do I Do?

If you really don't want to do any calculations, use this cheat sheet: Most of the recipes in this book have a desired dough temperature (DDT) of 78°F (25°C). Since the kitchen temperature usually has the largest impact, we use that and the fact that the pre-ferment (levain) will also be 78°F (25°C) to arrive at the following table (using the DDT calculation, opposite):

IF YOUR KITCHEN TEMPERATURE IS	WARM OR COOL THE MIXING WATER TO
64°F (17°C)	106°F (41°C)
66°F (18°C)	102°F (39°C)
68°F (20°C)	98°F (37°C)
70°F (21°C)	94°F (34°C)
72°F (22°C)	90°F (32°C)
74°F (23°C)	86°F (30°C)
76°F (24°C)	82°F (28°C)
78°F (25°C)	78°F (26°C)
80°F (26°C)	74°F (23°C)
82°F (27°C)	70°F (21°C)

Calculations for a DDT of 78°F (25°C) assuming hand mixing and that the levain temperature is around 78°F (25°C).

WHAT IS FRICTION FACTOR?

The friction factor represents the amount of heat generated when mixing a dough mechanically (it's a representation of the conversion of kinetic energy into thermal energy—i.e., heat). When mixing dough by hand, this is typically set to 0 because mixing by hand isn't vigorous enough to significantly increase the temperature of the dough (in fact, it might cool the dough in the winter). Ultimately, the friction factor is found through experimentation with your mixer because each is different. To determine the friction factor, take the temperature of the dough before mixing, proceed with your usual mix time and speed, then measure the temperature when mixing is finished. Note the difference in degrees and you have your friction factor. For a KitchenAid running on low speed ("Stir") for 2 to 3 minutes, then medium speed ("2") for 3 to 4 minutes, I find a friction factor of about 20°F/10°C. Use this number in the future for this calculation—if your mixing speed and times are consistent, so, too, will the friction factor be. Over time, you'll internalize the effect your mixer has on your dough and how to adjust your mixing water temperature to compensate.

Hydration

DOUGH HYDRATION REPRESENTS THE amount of water added to a dough recipe and is an incredibly important topic in bread baking. As I've said throughout this book, flour is not a static ingredient: It changes from type to type, mill to mill, and even bag to bag. The weather also plays a role: A dough that mixed up smooth and elastic on one day might need adjustment the next if it's raining and extra humid. The hydration percentage—which is related to the total flour—helps bakers get an intuitive sense of the dough's consistency when taken into consideration with the flour in the recipe. Because of the ever-changing nature of flour, treat the hydration percentage and the amount of water in these recipes as a guideline instead of a hard-and-fast rule. You'll need to be on your toes when mixing, adjusting right there and then as necessary. Developing the feel for when a dough is hydrated *just enough* takes practice, and your familiarity with that sweet spot will develop over time (and don't worry, throughout the recipes in this book I'll point out what to look for when mixing).

The hydration level affects the characteristics of the final loaf. I find a lower-hydration bread has a slightly thicker crust, usually a taller rise, and a crumb that's more toothsome. In contrast, a higher-hydration bread tends to have a thinner, more brittle crust, a slightly squatter look (less rise), and a crumb that's more tender and custard-like. Depending on your preference, any of the recipes in this book can be adjusted to have a lower or higher hydration, but I would recommend making this adjustment slowly over the course of a few bakes to avoid pushing things too far in one direction or the other too quickly.

In general, I would say my baking tends to lean more toward the higher-hydration end of the spectrum. This certainly isn't true for every bread I bake, but I enjoy a loaf that has a very thin crust, tender crumb, and a melt-in-your-mouth quality that comes when a dough is sufficiently hydrated and fully fermented. However, there is a line that can be crossed with hydration: If the water is pushed too high, the resulting loaf will have an excessively soft texture. I find these loaves do not retain their structure long after baking and eventually stale faster.

Visual Guide to Dough Hydration

The following images are from Simple Sourdough (page 40), showing various hydration levels. Remember that the hydration percentage (the actual number in and of itself) isn't as important as how the dough looks and feels in the mixing bowl: What feels like a wet and soupy dough with one type of flour at 70% hydration might mean a stiff dough when using another flour. Note that the following example illustrates what I look for when determining if a dough is sufficiently hydrated for a specific recipe. The point of this guide is to increase your sensitivity to the visual and tactile cues for determining dough hydration, which I find many bakers have trouble with when they first start out. The goal is to use the example of the Simple Sourdough to give you a way to correlate how the dough looks and feels with whether it's in the ballpark hydration level for this bread.

UNDER-HYDRATED

≡ 62% HYDRATION

- Texture is incredibly strong, elastic, and hard to mix.

- In extreme cases, there may still be flour not completely hydrated.

- You should add more water, a splash at a time, until the dough loosens up and feels pliable and workable.

JUST RIGHT

≡ 69% HYDRATION

- The dough is smooth and extensible, but still showing signs of potential strength and elasticity.

- It will be glossy and shred apart, but remember, this is still the beginning stages of mixing; the gluten isn't sufficiently developed just yet.

- It should not feel "soupy" with puddles of water scattered about.

OVER-HYDRATED

≡ 75% HYDRATION

- The dough is very soupy and falling apart. It's clear there's been far too much water added. This is the very reason that I hold back water during mixing (see Adding Water in Phases, page 142).

- You should add more flour to the mixing bowl, a little at a time, until the dough comes back together.

Adding Water in Phases

Bassinage (aka "double hydration") is a technique in which water is added in several phases during mixing. Instead of adding all the mixing water up front, some is held in reserve and added slowly into the later parts of the mix as the starches in the flour are better able to absorb it and after the gluten matrix has been developed to some degree. Many of the recipes in this book use this method, as it has some benefits:

- **It makes it easier to develop gluten:** If all the water is added to the mix in the beginning, especially with higher-hydration recipes, it might be incredibly difficult to efficiently strengthen the dough. When the water content of a dough becomes too high before any gluten is developed, it's hard to get enough friction to further develop the gluten. So, instead of adding all the water straight away, add most (usually 80% to 90% of the total water) and mix the dough until it starts to show signs of gluten development. Then slowly add the remaining water while you continue mixing as the water is absorbed and the dough gains strength. This way, you can push the hydration of the dough (if desired) without excessively long mix times.

- **It gives you the chance to judge dough strength:** Holding back water during mixing also gives you a chance to assess the dough strength and decide if the reserved water should be added or omitted. Flour is not a static ingredient; the final hydration percentage of each dough almost always requires some measure of adjustment. By holding back water, you can get a feel for the dough near the end of mixing and adjust the hydration as necessary.

In this book you will notice many of the recipes have "Water 1" and "Water 2" lines in the formula tables. Water 1 is used for making the levain, any soakers, and the first part of mixing. Then, after mixing has proceeded for a while, Water 2 can be added if it feels like the dough can handle the addition.

I'm often asked why one can't just add more flour if the dough gets too wet. The answer is because the balance of all the ingredients in a bread recipe relate to the total flour weight. If you change the total flour weight, then you'll have to adjust the percentages and weights of all the other ingredients, too. Adjusting the total water amount, on the other hand, only affects the total hydration in isolation and does not impact the ratios of all the other ingredients. That said, if I've added all the water in a mix and the dough suddenly feels soupy and it's starting to fall apart, as a last resort I'll add a little flour until the dough comes together and strengthens, and I'll record this change for next time.

HIGH-HYDRATION DOUGH TIPS

As you increase the hydration of a dough, its stability decreases. Increasing water is like pushing the gluten matrix of the dough—kind of like its scaffolding—to the limit. Some points to look out for:

- High-hydration doughs are usually very slack and extensible and therefore require extra mixing to develop the gluten network for increased structure.

- As these doughs will naturally spread during proofing, they also require tighter preshaping and shaping.

- These doughs can have increased fermentation activity and are more sensitive to proofing, quickly overproofing if one is not attentive. Alleviate the risk of overproofing by reducing the pre-fermented flour percentage.

U

RECIPES

THE HOME BAKER'S ROUTINE

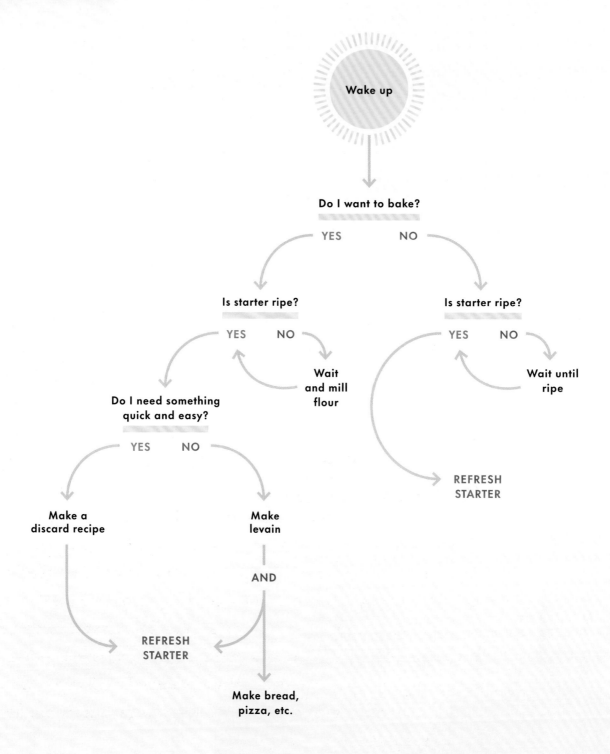

Wake up

Do I want to bake?

YES — NO

Is starter ripe?

YES — NO → Wait and mill flour

Is starter ripe?

YES — NO → Wait until ripe

Do I need something quick and easy?

YES — NO

Make a discard recipe

Make levain

AND

REFRESH STARTER

Make bread, pizza, etc.

REFRESH STARTER

My days almost always start the same: I wake early before the rest of the house and decide what I'm in the mood for. I head over to check on my starter: Is it ripe and ready to go? If so, I decide if I feel like baking today (almost always a yes), and if so, I figure out what bread I'm going to make and create the levain, perhaps also milling fresh flour at the same time. If I'm not in the mood for bread, I might instead make something simpler: Sourdough Pizza Dough (page 294) and Focaccia (page 304) are top choices and can come together in a single day. If it's a more laid-back kind of day, I might just use my ripe starter to make Buttermilk Waffles (page 412) or Sunday Morning Pancakes (page 410). If it's the most laid-back day possible, or if I have plans to go out and my starter is ready, I'll give it a refreshment, save the discard in my starter cache in the refrigerator to make something later (see Saving and Using Discard, page 37), and say good-bye until the next refreshment that night.

No matter your own routine—whether you're baking weekly or just once in a while—I hope you'll find great joy and learn from the recipes that follow.

How to Use the Recipes in the Book

If this is your first time using a bread baking book like this, you'll notice that the ingredient lists look very different from those in your average cookbook! I use two main tables (charts) to show both the essential features of the recipe (in a table called Vitals, below) and the ingredients and their baker's percentages (see opposite). Within the recipe method, smaller ingredient tables are presented next to the steps right where you'll use them. These tables show the ingredients that need to be added or combined at each specific step. Let's look at each of these tables using Simple Sourdough (page 40) as an example.

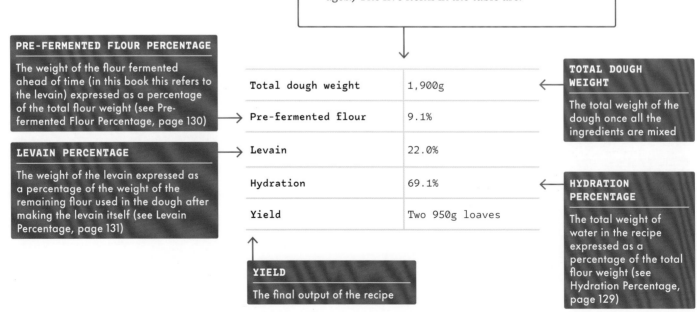

☰ **VITALS TABLE**

First, the vitals table gives you up front the important information about the bread you're about to bake. It's another way for a baker to get a *feel* for the bread before they even begin. Over time, these terms will carry significance for you when reading bread formulas. (See Baker's Percentages, page 129, for more on these percentages.) The five items in the table are:

PRE-FERMENTED FLOUR PERCENTAGE

The weight of the flour fermented ahead of time (in this book this refers to the levain) expressed as a percentage of the total flour weight (see Pre-fermented Flour Percentage, page 130)

LEVAIN PERCENTAGE

The weight of the levain expressed as a percentage of the weight of the remaining flour used in the dough after making the levain itself (see Levain Percentage, page 131)

Total dough weight	1,900g
Pre-fermented flour	9.1%
Levain	22.0%
Hydration	69.1%
Yield	Two 950g loaves

TOTAL DOUGH WEIGHT

The total weight of the dough once all the ingredients are mixed

HYDRATION PERCENTAGE

The total weight of water in the recipe expressed as a percentage of the total flour weight (see Hydration Percentage, page 129)

YIELD

The final output of the recipe

☰ TOTAL FORMULA TABLE

A snapshot of the bread you're making: the ingredients you'll need to mix the dough and the percentages of each ingredient in baker's math (which means all ingredients are a percentage of the total flour in the recipe). With this one table, you can get an intuitive feel for the bread before you even begin (see more about baker's percentages on page 129). I see each of the smaller tables that follow (levain and dough tables) as a piece of the total formula, everything that goes into your loaf of bread.

☰ LEVAIN TABLE

The levain table shows you only the ingredients you need to make the levain (the pre-ferment). This table also shows you the baker's percentages for the ingredients of the levain with respect to the total flour in the levain. Seeing the baker's percentages over time will give you an intuitive sense for the *characteristics* of the levain. For instance, the levain here calls for 100% white flour and 20% ripe sourdough starter—reading just this information, I know this levain is likely a longer-running levain (in this case, 12 hours) because of the reduced whole-grain flour and low inoculation percentage (see Inoculation Percentage, page 65).

☰ DOUGH TABLES

These tables are found at the autolyse and mixing steps. If the recipe doesn't have an autolyse, you'll simply find one table with all the dough ingredients needed for mixing: levain plus flour, water, salt, etc. If it does have an autolyse, you'll find a separate table where all the flour and most of the water (usually all of Water 1) are included for that process. There will then be a last table that shows any remaining ingredients that are added to the autolyse at the very end of mixing. Typically, this is any additional water needed (Water 2), salt, and the ripe levain.

TOTAL FORMULA

INGREDIENT	BAKER'S %	WEIGHT
White flour (~11.5% protein)	100.0%	1,100g
Water 1 (levain and autolyse)	63.6%	700g
Water 2 (mix)	5.5%	60g
Fine sea salt	1.8%	20g
Ripe sourdough starter, 100% hydration	1.8%	20g

LEVAIN

INGREDIENT	BAKER'S %	WEIGHT
White flour (~11.5% protein)	100.0%	100g
Water 1 (levain)	100.0%	100g
Ripe sourdough starter, 100% hydration	20.0%	20g

AUTOLYSE

INGREDIENT	WEIGHT
White flour (~11.5% protein)	1,000g
Water 1 (autolyse)	600g

MIX

INGREDIENT	WEIGHT
Water 2 (mix)	60g
Salt	20g
Levain	220g

IMPORTANT NOTES BEFORE YOU BEGIN BAKING

The recipes in this book (like most bread recipes) are more like guidelines: They might need some adjustment in your own kitchen. They will always include all the details you need to bake wonderful bread—what the dough should look like at each step and what it should feel like in your hands—but the chapters that have preceded this section were written to help you think like a baker and to adapt to the conditions in your kitchen in response to your starter and your dough. Depending on your altitude, climate, and flour, you may need to adjust the following in the recipes:

1. **Dough hydration**

    As discussed in the section on dough hydration (page 140), be ready to adjust the hydration of the recipes slightly to suit your climate and flour. I live in high-altitude, arid New Mexico, which means I typically need higher hydration percentages compared to those needed by someone living in a lower-altitude, more humid environment. Additionally, and in general, the flour here in the United States will be stronger (and usually requires more water) than flour found elsewhere in the world. Use the reserved water (Water 2) that's held back in mixing to adjust the consistency of your dough. For instance, if your dough feels incredibly wet, slack, and sloppy, don't add the reserved water at all; if the dough feels strong and like it can handle the water, add it in slowly while mixing.

2. **Pre-ferment and fermentation timeline**

    This is a very important point: Like hydration, the bulk fermentation and proof times listed in the recipes are a good starting point but might require adjustment based on your season, room temperature, and altitude. If you find

when following one of the recipes that the dough is sluggish and isn't displaying the same characteristics as those written, give it more time in bulk fermentation until it reaches a sufficiently fermented state, then proceed. Conversely, if you're at a very high altitude, you may find the dough is overactive so adjust accordingly.

3. **Baking time and temperature**

    The baking times and temperatures listed in the recipes that follow should suit most bakers at various altitudes. Living at a very high altitude might require either a longer bake time or a higher baking temperature. Between the two, I prefer to lengthen the bake time rather than adjust the temperature (which can have other side effects such as premature crust formation). If you live at a high altitude, use the temperatures I have listed in the recipes but be sure to let your bread bake as long as necessary to achieve a golden crust that crackles when gently squeezed. The loaf should feel light in your hand and not dense or heavy, which can be a sign that not enough water has baked off. Also note that if you live at a very high altitude, the internal temperature of your bread or other baked good may never reach the temperature listed in the recipe—and that's okay. Use the other visual and tactile cues provided in the recipe to help determine when your bread is fully baked.

Remember, one of the goals of this book is to prepare you to *think like a baker*, to adjust times, temperatures, and percentages to suit your location, flour, and schedule. The tips above and the material in this book have prepared you for the recipes to come—let's get baking.

FREE-FORM

LOAVES

Miche, Demi Baguettes,
and Sun-Dried Tomato and Olive

FIFTY-FIFTY

A wholesome loaf with an equal mix of whole wheat and white flours

THIS LOAF is a staple, one I turn to time and time again for a no-fuss, wholesome result. The flour mix yields a light textured loaf with amplified wheat flavors and assertive tang. This is a great starting point for many unaccustomed to working with higher percentages of whole grains, and you might find yourself quickly wanting to increase that percentage from here on out (see 100% Whole Wheat, page 219, for your next adventure).

You might look at the hydration of this recipe and wonder why it's so high, but remember, *hydration is always relative to the flour used*. In this bread, there is a higher percentage of whole-grain flour, which means more nutrition—and flavor—from the bran and germ in the dough. But it also means that the hydration needs to increase to compensate for these thirsty additions. For the high-protein flour portion of this recipe, a flour like King Arthur Baking Bread Flour at about 12.7% protein is a good choice.

BAKING TIMELINE

1 Levain

    3 hours

2 Autolyse

    1 hour

3 Mix

4 Bulk Fermentation

    3 hours 30 minutes

5 Divide, Preshape, Bench Rest

    35 minutes

6 Shape

7 Proof

    16 hours (overnight)

8 Bake

    55 minutes in the oven

TOTAL

24 hours

VITALS

Total dough weight	1,800g
Pre-fermented flour	5.0%
Levain	15.9%
Hydration	82.0%
Yield	Two 900g loaves

TOTAL FORMULA

INGREDIENT	BAKER'S %	WEIGHT
Whole wheat flour	50.0%	477g
White flour (~11.5% protein)	25.0%	238g
High-protein white flour (~12.7%–14% protein)	25.0%	238g
Water 1 (levain and autolyse)	72.0%	686g
Water 2 (mix)	10.0%	95g
Fine sea salt	1.9%	18g
Ripe sourdough starter, 100% hydration	5.0%	48g

INGREDIENT	BAKER'S %	WEIGHT
Whole wheat flour	50.0%	24g
White flour (~11.5% protein)	50.0%	24g
Water 1	100.0%	48g
Ripe sourdough starter, 100% hydration	100.0%	48g

INGREDIENT	WEIGHT
Whole wheat flour	453g
White flour (~11.5% protein)	214g
High-protein white flour (~12.7%-14% protein)	238g
Water 1	638g

INGREDIENT	WEIGHT
Water 2	95g
Fine sea salt	18g
Levain	144g

1. Levain

- **Duration:** 3 hours at warm room temperature: 74°–76°F (23°–24°C)

● **MIX THE LEVAIN:** Warm or cool the water to about 78°F (25°C). In a medium bowl, mix the levain ingredients until well incorporated. Use your hands to knead the mixture until all dry bits of flour are incorporated (this stiff levain will feel strong and dry). Transfer to a jar and loosely cover. Store in a warm place for 3 hours.

2. Autolyse

- **Duration:** 1 hour at warm room temperature: 74°–76°F (23°–24°C)
- **Desired dough temperature (DDT):** 78°F (25°C)

● **MIX THE AUTOLYSE:** About 1 hour before the levain is ready, warm or cool the autolyse water (see page 138 on how to calculate) so the temperature of the mixed dough meets the DDT for this recipe. Place the flour and water in a large bowl and use wet hands to mix until no dry bits remain. Use a bowl scraper to scrape down the sides of the bowl to keep all the dough in one area at the bottom. Cover the bowl and place it near your levain for 1 hour. Since this is a longer autolyse, be sure to keep the dough warm.

3. Mix

- **Desired dough temperature (DDT):** 78°F (25°C)

● **CHECK THE LEVAIN:** It should show signs of readiness: well aerated, risen, soft, sticky, and an assertive sour aroma. If the levain is not showing these signs, let it ferment 30 minutes more and check again.

● **ADJUST THE WATER TEMPERATURE:** Take the temperature of the dough and compare it to the DDT for this recipe: If it's higher, use cold water for the remaining water; if it's lower, use warm water.

● **MIX THE DOUGH:** To the autolyse, add about half of the water, the salt, and ripe levain. Using wet hands, mix the ingredients until well incorporated. If the dough feels very wet, slack, and loose, don't add the remaining water. Otherwise, add the rest of the water and continue to mix until the dough comes together and all the water is absorbed.

● **STRENGTHEN THE DOUGH:** With wet hands, use the slap and fold method (see page 83) for about 5 minutes to strengthen the dough. The dough should look smooth and begin to hold its shape. If it's still shaggy and loose, continue to strengthen for a few more minutes, but don't worry if it doesn't smooth out completely. Transfer back to the bowl or another container for bulk fermentation.

- **MEASURE THE TEMPERATURE OF THE DOUGH:** Compare it to the DDT and record it as the final dough temperature. Cover the dough.

4. Bulk fermentation

- **Duration:** About 3 hours 30 minutes at warm room temperature: 74°–76°F (23°–24°C)
- **Folds:** 5 sets of stretches and folds at 30-minute intervals

- **SET TIMER AND MAKE A NOTE:** Write down the current time as the start of bulk fermentation, set a timer for 30 minutes, and let the dough rest in a warm place.

- **STRETCH AND FOLD:** When your timer goes off, give the dough one set of stretches and folds. Using wet hands, grab one side of the dough and lift it up and over to the other side. Rotate the bowl 180 degrees and repeat. Then rotate the bowl a quarter turn and stretch and fold that side. Rotate the bowl 180 degrees again and finish with a stretch and fold on the last side. The dough should be folded up neatly. Cover and repeat these folds every 30 minutes for a total of 5 sets of stretches and folds.

- **LET THE DOUGH REST:** After the last set, cover the bowl and let the dough rest for the remainder of bulk fermentation, about 1 hour.

5. Divide and preshape

- **CHECK THE DOUGH:** At the end of bulk fermentation, the dough will have risen significantly; it may have bubbles on top and at the sides, it should look smoother and less shaggy, and at the edge of the dough where it meets the container, it should dome downward. If you wet a hand and gently tug on the surface of the dough, it will feel elastic and cohesive, resisting your pull. If you don't see dough that's airy, strong, and "alive," leave it for another 15 minutes in bulk fermentation and check again.

- **DIVIDE AND PRESHAPE THE DOUGH:** Using a bowl scraper, gently scrape the dough onto a clean work surface and use your bench knife to divide it directly in half. Using your bench knife in your dominant hand and with your other hand wet to reduce sticking, shape each piece of dough into a loose round. (See Preshaping, page 96, for more detail.) Let the rounds rest for 35 minutes, uncovered.

6. Shape

- **PREPARE THE PROOFING BASKETS:** Line two proofing baskets or bowls with clean kitchen towels. Dust lightly and evenly with white flour.

- **SHAPE THE DOUGH:** Shape each as a bâtard or a boule (see pages 102 to 107 for details). Gently transfer each piece to a proofing basket, seam-side up. Place each basket inside an airtight reusable plastic bag and seal.

RECIPE CONTINUES

FREE-FORM LOAVES

7. Proof

▪ **Duration:** About 16 hours (overnight) in a home refrigerator: 39°F (4°C)

● **LET THE DOUGH PROOF:** Place the baskets in the refrigerator to proof overnight.

8. Bake

▪ **Duration:** 50 to 55 minutes in the oven

● **PREPARE THE OVEN:** Place an oven rack in the bottom third of the oven with no rack above it. Place a Dutch oven/combo cooker inside the oven and preheat to 450°F (230°C) for at least 30 minutes. (Alternatively, bake directly on a baking stone/steel; see page 124 for details.)

● **SCORE THE DOUGH:** Take one of the proofing baskets out of the fridge, uncover, and put a piece of parchment paper over the basket. Place a pizza peel or inverted baking sheet on top of the parchment and, using both hands, flip everything over. Gently remove the basket and score the dough. (See Scoring, page 118, for details.)

● **BAKE THE DOUGH:** Slide the dough with the parchment into the preheated Dutch oven and cover with the lid. Bake for 20 minutes, then remove the lid. Continue to bake for 30 to 35 minutes, or until the internal temperature reaches 206°–210°F (96°–99°C) and the crust has a deep mahogany color and a crackle/crunch when gently squeezed.

● **FINISH AND COOL:** Let the loaf cool on a wire rack for 1 to 2 hours before slicing. For the second loaf, preheat the Dutch oven for 15 minutes and repeat.

HOW TO TINKER

REDUCE SOURNESS

To reduce the sour flavor of this bread, skip the overnight cold proof. Instead, proof the shaped dough on the counter in the proofing baskets, completely covered, at room temperature for 1½ to 3 hours, temperature depending. At an ambient temperature of 74°F (23°C) I would expect this dough to be ready for baking after about 2 hours; it should be puffy and risen, and a gentle poke to the surface will show a very slow bounce back (see the Poke Test, page 116, for more info).

TWENTY-FIVE RYE

Earthy and complex flavors with a tight crumb and beautiful crust

THIS BREAD has a deeply complex flavor profile with assertive fermentation flavors and an earthy backdrop—your mouth will water from the first bite. The crust bakes up dark with multifaceted coloring, ranging from light browns to deep chestnut and mahogany, and has the flavor of popped grains. I particularly love the denser crumb of this bread, which is partly a result of adding the rye, as it makes fantastic slices for sandwiches.

This recipe makes a single, large 1,000g loaf, which can be shaped as a bâtard (my preference) or a boule. However, you can also make two smaller 500g loaves.

BAKING TIMELINE

1. **Levain**

   5 hours

2. **Autolyse**

   1 hour

3. **Mix**

4. **Bulk Fermentation**

   3 hours 30 minutes

5. **Preshape, Bench Rest**

   35 minutes

6. **Shape**

7. **Proof**

   12 hours (overnight)

8. **Bake**

   55 minutes in the oven

TOTAL

22 hours

VITALS

Total dough weight	1,000g
Pre-fermented flour	5.7%
Levain	15.9%
Hydration	80.0%
Yield	One 1,000g loaf or two 500g loaves

TOTAL FORMULA

INGREDIENT	BAKER'S %	WEIGHT
White flour (~11.5% protein)	75.0%	406g
Whole rye flour	25.0%	135g
Water 1 (levain and autolyse)	70.0%	379g
Water 2 (mix)	10.0%	54g
Fine sea salt	1.8%	10g
Ripe sourdough starter, 100% hydration	3.0%	16g

INGREDIENT	BAKER'S %	WEIGHT
Whole rye flour	100.0%	31g
Water 1	110.0%	34g
Ripe sourdough starter, 100% hydration	50.0%	16g

INGREDIENT	WEIGHT
White flour (~11.5% protein)	406g
Whole rye flour	104g
Water 1	345g

INGREDIENT	WEIGHT
Water 2	54g
Fine sea salt	10g
Levain	81g

1. Levain

- Duration: 5 hours at warm room temperature: 74°–76°F (23°–24°C)

- **MIX THE LEVAIN:** Warm or cool the water to about 78°F (25°C). In a medium jar, mix the levain ingredients until well incorporated (this liquid levain will feel quite loose) and loosely cover. Store in a warm place for 5 hours.

2. Autolyse

- Duration: 1 hour at warm room temperature: 74°–76°F (23°–24°C)
- Desired dough temperature (DDT): 78°F (25°C)

- **MIX THE AUTOLYSE:** About 1 hour before the levain is ready, warm or cool the autolyse water (see page 138 on how to calculate) so the temperature of the mixed dough meets the DDT for this recipe. Place the flour and water in a large bowl and use wet hands to mix until no dry bits remain. Use a bowl scraper to scrape down the sides of the bowl to keep all the dough in one area at the bottom. Cover the bowl and place it near your levain for 1 hour. Since this is a longer autolyse, be sure to keep the dough warm.

3. Mix

- Desired dough temperature (DDT): 78°F (25°C)

- **CHECK THE LEVAIN:** This rye levain will present as an almost aerated paste when it's ready. You should see an aerated texture and moderate rise. There will be stickiness and a very assertive sour aroma. If the levain is not showing these signs, let it ferment 30 minutes more and check again.

- **ADJUST THE WATER TEMPERATURE:** Take the temperature of the dough and compare it to the DDT for this recipe: If it's higher, use cold water for the remaining water; if it's lower, use warm water.

- **MIX THE DOUGH:** To the autolyse, add about half of the water, the salt, and ripe levain. Using wet hands, mix the ingredients until well incorporated.

- **STRENGTHEN THE DOUGH:** With wet hands, use the slap and fold method (see page 83) for about 5 minutes to strengthen the dough. Due to the rye in the mix, the dough might feel tacky and paste-like, but it will strengthen, smooth, and begin to hold its shape. If it's still shaggy and loose, continue to strengthen for a few more minutes, but don't worry if it doesn't smooth out completely. Transfer back to the bowl or another container for bulk fermentation.

- **MEASURE THE TEMPERATURE OF THE DOUGH:** Compare it to the DDT and record it as the final dough temperature. Cover the dough.

4. Bulk fermentation

- **Duration:** About 3 hours 30 minutes at warm room temperature: 74°–76°F (23°–24°C)
- **Folds:** 4 sets of stretches and folds at 30-minute intervals

● **SET TIMER AND MAKE A NOTE:** Write down the current time as the start of bulk fermentation, set a timer for 30 minutes, and let the dough rest in a warm place.

● **STRETCH AND FOLD:** When your timer goes off, give the dough one set of stretches and folds. Using wet hands, grab one side of the dough and lift it up and over to the other side. Rotate the bowl 180 degrees and repeat. Then rotate the bowl a quarter turn and stretch and fold that side. Rotate the bowl 180 degrees again and finish with a stretch and fold on the last side. The dough should be folded up neatly. Cover the bowl and repeat these folds every 30 minutes for a total of 4 sets of stretches and folds.

● **LET THE DOUGH REST:** After the last set, cover the bowl and let the dough rest for the remainder of bulk fermentation, about 1 hour 30 minutes.

RECIPE CONTINUES →

5. Preshape

● **CHECK THE DOUGH:** At the end of bulk fermentation, the dough will have risen significantly; it may have bubbles on top and at the sides, it should look smoother and less shaggy, and at the edge of the dough where it meets the container, it should dome downward. If you wet a hand and gently tug on the surface of the dough, it will feel elastic and cohesive, resisting your pull. If you don't see dough that's airy, strong, and "alive," leave it for another 15 minutes in bulk fermentation and check again.

● **PRESHAPE THE DOUGH:** Using a bowl scraper, gently scrape the dough out onto a clean work surface. Using your bench knife in your dominant hand and with your other hand wet to reduce sticking, shape the dough into a taut round. (See Preshaping, page 96, for more detail.) Let the round rest for 35 minutes, uncovered.

6. Shape

● **PREPARE A PROOFING BASKET:** Line one large proofing basket or bowl with a clean kitchen towel. Dust lightly and evenly with white flour.

● **SHAPE THE DOUGH:** Shape as a bâtard or a boule (see pages 102 to 107 for details). Gently transfer the dough to the proofing basket, seam-side up. Place the basket inside a reusable plastic bag and seal.

7. Proof

▪ **Duration:** About 12 hours (overnight) in a home refrigerator: 39°F (4°C)

● **LET THE DOUGH PROOF:** Place the basket in the refrigerator to proof overnight.

8. Bake

▪ **Duration:** 50 to 55 minutes in the oven

● **PREPARE THE OVEN:** Place an oven rack in the bottom third of the oven with no rack above it. Place a Dutch oven/combo cooker inside the oven and preheat to 450°F (230°C) for at least 30 minutes. (Alternatively, bake directly on a baking stone/steel; see page 124 for details.)

● **SCORE THE DOUGH:** Take the proofing basket out of the fridge, uncover, and put a piece of parchment paper over the basket. Place a pizza peel or inverted sheet pan on top of the parchment and, using both hands, flip everything over. Gently remove the basket and score the dough. I prefer to score this with two offset parallel slashes to ensure optimal rise. (See Scoring, page 118, for details.)

● **BAKE THE DOUGH:** Slide the dough with the parchment into the preheated Dutch oven and cover with the lid. Bake for 20 minutes, then remove the lid. Continue to bake for 30 to 35 minutes, or until the internal temperature reaches 206°–210°F (96°–99°C) and the crust has a deep mahogany color and a crackle/crunch when gently squeezed.

● **FINISH AND COOL:** Let the loaf cool on a wire rack for 2 hours before slicing.

CRANBERRY AND WALNUT

A hefty loaf with meaty walnuts and slightly tart cranberries

I'VE BEEN baking this bread for so many years that it's a true staple in my kitchen. Upon reading the title, your first thought might be that the cranberries will bring a mouth-puckeringly sour flavor to this bread, but that's not the case—they add a reserved sweetness that complements the earthy flavor of the walnuts. I prefer leaving the walnuts whole when adding them to this dough; it's a nice surprise to get a large, toasted walnut in a single bite, and most of them end up cut to some degree when slicing the loaf anyway.

The addition of walnut oil brings a rich mouthfeel, softer crumb, and shiny crust. If you don't have walnut oil, feel free to omit it and keep the rest of the recipe the same. Additionally, if you don't have whole-grain rye flour on hand, substitute all the rye in the levain with the same amount of whole wheat flour.

Note that the longer autolyse helps this dough achieve greater extensibility, which I find helps when incorporating a high percentage of inclusions (mix-ins). The extensibility allows us to stretch the dough significantly during the first set of stretches and folds in bulk fermentation, making it easy to spread and work in the inclusions.

BAKING TIMELINE

1 Levain

   12 hours (overnight)

2 Autolyse

   1 hour

3 Mix

4 Bulk Fermentation

   3 hours

5 Divide, Preshape, Bench Rest

   30 minutes

6 Shape

7 Proof

   20 hours (overnight)

8 Bake

   55 minutes in the oven

TOTAL
36 hours 25 minutes

VITALS

Total dough weight	1,800g
Pre-fermented flour	10.0%
Levain	23.3%
Hydration	85.0%
Yield	Two 900g loaves

TOTAL FORMULA

INGREDIENT	BAKER'S %	WEIGHT
White flour (~11.5% protein)	80.0%	640g
Whole wheat flour	15.0%	120g
Whole rye flour	5.0%	40g
Walnut oil (optional)	3.0%	24g
Walnuts, raw	20.0%	160g
Sweetened dried cranberries	14.0%	112g
Water 1 (levain and autolyse)	75.0%	600g
Water 2 (mix)	10.0%	80g
Fine sea salt	1.9%	15g
Ripe sourdough starter, 100% hydration	1.0%	8g

1. Prepare the levain and walnuts

- Duration: 12 hours (overnight) at warm room temperature: 74°–76°F (23°–24°C)

● **MIX THE LEVAIN:** Warm or cool the water to about 78°F (25°C). In a medium bowl, mix the levain ingredients until well incorporated (this liquid levain is usually loose, but depending on your rye flour, it might be a little on the stiff side—and this is okay). Transfer to a jar and loosely cover. Store in a warm place for 12 hours.

● **TOAST THE WALNUTS:** Preheat the oven to 350°F (175°C). Spread the 160g walnuts out evenly on a sheet pan. Toast the walnuts, stirring occasionally, until they are fragrant and start to color, about 10 minutes. Set aside until bulk fermentation.

INGREDIENT	BAKER'S %	WEIGHT
White flour (~11.5% protein)	50.0%	40g
Whole rye flour	50.0%	40g
Water 1	100.0%	80g
Ripe sourdough starter, 100% hydration	10.0%	8g

2. Autolyse

- Duration: 1 hour at warm room temperature: 74°–76°F (23°–24°C)
- Desired dough temperature (DDT): 78°F (25°C)

● **MIX THE AUTOLYSE:** About 1 hour before the levain is ready, warm or cool the autolyse water (see page 138 on how to calculate) so the temperature of the mixed dough meets the DDT for this recipe. Place the flour and water in a large bowl and use wet hands to mix until no dry bits remain. Use a bowl scraper to scrape down the sides of the bowl to keep all the dough in one area at the bottom. Cover the bowl and place it near your levain for 1 hour.

INGREDIENT	WEIGHT
White flour (~11.5% protein)	600g
Whole wheat flour	120g
Water 1	520g

3. Mix

- Desired dough temperature (DDT): 78°F (25°C)

● **CHECK THE LEVAIN:** It should show signs of readiness: well aerated, soft, risen, though the high percentage of rye flour means this levain won't rise as much as others. If the levain is not showing these signs, let it ferment 1 hour more and check again.

● **ADJUST THE WATER TEMPERATURE:** Take the temperature of the dough and compare it to the DDT for this recipe: If it's higher, use cold water for the remaining water; if it's lower, use warm water.

● **MIX THE DOUGH:** To the autolyse, add the walnut oil (if using), about half of the water, the salt, and ripe levain. Using wet hands, mix the ingredients until well incorporated. While this dough is on the wetter side, if it feels very wet, slack, and loose, don't add the remaining water. Otherwise, add the rest of the water and continue to mix until the dough comes together and all the water is absorbed.

● **STRENGTHEN THE DOUGH:** With wet hands, use the slap and fold method (see page 83) for about 5 minutes to strengthen the dough. The dough should look smooth and begin to hold its shape. If it's still shaggy and loose, continue to strengthen for a few more minutes, but don't worry if it doesn't smooth out completely. Transfer back to the bowl or another container for bulk fermentation.

● **MEASURE THE TEMPERATURE OF THE DOUGH:** Compare it to the DDT and record it as the final dough temperature. Cover the dough.

INGREDIENT	WEIGHT
Walnut oil	24g
Water 2	80g
Fine sea salt	15g
Levain	168g

RECIPE CONTINUES →

4. Bulk fermentation

- **Duration:** About 3 hours at warm room temperature: 74°–76°F (23°–24°C)
- **Folds:** 3 sets of stretches and folds at 30-minute intervals

● **SET TIMER AND MAKE A NOTE:** Write down the current time as the start of bulk fermentation, set a timer for 30 minutes, and let the dough rest in a warm place.

● **ADD THE INCLUSIONS AND STRETCH AND FOLD:** When your timer goes off, spread about one-quarter of the toasted walnuts and one-quarter of the 112g cranberries evenly over the dough. Using wet hands, pick up one side of the dough and stretch it up and fold it over. Spread another one-quarter of the inclusions over the top. Rotate the bowl 180 degrees and perform another stretch and fold. Evenly spread on another one-quarter of the inclusions. Rotate the bowl a quarter turn, perform a stretch and fold, and spread on the remaining inclusions. Finally, rotate the bowl 180 degrees and perform the last stretch and fold. The dough should be folded up neatly. Cover and repeat these folds every 30 minutes for a total of 3 sets of stretches and folds.

● **LET THE DOUGH REST:** After the last set, cover the bowl and let the dough rest for the remainder of bulk fermentation, about 1 hour 30 minutes.

5. Divide and preshape

● **CHECK THE DOUGH:** At the end of bulk fermentation, the dough will have risen significantly; it may have bubbles on top and at the sides, it should look smoother and less shaggy, and at the edge of the dough where it meets the container, it should dome downward. If you wet a hand and gently tug on the surface of the dough, it will feel elastic and cohesive, resisting your pull. If you don't see dough that's airy, strong, and "alive," leave it for another 15 minutes in bulk fermentation and check again.

● **DIVIDE AND PRESHAPE THE DOUGH:** Using a bowl scraper, gently scrape the dough onto a clean work surface and use your bench knife to divide it directly in half. Using your bench knife in your dominant hand and with your other hand wet to reduce sticking, shape each piece of dough into a loose round. (See Preshaping, page 96, for more detail.) Let the rounds rest for 30 minutes, uncovered.

6. Shape

● **PREPARE THE PROOFING BASKETS:** Line two proofing baskets or bowls with clean kitchen towels. Dust lightly and evenly with white flour. I highly recommend using basket liners or kitchen towels in your proofing baskets with this dough, since the cranberries can sometimes leave red marks.

● **SHAPE THE DOUGH:** Shape each as a bâtard or a boule (see pages 102 to 107 for details). Gently transfer each piece to a proofing basket, seam-side up. Place each basket inside a reusable plastic bag and seal.

7. Proof

▪ **Duration:** About 20 hours (overnight) in a home refrigerator: 39°F (4°C)

● **LET THE DOUGH PROOF:** Place the baskets in the refrigerator to proof overnight.

8. Bake

▪ **Duration:** 50 to 55 minutes in the oven

● **PREPARE THE OVEN:** Place an oven rack in the bottom third of the oven with no rack above it. Place a Dutch oven/combo cooker inside the oven and preheat to 450°F (230°C) for at least 30 minutes. (Alternatively, bake directly on a baking stone/steel; see page 124 for details.)

● **SCORE THE DOUGH:** Take one of the proofing baskets out of the fridge, uncover, and put a piece of parchment paper over the basket. Place a pizza peel or inverted sheet pan on top of the parchment and, using both hands, flip everything over. Gently remove the basket and score the dough. (See Scoring, page 118, for details.)

● **BAKE THE DOUGH:** Slide the dough with the parchment into the preheated Dutch oven and cover with the lid. Bake for 20 minutes, then remove the lid. Continue to bake for 30 to 35 minutes, or until the internal temperature reaches 206°–210°F (96°–99°C) and the crust has a deep mahogany color and a crackle/crunch when gently squeezed.

● **FINISH AND COOL:** Let the loaf cool on a wire rack for 1 to 2 hours before slicing. For the second loaf, preheat the Dutch oven for 15 minutes and repeat.

Scoring a Dough That Has Inclusions

Because this dough has large, firm walnuts and soft cranberries, creating a clean score on the surface with a blade can be difficult. I find it easier to move slowly with the blade during the first cut, then perform a second pass with the blade to ensure any spots where it might have snagged on a nut or fruit are sufficiently deep. Alternatively, using scissors to make a series of snips from top to bottom also works very well with a dough such as this.

HOW TO TINKER

MAKE THIS LOAF MORE FESTIVE

This bread is already perfect for the winter holidays, but to make it even more so, add the grated zest of an orange to the dough at the end of mixing. The flavor of bright and citrusy orange with tangy cranberries and earthy walnuts is hard to resist.

SWAP OUT WALNUTS FOR PECANS

While walnuts are the cornerstone of this bread, toasted pecans (or a combination of both walnuts and pecans) also work very well when paired with dried cranberries.

SUNFLOWER AND SESAME

Prominent nutty flavor with a touch of sweetness

THIS IS one of my absolute favorite loaves to make. You see, I'm a nut butter devotee. Whether it's peanut butter, cashew butter, or almond butter, I could eat the stuff by the spoonful until someone finally wrests the spoon from my hand. The combination of roasted sunflower seeds and umami-rich sesame comes together with the touch of honey to make the entire loaf taste like one large serving of nut butter—the irony is, this loaf contains zero nuts, only seeds.

This bread is delightful toasted and works equally well in sandwiches. I don't even have to mention how good it is as a peanut butter and jelly sandwich—you have probably already guessed.

BAKING TIMELINE

1. Levain

   5 hours

2. Autolyse

   1 hour

3. Mix

4. Bulk Fermentation

   3 hours 30 minutes

5. Divide, Preshape, Bench Rest

   35 minutes

6. Shape

7. Proof

   20 hours (overnight)

8. Bake

   55 minutes in the oven

TOTAL

30 hours

VITALS

Total dough weight	1,800g
Pre-fermented flour	6.2%
Levain	16.7%
Hydration	77.0%
Yield	Two 900g loaves

TOTAL FORMULA

INGREDIENT	BAKER'S %	WEIGHT
White flour (~11.5% protein)	70.0%	614g
Whole wheat flour	30.0%	263g
Honey	4.0%	35g
Sunflower seeds, raw	15.0%	132g
Black sesame seeds (soaker)	4.0%	35g
Water 1 (soaker, levain, and autolyse)	72.0%	632g
Water 2 (mix)	5.0%	44g
Fine sea salt	1.8%	16g
Ripe sourdough starter, 100% hydration	3.1%	27g

ADDITIONAL INGREDIENT

White sesame seeds, for topping (optional)

INGREDIENT	BAKER'S %	WEIGHT
White flour (~11.5% protein)	50.0%	27g
Whole wheat flour	50.0%	27g
Water 1	100.0%	55g
Ripe sourdough starter, 100% hydration	50.0%	27g

INGREDIENT	WEIGHT
White flour (~11.5% protein)	587g
Whole wheat flour	236g
Water 1	542g

INGREDIENT	WEIGHT
Honey	35g
Water 2	44g
Fine sea salt	16g
Levain	136g

1. Prepare the levain, soaker, and sunflower seeds

◾ **Duration:** 5 hours at warm room temperature: 74°–76°F (23°–24°C)

● **MIX THE LEVAIN:** Warm or cool the water to about 78°F (25°C). In a medium jar, mix the levain ingredients until well incorporated (this liquid levain will feel quite loose) and loosely cover. Store in a warm place for 5 hours.

● **SOAK THE BLACK SESAME SEEDS:** In a small heatproof mixing bowl, combine the 35g black sesame seeds and 35g boiling water. Let cool and then cover the bowl. Set aside until bulk fermentation.

● **TOAST THE SUNFLOWER SEEDS:** Preheat the oven to 350°F (175°C). Spread the 132g sunflower seeds onto a sheet pan in an even layer. Toast until fragrant and beginning to brown, about 10 minutes. Let cool until bulk fermentation.

2. Autolyse

◾ **Duration:** 1 hour at warm room temperature: 74°–76°F (23°–24°C)
◾ **Desired dough temperature (DDT):** 78°F (25°C)

● **MIX THE AUTOLYSE:** About 1 hour before the levain is ready, warm or cool the autolyse water (see page 138 on how to calculate) so the temperature of the mixed dough meets the DDT for this recipe. Place the flour and water in a large bowl and use wet hands to mix until no dry bits remain. Use a bowl scraper to scrape down the sides of the bowl to keep all the dough in one area at the bottom. Cover the bowl and place it near your levain for 1 hour.

3. Mix

◾ **Desired dough temperature (DDT):** 78°F (25°C)

● **CHECK THE LEVAIN:** It should show signs of readiness: well aerated, risen, bubbly on top and at the sides, loose, and with a sour aroma. If the levain is not showing these signs, let it ferment 30 minutes more and check again.

● **ADJUST THE WATER TEMPERATURE:** Take the temperature of the dough and compare it to the DDT for this recipe: If it's higher, use cold water for the remaining water; if it's lower, use warm water.

● **MIX THE DOUGH:** To the autolyse, add the honey, about half of the water, the salt, and ripe levain. Using wet hands, mix the ingredients until well incorporated. If the dough feels very wet, slack, and loose, don't add the remaining water. Otherwise, add the rest of the water and continue to mix until the dough comes together and all the water is absorbed.

● **STRENGTHEN THE DOUGH:** With wet hands, use the slap and fold method (see page 83) for about 5 minutes to strengthen the dough. The dough should look smooth and begin to hold its shape. If it is still shaggy and loose, continue to strengthen for a few more minutes, but don't worry if it doesn't smooth out completely. Transfer back to the bowl or another container for bulk fermentation.

- **MEASURE THE TEMPERATURE OF THE DOUGH:** Compare it to the DDT and record it as the final dough temperature. Cover the dough.

4. Bulk fermentation

- **Duration:** About 3 hours 30 minutes at warm room temperature: 74°–76°F (23°–24°C)
- **Folds:** 3 sets of stretches and folds at 30-minute intervals

- **SET TIMER AND MAKE A NOTE:** Write down the current time as the start of bulk fermentation, set a timer for 30 minutes, and let the dough rest in a warm place.

- **ADD THE INCLUSIONS AND STRETCH AND FOLD:** In a bowl, stir together the toasted sunflower seeds and black sesame seed soaker (seeds and any water). When your timer goes off, spread about one-quarter of the seeds evenly over the dough. Using damp hands, pick up one side of the dough and stretch it up and fold it over. Spread another one-quarter of the seeds over the top. Rotate the bowl 180 degrees and perform another stretch and fold. Spread on another one-quarter of the seeds. Rotate the bowl a quarter turn, perform a stretch and fold, and spread on the remaining seeds. Rotate the bowl 180 degrees and perform the last stretch and fold. The dough should be folded up neatly. Cover and repeat these folds every 30 minutes for a total of 3 sets of stretches and folds.

- **LET THE DOUGH REST:** After the last set, cover the bowl and let the dough rest for the remainder of bulk fermentation, about 2 hours.

5. Divide and preshape

- **CHECK THE DOUGH:** At the end of bulk fermentation, the dough will have risen significantly; it may have bubbles on top and at the sides, it should look smoother and less shaggy, and at the edge where it meets the container, it should dome downward. If you wet a hand and gently tug on the surface of the dough, it will feel elastic and cohesive, resisting your pull. If you don't see dough that's airy, strong, and "alive," leave it for another 15 minutes in bulk fermentation and check again.

- **DIVIDE AND PRESHAPE THE DOUGH:** Using a bowl scraper, gently scrape the dough onto a clean work surface and use your bench knife to divide it directly in half. Using your bench knife in your dominant hand and with your other hand wet to reduce sticking, shape each piece of dough into a loose round. (See Preshaping, page 96, for more detail.) Let the rounds rest for 35 minutes, uncovered.

6. Shape

- **PREPARE THE PROOFING BASKETS:** Line two proofing baskets or bowls with clean kitchen towels. Dust lightly and evenly with white flour.

- **SHAPE THE DOUGH:** Shape each as a bâtard or a boule (see pages 102 to 107 for details).

RECIPE CONTINUES ›

Black sesame seeds have their dark hull still intact, whereas white sesame seeds are hull-less. I find black sesame to have a slightly more intense, nutty flavor than white, and I usually use black mixed into a dough and white as a topping. Since the hull is quite tough, I like to soak black sesame seeds in boiling water for several hours to soften, making them more palatable in the final loaf of bread. The white sesame seeds toast on the exterior of the loaf while it's baking, which amplifies their flavor considerably.

● **ADD THE TOPPING (OPTIONAL BUT RECOMMENDED):** Spread an even layer of white sesame seeds in a sheet pan or clean kitchen towel. After shaping each piece of dough, quickly roll the top side in the seeds so they stick. (See Add Toppings to Your Bread Dough, page 109, for more detail.) Gently transfer each piece to a proofing basket, seam-side up. Place each basket inside a reusable plastic bag and seal.

7. Proof

▪ **Duration:** About 20 hours (overnight) in a home refrigerator: 39°F (4°C)

● **LET THE DOUGH PROOF:** Place the baskets in the refrigerator to proof overnight.

8. Bake

▪ **Duration:** 50 to 55 minutes in the oven

● **PREPARE THE OVEN:** Place an oven rack in the bottom third of the oven with no rack above it. Place a Dutch oven/combo cooker inside the oven and preheat to 450°F (230°C) for at least 30 minutes. (Alternatively, bake directly on a baking stone/steel; see page 124 for details.)

● **SCORE THE DOUGH:** Take one of the proofing baskets out of the fridge, uncover, and put a piece of parchment paper over the basket. Place a pizza peel or inverted sheet pan on top of the parchment and, using both hands, flip everything over. Gently remove the basket and score the dough. (See Scoring, page 118, for details.)

● **BAKE THE DOUGH:** Slide the dough with the parchment into the preheated Dutch oven and cover with the lid. Bake for 20 minutes, then remove the lid. Continue to bake for 30 to 35 minutes, or until the internal temperature reaches 206°–210°F (96°–99°C) and the crust is a deep mahogany color specked with white sesame and has a crackle/crunch when gently squeezed.

● **FINISH AND COOL:** Let the loaf cool on a wire rack for 1 to 2 hours before slicing. For the second loaf, preheat the Dutch oven or baking surface for 15 minutes and repeat.

ROSEMARY AND OLIVE OIL

A mild-flavored bread with a pungent rosemary aroma and a golden crust

THIS SATISFYING bread calls for two kitchen staples that are often intertwined: rosemary and olive oil. The olive oil softens the crumb and crust, while the rosemary, with its pungent aroma and woodsy flavor, brings a backdrop of earthy notes. The overall flavor of this bread is kept mild with the same-day proof, but the overnight levain and added whole rye and whole wheat bring a little extra fermentation and grain flavor to the loaf.

While I don't typically add rosemary to my bruschetta, this bread makes a wonderful base for the easy-to-put-together appetizer: Brush slices with olive oil and toast in the oven until golden, then remove and use a garlic clove to rub on the toasted surface. Finish with a mixture of chopped tomatoes, red onion, basil, olive oil, vinegar, salt, and pepper.

BAKING TIMELINE

1. Levain

    12 hours (overnight)

2. Autolyse

    1 hour

3. Mix

4. Bulk Fermentation

    3 hours 30 minutes

5. Divide, Preshape, Bench Rest

    35 minutes

6. Shape

7. Proof

    2 hours

8. Bake

    55 minutes in the oven

TOTAL

19 hours

VITALS

Total dough weight	1,800g
Pre-fermented flour	10.0%
Levain	24.1%
Hydration	70.0%
Yield	Two 900g loaves

TOTAL FORMULA

INGREDIENT	BAKER'S %	WEIGHT
White flour (~11.5% protein)	85.0%	860g
Whole wheat flour	10.0%	101g
Whole rye flour	5.0%	50g
Extra-virgin olive oil	4.0%	40g
Fresh rosemary, finely chopped	1.0%	10g
Water 1 (levain and autolyse)	65.0%	657g
Water 2 (mix)	5.0%	51g
Fine sea salt	1.9%	19g
Ripe sourdough starter, 100% hydration	1.0%	10g

INGREDIENT	BAKER'S %	WEIGHT
White flour (~11.5% protein)	80.0%	81g
Whole rye flour	20.0%	20g
Water 1	100.0%	101g
Ripe sourdough starter, 100% hydration	10.0%	10g

INGREDIENT	WEIGHT
White flour (~11.5% protein)	779g
Whole wheat flour	101g
Whole rye flour	30g
Water 1	556g

INGREDIENT	WEIGHT
Extra-virgin olive oil	40g
Fresh rosemary, finely chopped	10g
Water 2	51g
Fine sea salt	19g
Levain	212g

1. Levain

- ▪ **Duration:** 12 hours (overnight) at warm room temperature: 74°–76°F (23°–24°C)

- ● **MIX THE LEVAIN:** Warm or cool the water to about 78°F (25°C). In a medium jar, mix the levain ingredients until well incorporated (this liquid levain will feel quite loose) and loosely cover. Store in a warm place for 12 hours.

2. Autolyse

- ▪ **Duration:** 1 hour at warm room temperature: 74°–76°F (23°–24°C)
- ▪ **Desired dough temperature (DDT):** 78°F (25°C)

- ● **MIX THE AUTOLYSE:** About 1 hour before the levain is ready, warm or cool the autolyse water (see page 138 on how to calculate) so the temperature of the mixed dough meets the DDT for this recipe. Place the flour and water in a large bowl and use wet hands to mix until no dry bits remain. Use a bowl scraper to scrape down the sides of the bowl to keep all the dough in one area at the bottom. Cover the bowl and place it near your levain for 1 hour.

3. Mix

- ▪ **Desired dough temperature (DDT):** 78°F (25°C)

- ● **CHECK THE LEVAIN:** It should show signs of readiness: well aerated, risen, bubbly on top and at the sides, loose, and with an assertive sour aroma. If the levain is not showing these signs, let it ferment 1 hour more and check again.

- ● **ADJUST THE WATER TEMPERATURE:** Take the temperature of the dough and compare it to the DDT for this recipe: If it's higher, use cold water for the remaining water; if it's lower, use warm water.

- ● **MIX THE DOUGH:** To the autolyse, add about half of the water, the salt, and ripe levain. Using wet hands, mix the ingredients until well incorporated. If the dough feels very wet, slack, and loose, don't add the remaining water. Otherwise, add the rest of the water and continue to mix until the dough comes together and all the water is absorbed.

- ● **STRENGTHEN THE DOUGH:** With wet hands, use the slap and fold method (see page 83) for about 5 minutes to strengthen the dough. The dough should look smooth and begin to hold its shape. If it's still shaggy and loose, continue to strengthen for a few more minutes. Transfer the dough to the bowl and add about half of the olive oil. Use your hands to mix, pinch, and massage the oil into the dough. Once all of the oil is absorbed, add the remaining olive oil and repeat, working the dough until all of the oil is absorbed and the dough comes back together. Then, spread the rosemary over the top of the dough and fold the dough until the rosemary is mostly dispersed. Transfer to another container, or keep it in the bowl, for bulk fermentation.

RECIPE CONTINUES →

- **MEASURE THE TEMPERATURE OF THE DOUGH:** Compare it to the DDT and record it as the final dough temperature. Cover the dough.

4. Bulk fermentation

- **Duration:** About 3 hours 30 minutes at warm room temperature: 74°–76°F (23°–24°C)
- **Folds:** 3 sets of stretches and folds at 30-minute intervals

- **SET TIMER AND MAKE A NOTE:** Write down the current time as the start of bulk fermentation, set a timer for 30 minutes, and let the dough rest in a warm place.

- **STRETCH AND FOLD:** When your timer goes off, give the dough one set of stretches and folds. Using wet hands, grab one side of the dough and lift it up and over to the other side. Rotate the bowl 180 degrees and repeat. Then rotate the bowl a quarter turn and stretch and fold that side. Rotate the bowl 180 degrees again and finish with a stretch and fold on the last side. The dough should be folded up neatly. Cover and repeat these folds every 30 minutes for a total of 3 sets of stretches and folds.

- **LET THE DOUGH REST:** After the last set, cover the bowl and let the dough rest for the remainder of bulk fermentation, about 2 hours.

5. Divide and preshape

- **CHECK THE DOUGH:** At the end of bulk fermentation, the dough will have risen significantly; it may have bubbles on top and at the sides, it should look smoother and less shaggy, and at the edge of the dough where it meets the container, it should dome downward. If you wet a hand and gently tug on the surface of the dough, it will feel elastic and cohesive, resisting your pull. If you don't see dough that's airy, strong, and "alive," leave it for another 15 minutes in bulk fermentation and check again.

- **DIVIDE AND PRESHAPE THE DOUGH:** Using a bowl scraper, gently scrape the dough onto a clean work surface and use your bench knife to divide it directly in half. Using your bench knife in your dominant hand and with your other hand wet to reduce sticking, shape each piece of dough into a loose round. (See Preshaping, page 96, for more detail.) Let the rounds rest for 35 minutes, uncovered.

6. Shape

● **PREPARE THE PROOFING BASKETS:** Line two proofing baskets or bowls with clean kitchen towels. Dust lightly and evenly with white flour.

● **SHAPE THE DOUGH:** Shape each as a bâtard or a boule (see pages 102 to 107 for details). Note that since this dough is proofed at room temperature, as opposed to overnight in the refrigerator, you need to shape it tightly. Gently transfer each piece to a proofing basket, seam-side up. Place each basket inside a reusable plastic bag and seal.

7. Proof

▪ **Duration:** About 2 hours at warm room temperature: 74°–76°F (23°–24°C)

● **LET THE DOUGH PROOF:** Put the baskets in a warm place to proof for about 2 hours. Check on the dough periodically. It is ready when it is puffy and soft, but not excessively bubbly or weak. You can also try the Poke Test (page 116).

8. Bake

▪ **Duration:** 50 minutes in the oven

● **PREPARE THE OVEN:** Place an oven rack in the bottom third of the oven with no rack above it. Place a Dutch oven/combo cooker inside the oven and preheat to 450°F (230°C) for at least 30 minutes. (Alternatively, bake directly on a baking stone/steel; see page 124 for details.)

● **SCORE THE DOUGH:** Take one of the proofing baskets out of the fridge, uncover, and put a piece of parchment paper over the basket. Place a pizza peel or inverted sheet pan on top of the parchment and, using both hands, flip everything over. Gently remove the basket and score the dough. (See Scoring, page 118, for details.)

● **BAKE THE DOUGH:** Slide the dough with the parchment into the preheated Dutch oven and cover with the lid. Bake for 20 minutes, then remove the lid. Continue to bake for 30 to 35 minutes, or until the internal temperature reaches 206°-210°F (96°-99°C) and the crust has a deep golden brown color and a crackle/crunch when gently squeezed.

● **FINISH AND COOL:** Let the loaf cool on a wire rack for 1 to 2 hours before slicing. For the second loaf, preheat the Dutch oven or baking surface for 15 minutes and repeat.

MEDITERRANEAN
OLIVE AND ROSEMARY

A dark, olive-studded
loaf with a hint of
piney rosemary

THIS LOAF screams *Mediterranean* to me and has just enough olives to ensure you get one in every bite without the loaf becoming burdened with too many inclusions. I love serving it with a charcuterie board: I slice it into cubes and set them out among cheese, cured meat, and pickles. Kalamata olives are always my first choice for this bread as I love their intense, briny flavor. But green Castelvetrano olives are also wonderful. You can either completely replace the kalamatas or use a mixture of both kinds.

BAKING TIMELINE

1 Levain

    12 hours (overnight)

2 Autolyse

    30 minutes

3 Mix

4 Bulk Fermentation

    4 hours

5 Divide, Preshape, Bench Rest

    35 minutes

6 Shape

7 Proof

    19 hours (overnight)

8 Bake

    55 minutes in the oven

TOTAL

36 hours 30 minutes

VITALS

Total dough weight	1,800g
Pre-fermented flour	7.5%
Levain	17.0%
Hydration	76.0%
Yield	Two 900g loaves

TOTAL FORMULA

INGREDIENT	BAKER'S %	WEIGHT
White flour (~11.5% protein)	85.0%	771g
Whole wheat flour	15.0%	136g
Kalamata olives, pitted and coarsely chopped	20.0%	181g
Fresh rosemary, finely chopped	1.0%	9g
Water 1 (levain and autolyse)	70.0%	635g
Water 2 (mix)	5.0%	45g
Fine sea salt	1.8%	16g
Ripe sourdough starter, 100% hydration	0.8%	7g

INGREDIENT	BAKER'S %	WEIGHT
White flour (~11.5% protein)	50.0%	34g
Whole wheat flour	50.0%	34g
Water 1	100.0%	68g
Ripe sourdough starter, 100% hydration	10.0%	7g

INGREDIENT	WEIGHT
White flour (~11.5% protein)	737g
Whole wheat flour	102g
Water 1	567g

INGREDIENT	WEIGHT
Water 2	45g
Fine sea salt	16g
Levain	143g

1. Levain

- **Duration:** 12 hours (overnight) at warm room temperature: 74°–76°F (23°–24°C)

● **MIX THE LEVAIN:** Warm or cool the water to about 78°F (25°C). In a medium jar, mix the levain ingredients until well incorporated (this liquid levain will feel quite loose) and loosely cover. Store in a warm place for 12 hours.

2. Autolyse

- **Duration:** 30 minutes at warm room temperature: 74°–76°F (23°–24°C)
- **Desired dough temperature (DDT):** 78°F (25°C)

● **MIX THE AUTOLYSE:** About 30 minutes before the levain is ready, warm or cool the autolyse water (see page 138 on how to calculate) so the temperature of the mixed dough meets the DDT for this recipe. Place the flour and water in a large bowl and use wet hands to mix until no dry bits remain. Use a bowl scraper to scrape down the sides of the bowl to keep all the dough in one area at the bottom. Cover the bowl and place it near your levain for 30 minutes.

3. Mix

- **Desired dough temperature (DDT):** 78°F (25°C)

● **CHECK THE LEVAIN:** It should show signs of readiness: well aerated, risen, bubbly on top and at the sides, loose, and an assertive sour aroma. If the levain is not showing these signs, let it ferment 1 hour more and check again.

● **ADJUST THE WATER TEMPERATURE:** Take the temperature of the dough and compare it to the DDT for this recipe: If it's higher, use cold water for the remaining water; if it's lower, use warm water.

● **MIX THE DOUGH:** To the autolyse, add about half of the water, the salt, and ripe levain. Using wet hands, mix the ingredients until well incorporated. If the dough feels very wet, slack, and loose, don't add the remaining water. Otherwise, add the rest of the water and continue to mix until the dough comes together and all the water is absorbed.

● **STRENGTHEN THE DOUGH:** With wet hands, use the slap and fold method (see page 83) for about 5 minutes to strengthen the dough. The dough should look smooth and begin to hold its shape. If the dough is still shaggy and loose, continue to strengthen for a few more minutes, but don't worry if the dough doesn't smooth out completely. Transfer back to the bowl or another container for bulk fermentation.

● **MEASURE THE TEMPERATURE OF THE DOUGH:** Compare it to the DDT and record it as the final dough temperature. Cover the dough.

4. Bulk fermentation

Duration: About 4 hours at warm room temperature: 74°–76°F (23°–24°C)

Folds: 3 sets of stretches and folds at 30-minute intervals

● **SET TIMER AND MAKE A NOTE:** Write down the current time as the start of bulk fermentation, set a timer for 30 minutes, and let the dough rest in a warm place.

● **ADD THE INCLUSIONS AND STRETCH AND FOLD:** In a medium bowl, mix the 181g olives and 9g rosemary. When your timer goes off, spread the olive and rosemary mixture evenly over the surface of the dough, tucking some down the sides of the dough where it meets the bowl. Using wet hands, grab one side of the dough and lift it up and over to the other side, trapping some of the inclusions. Rotate the bowl 180 degrees and repeat. Then rotate the bowl a quarter turn and stretch and fold that side. Rotate the bowl 180 degrees again and finish with a stretch and fold on the last side. The dough should be folded up neatly. Cover and repeat these folds every 30 minutes for a total of 3 sets of stretches and folds.

● **LET THE DOUGH REST:** After the last set, cover the bowl and let the dough rest for the remainder of bulk fermentation, about 2 hours 30 minutes.

5. Divide and preshape

● **CHECK THE DOUGH:** At the end of bulk fermentation, the dough will have risen significantly; it may have bubbles on top and at the sides, it should look smoother and less shaggy, and at the edge of the dough where it meets the container, it should dome downward. If you wet a hand and gently tug on the surface of the dough, it will feel elastic and cohesive, resisting your pull. If you don't see dough that's airy, strong, and "alive," leave it for another 15 minutes in bulk fermentation and check again.

● **DIVIDE AND PRESHAPE THE DOUGH:** Using a bowl scraper, gently scrape the dough onto a clean work surface and use your bench knife to divide it directly in half. Using your bench knife in your dominant hand and with your other hand wet to reduce sticking, shape each piece of dough into a loose round. (See Preshaping, page 96, for more detail.) Let the rounds rest for 35 minutes, uncovered.

6. Shape

● **PREPARE THE PROOFING BASKETS:** Line two proofing baskets or bowls with clean kitchen towels. Dust lightly and evenly with white flour.

● **SHAPE THE DOUGH:** Shape each as a boule or a bâtard (see pages 102 to 107 for details). Gently transfer each piece to a proofing basket, seam-side up. Place each basket inside a reusable plastic bag and seal.

Preparing Olives

If the olives you are using are in a brine, be sure to drain them, rinse well, and pat them dry to remove excess water before incorporating them into the dough. This way, you will avoid an overly salty loaf of bread. I also like to slice the olives in half, for two reasons: The first is to ensure there are no pits hiding in the olives, and second, for a more even distribution of olives through the loaf of bread.

RECIPE CONTINUES →

FREE-FORM LOAVES

7. Proof

▪ **Duration:** About 19 hours (overnight) in a home refrigerator: 39°F (4°C)

● **LET THE DOUGH PROOF:** Place the baskets in the refrigerator to proof overnight.

8. Bake

▪ **Duration:** 50 to 55 minutes in the oven

● **PREPARE THE OVEN:** Place an oven rack in the bottom third of the oven with no rack above it. Place a Dutch oven/combo cooker inside the oven and preheat to 450°F (230°C) for at least 30 minutes. (Alternatively, bake directly on a baking stone/steel; see page 124 for details.)

● **SCORE THE DOUGH:** Take one of the proofing baskets out of the fridge, uncover, and put a piece of parchment paper over the basket. Place a pizza peel or inverted sheet pan on top of the parchment and, using both hands, flip everything over. Gently remove the basket and score the dough. (See Scoring, page 118, for details.)

● **BAKE THE DOUGH:** Slide the dough with the parchment into the preheated Dutch oven and cover with the lid. Bake for 20 minutes, then remove the lid. Continue to bake for 30 to 35 minutes, or until the internal temperature reaches 206°-210°F (96°-99°C) and the crust has a deep mahogany color and a crackle/crunch when gently squeezed.

● **FINISH AND COOL:** Let the loaf cool on a wire rack for 1 to 2 hours before slicing. For the second loaf, preheat the Dutch oven or baking surface for 15 minutes and repeat.

LEMON AND HERB

A mild-flavored loaf with pops of flavor from the woodsy herbes de Provence, bright lemon zest, and nutty white sesame

AT FIRST glance, it might seem like this bread doesn't have much in the way of extra ingredients given the low percentages of herbs and lemon zest, but each of these is quite powerful. Commonly used in southern France, herbes de Provence is a mixture of dried marjoram, thyme, oregano, rosemary, savory, and sometimes lavender. The bright lemon zest complements the herbes de Provence, bringing a sweet taste and floral aroma to the bread, and the rye flour not only contributes flavor, but also adds to the beautiful crust color.

The dough for this recipe is rolled in white sesame seeds before an overnight, cold proof. The white sesame brings another layer of flavor to this bread, and its nuttiness complements the lemon and herbs. There's also something visually striking about a white sesame–encrusted loaf.

I like to shape this dough into smaller oval shapes, which means more crust overall, and the size is perfect for setting several directly out on the dinner table. If you'd like to make only two loaves, divide all the ingredients in half for a total dough weight of 1,200g and simply divide that dough in half to make two 600g loaves when preshaping.

BAKING TIMELINE

1. **Levain**

   5 hours

2. **Autolyse**

   30 minutes

3. **Mix**

4. **Bulk Fermentation**

   3 hours 30 minutes

5. **Divide, Preshape, Bench Rest**

   35 minutes

6. **Shape**

7. **Proof**

   15 hours (overnight)

8. **Bake**

   50 minutes in the oven

TOTAL

24 hours 55 minutes

VITALS

Total dough weight	2,400g
Pre-fermented flour	8.0%
Levain	21.7%
Hydration	71.0%
Yield	Four 600g loaves

TOTAL FORMULA

INGREDIENT	BAKER'S %	WEIGHT
White flour (~11.5% protein)	92.0%	1,242g
Whole rye flour	8.0%	108g
Herbes de Provence	0.8%	11g
Lemon zest	0.2%	3g (about 4 medium lemons)
Water 1 (levain and autolyse)	66.0%	891g
Water 2 (mix)	5.0%	67g
Fine sea salt	1.8%	24g
Ripe sourdough starter, 100% hydration	4.0%	54g

ADDITIONAL INGREDIENT

White sesame seeds, for topping (optional)

INGREDIENT	BAKER'S %	WEIGHT
White flour (~11.5% protein)	75.0%	81g
Whole rye flour	25.0%	27g
Water 1	100.0%	108g
Ripe sourdough starter, 100% hydration	50.0%	54g

INGREDIENT	WEIGHT
White flour (~11.5% protein)	1,161g
Whole rye flour	81g
Water 1	783g

INGREDIENT	WEIGHT
Herbes de Provence	11g
Lemon zest	3g (about 4 medium lemons)
Water 2	67g
Fine sea salt	24g
Levain	270g

1. Levain

▪ **Duration:** 5 hours at warm room temperature: 74°–76°F (23°–24°C)

● **MIX THE LEVAIN:** Warm or cool the water to about 78°F (25°C). In a medium bowl, mix the ingredients until well incorporated (this liquid levain will feel quite loose). Transfer to a jar and loosely cover. Store in a warm place for 5 hours.

2. Autolyse

▪ **Duration:** 30 minutes at warm room temperature: 74°–76°F (23°–24°C)
▪ **Desired dough temperature (DDT):** 78°F (25°C)

● **MIX THE AUTOLYSE:** About 30 minutes before the levain is ready, warm or cool the autolyse water (see page 138 on how to calculate) so the temperature of the mixed dough meets the DDT for this recipe. Place the flour and water in a large bowl and use wet hands to mix until no dry bits remain. Use a bowl scraper to scrape down the sides of the bowl to keep all the dough in one area at the bottom. Cover the bowl and place it near your levain for 30 minutes.

3. Mix

▪ **Desired dough temperature (DDT):** 78°F (25°C)

● **CHECK THE LEVAIN:** It should show signs of readiness: well aerated, risen, bubbly on top and at the sides, loose, and with a sour aroma. If the levain is not showing these signs, let it ferment 30 minutes more and check again.

● **ADJUST THE WATER TEMPERATURE:** Take the temperature of the dough and compare it to the DDT for this recipe: If it's higher, use cold water for the remaining water; if it's lower, use warm water.

● **MIX THE DOUGH:** To the autolyse, add about half of the water, the salt, and ripe levain. Using wet hands, mix the ingredients until well incorporated. If the dough feels very wet, slack, and loose, don't add the remaining water. Otherwise, add the rest of the water and continue to mix until the dough comes together and all the water is absorbed.

● **STRENGTHEN THE DOUGH:** With wet hands, use the slap and fold method (see page 83) for about 5 minutes to strengthen the dough. The dough should look smooth and begin to hold its shape. If the dough is still shaggy and loose, continue to strengthen for a few more minutes, but don't worry if it doesn't smooth out completely.

● **ADD THE INCLUSIONS:** Spread the herbes de Provence and lemon zest evenly over the surface of the dough. Using wet hands, gently massage the inclusions into it. Transfer the dough back to the bowl or another container for bulk fermentation.

RECIPE CONTINUES →

WINTERTIME SOURDOUGH

Earthy sage, sweet-tart cranberries, and buttery pecans with increased fermentation flavors

THIS BREAD is a comforting mix of flavors that just feels right during the colder months of the year. Using a small percentage of fresh sage in this mix brings an undeniable earthy flavor. Sage pairs very well with cranberry—further reinforcing that winter theme—and the buttery, warm pecans balance out the equation. This bread will make you want to throw on your favorite chunky-knit sweater and fuzzy socks, grab a thick book with a leather cover, and eat a toasted and buttered slice next to a roaring fireplace.

BAKING TIMELINE

1 Levain

    12 hours (overnight)

2 Mix

3 Bulk Fermentation

    3 hours 30 minutes

4 Divide, Preshape, Bench Rest

    35 minutes

5 Shape

6 Proof

    19 hours (overnight)

7 Bake

    55 minutes in the oven

TOTAL

36 hours

VITALS

Total dough weight	1,800g
Pre-fermented flour	7.5%
Levain	17.0%
Hydration	75.0%
Yield	Two 900g loaves

TOTAL FORMULA

INGREDIENT	BAKER'S %	WEIGHT
White flour (~11.5% protein)	80.0%	683g
Whole wheat flour	20.0%	171g
Sweetened dried cranberries	18.0%	154g
Pecans, raw	15.0%	128g
Fresh sage, finely chopped	0.4%	3g
Water	75.0%	640g
Fine sea salt	1.8%	15g
Ripe sourdough starter, 100% hydration	0.7%	6g

INGREDIENT	BAKER'S %	WEIGHT
White flour (~11.5% protein)	50.0%	32g
Whole wheat flour	50.0%	32g
Water	100.0%	64g
Ripe sourdough starter, 100% hydration	10.0%	6g

INGREDIENT	WEIGHT
White flour (~11.5% protein)	651g
Whole wheat flour	139g
Water	576g
Fine sea salt	15g
Levain	134g

1. Prepare the levain and pecans

▪ **Duration:** 12 hours (overnight) at warm room temperature: 74°–76°F (23°–24°C)

● **MIX THE LEVAIN:** Warm or cool the water to about 78°F (25°C). In a medium jar, mix the levain ingredients until well incorporated (this liquid levain will feel quite loose) and loosely cover. Store in a warm place for 12 hours.

● **TOAST THE PECANS:** Preheat the oven to 425°F (220°C). Spread the 128g pecans evenly on a sheet pan. Toast, stirring occasionally, until fragrant, about 10 minutes. Let them cool, then chop and set aside until bulk fermentation.

2. Mix

▪ **Desired dough temperature (DDT):** 78°F (25°C)

● **CHECK THE LIQUID LEVAIN:** It should show signs of readiness: well aerated, risen, bubbly on top and at the sides, loose, and an assertive sour aroma. If the levain is not showing these signs, let it ferment 1 hour more and check again.

● **MIX THE DOUGH:** Warm or cool the water (see page 138 on how to calculate) so the temperature of the mixed dough meets the DDT of this recipe. Place the flour, water, salt, and ripe levain in a large bowl. Using wet hands, mix until well incorporated.

● **STRENGTHEN THE DOUGH:** With wet hands, use the slap and fold method (see page 83) for about 5 minutes to strengthen the dough. The dough should look smooth and begin to hold its shape. If it's still shaggy and loose, continue to strengthen for a few more minutes, but don't worry if it doesn't smooth out completely. Transfer back to the bowl or another container for bulk fermentation. Cover the dough.

3. Bulk fermentation

▪ **Duration:** About 3 hours 30 minutes at warm room temperature: 74°–76°F (23°–24°C)
▪ **Folds:** 3 sets of stretches and folds at 30-minute intervals

● **SET TIMER AND MAKE A NOTE:** Write down the current time as the start of bulk fermentation, set a timer for 30 minutes, and let the dough rest in a warm place.

● **ADD THE INCLUSIONS AND STRETCH AND FOLD:** In a bowl, combine the 154g cranberries, toasted pecans, and 3g sage. When your timer goes off, spread one-quarter of the inclusions evenly over the dough. Using damp hands, pick up one side of the dough and stretch it up and fold it over. Spread another one-quarter of the inclusions over top. Rotate the bowl 180 degrees and perform another stretch and fold. Spread on another one-quarter of the inclusions. Rotate the bowl a quarter turn, perform a stretch and fold, and spread on the remaining inclusions. Rotate the bowl 180 degrees and perform the last stretch and fold. The dough should be folded up neatly. Cover and repeat every 30 minutes for a total of 3 sets of stretches and folds.

● **LET THE DOUGH REST:** After the last set, cover the bowl and let the dough rest for the remainder of bulk fermentation, about 1 hour 30 minutes.

4. Divide and preshape

● **CHECK THE DOUGH:** At the end of bulk fermentation, the dough will have risen significantly; it may have bubbles on top and at the sides, it should look smoother and less shaggy, and at the edge of the dough where it meets the container, it should dome downward. If you wet a hand and gently tug on the surface of the dough, it will feel elastic and cohesive, resisting your pull. If you don't see dough that's airy, strong, and "alive," leave it for another 15 minutes in bulk fermentation and check again.

● **DIVIDE AND PRESHAPE THE DOUGH:** Using a bowl scraper, gently scrape the dough onto a clean work surface and use your bench knife to divide it directly in half. Using your bench knife in your dominant hand and with your other hand wet to reduce sticking, shape each piece of dough into a loose round. (See Preshaping, page 96, for more detail.) Let the rounds rest for 35 minutes, uncovered.

5. Shape

● **PREPARE THE PROOFING BASKETS:** Line two proofing baskets or bowls with clean kitchen towels. Dust lightly and evenly with white flour.

● **SHAPE THE DOUGH:** Shape each as a bâtard or a boule (see pages 102 to 107 for details). Gently transfer each piece to a proofing basket, seam-side up. Place each basket inside a reusable plastic bag and seal.

6. Proof

▨ **Duration:** About 19 hours (overnight) in a home refrigerator: 39°F (4°C)

● **LET THE DOUGH PROOF:** Place the baskets in the refrigerator to proof overnight.

7. Bake

▨ **Duration:** 50 to 55 minutes in the oven

● **PREPARE THE OVEN:** Place an oven rack in the bottom third of the oven with no rack above it. Place a Dutch oven/combo cooker inside the oven and preheat to 450°F (230°C) for at least 30 minutes. (Alternatively, bake directly on a baking stone/steel; see page 124 for details.)

● **SCORE THE DOUGH:** Take one of the proofing baskets out of the fridge, uncover, and put a piece of parchment paper over the basket. Place a pizza peel or inverted sheet pan on top of the parchment and, using both hands, flip everything over. Gently remove the basket and score the dough. (See Scoring, page 118, for details.)

● **BAKE THE DOUGH:** Slide the dough with the parchment into the preheated Dutch oven and cover with the lid. Bake for 20 minutes, then remove the lid. Continue to bake for 30 to 35 minutes, or until the internal temperature reaches 206°–210°F (96°–99°C) and the crust has a deep mahogany color and a crackle/crunch when gently squeezed.

● **FINISH AND COOL:** Let the loaf cool on a wire rack for 1 to 2 hours before slicing. For the second loaf, preheat the Dutch oven for 15 minutes and repeat.

SEEDED SPELT

A deeply flavorful bread
with whole spelt and rye,
plus mixed seeds

A BLEND of whole-grain spelt and rye flour lays the foundation for a hearty sourdough bread with a deeply colored crust and dark-hued interior. The sesame and flaxseed soaker brings not only additional nutrition to an already wholesome bread, but also more flavor through its earthy and nutty notes. The whole package is a loaf to savor, a top choice to pair with aged and soft cheeses alike, and really anything on a charcuterie board.

BAKING TIMELINE

1. Levain

   5 hours

2. Mix

3. Bulk Fermentation

   4 hours

4. Divide, Preshape, Bench Rest

   30 minutes

5. Shape

6. Proof

   20 hours (overnight)

7. Bake

   55 minutes in the oven

TOTAL
30 hours 25 minutes

VITALS

Total dough weight	1,800g
Pre-fermented flour	5.0%
Levain	13.2%
Hydration	77.0%
Yield	Two 900g loaves

TOTAL FORMULA

INGREDIENT	BAKER'S %	WEIGHT
White flour (~11.5% protein)	62.0%	596g
Whole spelt flour	30.0%	288g
Whole rye flour	8.0%	76g
Black sesame seeds (soaker)	3.0%	29g
Whole flaxseeds (soaker)	3.0%	29g
Water 1 (soaker, levain, and mix)	72.0%	692g
Water 2 (mix)	5.0%	48g
Fine sea salt	1.8%	17g
Ripe sourdough starter, 100% hydration	2.5%	24g

1. Prepare the levain and soaker

Duration: 5 hours at warm room temperature: 74°–76°F (23°–24°C)

● **MIX THE LEVAIN:** Warm or cool the water to about 78°F (25°C). In a medium jar, mix the levain ingredients until well incorporated (this liquid levain will feel quite loose) and loosely cover. Store in a warm place for 5 hours.

● **PREPARE THE SOAKER:** In a heatproof bowl, combine the 29g black sesame seeds, 29g flaxseeds, and 58g boiling water. Set aside until bulk fermentation.

INGREDIENT	BAKER'S %	WEIGHT
White flour (~11.5% protein)	70.0%	34g
Whole rye flour	30.0%	14g
Water 1	100.0%	48g
Ripe sourdough starter, 100% hydration	50.0%	24g

INGREDIENT	WEIGHT
White flour (~11.5% protein)	562g
Whole spelt flour	288g
Whole rye flour	62g
Water 1	586g
Fine sea salt	17g
Levain	120g
Water 2	48g

2. Mix

Desired dough temperature (DDT): 78°F (25°C)

● **CHECK THE LEVAIN:** It should show signs of readiness: well aerated, risen, bubbly on top and at the sides, loose, and with a sour aroma. If you don't see these signs, let it ferment 30 minutes more and check again.

● **MIX THE DOUGH:** Warm or cool the water (see page 138 on how to calculate) so the temperature of the mixed dough meets the DDT of this recipe. In a large bowl, add the flour, water 1, salt, and ripe levain. Using wet hands, mix the ingredients until incorporated. If the dough feels very wet, slack, and loose, don't add the remaining water 2. Otherwise, add the rest of the water and continue to mix until the dough comes together and all the water is absorbed.

● **STRENGTHEN THE DOUGH:** With wet hands, use the slap and fold method (see page 83) for about 5 minutes to strengthen the dough. The dough should look smooth and begin to hold its shape. If it is still shaggy and weak, continue to strengthen for a few more minutes, but don't worry if it doesn't smooth out completely. Transfer back to the bowl or another container for bulk fermentation.

● **MEASURE THE TEMPERATURE OF THE DOUGH:** Compare it to the DDT and record it as the final dough temperature. Cover the dough.

3. Bulk fermentation

Duration: About 4 hours at warm room temperature: 74°–76°F (23°–24°C)

Folds: 4 sets of stretches and folds at 30-minute intervals

● **SET TIMER AND MAKE A NOTE:** Write down the current time as the start of bulk fermentation, set a timer for 30 minutes, and let the dough rest in a warm place.

● **ADD THE INCLUSIONS AND STRETCH AND FOLD:** When your timer goes off, spread about one-quarter of the seed soaker (seeds and any water) evenly over the dough. Using damp hands, pick up one side of the dough and stretch it up and fold it over. Spread another one-quarter of the soaker over the top. Rotate the bowl 180 degrees and perform another stretch and fold. Evenly spread on another one-quarter of the soaker. Rotate the bowl a quarter turn, perform a stretch and fold, and spread on the remaining soaker. Rotate the bowl 180 degrees and perform the last stretch and fold. The dough should be folded up neatly. Cover and repeat these folds every 30 minutes for a total of 4 sets of stretches and folds.

- **LET THE DOUGH REST:** After the last set, cover the bowl and let the dough rest for the remainder of bulk fermentation, about 2 hours.

4. Divide and preshape

- **CHECK THE DOUGH:** At the end of bulk fermentation, the dough will have risen significantly; it may have bubbles on top and at the sides, it should look smoother and less shaggy, and at the edge of the dough where it meets the container, it should dome downward. If you wet a hand and gently tug on the surface of the dough, it will feel elastic and cohesive, resisting your pull. If you don't see dough that's airy, strong, and "alive," leave it for another 15 minutes in bulk fermentation and check again.

- **DIVIDE AND PRESHAPE THE DOUGH:** Using a bowl scraper, gently scrape the dough onto a clean work surface and use your bench knife to divide it directly in half. Using your bench knife in your dominant hand and with your other hand wet to reduce sticking, shape each piece of dough into a loose round. (See Preshaping, page 96, for more detail.) Let the rounds rest for 30 minutes, uncovered.

5. Shape

● **PREPARE THE PROOFING BASKETS:** Line two proofing baskets or bowls with clean kitchen towels. Dust lightly and evenly with white flour.

● **SHAPE THE DOUGH:** Shape each as a boule or a bâtard (see pages 102 to 107 for details). Gently transfer each piece to a proofing basket, seam-side up. Place each basket inside a reusable plastic bag and seal.

6. Proof

Duration: About 20 hours (overnight) in a home refrigerator: 39°F (4°C)

● **LET THE DOUGH PROOF:** Place the baskets in the refrigerator to proof overnight.

7. Bake

Duration: 50 to 55 minutes in the oven

● **PREPARE THE OVEN:** Place an oven rack in the bottom third of the oven with no rack above it. Place a Dutch oven/combo cooker inside the oven and preheat to 450°F (230°C) for at least 30 minutes. (Alternatively, bake directly on a baking stone/steel; see page 124 for details.)

● **SCORE THE DOUGH:** Take one of the proofing baskets out of the fridge, uncover, and put a piece of parchment paper over the basket. Place a pizza peel or inverted sheet pan on top of the parchment and, using both hands, flip everything over. Gently remove the basket and score the dough. (See Scoring, page 118, for details.)

● **BAKE THE DOUGH:** Slide the dough with the parchment into the preheated Dutch oven and cover with the lid. Bake for 20 minutes, then remove the lid. Continue to bake for 30 to 35 minutes, or until the internal temperature reaches 206°–210°F (96°–99°C) and the crust has a very deep mahogany color and a crackle/crunch when gently squeezed.

● **FINISH AND COOL:** Let the loaf cool on a wire rack for 1 to 2 hours before slicing. For the second loaf, preheat the Dutch oven for 15 minutes and repeat.

TROUBLESHOOTING

MY DOUGH WAS SUPER STICKY AND WET!

In my experience, spelt is very sensitive to overhydration. When mixing, hold back some of the Water 1 and only add more if it feels like the dough can handle the addition.

RUSTICO

Open-textured with a deeply colored, crisp crust, and mellow flavor

I CALL this bread *rustico*, which, naturally, means "rustic" in Italian. It's a casual loaf that's meant for any place and any occasion. I've been tinkering with this recipe for years; it's my most baked, most changed, and most obsessed-over formula. I think every baker has a go-to recipe they'd choose over others—whether it's because of the striking flavor or elegant aesthetic, it's a challenging and satisfying dough to work with, or it simply is a crowd-pleaser. For me, this recipe is all of the above.

In playing the tinkerer, I've changed flour types from this to that, adjusted hydrations, levain build ratios, and temperatures. I've tried a variety of different final shapes and have also experimented with varying proof times—all with the goal of a bread that has maximal flavor and is still light in the hand. I also place heavy emphasis on the texture of any bread, and for this one I want significant contrast between a soft crumb and crunchy crust. Over the years it's evolved from a mostly white loaf to one with more and more whole grains.

If you don't have Type-85 flour, you can get close in crumb color by using 65% white flour (~11.5% protein) and 35% whole wheat. You may need to adjust hydration (up or down depending on dough consistency).

BAKING TIMELINE

1. **Levain**

   5 hours

2. **Autolyse**

   1 hour

3. **Mix**

4. **Bulk Fermentation**

   3 hours 30 minutes

5. **Divide, Preshape, Bench Rest**

   35 minutes

6. **Shape**

7. **Proof**

   14 hours (overnight)

8. **Bake**

   55 minutes in the oven

TOTAL

24 hours

VITALS

Total dough weight	1,800g
Pre-fermented flour	6.6%
Levain	17.5%
Hydration	80.0%
Yield	Two 900g loaves

TOTAL FORMULA

INGREDIENT	BAKER'S %	WEIGHT
White flour (~11.5% protein)	55.0%	535g
Type-85 flour (see headnote)	25.0%	243g
Whole spelt flour	20.0%	195g
Water 1 (levain and autolyse)	70.0%	681g
Water 2 (mix)	10.0%	97g
Fine sea salt	1.7%	17g
Ripe sourdough starter, 100% hydration	3.3%	32g

INGREDIENT	BAKER'S %	WEIGHT
White flour (~11.5% protein)	50.0%	32g
Whole spelt flour	50.0%	32g
Water 1	100.0%	63g
Ripe sourdough starter, 100% hydration	50.0%	32g

INGREDIENT	WEIGHT
White flour (~11.5% protein)	503g
Type-85 flour	243g
Whole spelt flour	163g
Water 1	618g

INGREDIENT	WEIGHT
Water 2	97g
Fine sea salt	17g
Levain	159g

Extra Strengthening

This dough is highly hydrated and requires additional kneading up front before bulk fermentation to help develop the gluten network. The mixing and kneading (using the slap and fold method) strengthen the dough enough for it to hold shape and trap the air incorporated during mixing and gasses generated during bulk fermentation. But we stop short of fully strengthening the dough by kneading; the remainder of the strength will be gained organically through fermentation and a series of stretch and fold sets during bulk fermentation.

1. Levain

- **Duration:** 5 hours at warm room temperature: 74°–76°F (23°–24°C)

- **MIX THE LEVAIN:** Warm or cool the water to about 78°F (25°C). In a medium jar, mix the levain ingredients until well incorporated (this liquid levain will feel quite loose) and loosely cover. Store in a warm place for 5 hours.

2. Autolyse

- **Duration:** 1 hour at warm room temperature: 74°–76°F (23°–24°C)
- **Desired dough temperature (DDT):** 78°F (25°C)

- **MIX THE AUTOLYSE:** About 1 hour before the levain is ready, warm or cool the autolyse water (see page 138 on how to calculate) so the temperature of the mixed dough meets the DDT for this recipe. Place the flour and water in a large bowl and use wet hands to mix until no dry bits remain. Use a bowl scraper to scrape down the sides of the bowl to keep all the dough in one area at the bottom. Cover the bowl and place it near your levain for 1 hour. Since this is a longer autolyse, be sure to keep the dough warm.

3. Mix

- **Desired dough temperature (DDT):** 78°F (25°C)

- **CHECK THE LIQUID LEVAIN:** It should show signs of readiness: well aerated, risen, bubbly on top and at the sides, loose, and an assertive sour aroma. If the levain is not showing these signs, let it ferment 30 minutes more and check again.

- **ADJUST THE WATER TEMPERATURE:** Take the temperature of the dough and compare it to the DDT for this recipe: If it's higher, use cold water for the remaining water; if it's lower, use warm water.

- **MIX THE DOUGH:** To the autolyse, add about half of the water, the salt, and ripe levain. Using wet hands, mix the ingredients until well incorporated.

- **STRENGTHEN THE DOUGH (FIRST PHASE):** With wet hands, use the slap and fold method (see page 83) for about 5 minutes to strengthen the dough. The dough should look smooth and begin to hold its shape. If it's still shaggy and loose, continue to strengthen for a few more minutes, but don't worry if it doesn't smooth out completely. Transfer the dough back to the bowl, cover, and let rest for 10 minutes.

- **STRENGTHEN THE DOUGH (SECOND PHASE):** If the dough feels very wet, slack, and loose, don't add the remaining water. Otherwise, add the rest of the water and pinch it into the dough until it is absorbed and the dough comes together. With wet hands, use the slap and fold method for 3 to 5 minutes to further strengthen the dough. The dough should be smoother and hold its shape more readily. Transfer back to the bowl or another container for bulk fermentation.

- **MEASURE THE TEMPERATURE OF THE DOUGH:** Compare it to the DDT and record it as the final dough temperature. Cover the dough.

4. Bulk fermentation

- **Duration:** About 3 hours 30 minutes at warm room temperature: 74°–76°F (23°–24°C)
- **Folds:** 4 sets of stretches and folds at 30-minute intervals

- **SET TIMER AND MAKE A NOTE:** Write down the current time as the start of bulk fermentation, set a timer for 30 minutes, and let the dough rest in a warm place.

- **STRETCH AND FOLD:** When your timer goes off, give the dough one set of stretches and folds. Using wet hands, grab one side of the dough and lift it up and over to the other side. Rotate the bowl 180 degrees and repeat. Then rotate the bowl a quarter turn and stretch and fold that side. Rotate the bowl 180 degrees again and finish with a stretch and fold on the last side. The dough should be folded up neatly. Cover the bowl and repeat these folds every 30 minutes for a total of 4 sets of stretches and folds.

- **LET THE DOUGH REST:** After the last set, cover the bowl and let the dough rest for the remainder of bulk fermentation, about 1 hour 30 minutes.

5. Divide and preshape

- **CHECK THE DOUGH:** At the end of bulk fermentation, the dough will have risen significantly; it may have some bubbles on top and at the sides, it should look smoother and less shaggy, and at the edge of the dough where it meets the container, it should dome downward. If you wet a hand and gently tug on the surface of the dough, it will feel elastic and cohesive, resisting your pull. If you don't see dough that's airy, strong, and "alive," leave it for another 15 minutes in bulk fermentation and check again.

- **DIVIDE AND PRESHAPE THE DOUGH:** Using a bowl scraper, gently scrape the dough out onto a clean work surface and use your bench knife to divide it directly in half. Using your bench knife in your dominant hand and with your other hand wet to reduce sticking, shape each piece of dough into a loose round. (See Preshaping, page 96, for more detail.) Let the rounds rest for 35 minutes, uncovered.

6. Shape

- **PREPARE THE PROOFING BASKETS:** Line two proofing baskets or bowls with clean kitchen towels. Dust lightly and evenly with white flour.

- **SHAPE THE DOUGH:** Shape each as a bâtard or a boule (see pages 102 to 107 for details). Gently transfer each piece to a proofing basket, seam-side up. Place each basket inside a reusable plastic bag and seal.

RECIPE CONTINUES

7. Proof

- ■ **Duration:** About 14 hours (overnight) in a home refrigerator: 39°F (4°C)

- ● **LET THE DOUGH PROOF:** Place the baskets in the refrigerator to proof overnight.

8. Bake

- ■ **Duration:** 50 to 55 minutes in the oven

- ● **PREPARE THE OVEN:** Place an oven rack in the bottom third of the oven with no rack above it. Place a Dutch oven/combo cooker inside the oven and preheat to 450°F (230°C) for at least 30 minutes. (Alternatively, bake directly on a baking stone/steel; see page 124 for details.)

- ● **SCORE THE DOUGH:** Take one of the proofing baskets out of the fridge, uncover, and put a piece of parchment paper over the basket. Place a pizza peel or inverted sheet pan on top of the parchment and, using both hands, flip everything over. Gently remove the basket and score the dough. (See Scoring, page 118, for details.)

- ● **BAKE THE DOUGH:** Slide the dough with the parchment into the preheated Dutch oven and cover with the lid. Bake for 20 minutes, then remove the lid. Continue to bake for 30 to 35 minutes, or until the internal temperature reaches 206°–210°F (96°–99°C) and the crust has a deep mahogany color and a crackle/crunch when gently squeezed.

- ● **FINISH AND COOL:** Let the loaf cool on a wire rack for 1 to 2 hours before slicing. For the second loaf, preheat the Dutch oven or baking surface for 15 minutes and repeat.

HOW TO TINKER

ALTERNATIVE GRAINS

While I adore the whole-grain spelt in this recipe, feel free to experiment with other grain varieties: emmer, Khorasan, or even other wheat varieties such as Red Fife. Alternatively, to take the flavor of spelt further, use freshly milled whole-grain spelt for the spelt portion of the recipe.

PUSH RESET ON YOUR BAKING

Sometimes after baking for a long stretch of time, you might find your results take a dip in quality. While this critical view is usually a self-imposed one—because I can guarantee others are still enjoying your bread as much as they always have—small mistakes sometimes find a way to add up in the mind, eroding your baking confidence. This is normal. This happens. The best way I've found to dig myself out of these slumps is to press reset on my baking. Pick a tried-and-true recipe—perhaps an easy one, or a recipe that is special to you in some way—and bake this bread to hoist you up out of whatever slump you're clawing to get out of. For me, this recipe is either this rustico or Miche (page 209), but the Simple Sourdough (page 40) would also be a great choice. Stepping back and working with these doughs, and later tasting the results, never fails to put a smile on my face and gets me back on track. Sometimes all it takes is a familiar approach, a way to let the hands reconnect with an old companion, and work without undue effort to produce bread that excites the senses. A way to begin again with renewed enthusiasm and a fresh perspective.

POLENTA

A loaf with a golden, crunchy crust and corn flavor

THIS BREAD is one of my absolute favorites. I ate polenta often growing up, a favorite of my grandmother's from northern Italy, and so, too, it became a regular dish at our house. In the winter months she would cook a big batch of it as a hot porridge and then pour the leftovers into a baking dish to cool and solidify. The next day, she'd cut the polenta into slices and pan-fry it to serve alongside meals. Polenta, with its wonderfully rich corn flavor, is delicious when incorporated into bread dough and results in a rustic loaf that shines golden in the sunlight. If there were a loaf that could give you a big, comforting hug, this would be it. I like to think my grandmother would have asked me to bake this often, and no doubt she'd still serve her polenta right alongside it.

I like to use *polenta integrale* for this bread, which is coarsely milled corn with some bran bits retained. My favorite source for polenta is Anson Mills—their rustic polenta is an heirloom red trentino flint corn that makes this bread extra special. Some might say using such high-quality corn in a loaf of bread is foolish, but then I give them a slice of this one, warm from the toaster, and the discussion is over.

BAKING TIMELINE

1 Levain

~ 5 hours

2 Autolyse

30 minutes

3 Mix

4 Bulk Fermentation

~ 3 hours 30 minutes

5 Divide, Preshape, Bench Rest

35 minutes

6 Shape

7 Proof

~ 13 hours (overnight)

8 Bake

55 minutes in the oven

TOTAL

23 hours

VITALS

Total dough weight	1,800g
Pre-fermented flour	6.4%
Levain	17.2%
Hydration	79.0%
Yield	Two 900g loaves

TOTAL FORMULA

INGREDIENT	BAKER'S %	WEIGHT
White flour (~11.5% protein)	65.0%	588g
Whole wheat flour	20.0%	181g
High-protein white flour (~12.7%-14% protein)	15.0%	136g
Polenta (cornmeal)	14.0%	127g
Fresh rosemary, finely chopped	0.8%	7g
Water 1 (polenta, levain, autolyse)	74.0%	670g
Water 2 (mix)	5.0%	45g
Fine sea salt	1.8%	16g
Ripe sourdough starter, 100% hydration	3.2%	29g

INGREDIENT	BAKER'S %	WEIGHT
White flour (~11.5% protein)	50.0%	29g
Whole wheat flour	50.0%	29g
Water 1	100.0%	59g
Ripe sourdough starter, 100% hydration	50.0%	29g

INGREDIENT	WEIGHT
White flour (~11.5% protein)	559g
Whole wheat flour	152g
High-protein white flour (~12.7%-14% protein)	136g
Water 1	478g

INGREDIENT	WEIGHT
Water 2	45g
Fine sea salt	16g
Levain	146g

1. Prepare the levain and polenta

▪ **Duration:** 5 hours at warm room temperature: 74°–76°F (23°–24°C)

● **MIX THE LEVAIN:** Warm or cool the water to about 78°F (25°C). In a medium jar, mix the levain ingredients until well incorporated (this liquid levain will feel quite loose) and loosely cover. Store in a warm place for 5 hours.

● **PREPARE THE POLENTA:** In a medium bowl, combine the 127g polenta and 133g boiling water and stir well. Cover and set aside until bulk fermentation.

2. Autolyse

▪ **Duration:** 30 minutes at warm room temperature: 74°–76°F (23°–24°C)
▪ **Desired dough temperature (DDT):** 78°F (25°C)

● **MIX THE AUTOLYSE:** About 30 minutes before the levain is ready, warm or cool the autolyse water (see page 138 on how to calculate) so the temperature of the mixed dough meets the DDT for this recipe. Place the flour and water in a large bowl and use wet hands to mix until no dry bits remain. Use a bowl scraper to scrape down the sides of the bowl to keep all the dough in one area at the bottom. Cover the bowl and place it near your levain for 30 minutes.

3. Mix

▪ **Desired dough temperature (DDT):** 78°F (25°C)

● **CHECK THE LEVAIN:** It should show signs of readiness: well aerated, risen, bubbly on top and at the sides, loose, and with a sour aroma. If the starter isn't showing these signs, let it ferment 15 minutes more and check again.

● **ADJUST THE WATER TEMPERATURE:** Take the temperature of the dough and compare it to the DDT for this recipe: If it's higher, use cold water for the remaining water; if it's lower, use warm water.

● **MIX THE DOUGH:** To the autolyse, add all of the water, the salt, and ripe levain. Using wet hands, mix the ingredients until well incorporated. Because a good portion of the mixing water was used to soak the polenta, the dough might feel a little dry. If it does, add a small splash of water. Continue to mix until the dough comes together and all the water is absorbed.

● **STRENGTHEN THE DOUGH:** With wet hands, use the slap and fold method (see page 83) for about 5 minutes to strengthen the dough. The dough should look smooth and begin to hold its shape. If it is still shaggy and loose, continue to strengthen for a few more minutes, but don't worry if it doesn't smooth out completely. Transfer back to the bowl or another container for bulk fermentation.

● **MEASURE THE TEMPERATURE OF THE DOUGH:** Compare it to the DDT and record it as the final dough temperature. Cover the dough.

RECIPE CONTINUES →

4. Bulk fermentation

- **Duration:** About 3 hours 30 minutes at warm room temperature: 74°–76°F (23°–24°C)
- **Folds:** 3 sets of stretches and folds at 30-minute intervals

● **SET TIMER AND MAKE A NOTE:** Write down the current time as the start of bulk fermentation, set a timer for 30 minutes, and let the dough rest in a warm place.

● **ADD THE INCLUSIONS AND STRETCH AND FOLD:** When your timer goes off, spread about one-quarter of the soaked polenta and one-quarter of the 7g rosemary evenly over the dough. Using wet hands, pick up one side of the dough and stretch it up and fold it over. Spread another one-quarter of the inclusions over the top. Rotate the bowl 180 degrees and perform another stretch and fold. Evenly spread on another one-quarter of the inclusions. Rotate the bowl a quarter turn, perform a stretch and fold, and spread on the remaining inclusions. Rotate the bowl 180 degrees and perform the last stretch and fold. The dough should be folded up neatly. Cover and repeat these folds every 30 minutes for a total of 3 sets of stretches and folds.

● **LET THE DOUGH REST:** After the last set, cover the bowl and let the dough rest for the remainder of bulk fermentation, about 2 hours.

5. Divide and preshape

● **CHECK THE DOUGH:** At the end of bulk fermentation, the dough will have risen significantly; it may have bubbles on top and at the sides, it should look smoother and less shaggy, and at the edge of the dough where it meets the container, it should dome downward. If you wet a hand and gently tug on the surface of the dough, it will feel elastic and cohesive, resisting your pull. If you don't see dough that's airy, strong, and "alive," leave it for another 15 minutes in bulk fermentation and check again.

● **DIVIDE AND PRESHAPE THE DOUGH:** Using a bowl scraper, gently scrape the dough onto a clean work surface and use your bench knife to divide it directly in half. Using your bench knife in your dominant hand and with your other hand wet to reduce sticking, shape each piece of dough into a loose round. (See Preshaping, page 96, for more detail.) Let the rounds rest for 35 minutes, uncovered.

6. Shape

● **PREPARE THE PROOFING BASKETS:** Line two proofing baskets or bowls with clean kitchen towels. Dust lightly and evenly with white flour.

● **SHAPE THE DOUGH:** Shape each as a bâtard or a boule (see pages 102 to 107 for details). Gently transfer each piece to a proofing basket, seam-side up. Place each basket inside a reusable plastic bag and seal.

7. Proof

◦ **Duration:** About 13 hours (overnight) in a home refrigerator: 39°F (4°C)

● **LET THE DOUGH PROOF:** Place the baskets in the refrigerator to proof overnight.

8. Bake

◦ **Duration:** 50 to 55 minutes in the oven

● **PREPARE THE OVEN:** Place an oven rack in the bottom third of the oven with no rack above it. Place a Dutch oven/combo cooker inside the oven and preheat to 450°F (230°C) for at least 30 minutes. (Alternatively, bake directly on a baking stone/steel; see page 124 for details.)

● **SCORE THE DOUGH:** Take one of the proofing baskets out of the fridge, uncover, and put a piece of parchment paper over the basket. Place a pizza peel or inverted sheet pan on top of the parchment and, using both hands, flip everything over. Gently remove the basket and score the dough. (See Scoring, page 118, for details.)

● **BAKE THE DOUGH:** Slide the dough with the parchment into the preheated Dutch oven and cover with the lid. Bake for 20 minutes, then remove the lid. Continue to bake for 30 to 35 minutes, or until the internal temperature reaches 206°-210°F (96°-99°C) and the crust has a golden brown color speckled with bits of toasted polenta and a crackle/crunch when gently squeezed.

● **FINISH AND COOL:** Let the loaf cool on a wire rack for 1 to 2 hours before slicing. For the second loaf, preheat the Dutch oven or baking surface for 15 minutes and repeat.

HOW TO TINKER

ADD OLIVES

Polenta, rosemary, and olives are made for one another. Add up to 90g kalamata or Castelvetrano olives (cut in half) along with the polenta and rosemary during bulk fermentation.

SUN-DRIED TOMATO AND OLIVE

Gentle tomato flavor accented by briny olives and mild fermentation flavors

WHILE I love everything tomato, and use sun-dried tomatoes often in my kitchen for topping Sourdough Pizza Dough (page 294) or tossing with pasta, adding tomatoes to a bread dough never struck me as something to try—until I did. The sweet-tart flavor of the sun-dried tomatoes and their rich preserving oil entwine themselves into the loaf, resulting in something less like bread with the occasional tomato, and more like a cohesive tomato-flavored loaf. The chopped kalamata olives add a splash of salty flavor that complements the tomato—there's a reason why olives and tomatoes so often go together. This is a versatile bread that can work with many dishes and is certainly great with any pasta dish, but it also surprisingly makes a mean tuna salad sandwich.

For this bread I like to use sun-dried tomatoes preserved in olive oil. The oil is packed with tomato flavor, and adding a small amount to the bread dough brings that flavor in tow and also results in a slightly softer crust and crumb (see How to Tinker, page 208). Be sure not to rinse them of their oil so that some of it will catch a ride into the final dough. As with the Mediterranean Olive and Rosemary bread (page 177), be sure to drain the olives of their brine, rinse them under running water, pat dry, and chop them before incorporating them into the dough with the tomatoes during bulk fermentation.

BAKING TIMELINE

1. Levain

   12 hours (overnight)

2. Autolyse

   30 minutes

3. Mix

4. Bulk Fermentation

   3 hours 30 minutes

5. Divide, Preshape, Bench Rest

   35 minutes

6. Shape

7. Proof

   19 hours (overnight)

8. Bake

   55 minutes in the oven

TOTAL

36 hours

VITALS

Total dough weight	1,800g
Pre-fermented flour	8.4%
Levain	19.5%
Hydration	70.0%
Yield	Two 900g loaves

TOTAL FORMULA

INGREDIENT	BAKER'S %	WEIGHT
White flour (~11.5% protein)	85.0%	766g
Whole wheat flour	15.0%	135g
Kalamata olives, pitted and coarsely chopped	14.0%	126g
Sun-dried tomatoes, preserved in olive oil, drained and finely chopped	13.0%	117g
Water 1 (levain and autolyse)	65.0%	586g
Water 2 (mix)	5.0%	45g
Fine sea salt	1.8%	16g
Ripe sourdough starter, 100% hydration	0.9%	8g

INGREDIENT	BAKER'S %	WEIGHT
White flour (~11.5% protein)	50.0%	38g
Whole wheat flour	50.0%	38g
Water 1	100.0%	77g
Ripe sourdough starter, 100% hydration	10.0%	8g

INGREDIENT	WEIGHT
White flour (~11.5% protein)	728g
Whole wheat flour	97g
Water 1	509g

INGREDIENT	WEIGHT
Water 2	45g
Fine sea salt	16g
Kalamata olives, pitted and coarsely chopped	126g
Sun-dried tomatoes, preserved in olive oil, drained and finely chopped	117g
Levain	161g

1. Levain

▪ **Duration:** 12 hours (overnight) at warm room temperature: 74°–76°F (23°–24°C)

● **MIX THE LEVAIN:** Warm or cool the water to about 78°F (25°C). In a medium jar, mix the levain ingredients until well incorporated (this liquid levain will feel quite loose) and loosely cover. Store in a warm place for 12 hours.

2. Autolyse

▪ **Duration:** 30 minutes at warm room temperature: 74°–76°F (23°–24°C)
▪ **Desired dough temperature (DDT):** 78°F (25°C)

● **MIX THE AUTOLYSE:** About 30 minutes before the levain is ready, warm or cool the autolyse water (see page 138 on how to calculate) so the temperature of the mixed dough meets the DDT for this recipe. Place the flour and water in a large bowl and use wet hands to mix until no dry bits remain. Use a bowl scraper to scrape down the sides of the bowl to keep all the dough in one area at the bottom. Cover the bowl and place it near your levain for 30 minutes.

3. Mix

▪ **Desired dough temperature (DDT):** 78°F (25°C)

● **CHECK THE LIQUID LEVAIN:** It should show signs of readiness: well aerated, risen, bubbly on top and at the sides, loose, and with an assertive sour aroma. If the levain is not showing these signs, let it ferment 30 minutes more and check again.

● **ADJUST THE WATER TEMPERATURE:** Take the temperature of the dough and compare it to the DDT for this recipe: If it's higher, use cold water for the remaining water; if it's lower, use warm water.

● **MIX THE DOUGH:** To the autolyse, add about half of the water, the salt, and ripe levain. Using wet hands, mix the ingredients until well incorporated. If the dough feels very wet, slack, and loose, don't add the remaining water. Otherwise, add the rest of the water and continue to mix until the dough comes together and all the water is absorbed.

● **STRENGTHEN THE DOUGH:** With wet hands, use the slap and fold method (see page 83) for about 5 minutes to strengthen the dough. The dough should look smooth and begin to hold its shape. If it's still shaggy and loose, continue to strengthen for a few more minutes, but don't worry if it doesn't smooth out completely. Transfer back to the bowl or another container for bulk fermentation.

● **ADD THE INCLUSIONS:** Spread the olives and sun-dried tomatoes evenly over the surface of the dough. Using wet hands, gently massage the inclusions into the dough.

- **MEASURE THE TEMPERATURE OF THE DOUGH:** Compare it to the DDT and record it as the final dough temperature. Cover the dough.

4. Bulk fermentation

- **Duration:** About 3 hours 30 minutes at warm room temperature: 74°–76°F (23°–24°C)
- **Folds:** 3 sets of stretches and folds at 30-minute intervals

- **SET TIMER AND MAKE A NOTE:** Write down the current time as the start of bulk fermentation, set a timer for 30 minutes, and let the dough rest in a warm place.

- **STRETCH AND FOLD:** When your timer goes off, give the dough one set of stretches and folds. Using wet hands, grab one side of the dough and lift it up and over to the other side. Rotate the bowl 180 degrees and repeat. Then rotate the bowl a quarter turn and stretch and fold that side. Rotate the bowl 180 degrees again and finish with a stretch and fold on the last side. The dough should be folded up neatly. Cover and repeat these folds every 30 minutes for a total of 3 sets of stretches and folds.

- **LET THE DOUGH REST:** After the last set, cover the bowl and let the dough rest for the remainder of bulk fermentation, about 2 hours.

5. Divide and preshape

- **CHECK THE DOUGH:** At the end of bulk fermentation, the dough will have risen significantly; it may have bubbles on top and at the sides, it should look smoother and less shaggy, and at the edge of the dough where it meets the container, it should dome downward. If you wet a hand and gently tug on the surface of the dough, it will feel elastic and cohesive, resisting your pull. If you don't see dough that's airy, strong, and "alive," leave it for another 15 minutes in bulk fermentation and check again.

- **DIVIDE AND PRESHAPE THE DOUGH:** Using a bowl scraper, gently scrape the dough onto a clean work surface and use your bench knife to divide it directly in half. Using your bench knife in your dominant hand and with your other hand wet to reduce sticking, shape each piece of dough into a loose round. (See Preshaping, page 96, for more detail.) Let the rounds rest for 35 minutes, uncovered.

6. Shape

- **PREPARE THE PROOFING BASKETS:** Line two proofing baskets or bowls with clean kitchen towels. Dust lightly and evenly with white flour.

- **SHAPE THE DOUGH:** Shape each as a boule or a bâtard (see pages 102 to 107 for details). Gently transfer each piece to a proofing basket, seam-side up. Place each basket inside a reusable plastic bag and seal.

RECIPE CONTINUES →

7. Proof

▪ **Duration:** About 19 hours (overnight) in a home refrigerator: 39°F (4°C)

● **LET THE DOUGH PROOF:** Place the baskets in the refrigerator to proof overnight.

8. Bake

▪ **Duration:** 50 to 55 minutes in the oven

● **PREPARE THE OVEN:** Place an oven rack in the bottom third of the oven with no rack above it. Place a Dutch oven/combo cooker inside the oven and preheat to 450°F (230°C) for at least 30 minutes. (Alternatively, bake directly on a baking stone/steel; see page 124 for details.)

● **SCORE THE DOUGH:** Take one of the proofing baskets out of the fridge, uncover, and put a piece of parchment paper over the basket. Place a pizza peel or inverted sheet pan on top of the parchment and, using both hands, flip everything over. Gently remove the basket and score the dough. (See Scoring, page 118, for details.)

● **BAKE THE DOUGH:** Slide the dough with the parchment into the preheated Dutch oven and cover with the lid. Bake for 20 minutes, then remove the lid. Continue to bake for 30 to 35 minutes, or until the internal temperature reaches 206°-210°F (96°-99°C) and the crust has a deep mahogany color and a crackle/crunch when gently squeezed.

● **FINISH AND COOL:** Let the loaf cool on a wire rack for 1 to 2 hours before slicing. For the second loaf, preheat the Dutch oven or baking surface for 15 minutes and repeat.

HOW TO TINKER

CASTELVETRANO OLIVES

Substitute chopped Castelvetrano olives for the kalamata olives.

A SOFTER LOAF

To increase the tomato flavor and further soften the crust and crumb, add up to 25g of the sun-dried tomato preserving oil during mixing.

MICHE

A large and rustic loaf with a deep wheat flavor, creamy crumb, and substantial crust

A MICHE is typically quite large—sometimes pushing 2,000 grams—but this adaptation is more approachable for the typical home kitchen and still brings with it all the qualities of a great miche. There's a tangible joy in handling this dough during shaping; the large dough weight requires the baker to approach shaping with a confident yet delicate hand, gently folding and nudging it into its final round form. The result is a beautiful mahogany-colored crust contrasted with a creamy, soft crumb. The flavor is abundant with the complex bouquet of well-fermented wheat.

This miche is among my favorite breads to make; it is one that represents a baker's skill in balancing all variables in the breadmaking equation and one I return to when I sometimes need to reset and sharpen my baking (see Push Reset on Your Baking, page 198). That practice of balance is evident here: Do not be afraid to push all stages of fermentation to the point of almost overproofing; you might ultimately have less rise in the final loaf, which is typical for a miche anyway, but with less rise comes maximum flavor and tenderness.

The Type-85 flour called for here is malted. If your Type-85 flour does not contain malt, add malt at 0.2% to total flour weight. Alternatively, if you do not have diastatic malt, try the recipe without it and then try it again in the future if you pick up some malt. I like adding some to bring additional color and flavor to this miche. If you don't have Type-85 flour, see page 18 on how to substitute.

BAKING TIMELINE

1 Levain

12 hours (overnight)

2 Autolyse

30 minutes

3 Mix

4 Bulk Fermentation

3 hours 30 minutes

5 Divide, Preshape, Bench Rest

35 minutes

6 Shape

7 Proof

2 hours

8 Bake

1 hour 5 minutes in the oven

TOTAL

19 hours 10 minutes

VITALS

Total dough weight	1,250g
Pre-fermented flour	10.0%
Levain	18.3%
Hydration	84.0%
Yield	One large miche

TOTAL FORMULA

INGREDIENT	BAKER'S %	WEIGHT
Type-85 flour, malted (see headnote)	84.0%	562g
Whole wheat flour	10.0%	67g
Whole rye flour	6.0%	40g
Water 1 (levain and autolyse)	74.0%	495g
Water 2 (mix)	10.0%	67g
Fine sea salt	1.9%	13g
Ripe sourdough starter, 100% hydration	1.0%	7g

INGREDIENT	BAKER'S %	WEIGHT
Type-85 flour, malted	100.0%	67g
Water 1	55.0%	37g
Ripe sourdough starter, 100% hydration	10.0%	7g

INGREDIENT	WEIGHT
Type-85 flour, malted	495g
Whole wheat flour	67g
Whole rye flour	40g
Water 1	458g

INGREDIENT	WEIGHT
Water 2	67g
Fine sea salt	13g
Levain	111g

1. Levain

■ **Duration:** 12 hours (overnight) at warm room temperature: 74°–76°F (23°–24°C)

● **MIX THE LEVAIN:** Warm or cool the water to about 78°F (25°C). In a medium bowl, mix the levain ingredients until well incorporated. Use your hands to knead the mixture until all dry bits of flour are incorporated (this stiff levain will feel strong and dry). Transfer the levain to a jar and loosely cover. Store in a warm place for 12 hours.

2. Autolyse

■ **Duration:** 30 minutes at warm room temperature: 74°–76°F (23°–24°C)
■ **Desired dough temperature (DDT):** 78°F (25°C)

● **MIX THE AUTOLYSE:** About 30 minutes before the levain is ready, warm or cool the autolyse water (see page 138 on how to calculate) so the temperature of the mixed dough meets the DDT for this recipe. Place the flour and water in a large bowl and use wet hands to mix until no dry bits remain. Use a bowl scraper to scrape down the sides of the bowl to keep all the dough in one area at the bottom. Cover the bowl and place it near your levain for 30 minutes.

3. Mix

■ **Desired dough temperature (DDT):** 78°F (25°C)

● **CHECK THE LEVAIN:** It should show signs of readiness: well aerated, risen, soft, sticky, and an assertive sour aroma. If the levain is not showing these signs, let it ferment 1 hour more and check again.

● **ADJUST THE WATER TEMPERATURE:** Take the temperature of the dough and compare it to the DDT for this recipe: If it's higher, use cold water for the remaining water; if it's lower, use warm water.

● **MIX THE DOUGH:** To the autolyse, add about half of the water, the salt, and ripe levain. Using wet hands, mix the ingredients until well incorporated. If the dough feels very wet, slack, and loose, don't add the remaining water. Otherwise, add the rest of the water and continue to mix until the dough comes together and all the water is absorbed.

● **STRENGTHEN THE DOUGH:** With wet hands, use the slap and fold method (see page 83) for about 5 minutes to strengthen the dough. The dough should look smooth and begin to hold its shape. If it's still shaggy and loose, continue to strengthen for a few more minutes, but don't worry if it doesn't smooth out completely. Transfer back to the bowl or another container for bulk fermentation.

● **MEASURE THE TEMPERATURE OF THE DOUGH:** Compare it to the DDT and record it as the final dough temperature. Cover the dough.

RECIPE CONTINUES →

4. Bulk fermentation

- **Duration:** About 3 hours 30 minutes at warm room temperature: 74°–76°F (23°–24°C)
- **Folds:** 3 sets of stretches and folds at 30-minute intervals

● **SET TIMER AND MAKE A NOTE:** Write down the current time as the start of bulk fermentation, set a timer for 30 minutes, and let the dough rest in a warm place.

● **STRETCH AND FOLD:** When your timer goes off, give the dough one set of stretches and folds. Using wet hands, grab one side of the dough and lift it up and over to the other side. Rotate the bowl 180 degrees and repeat. Then rotate the bowl a quarter turn and stretch and fold that side. Rotate the bowl 180 degrees again and finish with a stretch and fold on the last side. The dough should be folded up neatly. Cover and repeat these folds every 30 minutes for a total of 3 sets of stretches and folds.

● **LET THE DOUGH REST:** After the last set, cover the bowl and let the dough rest for the remainder of bulk fermentation, about 2 hours.

5. Preshape

● **CHECK THE DOUGH:** At the end of bulk fermentation, the dough will have risen significantly; it may have bubbles on top and at the sides, it should look smoother and less shaggy, and at the edge of the dough where it meets the container, it should dome downward. If you wet a hand and gently tug on the surface of the dough, it will feel elastic and cohesive, resisting your pull. If you don't see dough that's airy, strong, and "alive," leave it for another 15 minutes in bulk fermentation and check again.

● **PRESHAPE THE DOUGH:** Using a bowl scraper, gently scrape the dough onto a clean work surface. Using your bench knife in your dominant hand and with your other hand wet to reduce sticking, shape it into a loose round. (See Preshaping, page 96, for more detail.) Let the round rest for 35 minutes, uncovered.

TROUBLESHOOTING

MY MICHE IS SUPER FLAT WITH VERY LITTLE OVEN SPRING.

If you want more oven spring, try reducing the proof time by 15 to 30 minutes and be sure to shape the dough tightly enough so it doesn't spread in the oven when baking. Before baking, you can also chill the dough in the refrigerator, uncovered, for about 10 minutes, until slightly firm.

THE INTERIOR OF THE MICHE WAS GUMMY AND "WET" WHEN I SLICED INTO IT.

This is a large loaf that requires hours to properly cool. If you slice it too early, you'll almost certainly find that the interior hasn't properly set. Give it more time to cool before slicing. I actually prefer to bake it the day before I plan to serve it to give it time to set and let the flavors amplify.

6. Shape

- **PREPARE A PROOFING BASKET:** Line a 12-inch proofing basket or bowl with a clean kitchen towel. Dust lightly and evenly with white flour.

- **SHAPE THE DOUGH:** Classically, a miche is a large boule (round shape), and because the dough is large, it can be challenging to shape tightly—so be confident when shaping! I shape a miche in the same way as a smaller boule (see Shaping a Boule, page 106). When shaped, gently transfer the dough to the prepared proofing basket, seam-side up. Place the large basket inside a reusable plastic bag and seal.

7. Proof

- Duration: 2 hours at warm room temperature: 74°–76°F (23°–24°C)

- **LET THE DOUGH PROOF:** Put the basket in a warm place for about 2 hours. Check on the dough periodically after the first 1½ hours, using the Poke Test (page 116) to assess when it's ready.

8. Bake

- Duration: 60 to 65 minutes in the oven

- **PREPARE THE OVEN:** Place an oven rack in the bottom third of the oven. Place a baking stone/steel on the rack and a roasting pan with lava rocks on the bottom of the oven (see Baking Directly on a Surface, page 124, for more detail). Preheat the oven to 450°F (230°C) for 1 hour.

- **SCORE THE DOUGH:** Uncover and score the dough. (See Scoring, page 118, for details.)

- **BAKE THE DOUGH:** Slide the dough with the parchment onto the preheated baking surface. Steam the oven by pouring a cup of ice into the roasting pan with lava rocks and quickly close the oven door. Bake for 20 minutes. Vent the oven of steam by removing the roasting pan. Continue to bake for 40 to 45 minutes, or until the internal temperature reaches 206°–210°F (96°–99°C) and the crust has a deep walnut color and a crackle/crunch when gently squeezed.

- **FINISH AND COOL:** Let the miche cool on a wire rack for 6 to 8 hours before slicing, though letting it cool overnight is best.

Your Miche as a Canvas

One beautiful thing about this large miche is the roomy blank canvas of its expansive, round shape—a place to express your creativity as a baker. If you are looking for a high-contrast design, right before scoring and baking, dust a light layer of white flour on the top of the dough and rub the flour gently with your hand to even it out. Now, any scoring will show up clearly and in great detail once the loaf is baked. My favorite style is a crosshatch pattern, typical of a miche, but many bakers use this opportunity to impart their own unique signature. Get creative and find your own! (See Decorative Scoring, page 120, for more detail.)

HOW TO TINKER

INCREASE WHOLE-GRAIN RYE PERCENTAGE

I love the flavor and color that whole-grain rye flour brings to this bread. Experiment with increasing the percentage up to 12%, reducing the whole wheat flour commensurately. The added rye might tighten up the interior a bit more, but the increased flavor is a welcome tradeoff.

EARTHY BUCKWHEAT MICHE

Replace the 5% rye with 5% whole-grain buckwheat flour. Buckwheat lacks gluten, but it brings a deep, earthy flavor that works very well in this miche. While not a traditional addition, this small percentage of buckwheat makes for a hearty loaf of bread that's wonderful during colder months.

POTATO ROSEMARY
(Pane di Patate)

A hearty loaf with potato
and rosemary, perfect
for cold months, stews,
and soups

I CREATED this recipe for my dad one Father's Day. He grew up in the Puglia region of southern Italy, where cooked and mashed potatoes were mixed into a bread dough for a nourishing and filling loaf that was common at many meals. This recipe is my take on that bread, and it's a hefty, savory, and dense loaf. But the density gives way to an interior that's remarkably tender, bringing with it a melt-in-your-mouth quality punctuated by the pop of flavor from the rosemary. It pairs well with heavy dishes like soups and stews and is a wintertime staple in my house, when we almost subconsciously start to stock up on tubers to prepare for the coming cold months.

Note that this recipe has a slightly higher salt percentage than you will find in many of the other recipes in this book. The increased salt is necessary to bring additional flavor to the large percentage of potato.

BAKING TIMELINE

1. **Levain**

   5 hours

2. **Autolyse**

   30 minutes

3. **Mix**

4. **Bulk Fermentation**

   3 hours

5. **Divide, Preshape, Bench Rest**

   35 minutes

6. **Shape**

7. **Proof**

   18 hours (overnight)

8. **Bake**

   55 minutes in the oven

   TOTAL
   27 hours 30 minutes

VITALS

Total dough weight	1,800g
Pre-fermented flour	6.0%
Levain	15.8%
Hydration	77.0%
Yield	Two 900g loaves

TOTAL FORMULA

INGREDIENT	BAKER'S %	WEIGHT
White flour (~11.5% protein)	65.0%	524g
Whole wheat flour	20.0%	161g
High-protein white flour (~12.7%-14% protein)	15.0%	121g
Yukon Gold potato, baked, peeled, mashed, and cooled (see page 351)	40.0%	323g (about 3 medium)
Fresh rosemary, finely chopped	1.0%	8g
Water 1 (levain and autolyse)	72.0%	581g
Water 2 (mix)	5.0%	40g
Fine sea salt	2.0%	16g
Ripe sourdough starter, 100% hydration	3.0%	24g

1. Levain

▪ **Duration:** 5 hours at warm room temperature: 74°–76°F (23°–24°C)

● **MIX THE LEVAIN:** Warm or cool the water to about 78°F (25°C). In a medium jar, mix the levain ingredients until well incorporated (this liquid levain will feel quite loose) and loosely cover. Store in a warm place for 5 hours. (If you haven't baked your potatoes yet, do so now. See note on page 351 for details.)

INGREDIENT	BAKER'S %	WEIGHT
White flour (~11.5% protein)	50.0%	24g
Whole wheat flour	50.0%	24g
Water 1	100.0%	48g
Ripe sourdough starter, 100% hydration	50.0%	24g

2. Autolyse

▪ **Duration:** 30 minutes at warm room temperature: 74°–76°F (23°–24°C)
▪ **Desired dough temperature (DDT):** 78°F (25°C)

● **MIX THE AUTOLYSE:** About 30 minutes before the levain is ready, warm or cool the autolyse water (see page 138 on how to calculate) so the temperature of the mixed dough meets the DDT for this recipe. Place the flour and water in a large bowl and use wet hands to mix until no dry bits remain. Use a bowl scraper to scrape down the sides of the bowl to keep all the dough in one area at the bottom. Cover the bowl and place it near your levain for 30 minutes.

INGREDIENT	WEIGHT
White flour (~11.5% protein)	500g
Whole wheat flour	137g
High-protein white flour (~12.7%–14% protein)	121g
Water 1	533g

3. Mix

▪ **Desired dough temperature (DDT):** 78°F (25°C)

● **CHECK THE LEVAIN:** It should show signs of readiness: well aerated, risen, bubbly on top and at the sides, loose, and a sour aroma. If the levain is not showing these signs, let it ferment 30 minutes more and check again.

● **ADJUST THE WATER TEMPERATURE:** Take the temperature of the dough and compare it to the DDT for this recipe: If it's higher, use cold water for the remaining water; if it's lower, use warm water.

● **MIX THE DOUGH:** To the autolyse, add about half of the water, the salt, and ripe levain. Using wet hands, mix the ingredients until well incorporated. If the dough feels very wet, slack, and loose, don't add the remaining water. Otherwise, add the rest of the water and continue to mix until the dough comes together and all the water is absorbed. (Be conservative with the water in this recipe, since the dough will feel even more slack and wet when the potato is added and as bulk fermentation progresses.)

● **STRENGTHEN THE DOUGH:** With wet hands, use the slap and fold method (see page 83) for about 5 minutes to strengthen the dough. The dough should look smooth and begin to hold its shape. If it's still shaggy and loose, continue to strengthen for a few more minutes, but don't worry if it doesn't smooth out completely. Transfer back to the bowl or another container for bulk fermentation.

● **ADD THE INCLUSIONS:** Spread the rosemary and mashed potato on top of the dough. Using wet hands, pinch the ingredients through the dough and fold it over

INGREDIENT	WEIGHT
Yukon Gold potato, baked, peeled, mashed, and cooled	323g (about 3 medium)
Fresh rosemary, finely chopped	8g
Water 2	40g
Fine sea salt	16g
Levain	120g

RECIPE CONTINUES →

until everything is incorporated. Perform a series of stretches and folds in the bowl until the dough comes back together and the ingredients look well distributed. Cover the dough.

4. Bulk fermentation

- ▪ **Duration:** About 3 hours at warm room temperature: 74°–76°F (23°–24°C)
- ▪ **Folds:** 3 sets of stretches and folds at 30-minute intervals

- ● **SET TIMER AND MAKE A NOTE:** Write down the current time as the start of bulk fermentation, set a timer for 30 minutes, and let the dough rest in a warm place.

- ● **STRETCH AND FOLD:** When your timer goes off, give the dough one set of stretches and folds. Using wet hands, grab one side of the dough and lift it up and over to the other side. Rotate the bowl 180 degrees and repeat. Then rotate the bowl a quarter turn and stretch and fold that side. Rotate the bowl 180 degrees again and finish with a stretch and fold on the last side. The dough should be folded up neatly. Cover and repeat every 30 minutes for a total of 3 sets.

- ● **LET THE DOUGH REST:** After the last set, cover the bowl and let the dough rest for the remainder of bulk fermentation, about 1 hour 30 minutes.

5. Divide and preshape

- ● **CHECK THE DOUGH:** At the end of bulk fermentation, the dough will have risen significantly; it may have bubbles on top and at the sides, it should look smoother and less shaggy, and at the edge of the dough where it meets the container, it should dome downward. If you wet a hand and gently tug on the surface of the dough, it will feel elastic and cohesive, resisting your pull. If you don't see dough that's airy, strong, and "alive," leave it for another 15 minutes in bulk fermentation and check again.

- ● **DIVIDE AND PRESHAPE THE DOUGH:** Using a bowl scraper, gently scrape the dough onto a clean work surface and use your bench knife to divide it directly in half. Using your bench knife in your dominant hand and with your other hand wet to reduce sticking, shape each piece of dough into a loose round. (See Preshaping, page 96, for more detail.) Let the rounds rest for 35 minutes, uncovered.

Rosemary Garnish

When shaped as a boule, this bread looks very nice with a short, thin sprig of rosemary placed into the bottom of the proofing basket before the dough is placed inside. The sprig will press into the dough during proofing and bake onto the top of the loaf in the oven.

6. Shape

- ● **PREPARE THE PROOFING BASKETS:** Line two proofing baskets or bowls with clean kitchen towels. Dust lightly and evenly with white flour.

- ● **SHAPE THE DOUGH:** Shape each as a boule or a bâtard (see pages 102 to 107 for details). Gently transfer each piece to a proofing basket, seam-side up. Place each basket inside a reusable plastic bag and seal.

7. Proof

- ▪ **Duration:** About 18 hours (overnight) in a home refrigerator: 39°F (4°C)

- ● **LET THE DOUGH PROOF:** Place the baskets in the refrigerator to proof overnight.

8. Bake

■ **Duration:** 50 to 55 minutes in the oven

● **PREPARE THE OVEN:** Place an oven rack in the bottom third of the oven with no rack above it. Place a Dutch oven/combo cooker inside the oven and preheat to 450°F (230°C) for at least 30 minutes. (Alternatively, bake directly on a baking stone/steel; see page 124 for details.)

● **SCORE THE DOUGH:** Take one of the proofing baskets out of the fridge, uncover, and put a piece of parchment paper over the basket. Place a pizza peel or inverted sheet pan on top of the parchment and, using both hands, flip everything over. Gently remove the basket and score the dough. (See Scoring, page 118, for details.)

● **BAKE THE DOUGH:** Slide the dough with the parchment into the preheated Dutch oven and cover with the lid. Bake for 20 minutes, then remove the lid. Continue to bake for 30 to 35 minutes, or until the internal temperature reaches 206°-210°F (96°-99°C) and the crust is a deep golden brown. Let cool on a wire rack for 3 to 4 hours before slicing. For the second loaf, preheat the Dutch oven for 15 minutes and repeat.

100% WHOLE WHEAT

A wholesome loaf that's packed with whole-grain flavor and nutrition

THIS BREAD has such a rich flavor it might quickly jump to the top of your favorites. This recipe is comprised of only whole wheat flour, which is made from 100 percent of the wheat berry, so it's completely whole grain and perhaps the healthiest of loaves you can bake. This is bread that makes your body feel good when eating it, knowing you're getting the full nutrition the grain has to offer.

Just about any wheat variety—or a blend—will work well for this recipe, but if you can find a special variety, such as Red Fife, give it a try. Many local mills are now offering heritage wheat varieties; with this recipe, you have a chance to explore the flavor of each in the purest sense.

BAKING TIMELINE

1 Levain

   5 hours

2 Autolyse

   1 hour

3 Mix

4 Bulk Fermentation

   3 hours

5 Divide, Preshape, Bench Rest

   25 minutes

6 Shape

7 Proof

   2 hours or
   15 hours (overnight)

8 Bake

   55 minutes in the oven

TOTAL

11 hours 20 minutes
or 24 hours 20 minutes

VITALS

Total dough weight	1,800g
Pre-fermented flour	7.0%
Levain	15.1%
Hydration	90.0%
Yield	Two 900g loaves

TOTAL FORMULA

INGREDIENT	BAKER'S %	WEIGHT
Whole wheat flour	100.0%	921g
Water 1 (levain and autolyse)	80.0%	737g
Water 2 (mix)	10.0%	92g
Fine sea salt	1.9%	18g
Ripe sourdough starter, 100% hydration	3.5%	32g

ADDITIONAL INGREDIENT

Wheat bran, for topping (optional)

INGREDIENT	BAKER'S %	WEIGHT
Whole wheat flour	100.0%	64g
Water 1	50.0%	32g
Ripe sourdough starter, 100% hydration	50.0%	32g

INGREDIENT	WEIGHT
Whole wheat flour	857g
Water 1	705g

INGREDIENT	WEIGHT
Water 2	92g
Fine sea salt	18g
Levain	128g

Water 2

Whole wheat flour can typically take on much more water than white flour due to the increased bran and germ (it is 100 percent of the wheat berry, after all), but as always, it's best to be conservative when adding the remaining water and adjust to suit your flour.

1. Levain

- **Duration:** 5 hours at warm room temperature: 74°–76°F (23°–24°C)

● **MIX THE LEVAIN:** Warm or cool the water to about 78°F (25°C). In a medium bowl, mix the levain ingredients until well incorporated. Use your hands to knead the mixture until all dry bits of flour are incorporated (this stiff levain will feel strong and dry). Transfer the levain to a jar and loosely cover. Store in a warm place for 5 hours.

2. Autolyse

- **Duration:** 1 hour at warm room temperature: 74°–76°F (23°–24°C)
- **Desired dough temperature (DDT):** 75°F (23°C)

● **MIX THE AUTOLYSE:** About 1 hour before the levain is ready, warm or cool the autolyse water (see page 138 on how to calculate) so the temperature of the mixed dough meets the DDT for this recipe. Place the flour and water in a large bowl and use wet hands to mix until no dry bits remain. Use a bowl scraper to scrape down the sides of the bowl to keep all the dough in one area at the bottom. Cover the bowl and place it near your levain for 1 hour.

3. Mix

- **Desired dough temperature (DDT):** 75°F (23°C)

● **CHECK THE LEVAIN:** It should show signs of readiness: well aerated, risen, soft, sticky, and an assertive sour aroma. If the levain is not showing these signs, let it ferment 30 minutes more and check again.

● **ADJUST THE WATER TEMPERATURE:** Take the temperature of the dough and compare it to the DDT for this recipe: If it's higher, use cold water for the remaining water; if it's lower, use warm water.

● **MIX THE DOUGH:** To the autolyse, add about half of the water, the salt, and ripe levain. Using wet hands, mix the ingredients until well incorporated.

● **STRENGTHEN THE DOUGH (FIRST PHASE):** With wet hands, use the slap and fold method (see page 83) for about 5 minutes to strengthen the dough. The dough should look smooth and begin to hold its shape. If it's still shaggy and loose, continue to strengthen for a few more minutes, but don't worry if it doesn't smooth out completely. Transfer back to the bowl, cover, and let rest for 10 minutes.

● **STRENGTHEN THE DOUGH (SECOND PHASE):** This should be a rather wet dough, but if it feels excessively wet and soupy, don't add the remaining water. Otherwise, add the rest of the water and pinch it into the rested dough until the water is absorbed and the dough comes together. With wet hands, use the slap and fold method for 3 to 5 minutes to further strengthen the dough. The dough should be smoother and hold its shape more readily, but it won't smooth out to the same degree at this stage as a recipe with more white flour. At the end of strengthening, the dough should still be cohesive, a little smoother, and elastic, but it will still need further strengthening during bulk fermentation through stretches and folds. Transfer the dough back to the bowl or another container for bulk fermentation.

- **MEASURE THE TEMPERATURE OF THE DOUGH:** Compare it to the DDT and record it as the final dough temperature. Cover the dough.

4. Bulk fermentation

- **Duration:** About 3 hours at warm room temperature: 74°–76°F (23°–24°C)
- **Folds:** 4 sets of stretches and folds at 30-minute intervals

- **SET TIMER AND MAKE A NOTE:** Write down the current time as the start of bulk fermentation, set a timer for 30 minutes, and let the dough rest in a warm place.

- **STRETCH AND FOLD:** When your timer goes off, give the dough one set of stretches and folds. Using wet hands, grab one side of the dough and lift it up and over to the other side. Rotate the bowl 180 degrees and repeat. Then rotate the bowl a quarter turn and stretch and fold that side. Rotate the bowl 180 degrees again and finish with a stretch and fold on the last side. The dough should be folded up neatly. Cover and repeat these folds every 30 minutes for a total of 4 sets of stretches and folds.

- **LET THE DOUGH REST:** After the last set, cover the bowl and let the dough rest for the remainder of bulk fermentation, about 1 hour.

5. Divide and preshape

- **CHECK THE DOUGH:** At the end of bulk fermentation, the dough will have risen in the bulk container, it may have bubbles on top and at the sides and should look smoother and less shaggy. Because of the high hydration and nature of whole wheat doughs, you won't see the same domed edge with this one—it will likely be there, but not as prominently. If you wet a hand and gently tug on the surface of the dough, it will feel elastic and cohesive, resisting your pull. If you don't see dough that's airy, strong, and "alive," leave it for another 15 minutes in bulk fermentation and check again.

- **DIVIDE AND PRESHAPE THE DOUGH:** Using a bowl scraper, gently scrape the dough onto a clean work surface and use your bench knife to divide it directly in half. Using your bench knife in your dominant hand and with your other hand wet to reduce sticking, shape each piece of dough into a moderately tight round. (See Preshaping, page 96, for more detail.) Let the rounds rest for 25 minutes, uncovered.

6. Shape

- **PREPARE THE PROOFING BASKETS:** Line two proofing baskets or bowls with clean kitchen towels. Dust lightly and evenly with white flour.

- **SHAPE THE DOUGH:** Shape each as a boule or a bâtard (see pages 102 to 107 for details). Gently transfer each piece to a proofing basket, seam-side up. Place each basket inside a reusable plastic bag and seal.

RECIPE CONTINUES ›

FREE-FORM LOAVES

Proofing Timing

Whole wheat is very sensitive to overproofing, so it might be best to err on the side of underproofing just slightly if doing the same-day bake—get it into the oven a little before you'd usually think it's sufficiently proofed.

7. Proof

- **Duration:** 1 to 2 hours at warm room temperature (74°–76°F/23°–24°C) or 15 hours (overnight) in a home refrigerator (39°F/4°C)

- **LET THE DOUGH PROOF:** You have two proofing options.

  - Same-day bake: Let the dough proof in a warm place for 1 to 2 hours, or until a finger pressed into the dough fills back in relatively quickly.

  - Next-day bake: Place the baskets in the refrigerator to proof overnight.

8. Bake

- **Duration:** 50 to 55 minutes in the oven

- **PREPARE THE OVEN:** Place an oven rack in the bottom third of the oven with no rack above it. Place a Dutch oven/combo cooker inside the oven and preheat to 450°F (230°C) for at least 30 minutes. (Alternatively, bake directly on a baking stone/steel; see page 124 for details.)

- **SCORE THE DOUGH:** Take one of the proofing baskets out of the fridge, uncover, and put a piece of parchment paper over the basket. Place a pizza peel or inverted sheet pan on top of the parchment and, using both hands, flip everything over. Gently remove the basket and score the dough. (See Scoring, page 118, for details.)

- **BAKE THE DOUGH:** Slide the dough into the preheated Dutch oven and cover with the lid. Bake for 20 minutes, then remove the lid. Continue to bake for 30 to 35 minutes, or until the internal temperature reaches 206°–210°F (96°–99°C) and the crust has a deep mahogany color and a crackle/crunch when gently squeezed.

- **FINISH AND COOL:** Let the loaf cool on a wire rack for at least 2 to 3 hours before slicing. For the second loaf, preheat the Dutch oven for 15 minutes and repeat.

TROUBLESHOOTING

MY LOAF DIDN'T RISE IN THE OVEN.

One hundred percent whole wheat can quickly overproof. Be sure to watch the dough and adjust the timing of each step as necessary, since the temperature in your kitchen and, more important, that of the dough itself will affect the proof time. On your next bake, try to keep everything as consistent as possible and reduce the final proof time by 30 minutes if proofing on the counter, and 2 to 3 hours if in the refrigerator.

THE CRUMB IS GUMMY AND "WET."

This could be a few things. First, be sure to fully bake the loaves. Second, don't cut the loaves too early—if you cut too soon with highly hydrated loaves like these, the interior will be gummy.

HOW TO TINKER

SIFT AND SCALD

To open the interior on this loaf, after making your levain, use a sifting screen to sift the larger bran and germ pieces from the whole wheat flour. Transfer the pieces left in the screen to a heatproof bowl and set on a scale. Tare the scale and pour in boiling water just until it has covered the grain pieces. Stir well. Write down how much water you used and deduct that amount from Water 1. Be sure to do this sifting and scalding at the same time as you make the levain to give the mixture time to cool before you add it to the dough. During bulk fermentation, spread the mixture over the dough and work it in during the sets of stretches and folds.

FIVE-GRAIN SOURDOUGH

A nourishing bread brimming with grains, seeds, and even a pseudocereal

IF YOU count the wheat and rye flours in this recipe, it should probably be called a seven-grain sourdough. To confuse things further, the name is kind of a misnomer anyway because I like to include flaxseed and buckwheat, both of which are not technically considered grains at all (flaxseed is, of course, a seed, and buckwheat is a pseudocereal). But these two are so nutritious and flavorful, they deserve a place in this wholesome bread. What this bread has in naming issues, it more than makes up for in flavor and healthfulness. It's an incredibly flavor-forward loaf that is hearty and toothsome—the perfect bread for a thick minestrone.

Feel free to swap out any of the "grains" in the soaker for whatever you might have in your pantry. Instead of cracked spelt you could use cracked wheat or another grain, and instead of steel-cut oats you could use rolled oats or even flaked or rolled barley.

BAKING TIMELINE

1. Levain

   12 hours (overnight)

2. Mix

3. Bulk Fermentation

   3 hours 30 minutes

4. Divide, Preshape, Bench Rest

   35 minutes

5. Shape

6. Proof

   19 hours (overnight)

7. Bake

   55 minutes in the oven

   TOTAL
   36 hours

VITALS

Total dough weight	1,800g
Pre-fermented flour	9.7%
Levain	17.3%
Hydration	85.0%
Yield	Two 900g loaves

TOTAL FORMULA

INGREDIENT	BAKER'S %	WEIGHT
White flour (~11.5% protein)	70.0%	606g
Whole rye flour	15.0%	130g
Whole wheat flour	15.0%	130g
Whole spelt, cracked	5.0%	43g
Steel-cut oats	5.0%	43g
Polenta	4.0%	35g
Buckwheat groats, cracked	4.0%	35g
Flaxseeds	2.0%	17g
Water	85.0%	736g
Fine sea salt	1.8%	16g
Ripe sourdough starter, 100% hydration	0.9%	8g

ADDITIONAL INGREDIENT

Instant or old-fashioned rolled oats, for topping (optional)

INGREDIENT	BAKER'S %	WEIGHT
White flour (~11.5% protein)	50.0%	42g
Whole rye flour	50.0%	42g
Water	50.0%	42g
Ripe sourdough starter, 100% hydration	10.0%	8g

INGREDIENT	WEIGHT
White flour (~11.5% protein)	564g
Whole rye flour	88g
Whole wheat flour	130g
Water	521g
Fine sea salt	16g
Levain	134g

1. Prepare the levain and soaker

▧ **Duration:** 12 hours (overnight) at warm room temperature: 74°–76°F (23°–24°C)

● **MIX THE LEVAIN:** Warm or cool the water to about 78°F (25°C). In a medium bowl, mix the levain ingredients until well incorporated. Use your hands to knead the mixture until all dry bits of flour are incorporated (this stiff levain will feel strong and dry). Transfer the levain to a jar and loosely cover. Store in a warm place for 12 hours.

● **PREPARE THE SOAKER:** In a small heatproof bowl, combine the 43g cracked spelt, 43g oats, 35g polenta, 35g cracked buckwheat, 17g flaxseeds, and 173g boiling water. Stir well and let cool. Cover and set aside at room temperature until called for in bulk fermentation.

2. Mix

▧ **Desired dough temperature (DDT):** 78°F (25°C)

● **CHECK THE LEVAIN:** It should show signs of readiness: well aerated, risen, soft, sticky, and an assertive sour aroma. If the levain is not showing these signs, let it ferment 1 hour more and check again.

● **MIX THE DOUGH:** Warm or cool the water (see page 138 on how to calculate) so the temperature of the mixed dough meets the DDT of this recipe. In a large bowl, add the flour, water, salt, and ripe levain. Using wet hands, mix the ingredients until well incorporated.

● **STRENGTHEN THE DOUGH:** With wet hands, use the slap and fold method (see page 83) for about 5 minutes to strengthen the dough. The dough should look smooth and begin to hold its shape. If it is still shaggy and loose, continue to strengthen for a few more minutes, but don't worry if it doesn't smooth out completely. Transfer back to the bowl or another container for bulk fermentation.

● **MEASURE THE TEMPERATURE OF THE DOUGH:** Compare it to the DDT and record it as the final dough temperature. Cover the dough.

3. Bulk fermentation

▧ **Duration:** About 3 hours 30 minutes at warm room temperature: 74°–76°F (23°–24°C)

▧ **Folds:** 3 sets of stretches and folds at 30-minute intervals

● **SET TIMER AND MAKE A NOTE:** Write down the current time as the start of bulk fermentation, set a timer for 30 minutes, and let the dough rest in a warm place.

● **ADD THE GRAIN SOAKER AND STRETCH AND FOLD:** When your timer goes off, spread about one-quarter of the grains evenly over the dough. Using wet hands, pick up one side of the dough and stretch it up and fold it over. Spread another one-quarter of the grains over the top. Rotate the bowl 180 degrees and perform another stretch and fold. Evenly spread on another one-quarter of the grains. Rotate the bowl a quarter turn, perform a stretch and fold, and spread on the remaining grains. Rotate the bowl 180 degrees and perform the last stretch and fold. The dough should be folded up neatly. Cover and repeat these folds every 30 minutes for a total of 3 sets of stretches and folds.

● **LET THE DOUGH REST:** After the last set, cover the bowl and let the dough rest for the remainder of bulk fermentation, about 2 hours.

4. Divide and preshape

● **CHECK THE DOUGH:** At the end of bulk fermentation, the dough will have risen significantly; it may have bubbles on top and at the sides, it should look smoother and less shaggy, and at the edge of the dough where it meets the container, it should dome downward. If you wet a hand and gently tug on the surface of the dough, it will feel elastic and cohesive, resisting your pull. If you don't see dough that's airy, strong, and "alive," leave it for another 15 minutes in bulk fermentation and check again.

● **DIVIDE AND PRESHAPE THE DOUGH:** Using a bowl scraper, gently scrape the dough onto a clean work surface and use your bench knife to divide it directly in half. Using your bench knife in your dominant hand and with your other hand wet to reduce sticking, shape each piece of dough into a loose round. (See Preshaping, page 96, for more detail.) Let the rounds rest for 35 minutes, uncovered.

5. Shape

● **PREPARE THE PROOFING BASKETS:** Line two proofing baskets or bowls with clean kitchen towels. Dust lightly and evenly with white flour.

● **SHAPE THE DOUGH:** Shape each as a boule or a bâtard (see pages 102 to 107 for details).

● **ADD THE TOPPING (OPTIONAL BUT RECOMMENDED):** Spread an even layer of oats in a sheet pan or on a clean kitchen towel. After shaping each piece of dough, quickly roll the top side in the oats so they stick. (See Add Toppings to Your Bread Dough, page 105, for more detail.) Gently transfer each piece to a proofing basket, seam-side up. Place each basket inside a reusable plastic bag and seal.

6. Proof

▪ **Duration:** About 19 hours (overnight) in a home refrigerator: 39°F (4°C)

● **LET THE DOUGH PROOF:** Place the baskets in the refrigerator to proof overnight.

RECIPE CONTINUES →

7. Bake

▪ **Duration:** 50 to 55 minutes in the oven

● **PREPARE THE OVEN:** Place an oven rack in the bottom third of the oven with no rack above it. Place a Dutch oven/combo cooker inside the oven and preheat to 450°F (230°C) for at least 30 minutes. (Alternatively, bake directly on a baking stone/steel; see page 124 for details.)

● **SCORE THE DOUGH:** Take one of the proofing baskets out of the fridge, uncover, and put a piece of parchment paper over the basket. Place a pizza peel or inverted sheet pan on top of the parchment and, using both hands, flip everything over. Gently remove the basket and score the dough. (See Scoring, page 118, for details.)

● **BAKE THE DOUGH:** Slide the dough with the parchment into the preheated Dutch oven and cover with the lid. Bake for 20 minutes, then remove the lid. Continue to bake for 30 to 35 minutes, or until the internal temperature reaches 206°–210°F (96°–99°C) and the crust has a deep mahogany color and a crackle/crunch when gently squeezed.

● **FINISH AND COOL:** Let the loaf cool on a wire rack for 1 to 2 hours before slicing. For the second loaf, preheat the Dutch oven or baking surface for 15 minutes and repeat.

OAT PORRIDGE

Hefty, hearty, and incredibly tender

I FIRST dabbled with this style of bread many years ago, inspired by the loaves made at Tartine Bakery in California. These days, it seems you can find a variation of this bread in many bakeries, and for good reason: The oat porridge brings softness, flavor, and added nutrition, producing a weighty loaf with a deeply caramelized crust that has a subtle browned-butter flavor. I used to cook the oats into a proper porridge, but these days I simply cover them with boiling water to soften while the levain is ripening. I love to top this bread with instant oats, which have a thinner, broken, rough texture, hinting at what the loaf carries—quite abundantly—inside.

BAKING TIMELINE

1. **Levain**

   5 hours

2. **Mix**

3. **Bulk Fermentation**

   3 hours 30 minutes

4. **Divide, Preshape, Bench Rest**

   35 minutes

5. **Shape**

6. **Proof**

   13 hours (overnight)

7. **Bake**

   55 minutes in the oven

TOTAL

23 hours

VITALS

Total dough weight	1,800g
Pre-fermented flour	6.5%
Levain	17.4%
Hydration	79.0%
Yield	Two 900g loaves

TOTAL FORMULA

INGREDIENT	BAKER'S %	WEIGHT
White flour (~11.5% protein)	55.0%	490g
Whole wheat flour	25.0%	223g
High-protein white flour (~12.7%–14% protein)	20.0%	178g
Old-fashioned rolled oats	18.0%	160g
Water	79.0%	703g
Fine sea salt	1.9%	17g
Ripe sourdough starter, 100% hydration	3.3%	29g

ADDITIONAL INGREDIENT

Instant oats, for topping (optional)

INGREDIENT	BAKER'S %	WEIGHT
White flour (~11.5% protein)	50.0%	29g
Whole wheat flour	50.0%	29g
Water	100.0%	58g
Ripe sourdough starter, 100% hydration	50.0%	29g

INGREDIENT	WEIGHT
White flour (~11.5% protein)	461g
Whole wheat flour	194g
High-protein white flour (~12.7%-14% protein)	178g
Water	445g
Fine sea salt	17g
Levain	145g

1. Prepare the levain and oat porridge

▪ **Duration:** 5 hours at warm room temperature: 74°–76°F (23°–24°C)

● **MIX THE LEVAIN:** Warm or cool the water to about 78°F (25°C). In a medium jar, mix the levain ingredients until well incorporated (this liquid levain will feel quite loose) and loosely cover. Store in a warm place for 5 hours.

● **PREPARE THE OAT PORRIDGE:** Put the 160g rolled oats in a medium bowl, pour 200g boiling water over them, and stir well. Let cool. Cover and set aside until bulk fermentation.

2. Mix

▪ **Desired dough temperature (DDT):** 78°F (25°C)

● **CHECK THE LEVAIN:** It should show signs of readiness: well aerated, risen, bubbly on top and at the sides, loose, and with a sour aroma. If the levain is not showing these signs, let it ferment 15 minutes more and check again.

● **MIX THE DOUGH:** Warm or cool the water (see page 138 on how to calculate) so the temperature of the mixed dough meets the DDT of this recipe. Place the flour, water, salt, and ripe levain in a large bowl. Using wet hands, mix the ingredients until well incorporated. Because a sizable portion of the water was used to soak the oats, the dough might feel a little dry. If it does, add a small splash of water to increase the hydration. Continue to mix until the dough comes together and all the water is absorbed.

● **STRENGTHEN THE DOUGH:** With wet hands, use the slap and fold method (see page 83) for about 5 minutes to strengthen the dough. The dough should look smooth and begin to hold its shape. If it is still shaggy and weak, continue to strengthen for a few more minutes, but don't worry if it doesn't smooth out completely. Transfer back to the bowl or another container for bulk fermentation.

● **MEASURE THE TEMPERATURE OF THE DOUGH:** Compare it to the DDT and record it as the final dough temperature. Cover the dough.

3. Bulk fermentation

▪ **Duration:** About 3 hours 30 minutes at warm room temperature: 74°–76°F (23°–24°C)
▪ **Folds:** 4 sets of stretches and folds at 30-minute intervals

● **SET TIMER AND MAKE A NOTE:** Write down the current time as the start of bulk fermentation, set a timer for 30 minutes, and let the dough rest in a warm place.

● **ADD THE OAT PORRIDGE AND STRETCH AND FOLD:** When your timer goes off, spread about one-quarter of the oat porridge evenly over the dough. Using damp hands, pick up one side of the dough and stretch it up and fold it over. Spread another one-quarter of the porridge over the top. Rotate the bowl 180 degrees and

RECIPE CONTINUES →

perform another stretch and fold. Evenly spread on another one-quarter of the porridge. Rotate the bowl a quarter turn, perform a stretch and fold, and spread on the remaining porridge. Rotate the bowl 180 degrees and perform the last stretch and fold. The dough should be folded up neatly. Cover and repeat these folds every 30 minutes for a total of 4 sets of stretches and folds.

● **LET THE DOUGH REST:** After the last set, cover the bowl and let the dough rest for the remainder of bulk fermentation, about 1 hour 30 minutes.

4. Divide and preshape

● **CHECK THE DOUGH:** At the end of bulk fermentation, the dough will have risen significantly; it may have bubbles on top and at the sides, it should look smoother and less shaggy, and at the edge of the dough where it meets the container, it should dome downward. If you wet a hand and gently tug on the surface of the dough, it will feel elastic and cohesive, resisting your pull. If you don't see dough that's airy, strong, and "alive," leave it for another 15 minutes in bulk fermentation and check again.

● **DIVIDE AND PRESHAPE THE DOUGH:** Using a bowl scraper, gently scrape the dough onto a clean work surface and use your bench knife to divide it directly in half. Using your bench knife in your dominant hand and with your other hand wet to reduce sticking, shape each piece of dough into a loose round. (See Preshaping, page 96, for more detail.) Let the rounds rest for 35 minutes, uncovered.

5. Shape

● **PREPARE THE PROOFING BASKETS:** Line two proofing baskets or bowls with clean kitchen towels. Dust lightly and evenly with white flour.

● **SHAPE THE DOUGH:** Shape each as a boule or a bâtard. (See pages 102 to 107 for more detail.)

● **ADD THE TOPPING (OPTIONAL BUT RECOMMENDED):** Spread an even layer of instant oats in a sheet pan or on a clean kitchen towel. After shaping each piece of dough, quickly roll the top side in the oats so they stick. (See Add Toppings to Your Bread Dough, page 105, for more detail.) Gently transfer each piece to a proofing basket, seam-side up. Place each basket inside a reusable plastic bag and seal.

TROUBLESHOOTING

THE DOUGH IS WAY TOO WET AND SLACK!

Incorporating a porridge can be challenging, especially as the soaked oats tend to release water into the dough during bulk fermentation. If you get to the shaping stage and the dough is just completely unmanageable, divide the dough in half and shape it as best you can to get each half into a loaf pan (a Pullman pan without the lid or standard loaf pan) and bake at 425°F (220°C) with steam for 20 minutes, vent the steam, then reduce the temperature to 375°F (190°C) and bake for 30 minutes, or until the internal temperature reaches 204°F (95°C). The result is pretty fantastic! Next time, hold back more water through mixing, even if the dough feels firm.

6. Proof

▫ **Duration:** About 13 hours (overnight) in a home refrigerator: 39°F (4°C)

● **LET THE DOUGH PROOF:** Place the baskets in the refrigerator to proof overnight.

7. Bake

▫ **Duration:** 50 to 55 minutes in the oven

● **PREPARE THE OVEN:** Place an oven rack in the bottom third of the oven with no rack above it. Place a Dutch oven/combo cooker inside the oven and preheat to 450°F (230°C) for at least 30 minutes. (Alternatively, bake directly on a baking stone/steel; see page 124 for details.)

● **SCORE THE DOUGH:** Take one of the proofing baskets out of the fridge, uncover, and put a piece of parchment paper over the basket. Place a pizza peel or inverted sheet pan on top of the parchment and, using both hands, flip everything over. Gently remove the basket and score the dough. (See Scoring, page 118, for details.)

● **BAKE THE DOUGH:** Slide the dough with the parchment into the preheated Dutch oven and cover with the lid. Bake for 20 minutes, then remove the lid. Continue to bake for 30 to 35 minutes, or until the internal temperature reaches 206°-210°F (96°-99°C) and the crust has a deep mahogany color and a crackle/crunch when gently squeezed.

● **FINISH AND COOL:** Let the loaf cool on a wire rack for 1 to 2 hours before slicing. For the second loaf, preheat the Dutch oven or baking surface for 15 minutes and repeat.

HOW TO TINKER

USE TOASTED STEEL-CUT OATS

Swap out the rolled oats for the same quantity of steel-cut oats that have been first toasted in a skillet or roasted in the oven until golden brown. Toasting the oats amplifies their flavor and adds a subtle nuttiness to this bread.

CHANGE THE TOPPER

Play with different flavors and textures: sesame seeds, wheat bran, or even pepitas.

TINKERING WITH SOURNESS

Techniques for increasing or decreasing the acidity of your loaves

At its heart, sourdough breadmaking revolves around tinkering with microbes. The goal is to balance the yeast and bacterial activity in your starter, levain, and final dough to produce bread with ample flavor, nutrition, and pleasing eating qualities. Some bakers want a strong sour taste, whether it's to pair the bread with other foods or simply to make the mouth water. Others desire a subtler sourness to help elevate the flavor inherent in the grain, to boost sweetness, or just for a mild flavor profile overall. There are many parts of a bread formula you can play with to shift this balance: dough temperature, total fermentation time, flour choice, inoculation percentages, and more.

As you know with breadmaking, each part of the process has an impact on every other thing. With so many interrelated components, it's very hard to isolate and change a single element and be able to correlate that with an outcome—and this holds true for changing the flavor profile. For instance, it's hard to make a blanket statement that a dough with a high final dough temperature will result in a sourer loaf than one with a cooler temperature. Why? Because many other inputs must be considered as well (e.g., flour choice, pre-fermented flour percentage, final dough temperature of

the pre-ferment, and so on). However, we can step back and look at this from a broader perspective: Think about what changing a single component might do to the overall dough system, then piece together a path forward for a recipe that'll get us to the flavor profile that we're after. For example, if we want to add a little more sourness to our bread, we could look at increasing the whole-grain percentage in the levain and final dough and see how that affects the outcome. If the result doesn't achieve our goal, then we can look at taking the same dough and increasing the total fermentation time with a cold bulk fermentation and cold proof, and taste the results. If the flavor is too sour, we could then adjust it by dropping the cold bulk fermentation but keeping the cold proof.

The challenge (and dare I say, fun!) for sourdough bakers is to weave together a plan for altering these components to create the tapestry of the final loaf they're after. So let's look at a few of the levers I like to pull when adjusting the sourness in a loaf of sourdough bread. Keep in mind the following holds true in doughs that are lean, i.e., without the presence of sugar, egg, or butter.

Then we'll move on to Extra-Sour Sourdough (page 237) where we can apply these modifications to a dough to increase sourness while still producing a loaf that's texturally pleasing and delicious.

LESS SOUR	MORE SOUR	WHY?
Fewer whole grains	More whole grains	Whole grains (specifically whole wheat) buffer acidity, which allows bacteria to function longer. Bacteria are sensitive to low pH and growth decreases as pH drops. Increasing whole grains allows bacteria to produce more acidity overall.
Lower dough temperature	Higher dough temperature	Most sourdough bacteria have optimal growth at around 89°-91°F (32°-33°C).
Shorter bulk fermentation (within reason)	Longer bulk fermentation (within reason)	Letting bacteria function longer allows for more acid accumulation in the dough.
Larger pre-fermented flour percentage (pH ↓)	Smaller pre-fermented flour percentage (pH ↑)	A larger pre-ferment starts the dough's pH at a lower level. Bacterial activity is reduced at low pH.
Use starter or levain earlier before it is overly ripe	Let starter or levain ripen longer and use when very ripe	By allowing fermentation to continue longer, bacteria can function longer, which means greater bacterial growth and total acid accumulation.

PFF Percentage and Sourness

A common misconception is that simply increasing the pre-fermented flour (PFF) percentage in a recipe will result in a sourer final loaf ("If you want a sour bread, use more starter!"). In my experience, *only* increasing the PFF percentage won't bring ample sourness. Other important factors must also be considered, such as flour choice, temperature, total fermentation time, and starter/levain maintenance.

EXTRA-SOUR SOURDOUGH

Bread with lingering
sourness, a crispy crust,
and a tighter crumb

BAKING TIMELINE

1 Levain

  12 hours (overnight)

2 Mix

3 Warm Bulk Fermentation

  2 hours 30 minutes

4 Cold Bulk Fermentation

  12 hours (overnight)

5 Divide, Preshape,
Bench Rest

  1 hour

6 Shape

7 Warm Proof

  1 hour

8 Cold Proof

  12 hours (overnight)

9 Bake

  50 minutes in the oven

TOTAL
41 hours 20 minutes

"SOUR" HERE isn't the mouth-puckering variety, but, rather, a sourness that builds quickly and lingers. It's the kind that gets your mouth watering, like a pleasantly mild vinegar; and when baked dark, as I often do, the crust takes on a toasted nut flavor that complements the increased sourness. This is a delicious bread, and one I find goes incredibly well with aged cheese and olives, seafood, hearty stews, and even a dark beer.

In the following formula, we're trying to create favorable conditions for increasing bacterial cell population and activity, all with the end goal of increasing the total accumulated acidity in the dough. These conditions are created in a few ways: altering the flour types and amounts, dough temperature, fermentation time, and inoculation percentages. Each of these aspects of breadmaking is a contributing factor to adjusting the sour flavor of a loaf (see Tinkering with Sourness, page 234, for more detail).

Keep in mind that the following formula and process is not the only way to make a loaf of extra-sour sourdough bread. My hope is that you'll take some of these lessons into your own baking, working to adjust your favorite recipe to be more or less sour as you desire.

VITALS

Total dough weight	1,800g
Pre-fermented flour	4.0%
Levain	9.2%
Hydration	75.0%
Yield	Two 900g loaves

TOTAL FORMULA

INGREDIENT	BAKER'S %	WEIGHT
White flour (~11.5% protein)	65.0%	660g
Whole wheat flour	20.0%	203g
Whole rye flour	15.0%	153g
Water	75.0%	761g
Fine sea salt	2.0%	20g
Ripe sourdough starter, 100% hydration	0.4%	4g

INGREDIENT	BAKER'S %	WEIGHT
Whole rye flour	100.0%	41g
Water	110.0%	45g
Ripe sourdough starter, 100% hydration	10.0%	4g

1. Levain

- ▪ **Duration:** 12 hours (overnight) at warm room temperature: 74°–76°F (23°–24°C)

- ● **MIX THE LEVAIN:** Temperature is very important with this levain, so be sure to warm the water to about 82°F (28°C)—yes, it's warm! In a medium jar, mix the levain ingredients until well incorporated (this liquid levain will feel quite loose) and loosely cover. Store in a warm place for 12 hours.

INGREDIENT	WEIGHT
White flour (~11.5% protein)	660g
Whole wheat flour	203g
Whole rye flour	112g
Water	716g
Fine sea salt	20g
Levain	90g

2. Mix

- ▪ **Desired dough temperature (DDT):** 82°F (28°C)

- ● **CHECK THE LEVAIN:** It should show signs of readiness: well aerated, risen, soft, sticky, and with very sharp sour aroma. If the levain is not showing these signs, let it ferment 1 hour more and check again.

- ● **MIX THE DOUGH:** Warm or cool the water (see page 138 on how to calculate) so the temperature of the mixed dough meets the DDT of this recipe. (As with the levain, we want a warm final dough temperature because warmth encourages bacterial activity.) Place the flour, water, salt, and ripe levain in a large bowl. Using wet hands, mix the ingredients until well incorporated.

A LEVAIN FOR MAXIMUM SOURNESS

It's long-running: A longer running levain helps shift the balance between yeasts and bacteria toward increased bacterial activity, and with the other parameters in this recipe, helps emphasize the effects of their products (increased sourness). In general, bacteria grow faster but start later, whereas yeasts grow more slowly but start earlier. Additionally, this levain has favorable conditions (temperature, pH, etc.) to allow bacteria to function for longer than in a shorter running levain. It takes time for the products of lactic fermentation to accumulate, and we want that accumulation to increase sourness.

It uses whole-grain flour and warm temperatures: Whole-grain flour, which is rich in phytate compounds that help buffer acidity, can take on more acid before the pH drops enough to reduce bacterial activity. This means an increase in lactic fermentation, contributing to greater acidity. There are many possible sourdough bacteria, and they all have their own ideal temperature range (optimal temperature for the most common bacteria found in sourdough starters is around 89°F/32°C), but a warm temperature of 82°F (28°C) is a good compromise; it's warm enough to encourage strong growth without exceeding temperatures that would hamper the yeast. So a warm levain (and final dough) temperature will ensure ample bacterial activity. With all of this, you'll certainly smell the effects when you check the levain after it has fermented for about 12 hours: It

will have a pungent sour aroma and, if tasted, a sharp tang on the tongue.

The levain amount is quite small: A ripe levain brings along with it a potentially high acidity level (low pH). If a substantial amount of that levain is mixed into the rest of the dough, it will start off in a more "spent" condition and can drop the pH of the dough relatively quickly, accelerating the dough-degrading process. Using less levain starts the dough at a higher pH and slows fermentation, so acidity increases more gradually, preserving the dough's structure by delaying breakdown. This may make it possible for more acid accumulation in the final loaf, before pH-activated enzymes can compromise dough structure.

- **STRENGTHEN THE DOUGH:** With wet hands, use the slap and fold method (see page 83) for 3 to 5 minutes to strengthen the dough. This is a lower hydration dough, so it may only take a few minutes to become smoother and begin to hold shape. If it is still shaggy and loose, continue to strengthen for a few more minutes, but don't worry if it doesn't smooth out completely. Transfer back to the bowl or another container for bulk fermentation.

- **MEASURE THE TEMPERATURE OF THE DOUGH:** Compare it to the DDT and record it as the final dough temperature. Cover the dough.

3. Warm bulk fermentation

- Duration: About 2 hours 30 minutes at warm room temperature: 74°–76°F (23°–24°C)
- Folds: 3 sets of stretches and folds at 30-minute intervals

- **SET TIMER AND MAKE A NOTE:** Write down the current time as the start of bulk fermentation, set a timer for 30 minutes, and let the dough rest in a warm place.

- **STRETCH AND FOLD:** When your timer goes off, give the dough one set of stretches and folds. Using wet hands, grab one side of the dough and lift it up and over to the other side. Rotate the bowl 180 degrees and repeat. Then rotate the bowl a quarter turn and stretch and fold that side. Rotate the bowl 180 degrees again and finish with a stretch and fold on the last side. The dough should be folded up neatly. Cover and repeat these folds every 30 minutes for a total of 3 sets of stretches and folds.

- **LET THE DOUGH REST:** After the last set, cover the bowl and let the dough rest for the remainder of the warm bulk fermentation, about 1 hour.

4. Cold bulk fermentation

- Duration: About 12 hours (overnight) in a home refrigerator: 39°F (4°C)
- Folds: None

- **MOVE THE DOUGH TO THE REFRIGERATOR:** After the warm bulk fermentation, place the covered bulk fermentation container in the refrigerator overnight.

5. Divide and preshape

- **DIVIDE AND PRESHAPE THE DOUGH:** Uncover the bulk fermentation container and, using a bowl scraper, gently scrape the dough onto a clean work surface and use your bench knife to divide it directly in half. The dough will feel firm and tacky. If it's too firm to divide and preshape, let it warm up for 15 minutes, uncovered. Using your bench knife in your dominant hand, and with your other hand wet to reduce sticking, shape each piece of dough into a loose round. (See Preshaping, page 96, for more detail.) Let the rounds rest for 45 minutes to 1 hour, uncovered. Proceed with shaping once the dough has relaxed outward and is just slightly cold to the touch.

Long Bulk Fermentation

Similar to the long-running levain for this recipe, a longer bulk fermentation—both warm and cold phases—gives the bacteria more time to work and produce more acid overall.

RECIPE CONTINUES →

6. Shape

● **PREPARE THE PROOFING BASKETS:** Line two proofing baskets or bowls with clean kitchen towels. Dust lightly and evenly with white flour.

● **SHAPE THE DOUGH:** Shape each as a boule or a bâtard (see pages 102 to 107 for details). Gently transfer each piece to a proofing basket, seam-side up. Place each basket inside an airtight reusable plastic bag and seal.

7. Warm proof

▪ **Duration:** 1 hour at warm room temperature: 74°–76°F (23°–24°C)

● **LET THE DOUGH PROOF:** Place the baskets in a warm place to proof for 1 hour.

8. Cold proof

▪ **Duration:** About 12 hours (overnight) in a home refrigerator: 39°F (4°C)

● **LET THE DOUGH PROOF:** Place the baskets in the refrigerator to proof overnight.

9. Bake

▪ **Duration:** 50 to 55 minutes in the oven

● **PREPARE THE OVEN:** Place an oven rack in the bottom third of the oven with no rack above it. Place a Dutch oven/combo cooker inside the oven and preheat to 450°F (230°C) for at least 30 minutes. (Alternatively, bake directly on a baking stone/steel; see page 124 for details.)

● **SCORE THE DOUGH:** Take one of the proofing baskets out of the fridge, uncover, and put a piece of parchment paper over the basket. Place a pizza peel or inverted baking sheet on top of the parchment and, using both hands, flip everything over. Gently remove the basket and score the dough. (See Scoring, page 118, for details.)

● **BAKE THE DOUGH:** Slide the dough with the parchment into the preheated Dutch oven and cover with the lid. Bake for 20 minutes, then remove the lid. Continue to bake for 30 to 35 minutes, or until the internal temperature reaches 206°–210°F (96°–99°C) and the crust has a deep mahogany color and a crackle/crunch when gently squeezed.

● **FINISH AND COOL:** Let the loaf cool on a wire rack for 1 to 2 hours before slicing. For the second loaf, preheat the Dutch oven for 15 minutes and repeat.

HOW TO TINKER

TAKE THE SOURNESS FURTHER

Instead of refreshing your starter twice a day, only refresh it once a day. For this refreshment, keep only a very small amount of ripe starter in the jar, and to that refresh with at least 50% whole-grain wheat or rye flour with respect to the total flour. Additionally, you could leave the dough in the refrigerator for an extra day after the overnight proof.

Cold Proofing = More Sour

Proofing the dough in a home refrigerator, which is usually around 39°F (4°C), allows bacteria to continue functioning (although at a reduced rate) while most yeast activity slows down significantly. The result is increased acid—especially acetic acid—accumulation in the final loaves.

COUNTRY ITALIAN
(Pane Pugliese)

Rustic bread with a golden crust and crumb

THIS RECIPE is reminiscent of the free-form bread I remember eating most often in the Puglia region of southern Italy where my family is from. I like to shape the dough into a large oval or tube shape, top it with raw wheat bran, score it a little wildly, and bake it boldly—this results in a rustic loaf with a craggy crust evoking the wild and expressive thousand-year-old olive trees grown in the region. This recipe does not call for an overnight cold proof: The dough is baked on the same day that it's mixed for a loaf with mild fermentation flavor. The interior is soft and airy, and the durum in the mix reveals itself prominently through the golden hue of the crumb—the contrast between rough-textured crust and delicate crumb is striking. This is bread meant for the dinner table: large, humble loaves that can be sliced or torn into pieces and placed into a basket or bowl lined with a napkin.

Durum wheat is often used in pasta making, usually labeled as semolina, which is coarsely milled durum. For breadmaking, source the more finely milled version, labeled as either "durum flour," "semolina rimacinata" (twice-milled semolina), or sometimes "durum, extra fancy." The consistency of the flour is key and should be like a powder—like other bread flour—and not like coarse beach sand, as is the case with semolina.

BAKING TIMELINE

1. **Levain**

   12 hours (overnight)

2. **Autolyse**

   1 hour

3. **Mix**

4. **Bulk Fermentation**

   3 hours

5. **Divide, Preshape, Bench Rest**

   30 minutes

6. **Shape**

7. **Proof**

   2 hours

8. **Bake**

   55 minutes in the oven

TOTAL
18 hours 25 minutes

VITALS

Total dough weight	1,800g
Pre-fermented flour	12.1%
Levain	22.0%
Hydration	81.0%
Yield	Two 900g loaves

TOTAL FORMULA

INGREDIENT	BAKER'S %	WEIGHT
White flour (~11.5% protein)	47.0%	460g
Durum flour, "extra fancy" (semolina rimacinata)	38.0%	372g
Whole wheat flour	15.0%	147g
Water 1 (levain and autolyse)	75.0%	734g
Water 2 (mix)	6.0%	59g
Fine sea salt	1.8%	18g
Ripe sourdough starter, 100% hydration	1.2%	12g

ADDITIONAL INGREDIENT

Wheat bran, for topping (optional)

INGREDIENT	BAKER'S %	WEIGHT
White flour (~11.5% protein)	50.0%	59g
Whole wheat flour	50.0%	59g
Water 1	50.0%	59g
Ripe sourdough starter, 100% hydration	10.0%	12g

INGREDIENT	WEIGHT
White flour (~11.5% protein)	401g
Durum flour	372g
Whole wheat flour	88g
Water 1	675g

INGREDIENT	WEIGHT
Water 2	59g
Fine sea salt	18g
Levain	189g

1. Levain

- ▦ **Duration:** 12 hours (overnight) at warm room temperature: 74°–76°F (23°–24°C)

- ● **MIX THE LEVAIN:** Warm or cool the water to about 78°F (25°C). In a medium bowl, mix the levain ingredients until well incorporated. Use your hands to knead the mixture until all dry bits of flour are incorporated (this stiff levain will feel strong and dry). Transfer the levain to a jar and loosely cover. Store in a warm place for 12 hours.

2. Autolyse

- ▦ **Duration:** 1 hour at warm room temperature: 74°–76°F (23°–24°C)
- ▦ **Desired dough temperature (DDT):** 78°F (25°C)

- ● **MIX THE AUTOLYSE:** About 1 hour before the levain is ready, warm or cool the autolyse water (see page 138 on how to calculate) so the temperature of the mixed dough meets the DDT for this recipe. Place the water and the flour in a large bowl and use wet hands to mix until no dry bits remain. Use a bowl scraper to scrape down the sides of the bowl to keep all the dough in one area at the bottom. Cover the bowl and place it near your levain for 1 hour.

3. Mix

- ▦ **Desired dough temperature (DDT):** 78°F (25°C)

- ● **CHECK THE LEVAIN:** It should show signs of readiness: well aerated, risen, soft, sticky, and an assertive sour aroma. If the levain is not showing these signs, let it ferment 1 hour more and check again.

- ● **ADJUST THE WATER TEMPERATURE:** Take the temperature of the dough and compare it to the DDT for this recipe: If it's higher, use cold water for the remaining water; if it's lower, use warm water.

- ● **MIX THE DOUGH:** To the autolyse, add about half of the water, the salt, and ripe levain. Using wet hands, mix the ingredients until well incorporated. If the dough feels very wet, slack, and loose, don't add the remaining water. Otherwise, add the rest of the water and continue to mix until the dough comes together and all the water is absorbed.

- ● **STRENGTHEN THE DOUGH:** With wet hands, use the slap and fold method (see page 83) to strengthen the dough for 6 to 8 minutes. The dough should look smooth and begin to hold its shape. If it's still shaggy and loose, continue to strengthen for a few more minutes, but don't worry if it doesn't smooth out completely. Transfer back to the bowl or another container for bulk fermentation.

- ● **MEASURE THE TEMPERATURE OF THE DOUGH:** Compare it to the DDT and record it as the final dough temperature. Cover the dough.

RECIPE CONTINUES →

4. Bulk fermentation

- **Duration:** About 3 hours at warm room temperature: 74°–76°F (23°–24°C)
- **Folds:** 3 sets of stretches and folds at 30-minute intervals

● **SET TIMER AND MAKE A NOTE:** Write down the current time as the start of bulk fermentation, set a timer for 30 minutes, and let the dough rest in a warm place.

● **STRETCH AND FOLD:** When your timer goes off, give the dough one set of stretches and folds. Using wet hands, grab one side of the dough and lift it up and over to the other side. Rotate the bowl 180 degrees and repeat. Then rotate the bowl a quarter turn and stretch and fold that side. Rotate the bowl 180 degrees again and finish with a stretch and fold on the last side. The dough should be folded up neatly. Cover and repeat these folds every 30 minutes for a total of 3 sets of stretches and folds.

● **LET THE DOUGH REST:** After the last set, cover the bowl and let the dough rest for the remainder of bulk fermentation, about 1 hour 30 minutes.

5. Divide and preshape

Tight Preshape

This dough may have risen significantly in the bulk fermentation container and be quite loose, so be sure to preshape it rather tightly.

● **CHECK THE DOUGH:** At the end of bulk fermentation, the dough will have risen significantly; it may have bubbles on top and at the sides, should look smoother and less shaggy, and at the edge of the dough where it meets the container, it should dome downward. If you wet a hand and gently tug on the surface of the dough, it will feel elastic and cohesive, resisting your pull. If you don't see dough that's airy, strong, and "alive," leave it for another 15 minutes in bulk fermentation and check again.

● **DIVIDE AND PRESHAPE THE DOUGH:** Using a bowl scraper, gently scrape the dough onto a clean work surface and use your bench knife to divide it directly in half. Using your bench knife in your dominant hand and with your other hand wet to reduce sticking, shape each piece of dough into a tight round. (See Preshaping, page 96, for more detail.) Let the rounds rest for 30 minutes, uncovered.

6. Shape

Baskets

For this recipe, I like to use 14-inch-long oval baskets to let the dough relax outward, making for a long oval or tube shape. But keep in mind that if you opt for a long shape, the dough may not fit inside of a Dutch oven for baking.

● **PREPARE THE PROOFING BASKETS:** Line two proofing baskets or bowls with clean kitchen towels. Dust lightly and evenly with white flour.

● **SHAPE THE DOUGH:** Shape each as a bâtard or a boule (see pages 102 to 107 for details).

● **ADD THE TOPPING (OPTIONAL BUT RECOMMENDED):** Spread a thin layer of wheat bran in a sheet pan or on a clean kitchen towel. After shaping each piece of dough, quickly roll the top side in the wheat bran so it sticks. Gently transfer each piece to a proofing basket, seam-side up. Place each basket inside a reusable plastic bag and seal.

7. Proof

■ **Duration:** 1 hour 30 minutes to 2 hours at warm room temperature: 74°–76°F (23°–24°C)

● **LET THE DOUGH PROOF:** Put the baskets in a warm place to proof for 1 hour 30 minutes to 2 hours. Check on the dough periodically after the first hour. It is ready when it is puffy and soft, but not excessively bubbly or weak. You can also use the Poke Test (page 116).

8. Bake

■ **Duration:** 50 to 55 minutes in the oven

● **PREPARE THE OVEN:** Place an oven rack in the bottom third of the oven with no rack above it. Preheat a Dutch oven/combo cooker or baking stone/steel along with the oven and if using a steaming pan with lava rocks, add it to the bottom of the oven. Preheat the oven to 450°F (230°C) for at least 30 minutes. (Alternatively, bake directly on a baking stone/steel; see page 124 for details.)

● **SCORE THE DOUGH:** Take one of the proofing baskets out of the fridge, uncover, and put a piece of parchment paper over the basket. Place a pizza peel or inverted sheet pan on top of the parchment and, using both hands, flip everything over. Gently remove the basket and score the dough. (See Scoring, page 118, for details.)

● **BAKE THE DOUGH:** Slide the dough with the parchment into the preheated Dutch oven and cover with the lid. Bake for 20 minutes, then remove the lid. Continue to bake for 30 to 35 minutes, or until the internal temperature reaches 206°–210°F (96°–99°C) and the crust has a very deep mahogany color and a crackle/crunch when gently squeezed.

● **FINISH AND COOL:** Let the loaf cool on a wire rack for 1 to 2 hours before slicing. For the second loaf, preheat the Dutch oven or baking surface for 15 minutes and repeat.

Scoring

I like to score this dough with X shapes, one (for a boule) or three (for a bâtard), starting from one end and working to the other (as below).

HOW TO TINKER

TOPPING CHANGES

While I love topping these loaves with wheat bran for added crunch and nutrition, another Italian-inspired option would be white sesame seeds.

CRACKED SPELT

Nutty, naturally sweet, and wholesome—a loaf with freshly milled spelt and a cracked spelt soaker

AS A SPELT enthusiast, this wholesome loaf is a favorite of mine—and the delicious grain appears in this recipe in two different ways. First, a sizable portion of the flour in the recipe is freshly milled whole spelt, and second, a freshly cracked spelt soaker is included. The soaker brings additional textural interest—a little chew and toothsomeness—that complements the soft crumb and crunchy crust. In using spelt, being the magical grain that it is, the result is a loaf with a distinct yet gentle sweetness, tempered by the robust flavors of the whole grain. This is an unmistakably nutritious bread, both from the natural, long fermentation and the freshly milled whole grains incorporated into the dough.

If you do not have a grain mill, use the same amount of store-bought (aged) spelt flour instead of the freshly milled (you may need to reduce the total water in the recipe) and see How to Tinker on page 249 for options for the cracked spelt soaker.

BAKING TIMELINE

1. **Levain**

   12 hours (overnight)

2. **Mix**

3. **Bulk Fermentation**

   3 hours 30 minutes

4. **Divide, Preshape, Bench Rest**

   35 minutes

5. **Shape**

6. **Proof**

   19 hours (overnight)

7. **Bake**

   55 minutes in the oven

   TOTAL

   36 hours

VITALS

Total dough weight	1,800g
Pre-fermented flour	8.4%
Levain	14.8%
Hydration	85.0%
Yield	Two 900g loaves

TOTAL FORMULA

INGREDIENT	BAKER'S %	WEIGHT
White flour (~11.5% protein)	70.0%	612g
Whole spelt berries, for milling	30.0%	262g
Whole spelt berries, for cracking (soaker)	18.0%	158g
Water	85.0%	743g
Fine sea salt	1.8%	16g
Ripe sourdough starter, 100% hydration	0.8%	7g

1. Mill the flour and prepare the levain and soaker

▨ **Duration:** 12 hours (overnight) at warm room temperature: 74°–76°F (23°–24°C)

● **MILL THE FLOUR:** Mill the 262g whole spelt berries to a very fine granularity—I typically go as fine as my electric mill permits. Use some of the flour in the levain, and leave the rest out on the counter, covered, until the next day.

● **MIX THE LEVAIN:** Warm or cool the water to about 78°F (25°C). In a medium bowl, mix the levain ingredients until well incorporated. Use your hands to knead the mixture until all dry bits of flour are incorporated (this stiff levain will feel strong and dry). Transfer the levain to a jar and loosely cover. Store in a warm place for 12 hours.

● **MAKE THE CRACKED SPELT SOAKER:** Set your mill to the coarsest setting and let it run for a moment to clear out any debris. Mill the 158g whole spelt berries coarsely. When cracking, it's okay to keep any fine spelt pieces along with the coarse. Transfer to a heatproof bowl, pour in 173g boiling water, and stir well. Let cool. Cover and leave it out on the counter overnight until bulk fermentation.

INGREDIENT	BAKER'S %	WEIGHT
White flour (~11.5% protein)	50.0%	37g
Whole spelt flour, freshly milled	50.0%	37g
Water	50.0%	37g
Ripe sourdough starter, 100% hydration	10.0%	7g

2. Mix

▨ **Desired dough temperature (DDT):** 76°F (24°C)

● **CHECK THE LEVAIN:** It should show signs of readiness: well aerated, risen, soft, sticky, and an assertive sour aroma. If the levain is not showing these signs, let it ferment 1 hour more and check again.

● **MIX THE DOUGH:** Warm or cool the water (see page 138 on how to calculate) so the temperature of the mixed dough meets the DDT of this recipe. In a large bowl, add the flour, water, salt, and ripe levain. Using wet hands, mix the ingredients until well incorporated.

● **STRENGTHEN THE DOUGH:** With wet hands, use the slap and fold method (see page 83) for about 5 minutes to strengthen the dough. The dough should look smooth, feel rather firm, and begin to hold its shape. If it is still shaggy and loose, continue to strengthen for a few more minutes, but don't worry if it doesn't smooth out completely. Transfer back to the bowl or another container for bulk fermentation.

● **MEASURE THE TEMPERATURE OF THE DOUGH:** Compare it to the DDT and record it as the final dough temperature. Cover the dough.

INGREDIENT	WEIGHT
White flour (~11.5% protein)	575g
Whole spelt flour, freshly milled	225g
Water	533g
Fine sea salt	16g
Levain	118g

High Hydration

Because of the relatively high percentage of freshly milled whole-grain spelt flour and the cracked spelt soaker in this loaf, increased water is needed to properly hydrate the dough. Spelt is notorious for not responding well to high hydration, but because we're using fresh flour—which tends to want additional water—it's appropriate.

3. Bulk fermentation

▨ **Duration:** About 3 hours 30 minutes at warm room temperature: 74°–76°F (23°–24°C)

▨ **Folds:** 3 sets of stretches and folds at 30-minute intervals

● **SET TIMER AND MAKE A NOTE:** Write down the current time as the start of bulk fermentation, set a timer for 30 minutes, and let the dough rest in a warm place.

RECIPE CONTINUES ➔

● **ADD THE SOAKER AND STRETCH AND FOLD:** When your timer goes off, spread about one-quarter of the cracked spelt soaker (including any remaining water) evenly over the dough. Using wet hands, pick up one side of the dough and stretch it up and fold it over. Spread another one-quarter of the spelt over the top. Rotate the bowl 180 degrees and perform another stretch and fold. Evenly spread on another one-quarter of the spelt. Rotate the bowl a quarter turn, perform a stretch and fold, and spread on the remaining spelt. Rotate the bowl 180 degrees and perform the last stretch and fold. The dough should be folded up neatly. Cover and repeat these folds every 30 minutes for a total of 3 sets of stretches and folds.

● **LET THE DOUGH REST:** After the last set, cover the bowl and let the dough rest for the remainder of bulk fermentation, about 2 hours.

4. Divide and preshape

● **CHECK THE DOUGH:** At the end of bulk fermentation, the dough will have risen significantly; it may have bubbles on top and at the sides, it should look smoother and less shaggy, and at the edge of the dough where it meets the container, it should dome downward. If you wet a hand and gently tug on the surface of the dough, it will feel elastic and cohesive, resisting your pull. If you don't see dough that's airy, strong, and "alive," leave it for another 15 minutes in bulk fermentation and check again.

● **DIVIDE AND PRESHAPE THE DOUGH:** Using a bowl scraper, gently scrape the dough onto a clean work surface and use your bench knife to divide it directly in half. Using your bench knife in your dominant hand and with your other hand wet to reduce sticking, shape each piece of dough into a loose round. (See Preshaping, page 96, for more detail.) Let the rounds rest for 35 minutes, uncovered.

5. Shape

● **PREPARE THE PROOFING BASKETS:** Line two proofing baskets or bowls with clean kitchen towels. Dust lightly and evenly with white flour.

● **SHAPE THE DOUGH:** Shape each as a bâtard or a boule (see pages 102 to 107 for details). Gently transfer each piece to a proofing basket, seam-side up. Place each basket inside a reusable plastic bag and seal.

6. Proof

▪ **Duration:** About 19 hours (overnight) in a home refrigerator: 39°F (4°C)

● **LET THE DOUGH PROOF:** Place the baskets in the refrigerator to proof overnight.

7. Bake

▪ **Duration:** 50 to 55 minutes in the oven

● **PREPARE THE OVEN:** Place an oven rack in the bottom third of the oven with no rack above it. Place a Dutch oven/combo cooker inside the oven and preheat to 450°F (230°C) for at least 30 minutes. (Alternatively, bake directly on a baking stone/steel; see page 124 for details.)

● **SCORE THE DOUGH:** Take one of the proofing baskets out of the fridge, uncover, and put a piece of parchment paper over the basket. Place a pizza peel or inverted sheet pan on top of the parchment and, using both hands, flip everything over. Gently remove the basket and score the dough. (See Scoring, page 118, for details.) I like to score the dough with a simple circle that creates a lifted top.

● **BAKE THE DOUGH:** Slide the dough with the parchment into the preheated Dutch oven and cover with the lid. Bake for 20 minutes, then remove the lid. Continue to bake for 30 to 35 minutes, or until the internal temperature reaches 206°–210°F (96°–99°C) and the crust has a chestnut color and a crackle/crunch when gently squeezed.

● **FINISH AND COOL:** Let the loaf cool on a wire rack for 1 to 2 hours before slicing. For the second loaf, preheat the Dutch oven or baking surface for 15 minutes and repeat.

HOW TO TINKER

CHANGE THE GRAIN IN THE SOAKER

While cracked spelt is kind of the hallmark for this bread, you can still play with it by swapping it out for cracked wheat, Khorasan, rye, einkorn, or any other grain variety you have on hand. If you don't have a grain mill for cracking grain, use buckwheat cereal, steel-cut oats, or any other finely cracked cereal or grain you can find at your local market and prepare it as indicated in the recipe.

CRACKED SPELT TOPPER

An attractive—and nutritious—adornment for this bread is to use some of the smaller cracked spelt bits to top the loaves. When you crack the spelt, lightly sift out the bigger pieces to keep in the soaker. Lay out the smaller bits that fell through the sifter in a sheet pan or on a clean kitchen towel and after shaping roll the dough in them so that they stick to the top.

DEMI BAGUETTES

Light, crunchy, and ephemeral, with just a subtle hint of sourness

BAGUETTES ARE a baker's true test of commitment to the craft. At first glance, they may seem pretty simple, but the truth is, they take considerable practice—successful baguettes come down to repetition and working with intention. However, this should not discourage you! Fresh baguettes pulled from the home oven are a splendid thing. Even on your first attempt the result will be great, and there's no limit to the use of this bread in the kitchen.

The goal for baguettes is to have a clean flavor profile with minimal sourness; an open, soft, and light interior; and a thin and crunchy crust. My formula achieves all of these ideals with a mild yogurt-like sourness at the end of each bite and a crust that has a taste reminiscent of sweet, popped grain. The subtle sourness brings a wonderful complexity to the overall flavor profile, even if it's a departure from a classic baguette.

Due to the size restrictions of the typical home oven, the closest we can get to making baguettes (which are usually between 25 and 40 inches long) at home is to make demi baguettes—the word "demi" means half or half-size. In my oven, my baking surfaces typically run 14 inches deep, so my demi baguettes are also that length. Be sure to measure your baking surface and shape these baguettes no larger than its longest dimension.

BAKING TIMELINE

1. Levain

   5 hours

2. Autolyse

   1 hour

3. Mix

4. Warm Bulk Fermentation

   2 hours 30 minutes

5. Cold Bulk Fermentation

   17 hours (overnight)

6. Divide, Preshape, Bench Rest

   35 minutes

7. Shape

8. Proof

   1 hour 45 minutes

9. Bake

   40 minutes in the oven

TOTAL

27 hours 30 minutes

VITALS

Total dough weight	2,000g
Pre-fermented flour	6.5%
Levain	17.3%
Hydration	70.0%
Yield	Six 325g demi baguettes (about 14 inches long)

TOTAL FORMULA

INGREDIENT	BAKER'S %	WEIGHT
White flour (~11.5% protein)	100.0%	1,142g
Water 1 (levain and autolyse)	65.0%	742g
Water 2 (mix)	5.0%	57g
Fine sea salt	1.8%	21g
Ripe sourdough starter, 100% hydration	3.2%	37g

INGREDIENT	BAKER'S %	WEIGHT
White flour (~11.5% protein)	100.0%	74g
Water 1	100.0%	74g
Ripe sourdough starter, 100% hydration	50.0%	37g

INGREDIENT	WEIGHT
White flour (~11.5% protein)	1,068g
Water 1	668g

INGREDIENT	WEIGHT
Water 2	57g
Fine sea salt	21g
Levain	185g

1. Levain

■ **Duration:** 5 hours at warm room temperature: 74°–76°F (23°–24°C)

● **MIX THE LEVAIN:** Warm or cool the water to about 78°F (25°C). In a medium jar, mix the levain ingredients until well incorporated (this liquid levain will feel quite loose) and loosely cover. Store in a warm place for 5 hours.

2. Autolyse

■ **Duration:** 1 hour at warm room temperature: 74°–76°F (23°–24°C)
■ **Desired dough temperature (DDT):** 78°F (25°C)

● **MIX THE AUTOLYSE:** About 1 hour before the levain is ready, warm or cool the autolyse water (see page 138 on how to calculate) so the temperature of the mixed dough meets the DDT for this recipe. Place the flour and water in a large bowl and use wet hands to mix until no dry bits remain. Use a bowl scraper to scrape down the sides of the bowl to keep all the dough in one area at the bottom. Cover the bowl and place it near your levain for 1 hour.

3. Mix

■ **Desired dough temperature (DDT):** 78°F (25°C)

● **CHECK THE LEVAIN:** It should show signs of readiness: well aerated, risen, bubbly on the top and at the sides, loose, and with a mild sour aroma. If the levain is not showing these signs, let it ferment 30 minutes more and check again.

● **ADJUST THE WATER TEMPERATURE:** Take the temperature of the dough and warm it to the DDT for this recipe: If it's higher, use cold water for the remaining water; if it's lower, use warm water.

● **MIX THE DOUGH:** To the autolyse, add about half of the water, the salt, and ripe levain. Using wet hands, mix the ingredients until well incorporated. If the dough feels very wet, slack, and loose, don't add the remaining water. Otherwise, add the rest of the water and continue to mix until the dough comes together and all the water is absorbed.

● **STRENGTHEN THE DOUGH:** With wet hands, use the slap and fold method (see page 83) for about 5 minutes to strengthen the dough. The dough should look smooth and begin to hold its shape. If it's still shaggy and loose, continue to strengthen for a few more minutes, but don't worry if it doesn't smooth out completely. Transfer back to the bowl or another container for bulk fermentation.

● **MEASURE THE TEMPERATURE OF THE DOUGH:** Compare it to the DDT and record it as the final dough temperature. Cover the dough.

4. Warm bulk fermentation

■ **Duration:** 2 hours 30 minutes at warm room temperature: 74°–76°F (23°–24°C)
■ **Folds:** 3 sets of stretches and folds at 30-minute intervals

- **SET TIMER AND MAKE A NOTE:** Write down the current time as the start of bulk fermentation, set a timer for 30 minutes, and let the dough rest in a warm place.

- **STRETCH AND FOLD:** When your timer goes off, give the dough one set of stretches and folds. Using wet hands, grab one side of the dough and lift it up and over to the other side. Rotate the bowl 180 degrees and repeat. Then rotate the bowl a quarter turn and stretch and fold that side. Rotate the bowl 180 degrees again and finish with a stretch and fold on the last side. The dough should be folded up neatly. Cover and repeat these folds every 30 minutes for a total of 3 sets of stretches and folds.

- **LET THE DOUGH REST:** After the last set, cover the bowl and let the dough rest for the remainder of bulk fermentation, about 1 hour.

5. Cold bulk fermentation

- **Duration:** About 17 hours (overnight) in a home refrigerator: 39°F (4°C)
- **Folds:** None

- **MOVE THE DOUGH TO THE REFRIGERATOR:** After the warm bulk fermentation, place the covered bulk fermentation container in the refrigerator overnight.

6. Divide and preshape

- **DIVIDE AND PRESHAPE THE DOUGH:** Uncover the bulk container and gently scrape the dough out to a clean work surface. The dough will feel firm and slightly damp. Using a bench knife, divide it into 6 pieces of 325g each (you may have a small piece of dough left over). Shape each piece into a very loose round or small rectangle. Let the rounds rest for 35 minutes, uncovered.

7. Shape

- **PREPARE A PROOFING SURFACE:** Cover a large cutting board or proofing board with a couche (aka baker's linen) or large kitchen towel and place this next to your work surface. At one side where you will start laying down shaped baguettes, roll a section so that it stands up by itself, creating a strong edge. Then thoroughly and evenly dust flour on a 3- to 4-inch-wide strip down the couche, from farthest from you to nearest, where the first piece of shaped dough will sit.

- **SHAPE THE DOUGH:** Before you start, measure the width of your baking surface so you know how long your loaves can be. Flour the work surface and your hands. Using a bench knife, flip one round of dough upside down on your work surface. First, fold the top half down to the middle and press to seal (A) (see page 255). Rotate the dough 180 degrees and fold the new top down to the middle again, slightly overlapping the first fold, and press to seal. Using your left hand, place your thumb horizontally in line with the middle seam on the far right edge of the dough and, using your fingers on the left hand, pick up and curl the top edge of the dough up and over your thumb (B). Use your right palm to press down and seal the dough. Work

RECIPE CONTINUES →

Double Bulk Fermentation

This baguette dough has two phases of bulk fermentation: an up-front warm phase for about 2 hours 30 minutes, and then a second phase in the fridge overnight. The benefit of this split bulk fermentation is twofold: First, the long proof at a cold temperature imparts more depth of flavor; and second, by retarding the dough in bulk fermentation, instead of in shape, we encourage the final baguettes to have a thinner and more brittle crust. Additionally, dividing and preshaping a cold dough straight from the fridge makes for easier dough handling.

Shaping a baguette

your way from the right side of the dough all the way to the left, curling and sealing. Next, rotate the dough 180 degrees and repeat. You should have a uniform cylinder shape. Place one hand on the middle of the dough and roll it back and forth a few times (like rolling a rolling pin under your hand) (C). Then start using both hands to roll the dough while you work your way outward from the middle to the edges, keeping your fingertips and palms in contact with the work surface as you roll away and then toward your body (D). You're aiming to reduce the diameter of the dough while at the same time elongating it (E). Be sure you roll the dough only as wide as your baking surface is deep, so the loaf will fit when baking. As you begin to roll the dough toward the extreme edges, place more pressure down as you roll to taper the ends to a point. I like to make the end very pointy, but some prefer a blunter tip.

● **TRANSFER THE DOUGH:** Using both hands, one at each end, transfer the dough to the part of the couche that's dusted with flour, seam-side up. Then using both hands at the edges, pick up and drag a little of the couche toward the dough (like making a pleat in the couche) so that it forms a matching wall of the channel to hold the dough while it's proofing (F). Once the new wall is formed, it will look like the dough is nestled between two straight walls. Flour a new strip down the couche on the other side of the newly formed wall in preparation for another piece of dough. Repeat this process for all the preshaped rounds.

8. Proof

▪ **Duration:** About 1 hour 45 minutes at warm room temperature: 74°–76°F (23°–24°C)

● **LET THE DOUGH PROOF:** Fold the ends of the couche up and over the baguettes to totally cover them (this helps prevent a dry skin from forming). Put the couche on its board in a warm place to proof for about 1 hour 45 minutes. Check in on the loaves periodically toward the end of this period. When the dough pieces are very puffy, soft, and pass the Poke Test (page 116), they are ready to bake.

9. Bake

▪ **Duration:** 40 minutes in the oven

● **PREPARE THE OVEN:** Place an oven rack in the bottom third of the oven. Place a baking stone/steel on the rack to preheat along with the oven. Set a roasting pan with lava rocks on one side of the bottom of the oven (see Baking Directly on a Surface, page 124, for more detail). Preheat the oven to 450°F (230°C). Roll up 3 or 4 kitchen towels and place them in a second roasting pan and set near the oven. Boil 1 cup of water and have it at the ready.

● **TRANSFER THE DOUGH:** Line a pizza peel or large cutting board with a piece of parchment paper. Grab the right end of the couche and pull it out, moving one baguette away from the rest. Place a small cutting board to the inside of the baguette (the side closest to the rest of the dough pieces). Quickly flip the dough onto the board by tugging the couche up and slightly over the board. The dough should now be seam-side down. Slide the dough onto the lined pizza peel, seam-side down. Repeat with two more pieces. Cover the three remaining pieces of dough with the

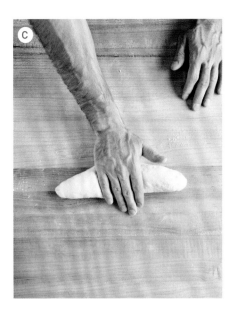

couche and place in the refrigerator. To score the dough, use a curved lame to make 3 cuts where each slightly overlaps the one previous. The cuts should run down the middle of the dough and be mostly parallel with the sides, with just a slight turn (perhaps 3 to 5 degrees); see page 120.

● **BAKE THE DOUGH:** Slide the parchment paper onto your baking surface. Steam the oven: Pour the boiling water over the rolled-up kitchen towels. Pour the ice into the pan with the lava rocks, then add the pan with the kitchen towels next to it. Quickly close the oven door and bake for 20 minutes. Vent the oven of steam by removing the steaming pans. Bake for 20 minutes more. When done, the baguettes will be light in hand and the crust should be golden brown and produce a satisfying crunch if gently squeezed.

● **FINISH AND COOL:** Let the baguettes cool on wire racks for 10 minutes. They are best eaten the day they're baked. For the remaining three baguettes, preheat the baking surface for 15 minutes and repeat.

HOW TO TINKER

MAKE SAME-DAY BAGUETTES

Instead of splitting the bulk fermentation into two phases—one warm and one cold—you can make same-day baguettes by bulk fermenting only at room temperature. To do this, skip the cold bulk fermentation and instead extend the warm bulk fermentation to a total of 3 hours 30 minutes to 4 hours. The result will be baguettes with an even milder sour flavor, highlighting sweetness and emphasizing grain flavor.

MY BEST SOURDOUGH
(High-Hydration White)

A highly hydrated dough yielding bread with a tender and open interior, subtle fermentation flavors, and a thin, crispy crust

THIS RECIPE has been on my website for many years and is still a favorite. Countless tests and trials culminated in the bread I was after: a loaf with a glossy and custard-like interior with mild lactic sourness, and a decidedly crispy crust with toasted grain and malty notes. The exterior of the loaf is usually more wabi-sabi in its expression: the high water content means less rigidity and structure, so the score isn't sharp and precise, but rather more of a relaxed opening.

This is a slightly more advanced recipe due to the high hydration, which makes the dough sticky and harder to handle; see page 101 for more detail on dough hydration and tips for working with a sticky and slack dough.

BAKING TIMELINE

1. **Levain**

   5 hours

2. **Autolyse**

   1 hour 30 minutes

3. **Mix**

4. **Bulk Fermentation**

   4 hours

5. **Divide, Preshape, Bench Rest**

   35 minutes

6. **Shape**

7. **Proof**

   18 hours (overnight)

8. **Bake**

   55 minutes in the oven

TOTAL
28 hours 30 minutes

VITALS

Total dough weight	1,800g
Pre-fermented flour	6.3%
Levain	17.0%
Hydration	85.0%
Yield	Two 900g loaves

TOTAL FORMULA

INGREDIENT	BAKER'S %	WEIGHT
White flour (~11.5% protein)	90.0%	852g
Whole wheat flour	10.0%	94g
Water 1 (levain and autolyse)	75.0%	711g
Water 2 (mix)	10.0%	95g
Fine sea salt	1.8%	17g
Ripe sourdough starter, 100% hydration	3.2%	30g

INGREDIENT	BAKER'S %	WEIGHT
White flour (~11.5% protein)	50.0%	30g
Whole wheat flour	50.0%	30g
Water 1	100.0%	61g
Ripe sourdough starter, 100% hydration	50.0%	30g

INGREDIENT	WEIGHT
White flour (~11.5% protein)	822g
Whole wheat flour	64g
Water 1	650g

INGREDIENT	WEIGHT
Water 2	95g
Fine sea salt	17g
Levain	151g

1. Levain

- **Duration:** 5 hours at warm room temperature: 74°–76°F (23°–24°C)

● **MIX THE LEVAIN:** Warm or cool the water to about 78°F (25°C). In a medium jar, mix the levain ingredients until well incorporated (this liquid levain will feel quite loose) and loosely cover. Store in a warm place for 5 hours.

2. Autolyse

- **Duration:** 1 hour 30 minutes at warm room temperature: 74°–76°F (23°–24°C)
- **Desired dough temperature (DDT):** 78°F (25°C)

● **MIX THE AUTOLYSE:** About 1 hour 30 minutes before the levain is ready, warm or cool the autolyse water (see page 138 on how to calculate) so the temperature of the mixed dough meets the DDT for this recipe. Place the flour and water in a large bowl and use wet hands to mix until no dry bits remain. Use a bowl scraper to scrape down the sides of the bowl to keep all the dough in one area at the bottom. Cover the bowl and place it near your levain for 1 hour 30 minutes. Since this is a longer autolyse, be sure to keep the dough warm.

3. Mix

- **Desired dough temperature (DDT):** 78°F (25°C)

● **CHECK THE LEVAIN:** It should show signs of readiness but not be overly ripe: moderate bubbles on the surface and a mild sour aroma. If the levain is not showing these signs, let it ferment 15 minutes more and check again.

● **ADJUST THE WATER TEMPERATURE:** Take the temperature of the dough and compare it to the DDT for this recipe: If it's higher, use cold water for the remaining water; if it's lower, use warm water.

HYDRATION

A dough's final hydration percentage is always relative to the flour used, but increasing the hydration to see how high you can go isn't the point. The goal is to find a hydration level that results in the texture and flavor you're after in the final bread. This might mean your flour makes better bread at 75% hydration, or it might be 95%—it's all relative to the flour, which is always the case when baking bread, but with this recipe it's especially true. The water percentages listed in the recipe are more of a guideline, requiring you to adjust during mixing based on the dough's consistency—be sure to hold back most of Water 2 and add it in only if it feels like the dough can handle the addition.

● **MIX THE DOUGH:** To the autolyse, add a splash of the water (with this recipe, add water only a little at a time to avoid overhydration), the salt, and ripe levain. Using wet hands, mix the ingredients until well incorporated. If at any point the dough feels excessively wet, slack, and possibly falling apart, don't add the remaining water. Otherwise, add the rest of the water, a little at a time, and continue to mix until the dough comes together, and all the water is absorbed.

● **STRENGTHEN THE DOUGH:** Depending on how the dough feels, you can slap and fold it (see page 83) on the counter for about 5 minutes, or you can perform 5 minutes of repeated folding in the bowl (see Dough Strengthening Methods, page 82). The slap and fold technique is effective for highly hydrated doughs, but it can be a bit of work and a bit messy. The dough should smooth out a little and gain some elasticity, but still be quite shaggy. Transfer back to the bowl or another container for bulk fermentation.

● **MEASURE THE TEMPERATURE OF THE DOUGH:** Compare it to the DDT and record it as the final dough temperature. Cover the dough.

4. Bulk fermentation

▪ **Duration:** About 4 hours at warm room temperature: 74°–76°F (23°–24°C)
▪ **Folds:** 6 sets of stretches and folds, the first 3 at 15-minute intervals, and the remaining 3 at 30-minute intervals

● **SET TIMER AND MAKE A NOTE:** Write down the current time as the start of bulk fermentation, set a timer for 15 minutes, and let the dough rest in a warm place.

● **STRETCH AND FOLD:** When your timer goes off, give the dough one set of stretches and folds. Using wet hands, grab one side of the dough and lift it up and over to the other side. Rotate the bowl 180 degrees and repeat. Then rotate the bowl a quarter turn and stretch and fold that side. Rotate the bowl 180 degrees again and finish with a stretch and fold on the last side. The dough should be folded up neatly. Cover and repeat for 2 more sets at 15-minute intervals. Then perform 3 additional sets at 30-minute intervals.

● **LET THE DOUGH REST:** After the last set, cover the bowl and let the dough rest for the remainder of bulk fermentation, about 1 hour 45 minutes.

5. Divide and preshape

● **CHECK THE DOUGH:** At the end of bulk fermentation, the dough will have risen some in the bulk container. Because of the high hydration, it might not be significantly risen, but it may have bubbles on top and at the sides, it should look smoother and less shaggy, and at the edge of the dough where it meets the container, it should dome downward. If you wet a hand and gently tug on the surface of the dough, it will feel elastic and cohesive, resisting your pull. If you don't see dough that's airy, strong, and "alive," leave it for another 15 minutes in bulk fermentation and check again.

Mixing

This recipe can be mixed in a stand mixer or by hand. Because of the high hydration, this dough requires extra development, either through a longer mechanical mix or some kneading up front and more than the usual sets of stretches and folds during bulk fermentation.

RECIPE CONTINUES →

FREE-FORM LOAVES

- **DIVIDE AND PRESHAPE THE DOUGH:** Using a bowl scraper, gently scrape the dough onto a clean work surface and use your bench knife to divide it directly in half. Using your bench knife in your dominant hand and with your other hand wet to reduce sticking, shape each piece of dough into a tight round. The dough will feel sticky and slack, so be sure to preshape it tightly to give it additional strength. (See Preshaping, page 96, for more detail.) Let the rounds rest for 35 minutes, uncovered. Keep an eye on this dough during the rest; if it looks like it's beginning to spread out into a thin pancake, skip the remaining bench rest time and proceed directly to shaping.

Tight Shaping

It's important that this dough be shaped very tightly with sufficient tension. If it is shaped loosely, it will spread excessively during proofing and oven spring will be compromised.

6. Shape

- **PREPARE THE PROOFING BASKETS:** Line two proofing baskets or bowls with clean kitchen towels. Dust lightly and evenly with white flour.

- **SHAPE THE DOUGH:** Shape each as a boule or a bâtard (see pages 102 to 107 for details). Gently transfer each piece to a proofing basket, seam-side up. Place each basket inside an airtight reusable plastic bag and seal.

7. Proof

- Duration: About 18 hours (overnight) in a home refrigerator: 39°F (4°C)

- **LET THE DOUGH PROOF:** Place the baskets in the refrigerator to proof overnight.

8. Bake

- Duration: 50 to 55 minutes in the oven

- **PREPARE THE OVEN:** Place an oven rack in the bottom third of the oven with no rack above it. Place a Dutch oven/combo cooker inside the oven and preheat to 450°F (230°C) for at least 30 minutes. (Alternatively, bake directly on a baking stone/steel; see page 124 for details.)

- **SCORE THE DOUGH:** Take one of the proofing baskets out of the fridge and uncover. Use your finger to gently poke around the dough to assess the strength. If it feels very fragile and weak, use a lighter hand when scoring to prevent the dough from collapsing when baking—don't score in excessively deeply, only enough to cut through the outer skin of the dough. Put a piece of parchment paper over the basket. Place a pizza peel or inverted baking sheet on top of the parchment and, using both hands, flip everything over. Gently remove the basket and score the dough. (See Scoring, page 118, for details.)

- **BAKE THE DOUGH:** Slide the dough with the parchment into the preheated Dutch oven and cover with the lid. Bake for 20 minutes, then remove the lid. Continue to bake for 30 to 35 minutes, or until the internal temperature reaches 206°-210°F (96°-99°C) and the crust has a deep mahogany color and a crackle/crunch when gently squeezed.

- **FINISH AND COOL:** Let the loaf cool on a wire rack for 1 to 2 hours before slicing. For the second loaf, preheat the Dutch oven for 15 minutes and repeat.

TROUBLESHOOTING

MY DOUGH SPREAD OUT LIKE A PANCAKE WHEN BAKING!

This is a typical issue when pushing the water percentage in a recipe. Next time, I'd suggest you drop the hydration of the recipe by 5% and still hold back 10% as instructed. Only add in that reserved water if it feels like your dough can handle it during mixing—it should not feel excessively soupy or never come together when mixing.

It's also important that this dough is sufficiently developed by the time you get to preshaping and shaping. If the dough feels very slack and weak when preshaping, preshape it and let it rest for 30 minutes. Then preshape it again to give it more strength, but this time preshape it into an even tighter round. Then proceed with another 30-minute rest. Finally, be sure to shape it tightly. Next time, either reduce the water in the mix or develop the dough further through slap and fold up front or a longer mix time in a mechanical mixer.

HOW TO TINKER

ADD INCLUSIONS

This dough is great for adding 10% to 15% (of the total flour weight) pecans, walnuts, or any other nut and seed—or a combination of nuts and seeds.

ADD TOPPINGS

Top with a combination of black and white sesame seeds or instant oats.

PAN

LOAVES

Naturally Leavened Brioche

EVERYDAY SANDWICH BREAD

A healthy and flavorful pan bread that's easy to make for weekly toast and sandwiches

THIS "SQUARE BREAD," as my kids have affectionately dubbed it, is a loaf I bake weekly. It's such a routine that I hardly even think about it, baking it each weekend in preparation for the week—and so many PB&Js—to come. The loaf has mild fermentation flavors for a relatively sweeter slant, but still a subtle sourness that brings added richness—an overall balanced and versatile loaf of bread.

This bread works well with any number of toppings (sesame, oat, poppy, flax, etc.), but my favorite is white sesame seeds. They bring a distinct nutty flavor, especially when a slice is toasted, and it's another way for me to sneak in a little extra nutrition for my kids; for them, the seeds seem to elevate the appeal of this loaf further, and I have to say, for me, too.

BAKING TIMELINE

1 Levain

　12 hours (overnight)

2 Mix

3 Bulk Fermentation

　3 hours

4 Divide, Preshape, Bench Rest

　35 minutes

5 Shape

6 Proof

　1 hour 30 minutes

7 Bake

　50 minutes in the oven

TOTAL

17 hours 55 minutes

VITALS

Total dough weight	1,800g
Pre-fermented flour	8.0%
Levain	18.3%
Hydration	74.0%
Yield	Two 900g loaves (each in a 9 x 4 x 4-inch Pullman pan)

TOTAL FORMULA

INGREDIENT	BAKER'S %	WEIGHT
White flour (~11.5% protein)	75.0%	729g
Whole wheat flour	25.0%	243g
Olive oil	4.5%	44g
Honey	4.0%	39g
Water	74.0%	720g
Fine sea salt	1.9%	18g
Ripe sourdough starter, 100% hydration	0.8%	8g

ADDITIONAL INGREDIENT

White sesame seeds or old-fashioned rolled oats, for topping (optional)

INGREDIENT	BAKER'S %	WEIGHT
White flour (~11.5% protein)	50.0%	39g
Whole wheat flour	50.0%	39g
Water	100.0%	78g
Ripe sourdough starter, 100% hydration	10.0%	8g

INGREDIENT	WEIGHT
White flour (~11.5% protein)	690g
Whole wheat flour	204g
Olive oil	44g
Honey	39g
Water	642g
Fine sea salt	18g
Levain	164g

1. Levain

■ **Duration:** 12 hours (overnight) at warm room temperature: 74°–76°F (23°–24°C)

● **MIX THE LEVAIN:** Warm or cool the water to about 78°F (25°C). In a medium jar, mix the levain ingredients until well incorporated (this liquid levain will feel quite loose) and loosely cover. Store in a warm place for 12 hours.

2. Mix

■ **Desired dough temperature (DDT):** 78°F (25°C)

● **CHECK THE LEVAIN:** It should show signs of readiness: well aerated, risen, bubbly on top and at the sides, loose, and with a sour aroma. If the levain is not showing these signs, let it ferment 1 hour more and check again.

● **ADJUST THE WATER TEMPERATURE:** Warm or cool the water (see page 138 on how to calculate) so the temperature of the mixed dough meets the DDT of this recipe.

● **MIX THE DOUGH:** You have two mixing options.

■ By hand: Place the flour, honey, water, salt, and ripe levain in a large bowl. Using wet hands, mix thoroughly. Use the slap and fold method (see page 83) for about 6 minutes to strengthen the dough. The dough should look smooth and begin to hold its shape. If it's still shaggy and loose, continue to strengthen for a few more minutes. Transfer back to the bowl, add the olive oil, and massage it into the dough while also stretching and folding the dough up and over onto itself, until the oil is completely absorbed.

■ With a mixer: Place the flour, honey, water, salt, and ripe levain in the bowl of a stand mixer fitted with the dough hook. Turn the mixer on to low speed and mix for 1 to 2 minutes until well incorporated. Increase the speed to medium and mix for 4 to 5 minutes until the dough begins to cling to the hook, but it won't completely clear the sides of the bowl. Add the olive oil, reduce the speed to low, and mix for 1 to 2 minutes until the oil is absorbed. Increase the speed to medium and mix for 2 to 3 minutes until the dough is smooth. Transfer to another container, or keep in the bowl, for bulk fermentation.

● **MEASURE THE TEMPERATURE OF THE DOUGH:** Compare it to the DDT and record it as the final dough temperature. Cover the dough.

3. Bulk fermentation

- **Duration:** About 3 hours at warm room temperature: 74°–76°F (23°–24°C)
- **Folds:** 3 sets of stretches and folds at 30-minute intervals

- **SET TIMER AND MAKE A NOTE:** Write down the current time as the start of bulk fermentation, set a timer for 30 minutes, and let the dough rest in a warm place.

- **STRETCH AND FOLD:** When your timer goes off, give the dough its first set of stretches and folds. Using wet hands, grab one side of the dough and lift it up and over to the other side. Rotate the bowl 180 degrees and repeat. Then rotate the bowl a quarter turn and stretch and fold that side. Rotate the bowl 180 degrees again and finish with a stretch and fold on the last side. The dough should be folded up neatly. Cover and repeat these folds every 30 minutes for a total of 3 sets of stretches and folds.

- **LET THE DOUGH REST:** After the last set, cover the bowl and let the dough rest for the remainder of bulk fermentation, 1 hour 30 minutes.

4. Divide and preshape

- **CHECK THE DOUGH:** At the end of bulk fermentation, the dough will have risen significantly; it may have some bubbles on top and at the sides, it should look smoother and less shaggy, and at the edge of the dough where it meets the container, it should dome downward. If you wet a hand and gently tug on the surface of the dough, it will feel elastic and cohesive, resisting your pull. If you don't see dough that's airy, strong, and "alive," leave it for another 15 minutes in bulk fermentation and check again.

- **DIVIDE AND PRESHAPE THE DOUGH:** Using a bowl scraper, gently scrape the dough out onto a clean work surface and use your bench knife to divide it directly in half. Using your bench knife in your dominant hand and with your other hand wet to reduce sticking, shape each piece of dough into a loose round. (See Preshaping, page 96, for more detail.) Let the rounds rest for 35 minutes, uncovered.

5. Shape

- **PREPARE THE BAKING PANS:** Liberally grease two 9 × 4 × 4-inch Pullman pans with olive oil (or use pans with silicone liners; see Resources, page 424).

- **SHAPE THE DOUGH:** Use your hands to shape each round into a long tube the same length as your pan. (See Shaping a Pan Loaf, page 108, for more detail.)

- **ADD THE OPTIONAL TOPPINGS:** Spread an even layer of either white sesame seeds or rolled oats in a sheet pan or on a clean kitchen towel. After shaping each piece of dough, quickly roll the top side in the seeds so they stick. (See Add Toppings to Your Bread Dough, page 105, for more detail.) Using both hands, or one hand and a bench knife, scoop each piece of dough into a Pullman pan. Place each pan inside a reusable plastic bag and seal.

RECIPE CONTINUES →

6. Proof

▪ **Duration:** About 1 hour 30 minutes at warm room temperature: 74°–76°F (23°–24°C)

● **LET THE DOUGH PROOF:** Put the pans in a warm place to proof for about 1 hour 30 minutes. The dough should be baked when it has risen to the top rim of the pan and is very soft when gently poked.

7. Bake

▪ **Duration:** 45 to 50 minutes in the oven

● **PREPARE THE OVEN:** Preheat the oven to 425°F (220°C) with a rack in the bottom third. Place a roasting pan with lava rocks below the empty oven rack (see Baking Directly on a Surface, page 124, for more detail).

● **BAKE THE DOUGH:** Uncover the pans and put them into the oven. Pour a cup of ice into the pan with lava rocks at the bottom of the oven, quickly close the oven door, and bake for 15 minutes at 425°F (220°C). Vent the steam by removing the steaming pan. Reduce the temperature to 375°F (190°C) and bake for 30 to 35 minutes more, or until the internal temperature reaches 204°F (95°C) and the crust has a dark mahogany color.

● **FINISH AND COOL:** Carefully turn the loaves out to a wire rack and let cool for 1 to 2 hours before slicing.

HOW TO TINKER

OVERNIGHT FERMENTATION

To add more fermentation flavors, or to spread the recipe over two days, retard the dough in shape overnight. Instead of proofing on the counter, put the covered pans in the refrigerator. The next morning or early afternoon, remove the pans from the refrigerator, uncover, and continue with the baking.

ALTERNATIVE GRAINS

The 25% whole wheat can be substituted with other wheat varieties (Red Fife or Turkey Red, for example), spelt, einkorn, or Khorasan wheat. If using spelt or einkorn, you might need to hold back some water during mixing to avoid overhydration.

SOFT WHITE SANDWICH BREAD
(Pain de Mie)

Soft and slightly sweet sandwich bread with a hint of buttery richness

TRADITIONALLY, PAIN DE MIE is a bread that exhibits little to no crust. The long, narrow Pullman pan in which it's customarily baked has a tight-fitting lid that ensures this, but it's also nice to bake the bread without the lid and topped with an egg wash for a glistening brown crust. Whichever path you take, this same-day (except the overnight levain) recipe yields a loaf that's subtly sweet, a little buttery, and far softer than a traditional free-form loaf.

I originally developed this bread to satisfy my two kids. After eating loaf after loaf of sourdough with a crunchy crust and deep, complex flavor profile, they wanted something light, soft, and a little sweet. While I'm a lover of thick-crusted bread, sometimes a delicate loaf brings a nice reprieve. The not-so-secret secret is that I also kind of bake this for myself: It makes an epic grilled cheese and the best buttered toast.

BAKING TIMELINE

1 Levain

　　12 hours (overnight)

2 Autolyse

　　30 minutes

3 Mix

4 Bulk Fermentation

　　4 hours

5 Divide, Preshape, Bench Rest

　　35 minutes

6 Shape

7 Proof

　　3 hours

8 Bake

　　45 minutes in the oven

TOTAL

20 hours 50 minutes

VITALS

Total dough weight	1,600g
Pre-fermented flour	8.5%
Levain	19.5%
Hydration	48.0%
Yield	Two 800g loaves (each in a 9 × 4 × 4-inch Pullman pan)

TOTAL FORMULA

INGREDIENT	BAKER'S %	WEIGHT
White flour (~11.5% protein)	100.0%	835g
Whole milk	22.0%	184g
Unsalted butter	12.0%	100g
Honey	7.0%	58g
Water 1 (levain and autolyse)	45.0%	376g
Water 2 (mix)	3.0%	25g
Fine sea salt	1.8%	15g
Ripe sourdough starter, 100% hydration	0.9%	7g

ADDITIONAL INGREDIENT

Egg wash: 1 egg and 1 tablespoon whole milk or heavy cream (optional)

INGREDIENT	BAKER'S %	WEIGHT
White flour (~11.5% protein)	100.0%	71g
Water 1	100.0%	71g
Ripe sourdough starter, 100% hydration	10.0%	7g

INGREDIENT	WEIGHT
White flour (~11.5% protein)	764g
Whole milk	184g
Water 1	305g
Levain	149g

INGREDIENT	WEIGHT
Unsalted butter	100g
Honey	58g
Water 2	25g
Fine sea salt	15g

Mix by Hand

While I prefer mixing enriched doughs with a stand mixer, you can also mix this dough by hand. To do so, mix the ingredients in a wide bowl and use the slap and fold method (see page 83) for 5 to 8 minutes to strengthen the dough before adding the butter.

1. Levain

- **Duration:** 12 hours (overnight) at warm room temperature: 74°–76°F (23°–24°C)

- **MIX THE LEVAIN:** Warm or cool the water to about 78°F (25°C). In a medium jar, mix the levain ingredients until well incorporated (this liquid levain will feel quite loose) and loosely cover. Store in a warm place for 5 hours.

2. Autolyse

- **Duration:** 30 minutes at warm room temperature: 74°–76°F (23°–24°C)
- **Desired dough temperature (DDT):** 78°F (25°C)

- **CHECK THE LIQUID LEVAIN:** It should show signs of readiness: well aerated, risen, bubbly on top and at the sides, loose, and an assertive sour aroma. If the levain is not showing these signs, let it ferment 30 minutes more and check again.

- **MIX THE AUTOLYSE:** Warm or cool the autolyse water (see page 138 on how to calculate) so the temperature of the mixed dough meets the DDT for this recipe. Place the flour, milk, water, and ripe levain in the bowl of a stand mixer fitted with the dough hook. Mix on low speed until just incorporated. Cover the bowl and let sit for 30 minutes.

- **PREPARE THE BUTTER:** Cut the butter into ½-inch-thick pats and place them on a plate to warm to room temperature.

3. Mix

- **Desired dough temperature (DDT):** 78°F (25°C)

- **ADJUST THE WATER TEMPERATURE:** Take the temperature of the dough and compare it to the DDT for this recipe: If it's higher, use cold water for the remaining water; if it's lower, use warm water.

- **MIX THE DOUGH:** Put the honey and salt on top of the dough and pour the water over it to help dissolve. Mix on low speed until the salt and water are incorporated, then increase to medium speed and mix, stopping to scrape the sides of the bowl as needed, until the dough comes together and, while still shaggy, starts to cling to the dough hook, about 6 minutes.

RECIPE CONTINUES ➞

LEVAIN

By building a levain made with 100% white flour and using it before it's overly ripe, you can direct the final bread down the path toward a milder, less sour flavor profile. The high hydration of the levain also contributes to this mild flavor.

Since a high percentage of the recipe's total water is included in the levain itself, the levain is incorporated in the autolyse, which is unusual (see Should I Include My Pre-ferment (Levain) in My Autolyse?, page 79). Without the levain, the autolyse dough would be very stiff and difficult to mix.

• **INCORPORATE THE BUTTER:** Make sure that the butter is perfectly room temperature. If you gently press a butter pat with your finger, it should show indentation but not be mushy or melted. With the mixer on low speed, add the butter, one pat at a time, until absorbed into the dough, scraping down the sides of the bowl and the dough hook as needed. Continue mixing on medium speed until the dough smooths out and almost reaches full development (it will almost pass the Windowpane Test, page 83), 3 to 5 minutes. The dough will be silky smooth, elastic, and shiny. Transfer to a container for bulk fermentation.

• **MEASURE THE TEMPERATURE OF THE DOUGH:** Compare it to the DDT and record it as the final dough temperature. Cover the dough.

4. Bulk fermentation

▪ **Duration:** 4 hours at warm room temperature: 74°–76°F (23°–24°C)
▪ **Folds:** 3 sets of stretches and folds at 30-minute intervals

• **SET TIMER AND MAKE A NOTE:** Write down the current time as the start of bulk fermentation, set a timer for 30 minutes, and let the dough rest in a warm place.

• **STRETCH AND FOLD:** When your timer goes off, give the dough one set of stretches and folds. Using wet hands, grab one side of the dough and lift it up and over to the other side. Rotate the bowl 180 degrees and repeat. Then rotate the bowl a quarter turn and stretch and fold that side. Rotate the bowl 180 degrees again and finish with a stretch and fold on the last side. The dough should be folded up neatly. Cover the bowl and repeat these folds every 30 minutes for a total of 3 sets of stretches and folds.

• **LET THE DOUGH REST:** After the last set, cover the bowl and let the dough rest for the remainder of bulk fermentation, about 2 hours 30 minutes.

5. Divide and preshape

• **CHECK THE DOUGH:** At the end of bulk fermentation, the dough will have risen significantly; it may have bubbles on top and at the sides, it should look smoother and less shaggy, and at the edge of the dough where it meets the container, it should dome downward. If you wet a hand and gently tug on the dough, it will feel elastic and cohesive, resisting your pull. If you don't see dough that's airy, strong, and "alive," leave it for another 15 minutes in bulk fermentation and check again.

• **DIVIDE AND PRESHAPE THE DOUGH:** Using a bowl scraper, gently scrape the dough onto a clean work surface and use your bench knife to divide it directly in half. Using your bench knife in your dominant hand and with your other hand wet to reduce sticking, shape each piece of dough into a taut round that is well gathered and smooth on top. (See Preshaping, page 96, for more detail.) Let the rounds rest for 35 minutes, uncovered.

6. Shape

● **PREPARE THE BAKING PANS:** Liberally grease two 9 × 4 × 4-inch Pullman pans with a neutral oil or butter (or use pans with silicone liners; see Resources, page 424).

● **SHAPE THE DOUGH:** Shape each preshaped round into a long tube the same length as your Pullman pan. Using both hands, or one hand and a bench knife, scoop each piece of dough into a Pullman pan. (See Shaping a Pan Loaf, page 108, for more detail.) Place each pan inside a reusable plastic bag and seal.

7. Proof

▬ **Duration:** About 3 hours at warm room temperature: 74°–76°F (23°–24°C)

● **LET THE DOUGH PROOF:** Put the pans in a warm place to proof for about 3 hours. The dough should be baked when it's about 1 inch from the top rim of the pan (at which time it will also pass the Poke Test, page 116).

8. Bake

▬ **Duration:** 45 minutes in the oven

● **PREPARE THE OVEN:** Place an oven rack in the bottom third of the oven and preheat the oven to 425°F (220°C). (Note that steaming the oven is not necessary for this recipe because the pans will either be covered with a lid or an egg wash will be brushed on the dough's surface. See note at right for more detail.)

● **CHOOSE HOW TO BAKE EACH LOAF:**

▬ For a perfectly square loaf with a thin and light-colored crust: Slide on the Pullman pan lid and close it tightly.

▬ For a loaf with a domed, deeply colored top: Make an egg wash by whisking together 1 egg and 1 tablespoon whole milk (or heavy cream for a deeper color). Use a pastry brush to brush the wash evenly over the top of the dough and do not use the pan lid.

● **BAKE THE DOUGH:** Put the pans into the oven side by side (like the number "11," not like an "=" sign). Bake for 15 minutes. Reduce the temperature to 350°F (175°C) and bake for 30 minutes more, or until the internal temperature reaches 205°F (96°C)—carefully pop the lid open slightly to insert a thermometer into the loaf—and the crust is a light golden brown.

● **FINISH AND COOL:** Carefully remove the pans from the oven, uncover any pan that has a lid, and turn the loaves out onto a wire rack to cool for 1 to 2 hours before slicing. These loaves freeze exceptionally well. Wrap a completely cooled loaf tightly in plastic wrap several times, then place it in a plastic freezer bag and freeze for at least 12 hours. To thaw, refrigerate for a day or so until soft, then keep on the counter.

Egg Wash and the Maillard Reaction

The Maillard reaction is partly responsible for adding that characteristic brown color to bread's exterior crust during baking. It's a complex chemical reaction that occurs between amino acids and sugar molecules, adding color, flavor, and aroma to baked goods. Applying an egg wash amplifies this with extra proteins from the eggs and milk and sugars (lactose) from the milk or heavy cream. For an optimal Maillard reaction to take place, high heat and a dry oven—in other words, no steam—is best, because moisture reduces the effectiveness of the reaction. In any case, adding steam isn't necessary when using an egg wash because the water in the egg whites and dairy provides ample moisture to keep the dough from baking too fast. The baking temperature here starts off high to rapidly color the crust, but then is dropped partway through the bake after the crust begins to color to ensure the interior bakes thoroughly before the crust colors too far, entering pyrolysis—aka burning.

TROUBLESHOOTING

MY LOAF ROSE ERRATICALLY AND HAS FISSURES AND DEEP CRACKS ON TOP!

This can be a sign of underproofing. Next time, give the dough more time in bulk fermentation and/or during proof to ensure a fully proofed dough that passes the Poke Test (page 116).

HONEY WHOLE WHEAT
SANDWICH BREAD

A healthful loaf that's as soft as it is flavorful, making for some darn fine toast

ONE HUNDRED percent whole-grain pan loaves are something I'm always tinkering with. They're a fantastic way to push the limits because the pan provides a structural helping hand. Within the confines of a pan, it's fun to play with very high dough hydrations, high enrichment percentages, loads of inclusions, and very long proof times—all of which, if not kept in check, might otherwise result in a loaf that struggles to hold its form in the oven. But specifically with this loaf, and its use of tangzhong (see note on page 277), we "sneak" in an abundance of softness to the crumb, without making the dough any harder to handle.

One result of all my whole-grain pan loaf tinkering is this same-day bread, which has mild fermentation flavors, a little sweetness, and enjoyable earthy and nutty flavors from the high whole-grain percentage. The texture of the crumb has copious softness and, likewise, the crust is soft, but still assertive enough to provide structure for toast and sandwiches. For me, this bread might be the perfect whole-grain sandwich loaf.

BAKING TIMELINE

1 Levain

  12 hours (overnight)

2 Autolyse

  1 hour

3 Tangzhong

4 Mix

5 Bulk Fermentation

  3 hours 30 minutes

6 Divide, Preshape, Bench Rest

  35 minutes

7 Shape

8 Proof

  1 hour 30 minutes

9 Bake

  50 minutes in the oven

TOTAL
18 hours 25 minutes

VITALS

Total dough weight	2,000g
Pre-fermented flour	9.0%
Levain	16.8%
Hydration	68.0%
Yield	Two 1,000g loaves (each in a 9 × 4 × 4-inch Pullman pan)

TOTAL FORMULA

INGREDIENT	BAKER'S %	WEIGHT
Whole wheat flour	92.0%	867g
Whole wheat flour (tangzhong)	8.0%	75g
Whole milk (tangzhong)	32.0%	301g
Extra-virgin olive oil or neutral-flavored oil	5.0%	47g
Honey	5.0%	47g
Water 1 (levain and autolyse)	65.0%	612g
Water 2 (mix)	3.0%	28g
Fine sea salt	1.9%	18g
Ripe sourdough starter, 100% hydration	0.4%	4g

ADDITIONAL INGREDIENT

Old-fashioned rolled oats or white sesame seeds, for topping (optional)

INGREDIENT	BAKER'S %	WEIGHT
Whole wheat flour	100.0%	85g
Water 1	50.0%	42g
Ripe sourdough starter, 100% hydration	5.0%	4g

INGREDIENT	WEIGHT
Whole wheat flour	782g
Water 1	570g

Tangzhong Timing

Be sure to make the tangzhong with plenty of time to cool to room temperature before mixing. Alternatively, you can make the tangzhong the night before, let it cool for a few minutes on the counter, cover, and refrigerate it overnight. The next day, let it come to room temperature before mixing it into the dough.

INGREDIENT	WEIGHT
Tangzhong	All
Extra-virgin olive oil or neutral-flavored oil	47g
Honey	47g
Water 2	28g
Fine sea salt	18g
Levain	131g

1. Levain

◾ **Duration:** 12 hours (overnight) at warm room temperature: 74°–76°F (23°–24°C)

● **MIX THE LEVAIN:** Warm or cool the water to about 75°F (23°C). In a medium bowl, mix the levain ingredients until well incorporated. Use your hands to knead the mixture until all dry bits of flour are incorporated (this stiff levain will feel strong and dry). Transfer the levain to a jar and loosely cover. Store in a warm place for 12 hours.

2. Autolyse

◾ **Duration:** 1 hour at warm room temperature: 74°–76°F (23°–24°C)

◾ **Desired dough temperature (DDT):** 75°F (23°C)

● **MIX THE AUTOLYSE:** About 1 hour before the levain is ready, warm or cool the autolyse water (see page 138 on how to calculate) so the temperature of the mixed dough meets the DDT for this recipe. Place the flour and water in a large bowl and use wet hands to mix until no dry bits remain. Use a bowl scraper to scrape down the sides of the bowl to keep all the dough in one area at the bottom. Cover the bowl and place it near your levain for 1 hour. Since this is a longer autolyse, be sure to keep the dough warm.

3. Tangzhong

● **MAKE THE TANGZHONG:** Place the 75g whole wheat flour and 301g milk in a medium saucepan over medium-low heat. Cook, whisking constantly to ensure it does not burn, until the mixture thickens and becomes like a paste, 5 to 8 minutes. Be patient; the mixture won't seem to do anything until it reaches a critical heat point. Remove the pan from the heat, spread the paste out on a small plate, and let it cool completely.

4. Mix

◾ **Desired dough temperature (DDT):** 75°F (23°C)

● **CHECK THE LEVAIN:** It should show signs of readiness: well aerated, risen, soft, sticky, and a sharp sour aroma. If the levain is not showing these signs, let it ferment 1 hour more and check again.

● **ADJUST THE WATER TEMPERATURE:** Take the temperature of the dough and compare it to the DDT for this recipe: If it's higher, use cold water for the remaining water; if it's lower, use warm water.

● **MIX THE DOUGH:** To the dough, add the tangzhong, olive oil, honey, water, salt, and ripe levain. Using wet hands, mix the ingredients until well incorporated.

● **STRENGTHEN THE DOUGH:** Give the dough a series of folds in the bowl (see page 83) for 4 to 5 minutes to strengthen it. The dough should look a little smooth but still shaggy overall. Transfer to another container, or keep it in the bowl, for bulk fermentation.

- **MEASURE THE TEMPERATURE OF THE DOUGH:** Compare it to the DDT and record it as the final dough temperature. Cover the dough.

5. Bulk fermentation

- **Duration:** About 3 hours 30 minutes at warm room temperature: 74°–76°F (23°–24°C)
- **Folds:** 5 sets of stretches and folds at 30-minute intervals

- **SET TIMER AND MAKE A NOTE:** Write down the current time as the start of bulk fermentation, set a timer for 30 minutes, and let the dough rest in a warm place.

- **STRETCH AND FOLD:** When your timer goes off, give the dough one set of stretches and folds. Using wet hands, grab one side of the dough and lift it up and over to the other side. Rotate the bowl 180 degrees and repeat. Then rotate the bowl a quarter turn and stretch and fold that side. Rotate the bowl 180 degrees again and finish with a stretch and fold on the last side. The dough should be folded up neatly. Cover and repeat these folds every 30 minutes for a total of 5 sets of stretches and folds.

- **LET THE DOUGH REST:** After the last set, cover the bowl and let the dough rest for the remainder of bulk fermentation, about 1 hour.

6. Divide and preshape

- **CHECK THE DOUGH:** At the end of bulk fermentation, the dough will have risen moderately; it may have bubbles on top and at the sides, it should look smoother and less shaggy, and at the edge of the dough where it meets the container, it should dome downward, although not to a great degree due to the high hydration and high whole grain percentage of this dough. If you wet a hand and gently tug on the surface of the dough, it will feel elastic and cohesive, resisting your pull. If you don't see dough that's airy, strong, and "alive," leave it for another 15 minutes in bulk fermentation and check again.

- **DIVIDE AND PRESHAPE THE DOUGH:** Using a bowl scraper, gently scrape the dough onto a clean work surface and use your bench knife to divide it directly in half. Using your bench knife in your dominant hand and with your other hand wet to reduce sticking, shape each piece of dough into a loose round. (See Preshaping, page 96, for more detail.) Let the rounds rest for 35 minutes, uncovered.

TANGZHONG

Sometimes called "flour scald," tangzhong is an East Asian technique in which a portion of the raw flour in a recipe is cooked with a liquid (usually whole dairy milk but it can also be water or a nut milk) in advance of mixing. Tangzhong is classically used in breads like Japanese Hokkaido milk bread to bring tenderness and fluffiness without the need for (or with a reduced quantity of) other enrichments such as butter, oil, or eggs. Tangzhong is usually one part flour to five parts liquid. The mixture is cooked in a saucepan over medium heat to about 150°F (65°C), at which point the starches in the flour will gelatinize (i.e., the liquid is absorbed into the starch, which swells as the mixture becomes more viscous and gel-like). The resulting sticky starch-paste is added to the dough during mixing; be sure you give the tangzhong time to cool (see Tangzhong Timing note opposite). See Soft Dinner Rolls (page 333) for another recipe utilizing this technique.

RECIPE CONTINUES →

7. Shape

● **PREPARE THE BAKING PANS:** Liberally grease two 9 × 4 × 4-inch Pullman pans with olive oil (or use pans with silicone liners; see Resources, page 424).

● **SHAPE THE DOUGH:** Shape each round into a long cylinder the same length as your Pullman pans.

● **ADD THE TOPPING (OPTIONAL):** Spread an even layer of oats or sesame seeds in a sheet pan or on a clean kitchen towel. After shaping each piece of dough, quickly roll the top side in the toppings so they stick. (See Add Toppings to Your Bread Dough, page 105, for more detail.) Using both hands, or one hand and a bench knife, scoop the dough into the pans. (See Shaping a Pan Loaf, page 108, for more detail.) Place each pan inside an airtight reusable plastic bag and seal.

8. Proof

▪ **Duration:** About 1 hour 30 minutes at warm room temperature: 74°–76°F (23°–24°C)

● **LET THE DOUGH PROOF:** Put the pans in a warm place to proof for about 1 hour 30 minutes. The dough is ready to bake when it has relaxed to fill the entire pan, it's soft to the touch, and it has risen to the top rim of the pan.

9. Bake

▪ **Duration:** 50 minutes in the oven

● **PREPARE THE OVEN:** Place an oven rack in the bottom third of the oven with no rack above it. Place a roasting pan with lava rocks on the bottom of the oven. (See Baking Directly on a Surface, page 124, for more detail.) Preheat the oven to 425°F (220°C).

● **BAKE THE DOUGH:** Uncover the pans and place in the oven side by side (like the number "11," not an "=" sign). Steam the oven: Pour a cup of ice into the pan with lava rocks and quickly close the oven door. Bake for 15 minutes. Vent the oven of steam by removing the steaming pan. Reduce the oven temperature to 375°F (190°C) and bake for 35 minutes more, or until the internal temperature reads 205°F (96°C) and the crust is a chestnut color.

● **FINISH AND COOL:** Carefully turn the loaves out onto a wire rack to cool for at least 2 to 3 hours before slicing.

HOW TO TINKER

MAKE THIS RECIPE VEGAN

To remove all dairy from this recipe, substitute the whole milk in the tangzhong with full-fat oat milk, almond milk, or other nut milk. You can also substitute the honey with pure maple syrup.

WHOLE-GRAIN MAPLE SPELT PAN LOAF

Wholesome and healthy, whole-grain spelt flour is the star of this tender bread

I HAVE many recipes in this book using spelt in varying percentages, but this recipe is a pan loaf using 100% whole-grain spelt. To me, spelt is one of the most flavorful grains I've worked with, and this pan loaf uses the delightful grain to maximum effect. In addition to abundant flavor, spelt is high in protein and is a good source of fiber, vitamins, and minerals. The great news is, spelt is increasingly more available. I even see it regularly at my local market.

I find spelt to be naturally sweet and nutty, and coupled with the small addition of pure maple syrup and the same-day fermentation, this results in a naturally sweeter bread that's still full of complex flavors. I prefer using light maple syrup in my baking, but for a more pronounced maple flavor, go for a robust, darker maple syrup.

BAKING TIMELINE

1. **Levain**

   12 hours (overnight)

2. **Mix**

3. **Bulk Fermentation**

   3 hours

4. **Divide, Preshape, Bench Rest**

   35 minutes

5. **Shape**

6. **Proof**

   2 hours

7. **Bake**

   45 minutes in the oven

TOTAL
18 hours 20 minutes

VITALS

Total dough weight	2,000g
Pre-fermented flour	12.5%
Levain	23.6%
Hydration	75.0%
Yield	Two 1,000g loaves (each in a 9 × 4 × 4-inch Pullman pan)

TOTAL FORMULA

INGREDIENT	BAKER'S %	WEIGHT
Whole spelt flour	100.0%	1,074g
Pure maple syrup	8.0%	86g
Water	75.0%	806g
Fine sea salt	1.9%	20g
Ripe sourdough starter, 100% hydration	1.3%	14g

ADDITIONAL INGREDIENT

Instant oats, for topping (optional)

INGREDIENT	BAKER'S %	WEIGHT
Whole spelt flour	100.0%	134g
Water	55.0%	74g
Ripe sourdough starter, 100% hydration	10.0%	14g

INGREDIENT	WEIGHT
Whole spelt flour	940g
Pure maple syrup	86g
Water	732g
Fine sea salt	20g
Levain	222g

Extra Stretches and Folds

Spelt is naturally more extensible than modern wheat. To compensate, give this dough a few more sets of stretches and folds during bulk fermentation. I call for 4 sets in this recipe, but add another set if the dough still feels slack and extensible after the fourth set.

1. Levain

▪ **Duration:** 12 hours (overnight) at warm room temperature: 74°–76°F (23°–24°C)

● **MIX THE LEVAIN:** Warm or cool the water to about 78°F (25°C). In a medium bowl, mix the levain ingredients until well incorporated. Use your hands to knead the mixture until all dry bits of flour are incorporated (this stiff levain will feel strong and dry). Transfer the levain to a jar and loosely cover. Store in a warm place for 12 hours.

2. Mix

▪ **Desired dough temperature (DDT):** 78°F (25°C)

● **CHECK THE LEVAIN:** It should show signs of readiness: well aerated, risen, bubbly at the top and at the sides, loose, and an assertive sour aroma. If the levain is not showing these signs, let it ferment 1 hour more and check again.

● **MIX THE DOUGH:** Warm or cool the water (see page 138 on how to calculate) so the temperature of the mixed dough meets the DDT of this recipe. In a large bowl, add the flour, maple syrup, water, salt, and ripe levain. Using wet hands, mix the ingredients until well incorporated. Give the dough a series of folds in the bowl (see page 83) for about 5 minutes until the dough starts to smooth out and gain strength. For each fold, grab the side of the dough with one hand and lift it up and over to the other side. Rotate the bowl a little and repeat. Transfer the dough to another container, or keep it in the bowl, for bulk fermentation.

● **MEASURE THE TEMPERATURE OF THE DOUGH:** Compare it to the DDT and record it as the final dough temperature. Cover the dough.

3. Bulk fermentation

▪ **Duration:** About 3 hours at warm room temperature: 74°–76°F (23°–24°C)
▪ **Folds:** 4 sets of stretches and folds at 30-minute intervals

● **SET TIMER AND MAKE A NOTE:** Write down the current time as the start of bulk fermentation, set a timer for 30 minutes, and let the dough rest in a warm place.

● **STRETCH AND FOLD:** When your timer goes off, give the dough one set of stretches and folds. Using wet hands, grab one side of the dough and lift it up and over to the other side. Rotate the bowl 180 degrees and repeat. Then rotate the bowl a quarter turn and stretch and fold that side. Rotate the bowl 180 degrees again and finish with a stretch and fold on the last side. The dough should be folded up neatly. Cover and repeat these folds every 30 minutes for a total of 4 sets of stretches and folds (see note).

● **LET THE DOUGH REST:** After the last set, cover the bowl and let the dough rest for the remainder of bulk fermentation, about 1 hour.

4. Divide and preshape

● **CHECK THE DOUGH:** At the end of bulk fermentation, the dough will have risen; it may have bubbles on top and at the sides, it should look smoother and less shaggy, and at the edge of the dough where it meets the container, it should dome downward. Due to spelt's increased extensibility, the dough will still stretch out considerably if you tug on it, but it should be cohesive and smoother than when bulk fermentation began. If you don't see dough that's airy, strong, and "alive," leave it for another 15 minutes in bulk fermentation and check again.

● **DIVIDE AND PRESHAPE THE DOUGH:** Using a bowl scraper, gently scrape the dough onto a clean work surface and use your bench knife to divide it directly in half. Using your bench knife in your dominant hand and with your other hand wet to reduce sticking, shape each piece of dough into a loose round. (See Preshaping, page 96, for more detail.) Let the rounds rest for 35 minutes, uncovered.

RECIPE CONTINUES ➤

PAN LOAVES

281

5. Shape

● **PREPARE THE BAKING PANS:** Liberally grease two 9 × 4 × 4-inch Pullman pans with a neutral oil or olive oil.

● **SHAPE THE DOUGH:** This dough is soft and slack, so be a little forceful when working with it in order to shape it tightly. Shape each round into a long tube the same length as your pan. Using both hands, or one hand and a bench knife, scoop the dough into the Pullman pans. (See Shaping a Pan Loaf, page 108, for more detail.) If desired, sprinkle an even layer of instant oats on the top of the dough. Place each pan inside a reusable plastic bag and seal.

6. Proof

▪ **Duration:** 1 to 2 hours at warm room temperature: 74°–76°F (23°–24°C)

● **LET THE DOUGH PROOF:** Put the pans in a warm place to proof for 1 to 2 hours. The dough should be baked when it is right at the top rim of the pan.

7. Bake

▪ **Duration:** 45 minutes in the oven

● **PREPARE THE OVEN:** Place an oven rack in the bottom third of the oven with no rack above it. Place a roasting pan with lava rocks on the bottom of the oven. (See Baking Directly on a Surface, page 124, for more detail.) Preheat the oven to 425°F (220°C).

● **BAKE THE DOUGH:** Uncover the two pans and load them into the oven side by side (like the number "11," not an "=" sign). Steam the oven by pouring a cup of ice into the preheated steaming pan at the bottom of the oven. Bake for 15 minutes. Vent the oven of steam by removing the steaming pan. Reduce the oven temperature to 375°F (190°C) and bake for 30 minutes more, or until the internal temperature reaches 205°F (96°C) and the crust is a chestnut color.

● **FINISH AND COOL:** Carefully turn the baked loaves out onto a wire rack and let cool for at least 2 hours before slicing.

TROUBLESHOOTING

THE DOUGH IS WAY TOO STICKY TO HANDLE WHEN SHAPING!

Next time, reduce the hydration of the dough by 2% to 5%. The wonderful thing about a pan loaf, though, is that even if shaping was very difficult, the pan will give the loaf structure and you won't have to worry about excessive spreading in the oven.

HOW TO TINKER

MAPLE SYRUP VARIATIONS

Try using different types of maple syrup, from golden colored syrup for a delicate flavor to very dark colored syrup for a stronger, more robust maple flavor. I've also played with adding flavored versions, such as bourbon barrel–aged maple syrup—these are fun and especially delicious!

INCREASED FERMENTATION FLAVORS WITH OVERNIGHT FERMENTATION

To increase the sour flavor of the bread, proof the dough overnight in the refrigerator. Bake in the morning or early afternoon the next day as described in the recipe.

NATURALLY LEAVENED BRIOCHE

An ethereal loaf that's buttery, sweet, and decadent

THIS DELICATE loaf deserves all the superlatives. When baking, the aroma suffuses the oven, the kitchen, the house—there's no concealing a baking brioche. It's not something you casually pull from the oven in an empty kitchen and let cool on a rack. It's a bread that has a line waiting for every slice. I like to say, if you want to make friends with someone, bake them a loaf of sourdough bread. If you need to be forgiven, bake them a brioche.

Making this brioche is a practice in pushing the limits of what a dough can handle, a testament to the wonder of gluten, and the power of lengthy, natural fermentation. Successful execution requires careful attention to ingredients, temperatures, and process. First, it's important to fully strengthen the dough (it should pass the Windowpane Test, page 83) in a stand mixer before adding the butter. When mixing, it might seem like there's an impossible amount of butter to add, but by mixing it in slowly, and letting the dough rest during this process, if necessary, you'll be amazed at what the gluten can do. Second, be sure to proof the dough until it is extremely soft and well risen—it will feel like poking a balloon when it's ready to bake.

To make a loaf with straight sides and tall rise, I like to use a 9 × 4 × 4-inch Pullman pan. If you use a traditional loaf pan that has slanted sides, the loaf will have less upward rise and more of a gentle dome on top—equally beautiful. This recipe makes two large brioche loaves, but as always, you can halve all the ingredients to make a single loaf. I usually make two, though, since the second makes an excellent gift.

For the best texture and flavor, this recipe has long bulk fermentation and proof times at a warm room temperature. Therefore, I prefer to start making this very early in the day to ensure it's ready to bake before it gets too late in the evening. However, another option is to shift the baking schedule so you start the process later in the day; the long proof will happen overnight and the brioche will be ready to bake first thing in the morning.

I recommend using high-protein white flour for this recipe because the stronger flour will ensure the dough can support the high levels of enrichments, intensive development in the mixer, and lengthy fermentation time, which will result in a brioche with a tall rise and an open interior. King Arthur Baking Bread Flour at about 12.7% protein is a great option.

BAKING TIMELINE

1. **Levain**

    12 hours (overnight)

2. **Mix**

    30 minutes

3. **Bulk Fermentation**

    4 hours

4. **Divide and Shape**

5. **Proof**

    9 hours

6. **Bake**

    40 minutes in the oven

TOTAL

26 hours 10 minutes

VITALS

Total dough weight	1,320g
Pre-fermented flour	13.6%
Levain	40.7%
Hydration	13.5%
Yield	Two 660g loaves (each in a 9 × 4 × 4-inch Pullman pan)

TOTAL FORMULA

INGREDIENT	BAKER'S %	WEIGHT
High-protein white flour (~12.7%-14% protein)	100.0%	546g
Whole milk	16.0%	87g
Egg, beaten	42.0%	229g (4 to 5 medium)
Unsalted butter	42.0%	229g
Superfine sugar	21.0%	114g
Water	13.5%	74g
Diastatic malt powder	0.5%	3g
Fine sea salt	2.0%	11g
Ripe sourdough starter, 100% hydration	4.7%	26g

ADDITIONAL INGREDIENT

Egg wash: 1 egg and 1 tablespoon whole milk or heavy cream

1. Levain

▨ **Duration:** 12 hours (overnight) at warm room temperature: 74°–76°F (23°–24°C)

● **MIX THE LEVAIN:** Warm or cool the water to about 78°F (25°C). In a large bowl, mix the levain ingredients until well incorporated. This sweet levain (see page 76) will expand considerably, so be sure to use a container that has plenty of room. Cover loosely and store in a warm place for 12 hours.

INGREDIENT	BAKER'S %	WEIGHT
High-protein white flour (~12.7%-14% protein)	100.0%	74g
Superfine sugar	25.0%	18g
Water	100.0%	74g
Ripe sourdough starter, 100% hydration	35.0%	26g

2. Mix

▨ **Desired dough temperature (DDT):** 78°F (25°C)

● **CHECK THE LEVAIN:** It should show signs of readiness: It should have risen very high, be very bubbly, and be frothy with a sharp sour aroma. If your starter is not showing these signs, let it ferment 1 hour more and check again.

● **PREPARE THE BUTTER:** Cut the butter into ½-inch-thick pats and place them on a plate on the counter to warm to room temperature.

● **MIX THE DOUGH:** To the bowl of a stand mixer fitted with the paddle, add the flour, milk, egg, half the sugar, the diastatic malt powder, salt, and ripe levain. Turn the mixer on low speed and mix for 1 to 2 minutes until well mixed. If the dough is very dry, add more milk, a small splash at a time, until it comes together and no dry bits remain. However, the dough should be a little on the firm side at this stage. Increase the mixer to medium speed and mix for 10 to 12 minutes until the dough begins to cling to the paddle and pull from the sides. Let the dough rest uncovered for 10 minutes.

● **ADD THE REMAINING SUGAR:** Add the remaining sugar and mix on low speed for 1 to 2 minutes until it is absorbed and the dough comes back together. Increase the mixer to medium speed and mix for 5 to 6 minutes until the dough is smooth and strong; it should cling to the paddle but not completely remove from the sides of the bowl. Use the Windowpane Test (page 83) to see if the dough is ready. If the dough tears irregularly and feels weak, mix on medium speed for 2 to 4 minutes more and test again.

● **INCORPORATE THE BUTTER:** At this point, if your dough is strong enough and was clinging to the paddle, you might want to switch to the dough hook. With the mixer on low speed, add the butter, one pat at a time, until absorbed into the dough, scraping down the sides of the bowl and the paddle as needed. Continue until all the butter is added, 10 to 15 minutes. Increase the mixer to medium speed and mix for 2 minutes more until the dough smooths out and clings to the dough hook. The dough will be silky smooth, elastic, and shiny. Transfer to a container for bulk fermentation.

INGREDIENT	WEIGHT
High-protein white flour (~12.7%-14% protein)	472g
Whole milk	87g
Egg, beaten	229g (4 to 5 medium)
Unsalted butter	229g
Superfine sugar	96g
Diastatic malt powder	3g
Fine sea salt	11g
Levain	192g

Mixing

Due to the lengthy mixing time required to develop this dough, I highly recommend using a stand mixer with a paddle to start. If at any point the dough clings excessively to the paddle, switch to the dough hook. This process will take 20 to 30 minutes. Be patient and let the dough rest periodically if it begins to get too hot—you want to keep the temperature close to the DDT of 78°F (25°C).

RECIPE CONTINUES →

- **MEASURE THE TEMPERATURE OF THE DOUGH:** Compare it to the DDT and record it as the final dough temperature. Cover the dough.

3. Bulk fermentation

- **Duration:** About 4 hours at warm room temperature: 74°–76°F (23°–24°C)
- **Folds:** 1 set of stretches and folds after 1 hour of bulk fermentation

- **SET TIMER AND MAKE A NOTE:** Write down the current time as the start of bulk fermentation, set a timer for 1 hour, and let the dough rest in a warm place.

- **STRETCH AND FOLD:** When your timer goes off, give the dough one set of gentle stretches and folds. Wet your hands. Slip your fingers under the dough in the middle and pick it up to let one side of the dough fall under itself. Rotate the bowl 180 degrees and repeat. Then rotate the bowl a quarter turn and stretch and fold that side. Rotate the bowl 180 degrees and stretch and fold on the last side. The dough should be folded up neatly.

- **LET THE DOUGH REST:** Cover the bowl and let the dough rest for the remainder of bulk fermentation, about 3 hours.

4. Divide and shape

- **CHECK THE DOUGH:** At the end of bulk fermentation, the dough will have risen, you may see some bubbles on top and at the sides, and it should look smoother and supple. If you don't see dough that's airy and "alive," leave it for another 15 minutes in bulk fermentation and check again.

- **PREPARE THE BAKING PANS:** Grease two 9 × 4 × 4-inch Pullman pans with butter (even if they have a nonstick lining).

- **DIVIDE AND SHAPE THE DOUGH:** Using a bowl scraper, gently scrape the dough onto a clean work surface and use your bench knife to divide it into 6 pieces of 220g each (you might have a small piece of scrap dough left over; discard it). Using your bench knife in your dominant hand and with your other hand wet to reduce sticking, shape each piece of dough into a moderately tight round. (I like to gently degas the dough by tapping the pieces very lightly as I go.) Place 3 rounds in each Pullman pan. Cover the pans with reusable plastic.

5. Proof

- **Duration:** About 9 hours at very warm room temperature: 76°–80°F (24°–26°C)

- **LET THE DOUGH PROOF:** Put the pans in a very warm place to proof for about 9 hours. This is a slow-moving dough, so be sure to give it the time it needs to fully proof. At the end of proofing, the dough will be very soft to the touch, and if you gently poke it, it will feel like poking a balloon.

6. Bake

Duration: 40 minutes in the oven

● **PREPARE THE OVEN:** Place an oven rack in the bottom third of the oven and preheat the oven to 425°F (220°C).

● **BAKE THE DOUGH:** Make the egg wash by whisking together the egg and 1 tablespoon milk. Use a pastry brush to brush the egg wash evenly and gently on the top of the dough. Load the pans side by side into the oven (like the number "11," not an "=" sign). Bake for 15 minutes. Reduce the oven temperature to 375°F (190°C) and bake for 20 to 25 minutes more, or until the internal temperature reaches 204°F (95°C) and the loaves are golden brown with a soft crust. It can be difficult to tell when the loaves are fully baked, so taking the internal temperature is recommended.

● **FINISH AND COOL:** Carefully remove the pans from the oven. Let cool for 10 minutes. Then, gently transfer the loaves to a wire rack to cool for at least 2 hours before slicing.

TROUBLESHOOTING

I HAVE A LARGE HOLE OR GAP BETWEEN THE TOP CRUST AND THE INTERIOR CRUMB.

If the rest of the crumb in the loaf looks well aerated, this is usually from overproofing. Reduce the final proof time to eliminate this gap.

MY DOUGH EXPLODED TO ONE SIDE.

You may have shaped the dough balls a little *too* tightly. They need to have a taut, smooth skin to them, but do not overly tighten them when shaping.

THE DOUGH NEVER ROSE IN BULK FERMENTATION.

Be sure you use your sourdough starter when it's ripe to make the levain, and use the levain when it's ripe to mix into your dough. From there, it's very important you hit the final dough temperature since it sets the stage for fermentation through the entire process. If your final dough temperature comes in below 78°F (25°C), know that bulk fermentation and final proof will need to be lengthened to give the dough sufficient fermentation time.

MY DOUGH ROSE INCREDIBLY HIGH IN THE OVEN.

This dough is expected to rise dramatically, but if it goes too far, it is almost always due to underproofing. Be sure to let the dough proof as long as needed, until it becomes very soft to the touch, almost like poking a balloon.

GERMAN WHOLE RYE
(Roggenvollkornbrot)

One hundred percent
whole-grain rye with
deep earthy flavors
and malty notes

A FEW years back, I had the opportunity to take a week-long course with Jeffrey Hamelman (a Certified Master Baker and former bakery director at the King Arthur Baking Company) at the King Arthur Baking facility in Washington state, and to say I left moved to action would be an understatement. His book, *Bread*, has been an inspiration for me as a home baker for many years and having the chance to meet and bake with him in person was a deeply enriching experience. I can distinctly remember trying his rye bread in our class for the first time: It was everything I didn't know rye could be. I grew up with little exposure to rye bread, and the little I did have were caraway-laden loaves with a smidgen of rye flour as a façade.

Since taking the class, and with the flavors of his vollkornbrot ever on my mind, I've worked on this recipe. My 100% whole-grain rye bread relies on a large

sourdough pre-ferment, a mixed seed soaker, and a rye chop soaker to produce a bread with a deep, hearty flavor and captivating aroma—think flavors of baked chestnut, dark beer, and even a touch of sweet molasses.

Rye chops are essentially coarsely cracked whole rye berries. You can order rye chops online (see Resources, page 424) or crack your own if you have a home grain mill. Set the mill to a very coarse setting (I set it to the coarsest setting possible on my KoMo grain mill) and test cracking a few rye berries.

You want to still see some larger pieces of the berry but no whole pieces remaining; it will look similar to cracked wheat. It's okay if there are finer bits among the larger cracked pieces as well.

Aside from the overnight levain, this recipe is a same-day process where the skill in producing a good rye bread lies in managing fermentation effectively: Be sure your starter is strong and has fully ripened when you use it to make your levain, and similarly, that your levain is ripe when you mix it into your dough.

BAKING TIMELINE

1. Levain

   12 hours (overnight)

2. Mix

3. Bulk Fermentation

   15 minutes

4. Shape

5. Proof

   1 hour 30 minutes

6. Bake

   1 hour 25 minutes in the oven

   ___

   TOTAL

   15 hours 10 minutes

VITALS

Total dough weight	1,400g
Pre-fermented flour	40.1%
Levain	138.3%
Hydration	100.0%
Yield	One 1,400g loaf (in a 9 × 4 × 4-inch Pullman pan)

TOTAL FORMULA

INGREDIENT	BAKER'S %	WEIGHT
Whole rye flour	100.0%	584g
Rye chops (soaker; see headnote)	20.0%	117g
Flaxseeds (soaker)	5.0%	29g
Black sesame seeds (soaker)	5.0%	29g
Sunflower seeds, raw	5.0%	29g
Water	100.0%	584g
Fine sea salt	2.0%	12g
Ripe sourdough starter, 100% hydration	2.8%	16g

INGREDIENT	BAKER'S %	WEIGHT
Whole rye flour	100.0%	234g
Water	100.0%	234g
Ripe sourdough starter, 100% hydration	7.0%	16g

Pre-fermented Flour

This recipe uses a high percentage of pre-fermented flour (the flour in your pre-ferment, the levain) to bring high acidity to the dough from the start. When baking recipes with a high percentage of rye, this large, acidic pre-ferment (in combination with the salt added to the dough) staves off excessive starch breakdown during baking, which can result in a loaf with a dense and gummy interior that has separated from the top crust, forming a large hole running through the loaf.

INGREDIENT	WEIGHT
Whole rye flour	350g
Water	157g
Fine sea salt	12g
Levain	484g

A Very Different Bulk Fermentation

For this dough, there are two reasons why bulk fermentation is short. First, there is a high percentage of whole grains and pre-fermented flour in the dough. Second, rye has different protein characteristics than wheat, and doesn't benefit from stretches and folds during bulk fermentation.

1. Prepare the levain, soakers, and sunflower seeds

▦ **Duration:** 12 hours (overnight) at warm room temperature: 74°–76°F (23°–24°C)

● **MIX THE LEVAIN:** It is important for the levain to have a final dough temperature of 85°F (29°C) for this recipe, so to help with that, warm or cool the water to about 85°F (29°C). In a large bowl, mix the levain ingredients until well incorporated (this liquid levain will feel quite loose). This levain is quite large and may rise higher than expected, so be sure your bowl has a few inches of headspace. Loosely cover and store in a warm place for 12 hours.

● **MIX THE SEED SOAKER:** In a medium bowl, combine the 29g flaxseeds, 29g black sesame seeds, and 58g boiling water. (It is not necessary to soak the sunflower seeds, which are relatively soft.) Cover and let soak overnight at room temperature.

● **MIX THE RYE CHOP SOAKER:** In another medium bowl, combine the 117g rye chops and 135g boiling water. Cover and let soak overnight at room temperature.

● **TOAST THE SUNFLOWER SEEDS:** In a dry skillet, toast the 29g sunflower seeds over medium-low heat until they begin to take on color and are aromatic, 3 to 5 minutes. (Alternatively, toast them in a 350°F/175°C oven for 8 to 10 minutes.) Transfer to a bowl and let cool.

2. Mix

▦ **Desired dough temperature (DDT):** 85°F (29°C)

● **CHECK THE LEVAIN:** It should show signs of readiness: well aerated, risen, loose, a crackled texture on top, and a strong earthy aroma. If the levain is not showing these signs, let it ferment 1 hour more and check again.

● **MIX THE DOUGH:** Warm or cool the water (see page 138 on how to calculate) so the temperature of the mixed dough meets the DDT of this recipe. To the bowl of a stand mixer fitted with the paddle, add the flour, water, salt, toasted sunflower seeds, seed soaker, rye chop soaker, and ripe levain. Mix on low speed for 10 to 12 minutes until the mixture becomes smooth and slightly aerated. Scrape down the paddle and the sides of the bowl as needed. Over the course of mixing, you will notice the consistency of the mixture change from dense concrete to a soft, puffy substance that should lighten a little in color.

● **MEASURE THE TEMPERATURE OF THE DOUGH:** Compare it to the DDT and record it as the final dough temperature. Cover the dough.

3. Bulk fermentation

▦ **Duration:** 15 minutes at warm room temperature: 74°–76°F (23°–24°C)

● **SET TIMER AND MAKE A NOTE:** Write down the current time as the start of bulk fermentation, set a timer for 15 minutes, and let the dough rest in a warm place.

4. Shape

- **PREPARE THE BAKING PAN:** Lightly oil one 9 × 4 × 4-inch Pullman pan with a neutral oil like vegetable oil or grapeseed oil and dust it with a light coating of whole rye flour, tapping out any excess flour.

- **SHAPE THE DOUGH:** Using a bowl scraper, gently scrape the dough onto a floured work surface (I like to use rye flour to keep this recipe strictly 100% rye). Moderately flour the top of the dough. Using floured hands, fold the sides of the dough into the center at about the length of the pan. Then roll the dough down from top to bottom, tucking it into itself as you go. The dough should tighten up as it's rolled down and form a compact cylinder. Transfer the cylinder to the prepared pan seam-side down. Using a floured hand, smooth the top of the dough so it fills the pan edge to edge. If desired, liberally dust the top with whole rye flour, which will look rather pleasing as fissures form due to expansion during proof and bake. Place the pan inside an airtight reusable plastic bag and seal.

5. Proof

- **Duration:** 1 hour to 1 hour 30 minutes at very warm room temperature: 76°–80°F (24°–26°C)

- **LET THE DOUGH PROOF:** Put the pan in a warm place to proof for 60 to 90 minutes. The dough is ready when it has risen to the top of the pan, shows fissures where it has expanded, and is very soft in texture.

6. Bake

- **Duration:** 1 hour 25 minutes in the oven

- **PREPARE THE OVEN:** Place an oven rack in the bottom third of the oven with no rack above it. Place a roasting pan with lava rocks at the bottom of the oven to one side. (See Baking Directly on a Surface, page 124, for more detail). Preheat the oven to 475°F (245°C). Roll up 3 or 4 kitchen towels and place them in a second roasting pan and set near the oven. Boil 1 cup of water and have it at the ready.

- **BAKE THE DOUGH:** Uncover the pan and place it on the counter. Steam the oven: Pour the boiling water over the rolled-up kitchen towels and set next to the pan with the lava rocks. Next, slide the pan of dough (without the Pullman pan's lid) into the oven. Carefully pour the ice into the pan of lava rocks and quickly shut the oven door. Bake for 15 minutes. Vent the oven of steam by removing the steaming pans. Reduce the oven temperature to 375°F (190°C). Bake for 60 minutes more. Carefully remove the bread from the Pullman pan and place it on a sheet pan. Place the sheet pan into the oven and bake for 10 minutes more, or until the internal temperature reaches 204°F (95°C) and the crust is a deep chocolate brown color.

- **FINISH AND COOL:** Let the bread cool on a wire rack. Once cool, wrap the loaf in baker's linen or a clean kitchen towel and let it rest on the counter for 24 hours before slicing to ensure the loaf is fully set and to avoid a gummy interior. The loaf will keep tightly wrapped in a towel on the counter for several weeks. (If the crust becomes thick after a few days, wrap the loaf in a slightly damp kitchen towel and let it rest overnight.)

TROUBLESHOOTING

MY TOP CRUST SEPARATED FROM THE CRUMB!

A common issue when baking rye bread is the dreaded "flying crust," where the top crust of the bread separates from the interior crumb, causing a large gap at the top of the loaf. In my experience, this is usually due to insufficient acidification of the dough. Be sure to make the levain the night before baking with a sourdough starter that's strong and ripe and mixed to the warm dough temperature listed. Similarly, use the levain in the morning when it's very ripe (see When Is a Levain Ready to Use?, page 73, for more detail).

Conversely if your levain was sufficiently ripe, it could be due to overproofing—in this case the crumb typically separates from the top crust, but the top crust also droops downward. This is due to excessive acidification of the dough through lengthy fermentation. Next time, reduce the bulk fermentation and/or proof time to compensate.

PIZZAS

& FLATBREADS

Focaccia

SOURDOUGH PIZZA DOUGH

A delightfully chewy and flavorful pizza dough perfect for the home oven

IF THERE'S any food that should be classified as the perfect food, I would venture to say it's pizza. And armed with the right dough, pizza perfection is attainable in a home oven just as well as in a pizzeria. This naturally leavened dough is a blank slate, a canvas for experimentation and endless possibility. Your pizza can be a doorway into countless variations and permutations, mixing and matching toppings based on what's in season and making something delightfully balanced and delicious.

If four 12-inch pizzas is too much for one dinner, you can save the dough balls covered in the fridge and use them the next day to make a simple flatbread. Alternatively, you can divide the entire formula in half and make two pizzas.

If your sourdough starter is refreshed regularly and at 100% hydration, you can swap out the levain in this recipe for your starter. See note on page 302 for more detail.

BAKING TIMELINE

1. Levain

    } 12 hours (overnight)

2. Mix

3. Warm Bulk Fermentation

    } 2 hours 30 minutes

4. Cold Bulk Fermentation

    } 23 hours (overnight)

5. Divide and shape

6. Proof

    } 6 hours

7. Bake

    | 10 minutes in the oven per pizza

TOTAL

43 hours 40 minutes

VITALS

Total dough weight	1,200g
Pre-fermented flour	6.7%
Levain	15.2%
Hydration	69.0%
Yield	Four 12-inch pizzas (290g each dough ball)

TOTAL FORMULA

INGREDIENT	BAKER'S %	WEIGHT
Type 00 flour (see opposite) or white flour (~11.5% protein)	90.0%	629g
Whole wheat flour	10.0%	70g
Water	69.0%	482g
Fine sea salt	2.0%	14g
Ripe sourdough starter, 100% hydration	0.7%	5g

ADDITIONAL INGREDIENTS

Tomato sauce, low-moisture mozzarella (cut into ½-inch cubes), and toppings of your choice (see How to Tinker on page 298 for ideas)

1. Levain

- **Duration:** 12 hours (overnight) at warm room temperature: 74°–76°F (23°–24°C)

● **MIX THE LEVAIN:** Warm or cool the water to about 78°F (25°C). In a medium jar, mix the levain ingredients until well incorporated (this liquid levain will feel quite loose) and loosely cover. Store in a warm place for 12 hours.

INGREDIENT	BAKER'S %	WEIGHT
Type 00 flour or white flour (~11.5% protein)	100.0%	47g
Water	100.0%	47g
Ripe sourdough starter, 100% hydration	10.0%	5g

2. Mix

- **Desired dough temperature (DDT):** 78°F (25°C)

● **CHECK THE LEVAIN:** It should show signs of readiness: well aerated, soft, bubbly on top and at the sides, and an assertive sour aroma. If the levain is not showing these signs, let it ferment 1 hour more and check again.

● **MIX THE DOUGH:** Warm or cool the water (see page 138 on how to calculate) so the temperature of the mixed dough meets the DDT of this recipe. In the bowl of a stand mixer fitted with the dough hook, add the flour, water, salt, and ripe levain. Mix on low speed until just incorporated. Increase to medium speed and mix until the dough begins to strengthen and cling to the dough hook, 3 to 4 minutes. Transfer to a container for bulk fermentation.

● **MEASURE THE TEMPERATURE OF THE DOUGH:** Compare it to the DDT and record it as the final dough temperature. Cover the dough.

INGREDIENT	WEIGHT
Type 00 flour or white flour (~11.5% protein)	582g
Whole wheat flour	70g
Water	435g
Fine sea salt	14g
Levain	99g

Type 00 Flour

Type 00 (or tipo 00) flour is classified by the Italian flour system as flour that's been milled extremely fine and has much of the bran and germ sifted out. In fact, it's the whitest and finest flour you can find in Italy. Specifying a flour as type 00 does not indicate its protein percentage. This type of flour is typically used for pizza, some pasta, and Focaccia (page 304). If you don't have access to type 00 flour, white flour (~11.5% protein) or even an all-purpose flour will work in its place, but I've found using type 00 yields the lightest and most tender pizza in a home oven.

3. Warm bulk fermentation

- **Duration:** 2 hours 30 minutes at warm room temperature: 74°–76°F (23°–24°C)
- **Folds:** 3 sets of stretches and folds at 30-minute intervals

● **SET TIMER AND MAKE A NOTE:** Write down the current time as the start of bulk fermentation, set a timer for 30 minutes, and let the dough rest in a warm place.

● **STRETCH AND FOLD:** When your timer goes off, give the dough one set of stretches and folds. Using wet hands, grab one side of the dough and lift it up and over to the other side. Rotate the bowl 180 degrees and repeat. Then rotate the bowl a quarter turn and stretch and fold that side. Rotate the bowl 180 degrees again and finish with a stretch and fold on the last side. The dough should be folded up neatly. Cover and repeat these folds every 30 minutes for a total of 3 sets of stretches and folds.

● **LET THE DOUGH REST:** After the last set, cover the bowl and let the dough rest for the remainder of bulk fermentation, about 1 hour.

RECIPE CONTINUES →

4. Cold bulk fermentation

- ▪ **Duration:** About 23 hours (overnight) in a home refrigerator: 39°F (4°C)
- ▪ **Folds:** None

- ● **MOVE THE DOUGH TO THE REFRIGERATOR:** After the warm bulk fermentation, place the covered bulk fermentation container in the refrigerator overnight.

5. Divide and shape the pizza balls

- ● **PREPARE THE PROOFING VESSEL:** Lightly grease a large baking dish (a glass one works especially well) with olive oil.

Shaping small rounds, stiff dough, pinching method

- ● **DIVIDE THE DOUGH:** Using a bowl scraper, gently scrape the dough onto a clean work surface. Divide the dough into four 290g pieces. Shape each into a very tight ball: Pick up the dough with both hands and tuck the dough back and into itself as you rotate it around in your hand. Work your way around and around, stretching and tucking, then flip the ball over and pinch the bottom to seal. Place it on the work surface and lightly tug it toward you one or two times to ensure that it is sealed and perfectly round. It's important to shape each piece into a completely smooth ball with no breaks on the bottom: You want each dough ball to have a tight skin that completely surrounds it. Transfer to the prepared baking dish and repeat with the remaining dough pieces.

Overnight Option

Place the covered dough in the refrigerator to proof overnight. The next day, take the dough out 4 to 6 hours before you want to cook the pizza, temperature depending.

6. Proof

- ▪ **Duration:** About 6 hours at warm room temperature: 74°–76°F (23°–24°C)

- ● **LET THE DOUGH PROOF:** Cover the baking dish with reusable plastic wrap or a lid and put the dish in a warm place to proof for about 6 hours.

7. Bake

- ▪ **Duration:** 10 minutes in the oven for each pizza

- ● **PREPARE THE OVEN:** Place an oven rack in the top third of the oven. Place a baking stone/steel on the rack. Preheat the oven as hot as it goes—I set mine to 550°F (290°C)—for 1 hour.

- ● **PREPARE THE TOPPINGS:** While your oven is preheating, gather and prepare your pizza toppings.

Shaping a pizza crust

- ● **SHAPE THE CRUST:** Cut a piece of parchment paper to fit your pizza peel and place it on top. Flour a work surface and the top of one dough ball from the fridge. Using a dough scraper, gently remove the dough ball from the baking dish and place it upside down on your work surface. Using two floured hands shaped like an inverted letter V, and using your fingertips, press down the dough in a uniform fashion starting at the side farthest from you and working toward your body Ⓐ . Try not to press out any gas at the rim of the dough where the edge will form—you want this to rise as high as possible. After pressing, flip the dough over. Again, using your hands

RECIPE CONTINUES →

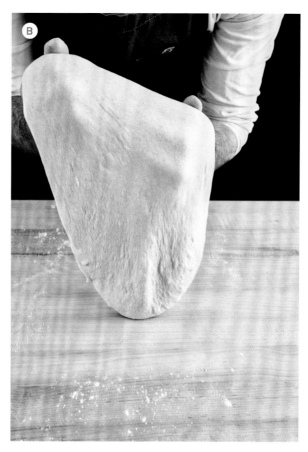

still shaped like an inverted V, press a few times in this way again. Then, using both hands, pick up the dough and drape it over your knuckles with your palms facing each other, grabbing the rim of the dough with your thumbs (B). Gently spread your hands apart to stretch and open the dough. Continue doing this until the pizza is about 12 inches in diameter, then place it on the parchment paper (C). Once finished, the flattened disc should be smooth and with a slightly pronounced rim around the disc (this will form the crust). If you have trouble shaping the crust, chill the dough balls for 30 minutes and proceed, using extra bench flour as needed.

● **BAKE THE PIZZAS:** Switch your oven setting from bake to high broil. Top the pizza dough with your desired toppings (D). Slide the parchment paper and pizza into your oven. Cook for 1½ to 2 minutes until you see the dough slightly color, then switch your oven back to bake (at maximum temperature, which is 550°F/290°C for my oven). Cook for 2 minutes. Using your pizza peel, carefully rotate the pizza 180 degrees. Continue cooking until done to your liking. I like to ever-so-slightly undercook these so that they are still very soft, 2 minutes more, but the crust should be evenly golden all over with a few scattered black spots. Remove from the oven using your pizza peel and transfer to a large plate. Top with any items not suitable for lengthy cooking in the oven (such as prosciutto, basil, or other fresh herbs).

● **FINISH AND COOL:** Let each pizza cool just a few minutes on the plate before cutting with a pizza wheel or mezzaluna. For the remaining pizzas, preheat the baking surface for 15 minutes and repeat.

HOW TO TINKER

MY GO-TO SAUCE FOR PIZZA

This simple *salsa di pomodoro* is my favorite tomato sauce for pizza. If you like it more *arrabbiata*, add a pinch of crushed red pepper flakes before blending. Any unused sauce can be cooked in a pan with olives, garlic, and capers for a quick and easy pasta sauce later in the week.

In a blender, combine 1 drained (28-ounce) can whole peeled tomatoes (San Marzano or Bianco DiNapoli), 20g (1½ tablespoons) extra-virgin olive oil, 3g (½ teaspoon) sea salt, and a pinch of crushed red pepper flakes (optional). Blend until very smooth. The sauce will keep for a week in the fridge.

MY FAVORITE PIZZA TOPPING COMBINATIONS

Really, the possibilities for pizza are endless, and it's the perfect canvas for anything ripe in the garden or from the farmers' market. I've had some pretty out-there pizza toppings in Italy (French fries being the strangest, perhaps, but I'd be lying if I didn't admit it was delicious). My favorite among favorites has to be the simplest of all, a Margherita pizza with just my *salsa di pomodoro*, mozzarella, and fresh basil. Here are a few other creative ideas:

■ Salsa di pomodoro / cubed mozzarella cheese / whole Peppadew peppers / coarsely chopped kalamata olives / fresh basil / drizzle of olive oil / light sprinkle of chunky salt

■ Chopped garlic confit / whole spinach leaves / crumbled feta cheese / cubed mozzarella cheese / a pinch of crushed red pepper flakes / drizzle of olive oil

■ Cubed mozzarella cheese / halved multicolored cherry tomatoes / coarsely chopped kalamata olives / fresh basil

ROMAN-STYLE PAN PIZZA
(Pizza in Teglia)

A thin, crispy-bottomed pizza
baked in a sheet pan

PIZZA IN TEGLIA, or "pizza in pan," can mean different things to different people, but for me it is a Roman-style rectangular pizza baked in a pan. This isn't focaccia (which is typically thicker, with fewer toppings, and proofed directly in the pan; see page 304), and it is certainly not bread, but rather, it is its own category. I prefer this pizza with a decidedly crispy bottom crust—but not so much it enters cracker territory—and it should not be as deep as a Sicilian-style pizza. Rather, it should be quite thin and *bassa*—low. A slice should feel light, airy, and yet have some structure to it, finished with a dramatic mix of toppings.

This is an accommodating recipe that can be mixed and made the same day, or made over two days, depending on your schedule. It's a flexible and low-maintenance dough: Mix it in the early morning when your levain is ripe, give it a few folds and attention here and there throughout the day, and then bake it that evening for dinner or retard the dough until lunch or dinner the next day. The small addition of extra-virgin olive oil keeps the center soft and chewy but makes the crust—especially the parts that come in contact with the pan—extra crisp.

BAKING TIMELINE

1 Levain

⎰ 12 hours (overnight)

2 Mix

3 Bulk Fermentation

⎰ 3 hours 30 minutes

4 Proof

⎰ 3 hours

5 Bake

⎰ 30 minutes in the oven

TOTAL

19 hours

VITALS

Total dough weight	900g
Pre-fermented flour	7.5%
Levain	17.0%
Hydration	72.0%
Yield	One 13 × 18-inch rectangular pizza (baked in a half-sheet pan)

TOTAL FORMULA

INGREDIENT	BAKER'S %	WEIGHT
Type 00 flour or white flour (~11.5% protein)	90.0%	458g
Whole spelt or whole wheat flour	10.0%	51g
Extra-virgin olive oil	2.3%	12g
Water	72.0%	366g
Fine sea salt	1.9%	10g
Ripe sourdough starter, 100% hydration	0.8%	4g

ADDITIONAL INGREDIENTS

Tomato sauce, low-moisture mozzarella (cut into ½-inch cubes), and toppings of your choice

INGREDIENT	BAKER'S %	WEIGHT
Type 00 flour or white flour (~11.5% protein)	100.0%	38g
Water	100.0%	38g
Ripe sourdough starter, 100% hydration	10.0%	4g

INGREDIENT	WEIGHT
Type 00 flour or white flour (~11.5% protein)	420g
Whole spelt or whole wheat flour	51g
Extra-virgin olive oil	12g
Water	328g
Fine sea salt	10g
Levain	80g

Using Ripe Sourdough Starter Instead of a Levain

If your sourdough starter is refreshed regularly and at 100% hydration, you can swap out the levain in this recipe for your starter. Give it a refreshment 12 hours before (i.e., the night before) you plan to mix this dough and omit the levain. If your starter is not made of a large portion of white flour, note that the final pizza will be a bit more sour than it would otherwise be.

1. Levain

- **Duration:** 12 hours (overnight) at warm room temperature: 74°–76°F (23°–24°C)

- **MIX THE LEVAIN:** Warm or cool the water to about 78°F (25°C). In a medium jar, mix the levain ingredients until well incorporated (this liquid levain will feel quite loose) and loosely cover. Store in a warm place for 12 hours.

2. Mix

- **Desired dough temperature (DDT):** 78°F (25°C)

- **CHECK THE LEVAIN:** It should show signs of readiness: well aerated, soft, bubbly on top and at the sides, and with a sour aroma. If the levain is not showing these signs, let it ferment 1 hour more and check again.

- **MIX THE DOUGH:** Warm or cool the water (see page 138 on how to calculate) so the temperature of the mixed dough meets the DDT of this recipe. In the bowl of a stand mixer fitted with the dough hook, add the flour, water, salt, and ripe levain. Mix on low speed until just incorporated. Increase the speed to medium and mix until the dough begins to strengthen and cling to the dough hook, 3 to 4 minutes. Let the dough rest in the bowl for 5 minutes.

- **ADD THE OLIVE OIL:** Mix on low speed until all the olive oil is incorporated, 1 to 2 minutes. Increase the mixer speed to medium and mix until the dough begins to smooth out and cling to the dough hook, 2 to 3 minutes. Transfer to a bulk fermentation container.

- **MEASURE THE TEMPERATURE OF THE DOUGH:** Compare it to the DDT and record it as the final dough temperature. Cover the dough.

3. Bulk fermentation

- **Duration:** About 3 hours 30 minutes at warm room temperature: 74°–76°F (23°–24°C)
- **Folds:** 3 sets of stretches and folds at 30-minute intervals

- **SET TIMER AND MAKE A NOTE:** Write down the current time as the start of bulk fermentation, set a timer for 30 minutes, and let the dough rest in a warm place.

- **STRETCH AND FOLD:** When your timer goes off, give the dough one set of stretches and folds. Using wet hands, grab one side of the dough and lift it up and over to the other side. Rotate the bowl 180 degrees and repeat. Then rotate the bowl a quarter turn and stretch and fold that side. Rotate the bowl 180 degrees again and finish with a stretch and fold on the last side. The dough should be folded up neatly. Cover and repeat these folds every 30 minutes for a total of 3 sets of stretches and folds.

- **LET THE DOUGH REST:** After the last set, cover the bowl and let the dough rest for the remainder of bulk fermentation, about 2 hours.

4. Proof

- **Duration:** 3 hours at warm room temperature: 74°–76°F (23°–24°C), or overnight in a home refrigerator: 39°F (4°C)

- **LET THE DOUGH PROOF:** You have two proofing options:

- Same-day bake: Proof the dough in a warm place for 3 hours.

- Next-day bake: Proof the dough in the refrigerator overnight. The next day, take the dough out and leave out on the counter for 2 hours to bring it back to room temperature before baking.

5. Bake

- **Duration:** 30 minutes in the oven

- **PREPARE THE OVEN:** Place a rack in the bottom third of the oven with a baking stone/steel on top. Preheat the oven to 500°F (260°C) for 1 hour.

- **PREPARE THE TOPPINGS:** While your oven is preheating and your dough is chilling in the fridge, gather and prepare your pizza sauce, cheese, and other toppings.

- **SHAPE THE DOUGH:** Have a 13 × 18-inch half-sheet pan at hand. Gently scrape the dough onto a floured work surface. Flour the top of the dough and your hands, and using your fingertips, gently press the dough out to a rectangle. Once pressed out to about 75 percent of the pan's length, transfer the dough to the pan. Gently stretch the dough as needed so it runs edge to edge. (Stretching the dough to 75 percent first makes it easier to transfer to the pan and then finish stretching.)

- **BAKE THE PIZZA:** Using a large spoon, spread a thin layer of pizza sauce over the dough from edge to edge. Slide the baking pan into the oven on top of the baking surface. Decrease the oven temperature to 425°F (220°C) and bake for 10 minutes. Transfer the pan to a wire rack and sprinkle on the grated cheese and any other toppings. Lightly drizzle some olive oil over the entire pizza. Slide the sheet pan back into the oven on the baking surface and bake for 15 to 20 minutes more. The cheese should be melted and the bottom crust well colored.

- **FINISH AND COOL:** Transfer the pan to a wire rack and let the pizza cool for 5 minutes before slicing.

Baking with Sauce Only

Baking the pizza first with only the sauce does two things: It gives the dough a chance to get a head start in baking, since the dough usually takes longer to bake than most of the toppings. Second, having only the tomato sauce on top means there isn't too much weight on the dough so that it can't rise (the full complement of toppings would prevent rising), but not so little weight that it rises too high.

FOCACCIA

A golden, flat, and thick bread with a slightly crispy top and chewy center

FOCACCIA WILL forever remind me of childhood trips to southern Italy to visit my family. Daily excursions to the beach in the late summer were our attempts at escaping the sweltering heat in the city—long days spent swimming, playing beach soccer, and, of course, *calcio balilla* (table soccer or foosball). Much like a small circus caravan, we would load four to six per car (if you know Italy, you know the cars are small) and make our way through the narrow winding streets to stop at the local baker's for whole sheet trays of freshly made focaccia topped with tomato, olive, salt, and rosemary. With coolers full of aranciata, light Italian beer, and anything else my aunts and uncles thought to bring, we'd stake our claim on a large swath of the beach with umbrellas and

blankets, and with that, the fun began. I'll never forget emerging from the water in a sprint toward my family, approaching with eager eyes and a voracious hunger. As I drew near, they would already know what I was after: a thick slice of focaccia, and not just any slice, always the corner where the oil pooled just a bit more, where the crust was thickest.

This recipe is my take on that southern Italian focaccia of my childhood. It's a same-day, naturally leavened dough that comes together so easily and is so fuss-free it'll shock you just how good it tastes. Topped with any fresh summer produce, it's the perfect thing to make for a group gathering, a park excursion, or, of course, a day trip to the beach.

If your sourdough starter is refreshed regularly and at 100% hydration, you can swap out the levain in this recipe for your starter. See note on page 302 for more detail.

BAKING TIMELINE

1 Levain

12 hours (overnight)

2 Mix

3 Bulk Fermentation

2 hours 30 minutes

4 Proof

4 hours

5 Bake

30 minutes in the oven

TOTAL

19 hours

VITALS

Total dough weight	1,300g
Pre-fermented flour	8.3%
Levain	19.1%
Hydration	76.0%
Yield	One 9 x 13-inch rectangular focaccia or two 10 × 2¼-inch round focaccia

TOTAL FORMULA

INGREDIENT	BAKER'S %	WEIGHT
White flour (~11.5% protein)	70.0%	504g
High-protein white flour (~12.7%-14% protein)	30.0%	216g
Extra-virgin olive oil	2.0%	14g
Water 1 (levain and mix)	71.0%	511g
Water 2 (reserve)	5.0%	36g
Fine sea salt	1.8%	13g
Ripe sourdough starter, 100% hydration	0.8%	6g

ADDITIONAL INGREDIENTS

Very good extra-virgin olive oil and coarse sea salt, for topping

Chopped fresh herbs, olives, and/or cherry tomatoes, for topping (optional)

INGREDIENT	BAKER'S %	WEIGHT
White flour (~11.5% protein)	100.0%	60g
Water 1	100.0%	60g
Ripe sourdough starter, 100% hydration	10.0%	6g

INGREDIENT	WEIGHT
White flour (~11.5% protein)	444g
High-protein white flour (~12.7%-14% protein)	216g
Extra-virgin olive oil	14g
Water 1	451g
Water 2 (reserve)	36g
Fine sea salt	13g
Levain	126g

1. Levain

▪ **Duration:** 12 hours (overnight) at warm room temperature: 74°–76°F (23°–24°C)

● **MIX THE LEVAIN:** Warm or cool the water to about 78°F (25°C). In a medium jar, mix the levain ingredients until well incorporated (this liquid levain will feel quite loose) and loosely cover. Store in a warm place for 12 hours.

2. Mix

▪ **Desired dough temperature (DDT):** 78°F (25°C)

● **CHECK THE LEVAIN:** It should show signs of readiness: well aerated, soft, bubbly on top and at the sides, and with a sour aroma. If the levain is not showing these signs, let it ferment 1 hour more and check again.

● **MIX THE DOUGH:** Warm or cool the water (see page 138 on how to calculate) so the temperature of the mixed dough meets the DDT of this recipe. To the bowl of a stand mixer fitted with a dough hook, add the flour, water 1, salt, and ripe levain. (This is a wet and sticky dough, so adding the water in two steps will help strengthen the dough before too much water is added.) Mix on low speed for 1 minute until combined. Increase to medium speed and mix for about 5 minutes. If the dough is starting to smooth out and cling to the dough hook, decrease to low speed and slowly add in water 2 over the course of 2 to 4 minutes. If the dough looks very shaggy and wet, leave out the remaining water 2. Then, with the mixer running, begin to drizzle in the olive oil. The dough should start to cling to the dough hook and show signs of strength. It will still be a little shaggy and sticky but should be smoother and more elastic—if in doubt, mix a few minutes longer. Transfer to another container, or keep it in the bowl, for bulk fermentation.

● **MEASURE THE TEMPERATURE OF THE DOUGH:** Compare it to the DDT and record it as the final dough temperature. Cover the dough.

MIXING

Due to their higher hydration, breads like focaccia benefit from extended mixing to develop an open and light interior. During mixing it will feel loose and extensible, especially with the added olive oil, but resist the urge to add more flour. The dough will eventually come together and strengthen sufficiently during bulk fermentation and the pan will help keep it in shape.

This dough can also be mixed by hand. Just make sure to look for the same signs of dough development. It should take 8 to 10 minutes of mixing by hand, but the dough may need a few minutes longer depending on your mixing and strengthening method (see Dough Strengthening Methods, page 82, for more detail).

3. Bulk fermentation

- **Duration:** 2 hours 30 minutes at warm room temperature: 74°–76°F (23°–24°C)
- **Folds:** 3 sets of stretches and folds at 30-minute intervals

● **SET TIMER AND MAKE A NOTE:** Write down the current time as the start of bulk fermentation, set a timer for 30 minutes, and let the dough rest in a warm place.

● **STRETCH AND FOLD:** When your timer goes off, give the dough one set of stretches and folds. For each set, wet your hands. Grab one side of the dough and lift it up and over to the other side. Rotate the bowl 180 degrees and repeat. Then rotate the bowl a quarter turn and stretch and fold that side. Rotate the bowl 180 degrees again and finish with a stretch and fold on the last side. The dough should be folded up neatly. Cover and repeat these folds every 30 minutes for a total of 3 sets of stretches and folds.

● **LET THE DOUGH REST:** After the last set, cover the bowl and let the dough rest for the remainder of bulk fermentation, about 1 hour.

RECIPE CONTINUES

Overnight Option

Cover the pan and place it in the refrigerator to proof overnight. The next day, take it out of the fridge and let it come to room temperature. Then stretch it out, if necessary, and let it finish proofing on the counter until ready to bake, about 1 hour longer. The dough is ready when it's very bubbly, well risen, and soft to the touch.

4. Proof

■ **Duration:** 3 to 4 hours at warm room temperature: 74°–76°F (23°–24°C)

● **TRANSFER THE DOUGH:** Generously grease a 9 × 13-inch rectangular pan or two 10 × 2¼-inch round pans with extra-virgin olive oil. If your baking pan is not nonstick, use greased parchment paper to line the pan to prevent sticking or oil the pan very generously. Using a bowl scraper, gently scrape the dough into the pan. Using wet hands, gently stretch the dough out toward the edges of the pan until it just begins to show signs of resistance. Cover.

● **LET THE DOUGH PROOF:** Set the focaccia in a warm place and set a timer for 30 minutes. Every 30 minutes for the first 2 hours during proofing, use wet hands to gently stretch the dough toward the edges of the pan. The dough will resist stretching and spring back but don't force it. Each time you do this the dough will stretch a little more, eventually filling the container. Let the dough proof, untouched and covered, for 1 to 2 more hours. It is ready when it has risen in the pan, is very bubbly, and when poked, is reminiscent of soft marshmallows.

5. Top and bake

■ **Duration:** 30 minutes in the oven

● **PREPARE THE OVEN:** Place a rack in the middle position and preheat the oven to 425°F (220°C).

● **DIMPLE THE DOUGH AND ADD TOPPINGS (IF USING):** Uncover the dough and dimple it by using your fingers to poke it all over, down to the pan. Drizzle 2 to 3 tablespoons of olive oil over the top, then sprinkle with coarse sea salt. If desired, sprinkle with chopped herbs and/or press olives and cherry tomatoes into the dough.

● **BAKE THE DOUGH:** Place the pan in the oven and bake for 15 minutes. Rotate the pan and bake for 15 minutes more. When done, the focaccia should be a deep golden brown and glistening. Let cool for a few minutes in the pan, then transfer to a wire rack to cool completely.

TROUBLESHOOTING

MY FOCACCIA IS NOT AIRY.

It's underproofed: Be sure to use your starter when it's fully ripe. If you use it too early, lengthen the bulk fermentation and/or proof time.

It's overhydrated or understrengthened: While this is a very wet dough, it's possible too much water was added. Reduce the water by 50g (~5%) and it should feel stronger and more elastic. Also, be sure you're mixing the dough until sufficiently strengthened.

HOW TO TINKER

ALTERNATE GRAIN

For a different flavor profile, try substituting 20% of the white flour with durum flour ("extra fancy"), whole-grain spelt, or white whole wheat—each will bring a slightly different character to the focaccia. Adding in whole grains will result in a slight increase in sourness (in a good way). Note that if you add whole-grain flour, your bulk fermentation and/or final proof might need to be slightly shortened due to the increased fermentation activity.

ALTERNATE TOPPING

Many toppings work for this focaccia besides my favorite of cherry tomatoes, olives, rosemary, and coarse sea salt. Here is another: Try thinly sliced Yukon Gold potatoes (sliced on a mandoline to ¹⁄₁₆ inch for the best texture) soaked in a brine solution of 1 liter (4¼ cups) water and 4 teaspoons salt for several hours or overnight in the refrigerator. Top the potatoes with chopped fresh thyme or rosemary.

TUSCAN FLATBREAD

(Schiacciata)

Focaccia's squished, crunchy sibling

SCHIACCIATA **(SKIAH-CHA-TAH)** hails from Tuscany, and while it's quite similar to the thicker—and often fancifully topped—focaccia, changing the hydration, flour, and reducing the dough weight results in a totally different bread. It's thinner and crunchier, making it perfect to slice in half for sandwiches (mortadella, tomato, provolone, and arugula being my favorite). Traditionally, this bread would be topped simply, with just salt and olive oil, but I completely understand if you have a bowl of ripe cherry tomatoes—who could resist? Or try prosciutto and olives: Add a handful of olives (kalamata or Castelvetrano) after you dimple the dough. When it has finished baking, spread on thin slices of prosciutto while it cools.

This recipe can be baked equally well in a single 9 × 13-inch baking pan or two 10-inch round pans—regardless, be sure to oil the pans well.

BAKING TIMELINE

1. Levain

   12 hours (overnight)

2. Mix

3. Bulk Fermentation

   3 hours 30 minutes

4. Shape

5. Proof

   3 hours

6. Bake

   30 minutes in the oven

TOTAL
19 hours

VITALS

Total dough weight	1,000g
Pre-fermented flour	8.7%
Levain	20.0%
Hydration	67.0%
Yield	One 9 × 13-inch rectangular schiacciata

TOTAL FORMULA

INGREDIENT	BAKER'S %	WEIGHT
White flour (~11.5% protein)	100.0%	576g
Extra-virgin olive oil	4.0%	23g
Water	67.0%	386g
Fine sea salt	1.7%	10g
Ripe sourdough starter, 100% hydration	0.9%	5g

ADDITIONAL INGREDIENTS

Olive oil and coarse sea salt, for topping

INGREDIENT	BAKER'S %	WEIGHT
White flour (~11.5% protein)	100.0%	50g
Water	100.0%	50g
Ripe sourdough starter, 100% hydration	10.0%	5g

INGREDIENT	WEIGHT
White flour (~11.5% protein)	526g
Extra-virgin olive oil	23g
Water	336g
Fine sea salt	10g
Levain	105g

Mix by Hand

The dough can also be mixed by hand using a strengthening technique like slap and fold (see page 83).

1. Levain

- ▪ **Duration:** 12 hours (overnight) at warm room temperature: 74°–76°F (23°–24°C)

- ● **MIX THE LEVAIN:** Warm or cool the water to about 78°F (25°C). In a medium jar, mix the levain ingredients until well incorporated (this liquid levain will feel quite loose) and loosely cover. Store in a warm place for 12 hours.

2. Mix

- ▪ **Desired dough temperature (DDT):** 78°F (25°C)

- ● **CHECK THE LEVAIN:** It should show signs of readiness: well aerated, soft, bubbly on top and at the sides, and with an assertive sour aroma. If the levain is not showing these signs, let it ferment 1 hour more and check again.

- ● **MIX THE DOUGH:** Warm or cool the water (see page 138 on how to calculate) so the temperature of the mixed dough meets the DDT of this recipe. To the bowl of a stand mixer fitted with a dough hook, add the flour, olive oil, water, salt, and ripe levain. Mix on low speed for 1 minute until combined. Increase to medium speed and mix for about 5 minutes until the dough starts to cling to the dough hook, but it is still shaggy and sticky. Transfer to another container, or keep it in the bowl, for bulk fermentation.

- ● **MEASURE THE TEMPERATURE OF THE DOUGH:** Compare it to the DDT and record it as the final dough temperature. Cover the dough.

3. Bulk fermentation

- ▪ **Duration:** 3 hours 30 minutes at warm room temperature: 74°–76°F (23°–24°C)
- ▪ **Folds:** 2 sets of stretches and folds at 30-minute intervals

- ● **SET TIMER AND MAKE A NOTE:** Write down the current time as the start of bulk fermentation, set a timer for 30 minutes, and let the dough rest in a warm place.

- ● **STRETCH AND FOLD:** When your timer goes off, give the dough one set of stretches and folds. Using wet hands, grab one side of the dough and lift it up and over to the other side. Rotate the bowl 180 degrees and repeat. Then rotate the bowl a quarter turn and stretch and fold that side. Rotate the bowl 180 degrees again and finish with a stretch and fold on the last side. The dough should be folded up neatly. Cover the bowl and repeat these folds one more time after another 30 minutes for a total of 2 sets of stretches and folds.

- ● **LET THE DOUGH REST:** After the last set, cover the bowl and let the dough rest for the remainder of bulk fermentation, about 2 hours 30 minutes.

RECIPE CONTINUES →

4. Shape

- **CHECK THE DOUGH:** At the end of bulk fermentation, the dough should have smoothed out and risen. If the dough still looks dense and not active, let ferment 15 minutes more and check again.

- **TRANSFER THE DOUGH:** If your baking pan is not nonstick, use parchment paper to line it to prevent sticking. Grease a 9 × 13-inch baking pan (or the parchment paper, if using) with extra-virgin olive oil. Gently scrape the dough directly into the greased pan. Wet your hands and gently stretch the dough out until it resists, but don't worry if it doesn't completely fill the pan at this point. Cover.

5. Proof

- **Duration:** 2 to 3 hours at warm room temperature: 74°–76°F (23°–24°C)

- **LET THE DOUGH PROOF:** Put the pan in a warm place to proof for 2 to 3 hours total. After the first hour in proof, you will stretch the dough out to help it fill the pan. Set a timer for 1 hour.

- **STRETCH THE DOUGH:** After the first hour in proof, uncover the pan, wet your hands, and gently pick up and stretch the dough outward. Avoid pressing the dough at this point; you want to scoop up a side and extend it outward toward the rim of the pan. After stretching, let the dough rest for the remaining 1- to 2-hour proof time.

6. Bake

- **Duration:** 30 minutes in the oven

- **CHECK THE DOUGH:** It should show bubbles on the surface, have relaxed to either fill the pans or come close, look slightly risen, and if you poke it gently, feel light and airy. If it still feels tight and dense, let proof 30 minutes more and check again before preheating the oven.

- **PREPARE THE OVEN:** Place a rack in the middle of the oven. Place a baking stone/steel on the rack (you can also bake it directly on the oven rack). Preheat the oven to 450°F (230°C) or 425°F (220°C) convection (which I prefer for a faster bake and a more golden crust) for 30 minutes.

- **TOP THE DOUGH:** Uncover the pan. Drizzle on a good measure of extra-virgin olive oil to cover, but not drench, the dough. Using wet fingers, dimple the dough by using your fingers to poke all over it all the way down to the pan. Sprinkle with coarse sea salt.

- **BAKE THE DOUGH:** Place the pan on your preheated baking surface and bake for 15 minutes. Rotate the pan 180 degrees and bake for 10 to 15 minutes more. Keep an eye on it in the last 10 minutes to avoid overbaking. When done, it will be a deep golden-brown color with a crunchy crust.

- **FINISH AND COOL:** Let cool for 15 minutes before slicing.

TROUBLESHOOTING

MY SCHIACCIATA CAME OUT VERY DRY AND CRACKER-LIKE!

The thinner your schiacciata is, the crisper it will be. If you're using a pan wider than the one called for in the recipe, the total dough weight for this recipe might need to be scaled up so the bread isn't too thin. Also, the longer you bake it, the drier it will become, so bake at a hotter temperature for a shorter time (this is why I prefer using the convection option).

FRENCH FLATBREAD
(Fougasse)

A uniquely shaped herbed bread perfect for sharing

WALKING INTO a friend's house with a large and intricate fougasse tucked under your arm might just make you everyone's favorite guest at the dinner table. Sure to elicit oohs and aahs, the labyrinth of crunchy parts winding here and there adds up to a striking whole. Think of this shape as a blank canvas that can be anything you dream up—I alternate between the traditional triangular leaf and a "ladder," or sometimes I simply let my hand and bench knife direct the cuts as in-the-moment inspiration strikes. What is the reason for all these cuts? To maximize the crust's surface area. A fougasse encourages sharing, as it breaks easily at the thinner points in the design, forming neat snackable segments. With that, have fun and cut away; you really cannot make a mistake.

This dough is versatile and accepting of many ingredients and toppings. I love adding kalamata or Castelvetrano olives to the dough and then finishing with a light brushing of olive oil as directed in the recipe. See How to Tinker (page 317) for more ideas.

BAKING TIMELINE

1. Levain

    12 hours (overnight)

2. Mix

3. Bulk Fermentation

    3 hours

4. Divide, Preshape, Bench Rest

    30 minutes

5. Shape

6. Proof

    1 hour 30 minutes

7. Cut and Top

8. Bake

    30 minutes in the oven

TOTAL
17 hours 30 minutes

VITALS

Total dough weight	1,600g
Pre-fermented flour	9.0%
Levain	20.6%
Hydration	64.0%
Yield	Two 800g fougasses or four 400g fougasses

TOTAL FORMULA

INGREDIENT	BAKER'S %	WEIGHT
White flour (~11.5% protein)	85.0%	796g
Whole wheat flour	15.0%	141g
Extra-virgin olive oil	4.0%	37g
Water	64.0%	600g
Fine sea salt	1.8%	17g
Ripe sourdough starter, 100% hydration	0.9%	8g

ADDITIONAL INGREDIENTS

Extra-virgin olive oil, coarse sea salt, and herbes de Provence, for topping (optional)

1. Levain

- Duration: 12 hours (overnight) at warm room temperature: 74°–76°F (23°–24°C)

● **MIX THE LEVAIN:** Warm or cool the water to about 78°F (25°C). In a medium jar, mix the levain ingredients until well incorporated (this liquid levain will feel quite loose) and loosely cover. Store in a warm place for 12 hours.

INGREDIENT	BAKER'S %	WEIGHT
White flour (~11.5% protein)	100.0%	84g
Water	100.0%	84g
Ripe sourdough starter, 100% hydration	10.0%	8g

2. Mix

- Desired dough temperature (DDT): 78°F (25°C)

● **CHECK THE LEVAIN:** It should show signs of readiness: well aerated, bubbly at the top and at the sides, loose, and with an assertive sour aroma. If the levain is not showing these signs, let it ferment 1 hour more and check again.

● **MIX THE DOUGH:** Warm or cool the water (see page 138 on how to calculate) so the temperature of the mixed dough meets the DDT of this recipe. To the bowl of a stand mixer fitted with a dough hook, add the water, flour, salt, and ripe levain. Mix on low speed for 1 to 2 minutes until combined. Increase the speed to medium and mix for 2 to 4 minutes until the dough starts to cling to the dough hook, showing signs of strength. Let the dough rest for 10 minutes, uncovered.

● **ADD THE OIL:** Turn the mixer on low speed and slowly drizzle in the olive oil while the mixer is running. It will take a few minutes to add all the oil. Once all the oil is added, increase the speed to medium and mix for 2 to 3 minutes until all the oil is absorbed. The dough won't completely cling to the dough hook, but it will be smoother and more elastic. Transfer to another container, or keep it in the bowl, for bulk fermentation.

● **MEASURE THE TEMPERATURE OF THE DOUGH:** Compare it to the DDT and record it as the final dough temperature. Cover the dough.

INGREDIENT	WEIGHT
White flour (~11.5% protein)	712g
Whole wheat flour	141g
Extra-virgin olive oil	37g
Water	516g
Fine sea salt	17g
Levain	176g

Mix by Hand

The dough can also be mixed by hand using a strengthening technique like slap and fold (see page 83).

3. Bulk fermentation

- Duration: About 3 hours at warm room temperature: 74°–76°F (23°–24°C)
- Folds: 3 sets of stretches and folds at 30-minute intervals

● **SET TIMER AND MAKE A NOTE:** Write down the current time as the start of bulk fermentation, set a timer for 30 minutes, and let the dough rest in a warm place.

● **STRETCH AND FOLD:** When your timer goes off, give the dough one set of stretches and folds. Using wet hands, grab one side of the dough and lift it up and over to the other side. Rotate the bowl 180 degrees and repeat. Then rotate the bowl a quarter turn and stretch and fold that side. Rotate the bowl 180 degrees again and finish with a stretch and fold on the last side. The dough should be folded up neatly. Cover and repeat these folds every 30 minutes for a total of 3 sets of stretches and folds.

RECIPE CONTINUES →

- **LET THE DOUGH REST:** After the last set, cover the bowl and let the dough rest for the remainder of bulk fermentation, about 1 hour 30 minutes.

4. Divide and preshape

- **CHECK THE DOUGH:** At the end of bulk fermentation, the dough will have risen significantly; it may have bubbles on top and at the sides, it should look smoother and less shaggy, and at the edge of the dough where it meets the container, it should dome downward. If you wet a hand and gently tug on the surface of the dough, it will feel elastic and cohesive, resisting your pull. If you don't see dough that's airy, strong, and "alive," leave it for another 15 minutes in bulk fermentation and check again.

- **DIVIDE AND PRESHAPE THE DOUGH:** Using a bowl scraper, gently scrape the dough onto a work surface and use your bench knife to divide it directly in half. Using your bench knife in your dominant hand and with your other hand wet to reduce sticking, shape each piece of dough into a loose round. (See Preshaping, page 96, for more detail.) Let the rounds rest for 30 minutes, uncovered.

5. Shape

- **PREPARE THE PROOFING AND BAKING SURFACE:** Cut two pieces of parchment paper, each to fit a 13 × 18-inch half-sheet pan. Grease each piece with olive oil from edge to edge. Using your bench knife, scoop up each round and place it in the center of a greased piece of parchment paper.

- **SHAPE THE DOUGH:** Lightly flour the top of each round of dough. Using a rolling pin, roll out the dough to an elongated oval that's just shy of two-thirds of your pan's width and length. Avoid excessively pressing down on the rolling pin and the dough; just apply enough pressure to push the dough outward without overly degassing it. Spread one end of the oval out to the left and right so that the dough resembles a triangle. Transfer the parchment paper and dough onto a half-sheet pan. Place each pan in a large reusable plastic bag and seal.

6. Proof

- **Duration:** About 1 hour 30 minutes at warm room temperature: 74°–76°F (23°–24°C)

- **LET THE DOUGH PROOF:** Put the pans in a warm place to proof for about 1 hour 30 minutes. Uncover to let the dough dry slightly during the last 30 minutes of proofing.

7. Cut and top

- **PREPARE THE OVEN:** Place an oven rack in the bottom third and one in the top third of the oven. Preheat the oven to 450°F (230°C).

- **CUT THE DOUGH:** Working with one piece of dough at a time, make 2 or 3 short vertical cuts from the base of the triangle to the top, leaving space between the cuts.

While cutting, use your other hand to gently spread the dough with your fingers to encourage it to open and prevent it from sticking back together. After cutting, spread the sides of the triangle outward to widen the cuts even further. Next, make diagonal cuts from the center cuts outward toward the sides of the triangle, while spreading the sides outward so the cuts open wide.

● **TOP THE DOUGH:** Using a pastry brush, cover the top of the dough with olive oil. Sprinkle with coarse sea salt and herbes de Provence, if desired. Repeat for the second fougasse.

8. Bake

▪ **Duration:** 25 to 30 minutes in the oven

● **BAKE THE DOUGH:** Slide the sheet pans into the oven and bake for 15 minutes. Rotate the pans 180 degrees, swap the pans between top and bottom racks, and bake for 10 to 15 minutes more. The fougasses are done when the top and bottom are golden. The longer you bake them, the crunchier they become.

● **FINISH AND COOL:** Transfer the fougasses to a wire rack and lightly brush on a little more olive oil. These are best eaten warm from the oven, or at least the day they're baked, though they will keep in an airtight container for 1 day. Reheat with a minute or two under the broiler.

HOW TO TINKER

GET CREATIVE

These fougasses are a blank canvas for many wonderful flavor combinations. Here are a few of my favorites:

▪ Olive: Add up to 90g of whole or coarsely chopped kalamata or Castelvetrano olives before the first set of stretches and folds during bulk fermentation.

▪ Black pepper and parmesan cheese: Instead of the herbes de Provence, sprinkle on a little freshly cracked black pepper and a lot of freshly grated parmesan cheese. Keep an eye on the fougasses as they're baking to ensure the cheese does not scorch; if you see this happening, turn the oven down to 425°F (220°C) and watch closely.

▪ Za'atar seasoning: Za'atar is a Middle Eastern spice mixture of salt, sesame seeds, sumac, and a combination of dried herbs. Instead of the herbes de Provence, sprinkle on za'atar (it's a fairly strong blend, so I am usually light-handed) and bake as directed.

NAAN

Tender and pillowy flatbreads with very mild fermentation flavors

THESE FLATBREADS are my sourdough take on Indian-style naan, something I could eat with almost any meal, especially those that have a sauce or liquid for sopping up. With a little planning the night before (for the overnight levain), they're quick to mix in the morning and have ready by dinner. I like to brush the finished naan with a melted herb butter right after cooking them in a hot skillet. At first, it might seem a little fussy to make a dedicated levain for these, but it results in a flavorful naan that's worth the extra effort.

The key to making naan is to use a preheated cast-iron skillet on the stove. If you don't have a cast-iron skillet, you can make them in the oven on a pizza stone or baking steel preheated to 500°F (260°C). Either way, once they are cooked, wrap the cooked flatbreads in a clean kitchen towel to keep warm while you finish shaping and cooking the rest of the dough.

BAKING TIMELINE

1. Levain

   12 hours (overnight)

2. Mix

3. Bulk Fermentation

   4 hours

4. Divide and Preshape

5. Proof

   1 hour 30 minutes

6. Shape and Cook

   30 minutes on the stovetop

TOTAL

18 hours

VITALS

Total dough weight	950g
Pre-fermented flour	13.0%
Levain	38.9%
Hydration	23.0%
Yield	Eight 115g naan

TOTAL FORMULA

INGREDIENT	BAKER'S %	WEIGHT
White flour (~11.5% protein)	100.0%	538g
Whole milk	36.0%	193g
Neutral-flavored oil, such as canola	8.0%	43g
Superfine sugar	2.6%	14g
Water	23.0%	124g
Fine sea salt	2.0%	11g
Ripe sourdough starter, 100% hydration	5.2%	28g

ADDITIONAL INGREDIENTS

2 tablespoons melted butter, for brushing

Chopped cilantro or parsley, for topping

INGREDIENT	BAKER'S %	WEIGHT
White flour (~11.5% protein)	100.0%	70g
Superfine sugar	20.0%	14g
Water	100.0%	70g
Ripe sourdough starter, 100% hydration	40.0%	28g

INGREDIENT	WEIGHT
White flour (~11.5% protein)	468g
Whole milk	193g
Neutral-flavored oil such as canola	43g
Water	54g
Fine sea salt	11g
Levain	182g

1. Levain

- **Duration:** 12 hours (overnight) at warm room temperature: 74°–76°F (23°–24°C)

● **MIX THE LEVAIN:** Warm or cool the water to about 78°F (25°C). In a large jar, mix the levain ingredients until well incorporated (this sweet levain will feel quite loose and have a sweet aroma). Be sure the jar has plenty of headspace, this levain will rise very high. Loosely cover and store in a warm place for 12 hours.

2. Mix

- **Desired dough temperature (DDT):** 78°F (25°C)

● **CHECK THE LEVAIN:** It should show signs of readiness: well aerated, risen, frothy, loose, and with a sweet-sour aroma. If the levain is not showing these signs, let it ferment 1 hour more and check again.

● **MIX THE DOUGH:** Warm the milk to 78°F (25°C). To the bowl of a stand mixer fitted with the dough hook, add the flour, milk, water, salt, and ripe levain. Mix on low speed for 3 to 4 minutes until combined. Increase the speed to medium and mix for 2 to 3 minutes until the dough begins to smooth. Turn the speed to low and slowly drizzle in the oil. Continue to mix on low for 2 minutes until all the oil is absorbed into the dough. Increase the speed to medium for 2 to 3 minutes until the dough comes together into a ball but doesn't completely cling to the dough hook. Transfer to another container, or keep it in the bowl, for bulk fermentation.

● **MEASURE THE TEMPERATURE OF THE DOUGH:** Compare it to the DDT and record it as the final dough temperature. Cover the dough.

3. Bulk fermentation

- **Duration:** About 4 hours at warm room temperature: 74°–76°F (23°–24°C)
- **Folds:** 1 set of stretches and folds after 1 hour of bulk fermentation

● **SET TIMER AND MAKE A NOTE:** Write down the current time as the start of bulk fermentation, set a timer for 1 hour, and let the dough rest in a warm place.

● **STRETCH AND FOLD:** When your timer goes off, give the dough one set of stretches and folds. This dough is rather stiff, so only a single set is necessary. Using wet hands, grab one side of the dough and lift it up and over to the other side. Rotate the bowl 180 degrees and repeat. Then rotate the bowl a quarter turn and stretch and fold that side. Rotate the bowl 180 degrees again and finish with a stretch and fold on the last side. The dough should be folded up neatly.

● **LET THE DOUGH REST:** After the set, cover the bowl and let the dough rest for the remainder of bulk fermentation, about 3 hours.

4. Divide and preshape

● **CHECK THE DOUGH:** At the end of bulk fermentation, the dough will have risen and feel soft and pillowy. If you wet a hand and gently tug on the surface of the dough, it will feel elastic and cohesive, resisting your pull. If you don't see dough that's airy, strong, and "alive," leave it for another 15 minutes in bulk fermentation and check again.

● **PREPARE THE PROOFING PAN:** Evenly dust a 13 × 18-inch half-sheet pan with white flour.

● **DIVIDE AND PRESHAPE THE DOUGH:** Using a bowl scraper, gently scrape the dough onto a clean work surface and use your bench knife to divide it into 8 pieces of 115g each (you might have a little extra scrap dough). Using your bench knife in your dominant hand and with your other hand wet to reduce sticking, shape each piece into a tight round. (See Preshaping, page 96, for more detail.) Transfer the rounds to the prepared sheet pan with plenty of space in between. Place the sheet pan inside a reusable plastic bag and seal.

5. Proof

▫ **Duration:** About 1 hour 30 minutes at warm room temperature: 74°–76°F (23°–24°C)

● **LET THE ROUNDS PROOF:** Put the pans in a warm place to proof for about 1 hour 30 minutes.

6. Shape and cook

▫ **Duration:** About 30 minutes

● **CHECK THE DOUGH:** The dough is ready when it's very soft to the touch. When you gently poke a round, there should be no tight spots. If the dough still feels tight, proof 15 minutes more and check again.

● **PREPARE THE HERB BUTTER AND THE PAN:** Melt 2 tablespoons of butter in a small bowl. Add 1 tablespoon of finely chopped cilantro or parsley. Set aside. Preheat a 10- or 12-inch cast-iron skillet on the stove over medium-high heat.

● **SHAPE THE NAAN:** Flour a work surface and uncover the dough. Place one round on the floured work surface and, using your hands, gently flatten it. Pick up the dough and stretch it apart into a round or teardrop shape using both hands, stopping when it's about 8 × 6 inches and ¼ to ½ inch thick (the thinner it's stretched, the crunchier and less rise you'll get).

● **COOK THE NAAN:** Put the dough into the skillet and cover the pan immediately to help steam the dough. Cook for 2 minutes. Flip the dough, cover, and cook for 2 minutes more, until both sides are well colored. Transfer the naan to a clean kitchen towel, brush on the herb butter, and cover with the towel while you cook the remaining pieces. These are best eaten immediately, though they will keep in an airtight container for 1 day.

HOW TO TINKER

FLAVORED BUTTER

Add any, or all, of the following to the herb butter: 1 minced garlic clove, 1 teaspoon nigella seeds, 1 teaspoon cumin seeds.

FLOUR TORTILLAS

A versatile and soft flatbread with additional flavor from the lengthy fermentation time and whole grains

HERE IN my hometown of Albuquerque, New Mexico, tortillas are ubiquitous. You can find local vendors making incredible fresh tortillas for farmers' markets and they're in every grocery store. My version has added flavor and a slight puff thanks to the natural leavening and yet still retains a supple texture, perfect for tearing, wrapping, and dipping. These tortillas also freeze well, making it economical to double this recipe and freeze an entire batch for later.

These tortillas turn out best when cooked in a preheated cast-iron skillet on the stove. If you don't have a cast-iron skillet, you can also make them in the oven on a pizza stone or baking steel preheated to 500°F (260°C). Wrap finished tortillas in a clean kitchen towel to keep warm while you cook the remaining dough pieces.

BAKING TIMELINE

1. **Levain**

   12 hours (overnight)

2. **Mix**

3. **Bulk Fermentation**

   4 hours

4. **Divide and Preshape**

5. **Proof**

   1 hour

6. **Shape and Cook**

   45 minutes on the stovetop

TOTAL

17 hours 45 minutes

VITALS

Total dough weight	800g
Pre-fermented flour	23.7%
Levain	65.1%
Hydration	58.0%
Yield	Twelve 8-inch tortillas (65g each dough ball)

TOTAL FORMULA

INGREDIENT	BAKER'S %	WEIGHT
White flour (~11.5% protein)	90.0%	395g
Whole wheat flour	10.0%	44g
Neutral-flavored oil, such as canola	20.0%	88g
Water	58.0%	255g
Fine sea salt	2.0%	9g
Ripe sourdough starter, 100% hydration	2.3%	10g

INGREDIENT	BAKER'S %	WEIGHT
White flour (~11.5% protein)	100.0%	104g
Water	100.0%	104g
Ripe sourdough starter, 100% hydration	10.0%	10g

INGREDIENT	WEIGHT
White flour (~11.5% protein)	291g
Whole wheat flour	44g
Neutral-flavored oil such as canola	88g
Water	151g
Fine sea salt	9g
Levain	218g

Using Ripe Sourdough Starter Instead of a Levain

If your sourdough starter is refreshed regularly and at 100% hydration, you can swap out the levain in this recipe for your starter. Give it a refreshment 12 hours before (i.e., the night before) you plan to mix this dough and omit the levain. If your starter is not made of a large portion of white flour, note that the final tortillas will be a bit more sour than they would otherwise be.

1. Levain

▪ **Duration:** 12 hours (overnight) at warm room temperature: 74°–76°F (23°–24°C)

● **MIX THE LEVAIN:** Warm or cool the water to about 78°F (25°C). In a medium jar, mix the levain ingredients until well incorporated (this liquid levain will feel quite loose) and loosely cover. Store in a warm place for 12 hours.

2. Mix

▪ **Desired dough temperature (DDT):** 78°F (25°C)

● **CHECK THE LEVAIN:** It should show signs of readiness: well aerated, bubbly on top and at the sides, loose, and with a sour aroma. If the levain is not showing these signs, let it ferment 1 hour more and check again.

● **MIX THE DOUGH:** Warm or cool the water (see page 138 on how to calculate) so the temperature of the mixed dough meets the DDT of this recipe. To the bowl of a stand mixer fitted with the dough hook, add the flour, oil, water, salt, and ripe levain. Mix on low speed for 1 to 2 minutes until combined. Increase the speed to medium and mix for 4 minutes until the dough begins to cling to the dough hook and is cohesive and smooth. Transfer to another container, or keep in the bowl, for bulk fermentation.

● **MEASURE THE TEMPERATURE OF THE DOUGH:** Compare it to the DDT and record it as the final dough temperature. Cover the dough.

3. Bulk fermentation

▪ **Duration:** 4 hours at warm room temperature: 74°–76°F (23°–24°C)
▪ **Folds:** 1 set of stretches and folds after 2 hours

● **SET TIMER AND MAKE A NOTE:** Write down the current time as the start of bulk fermentation, set a timer for 2 hours, and let the dough rest in a warm place.

● **STRETCH AND FOLD:** When your timer goes off, give the dough one set of stretches and folds. Using wet hands, grab one side of the dough and lift it up and over to the other side. Rotate the bowl 180 degrees and repeat. Then rotate the bowl a quarter turn and stretch and fold that side. Rotate the bowl 180 degrees again and finish with a stretch and fold on the last side. The dough should be folded up neatly.

● **LET THE DOUGH REST:** Cover the bowl and let the dough rest for the remainder of bulk fermentation, about 2 hours.

4. Divide and preshape

● **CHECK THE DOUGH:** At the end of bulk fermentation, the dough will have risen in the container, be smooth and strong, and perhaps a little bubbly. If you don't see these signs, check again in 30 minutes.

- **PREPARE THE PROOFING PAN:** Lightly flour a 13 × 18-inch half-sheet pan.

- **DIVIDE AND PRESHAPE THE DOUGH:** Using a bowl scraper, gently scrape the dough onto a clean work surface and use your bench knife to divide it into 12 pieces of 65g each (you might have a little scrap left over). Using two floured hands or your bench knife in your dominant hand and with your other hand lightly floured, shape each piece of dough into a very tight round. Place the rounds on the prepared sheet pan with a little space in between. (See Preshaping, page 96, for more detail.) Place the pan inside a reusable plastic bag and seal.

5. Proof

▪ **Duration:** About 1 hour at warm room temperature: 74°–76°F (23°–24°C)

- **LET THE DOUGH PROOF:** Put the pan in a warm place to proof for about 1 hour.

6. Shape and cook

▪ **Duration:** About 45 minutes

- **PREPARE THE PAN:** Preheat a heavy-bottomed cast-iron skillet on the stove over medium-low heat.

- **SHAPE THE TORTILLAS:** Flour a large cutting board or work surface. Flour one piece of dough and using a rolling pin, roll it out to a round about 8 inches in diameter. The dough should be rolled out very thin; use extra flour if needed to prevent sticking. If it tears, seal it up by overlapping some of the dough.

- **COOK THE TORTILLAS:** Place the tortilla in the preheated skillet. Let it cook for 2 to 3 minutes undisturbed. You'll notice bubbles begin to form, the dough will puff up, and the bottom should be deeply browned in spots. (If the tortillas are cooking too fast and the spots become black, reduce the heat.) Flip the tortilla and cook for 3 to 4 minutes more until golden brown in scattered areas.

- **FINISH AND SERVE:** Transfer the finished tortillas to a clean kitchen towel and wrap tightly to keep warm while you cook the remaining pieces of dough. The tortillas are wonderful while still warm from the pan. Alternatively, pile them on top of a single paper towel, wrap the stack in paper towels, then put the stack into a zip-top plastic bag. They will keep at room temperature for 2 to 3 days or in the refrigerator for up to 1 week. To reheat, warm under the broiler or over a direct flame on the stove. To freeze them, stack the tortillas with a piece of paper towel or parchment paper in between them, put the stack in a zip-top plastic freezer bag, and place in the freezer. They will keep for up to 3 months. Thaw in the refrigerator, then warm them under the broiler or over direct flame on the stove for a few minutes until pliable and well colored.

PITA

Soft, puffy clouds with
elevated wheat and
fermentation flavors

THESE SOFT, puffy pita breads can be eaten stuffed or used for a wrap. They have very gentle sour notes with a pleasant and assertive wheat flavor, especially if freshly milled or stone-ground wheat is used for the whole wheat called for in the recipe. For a soft pita, be sure to roll them thin, but not too thin—about ¼ inch thick. If they're rolled too thin, they will become crispy after they puff, and if left too thick, they could fail to puff altogether. Once you get the hang of rolling them out, these pita breads are very easy and quick to make. I find they are best the day they're made, but the recipe can be doubled and, once the cooked pitas are cooled, they can be frozen in a freezer bag for several months (reheat them under the broiler).

BAKING TIMELINE

1. **Levain**

   12 hours (overnight)

2. **Mix**

3. **Bulk Fermentation**

   3 hours 30 minutes

4. **Divide and Preshape**

5. **Proof**

   2 hours

6. **Shape and Bake**

   30 minutes in the oven

TOTAL
18 hours

VITALS

Total dough weight	1,040g
Pre-fermented flour	16.0%
Levain	40.1%
Hydration	66.0%
Yield	Ten 100g pitas

TOTAL FORMULA

INGREDIENT	BAKER'S %	WEIGHT
White flour (~11.5% protein)	85.0%	487g
Whole wheat flour	15.0%	86g
Neutral-flavored oil, such as canola	9.0%	52g
Superfine sugar	3.0%	17g
Water	66.0%	378g
Fine sea salt	2.0%	11g
Ripe sourdough starter, 100% hydration	1.6%	9g

INGREDIENT	BAKER'S %	WEIGHT
White flour (~11.5% protein)	100.0%	92g
Water	100.0%	92g
Ripe sourdough starter, 100% hydration	10.0%	9g

INGREDIENT	WEIGHT
White flour (~11.5% protein)	395g
Whole wheat flour	86g
Neutral-flavored oil such as canola	52g
Superfine sugar	17g
Water	286g
Fine sea salt	11g
Levain	193g

Using Ripe Sourdough Starter Instead of a Levain

If your sourdough starter is refreshed regularly and at 100% hydration, you can swap out the levain in this recipe for your starter. Give it a refreshment 12 hours before (i.e., the night before) you plan to mix this dough and omit the levain. If your starter is not made of a large portion of white flour, note that the final pita breads will be a bit more sour than they would otherwise be.

1. Levain

- **Duration:** 12 hours (overnight) at warm room temperature: 74°–76°F (23°–24°C)

- **MIX THE LEVAIN:** Warm or cool the water to about 78°F (25°C). In a medium jar, mix the levain ingredients until well incorporated (this liquid levain will feel quite loose) and loosely cover. Store in a warm place for 12 hours.

2. Mix

- **Desired dough temperature (DDT):** 78°F (25°C)

- **CHECK THE LEVAIN:** It should show signs of readiness: well aerated, risen, bubbly on top and at the sides, loose, and with a sour aroma. If the levain is not showing these signs, let it ferment 1 hour more and check again.

- **MIX AND STRENGTHEN THE DOUGH:** Warm or cool the water (see page 138 on how to calculate) so the temperature of the mixed dough meets the DDT of this recipe. To the bowl of a stand mixer fitted with the dough hook, add the flour, oil, sugar, water, salt, and ripe levain. Mix on low speed for 2 to 3 minutes until combined. Increase the speed to medium and mix for 3 minutes, until the dough begins to cling to the dough hook. Let the dough rest in the bowl for 10 minutes, covered.

- **CONTINUE MIXING:** Mix on medium speed for 3 minutes until the dough begins to smooth, gain strength, and cling to the dough hook. Transfer to another container for bulk fermentation.

- **MEASURE THE TEMPERATURE OF THE DOUGH:** Compare it to the DDT and record it as the final dough temperature. Cover the dough.

3. Bulk fermentation

- **Duration:** 3 hours 30 minutes at warm room temperature: 74°–76°F (23°–24°C)
- **Folds:** 2 sets of stretches and folds at 30-minute intervals

- **SET TIMER AND MAKE A NOTE:** Write down the current time as the start of bulk fermentation, set a timer for 30 minutes, and let the dough rest in a warm place.

- **STRETCH AND FOLD:** When your timer goes off, give the dough one set of stretches and folds. Using wet hands, grab one side of the dough and lift it up and over to the other side. Rotate the bowl 180 degrees and repeat. Then rotate the bowl a quarter turn and stretch and fold that side. Rotate the bowl 180 degrees again and finish with a stretch and fold on the last side. The dough should be folded up neatly. Cover and repeat 30 minutes later for a total of 2 sets of stretches and folds.

- **LET THE DOUGH REST:** After the last set, cover the bowl and let the dough rest for the remainder of bulk fermentation, about 2 hours 30 minutes.

4. Divide and preshape

- **CHECK THE DOUGH:** At the end of bulk fermentation, the dough will have risen in the container, be smooth and strong, and perhaps a little bubbly.

- **PREPARE THE PROOFING PAN:** Lightly flour a 13 × 18-inch half-sheet pan.

- **DIVIDE AND PRESHAPE THE DOUGH:** Using a bowl scraper, gently scrape the dough onto a clean work surface and use your bench knife to divide it into 10 pieces of 100g each (you might have a small bit of scrap left over). Using two floured hands or your bench knife in your dominant hand and with your other hand lightly floured, shape each piece of dough into a very tight round. (See Shaping Small Rounds, page 109, for more detail.) Place the rounds on the prepared sheet pan with a little space in between. Place the pan inside a reusable plastic bag and seal.

5. Proof

- **Duration:** About 2 hours at warm room temperature: 74°–76°F (23°–24°C)

- **LET THE DOUGH PROOF:** Put the pan in a warm place to proof for about 2 hours.

6. Shape and bake

- **Duration:** 30 minutes in the oven

- **CHECK THE DOUGH:** The rounds should be puffed up and feel very soft. Gently poke a few: There should be no dense or hard spots. If needed, let the dough proof 15 to 30 minutes more and check again.

- **PREPARE THE OVEN:** Place an oven rack in the bottom third of the oven with no rack above it. Place a baking stone/steel on the rack and preheat the oven to 500°F (260°C) for at least 30 minutes.

- **SHAPE THE PITA:** Lightly flour a large cutting board or work surface. Place one piece of dough upside down on the work surface and lightly flour the top. Using a rolling pin, roll it out into a round about ¼ inch thick and about 8 inches in diameter. If the dough feels sticky, use extra flour on the work surface and dough to make rolling easier.

- **BAKE THE PITA:** Carefully transfer the dough rounds to the baking surface. (Depending on the size of your baking surface, you should be able to bake 2 to 4 pitas at a time. You can also roll a few at a time first then load them into the oven together.) Bake for 2 minutes. The dough should puff up and form a balloon. Use a long spatula or pair of oven mitts to gently flip the pitas and bake for 1 to 2 minutes more. When done, the pita will be lightly browned on each side; if left too long in the oven, it will become hard and tough. Transfer to a clean kitchen towel and wrap tightly to keep warm; it will deflate. Repeat with the remaining dough rounds. These are best freshly made, but they will also keep well stacked and wrapped in a paper towel in a zip-top plastic bag for 1 to 2 days. To reheat, warm under the broiler or in a warm oven.

TROUBLESHOOTING

MY PITAS DIDN'T PUFF.

Be sure to roll the pieces of dough out to the dimensions given. If the dough is not rolled out thinly enough, the weight will be excessive and prevent the two layers from separating to form a balloon.

MY PITAS ARE TOO CRISPY.

Don't roll them out quite as thin and bake them for less time.

BUNS,

ROLLS

& MORE

Ⓓ

All of these recipes can be made using the discard from your sourdough starter, as they rely on the starter primarily for flavor rather than leavening.

Mini Herb Rolls

SOFT DINNER ROLLS

A shiny, soft, and buttery roll topped with coarse sea salt—perfect for Thanksgiving or any holiday meal

THE TEXTURE and flavor of these rolls are everything I look for in the archetypical buttery dinner roll. Using sourdough and added fermentation time, the rolls also exhibit very gentle sour notes reminiscent of mild buttermilk, which helps elevate the simple roll to something much more gratifying. To make these rolls, I opt for using a technique called tangzhong (see Tangzhong, page 277, for more information), which involves precooking some of the flour in the recipe with a liquid, typically milk, until the mixture turns into a thick paste. Adding this paste to the dough brings softness and a little extra sweetness, making for extraordinarily tender and squishy rolls.

One of my favorite uses for these rolls is as mini French toast slices. Slice the rolls in half vertically, let them sit out uncovered overnight to firm, then proceed with soaking them in your favorite French toast custard before cooking them on a griddle.

BAKING TIMELINE

1. **Levain**

   ⌇ 12 hours (overnight)

2. **Tangzhong**

   10 minutes

3. **Mix**

4. **Bulk Fermentation**

   ⌇ 3 hours 30 minutes

5. **Chill Dough**

   25 minutes

6. **Divide and Shape**

7. **Proof**

   ⌇ 3 hours

8. **Bake**

   40 minutes in the oven

TOTAL
19 hours 35 minutes

VITALS

Total dough weight	1,200g
Pre-fermented flour	12.5%
Levain	37.1%
Hydration	43.0% (see note on page 334)
Yield	Sixteen 70g pull-apart rolls baked in a 9-inch square pan

TOTAL FORMULA

INGREDIENT	BAKER'S %	WEIGHT
White flour (~11.5% protein)	68.0%	402g
High-protein white flour (~12.7%-14% protein)	25.0%	148g
White flour (~11.5% protein) (tangzhong)	7.0%	41g
Whole milk (tangzhong)	28.0%	166g
Unsalted butter	16.0%	95g
Superfine sugar	9.0%	53g
Water	43.0%	254g
Fine sea salt	1.9%	11g
Ripe sourdough starter, 100% hydration	5.0%	30g

ADDITIONAL INGREDIENTS

Egg wash: 1 egg and 1 tablespoon of milk or heavy cream

Coarse sea salt, for topping (optional)

INGREDIENT	BAKER'S %	WEIGHT
White flour (~11.5% protein)	100.0%	74g
Superfine sugar	20.0%	15g
Water	100.0%	74g
Ripe sourdough starter, 100% hydration	40.0%	30g

1. Levain

▦ **Duration:** 12 hours (overnight) at warm room temperature: 74°–76°F (23°–24°C)

● **MIX THE LEVAIN:** Warm or cool the water to about 78°F (25°C). In a medium jar, mix the levain ingredients until well incorporated (this sweet levain will expand and rise considerably, so be sure to use a container that has plenty of room). Loosely cover and store in a warm place for 12 hours.

Tangzhong Timing
Be sure to make the tangzhong with plenty of time for it to cool to room temperature before mixing it into the dough. Alternatively, you can make the tangzhong the night before, let it cool for a few minutes on the counter, cover, and refrigerate it overnight. The next day, let it come to room temperature before mixing into the dough.

2. Tangzhong

● **MAKE THE TANGZHONG:** Place the 41g white flour (~11.5% protein) and 166g milk in a medium saucepan set over medium-low heat. Cook, whisking constantly to ensure it does not burn, until the mixture thickens and becomes like a paste, 5 to 8 minutes. Be patient; the mixture won't seem to do anything until it reaches a critical heat point. Remove the pan from the heat, spread the paste out on a small plate, and let cool completely.

INGREDIENT	WEIGHT
Tangzhong	All
White flour (~11.5% protein)	328g
High-protein white flour (~12.7%-14% protein)	148g
Unsalted butter	95g
Superfine sugar	38g
Water	180g
Fine sea salt	11g
Levain	193g

3. Mix

▦ **Desired dough temperature (DDT):** 78°F (25°C)

● **CHECK THE LEVAIN:** It should show signs of readiness: well aerated, risen very high, very bubbly, and frothy. If the levain is not showing these signs, let it ferment 1 hour more and check again.

● **PREPARE THE BUTTER:** Cut the butter into ½-inch-thick pats. Place the pats on a plate on the counter to warm to room temperature.

● **MIX THE DOUGH:** Warm or cool the water (see page 138 on how to calculate) so the temperature of the mixed dough meets the DDT of this recipe. To the bowl of a stand mixer fitted with the dough hook, add the tangzhong, flour, sugar, water, salt, and ripe levain. Mix on low speed for 1 to 2 minutes until combined. Increase the mixer speed to medium and mix for 5 to 6 minutes until the dough begins to cling to the dough hook, but it doesn't completely clear the sides of the mixing bowl. Let the dough rest in the bowl, covered, for 10 minutes.

● **TEST THE BUTTER:** Gently press a butter pat with your finger: It should easily show an indentation but not be wet or melted. If the butter is too warm, place it in the freezer for 5 minutes and test again. Conversely, if the butter is too firm, microwave it for 10 seconds to warm it, then check again.

● **INCORPORATE THE BUTTER:** With the mixer running on low speed, add the butter, one pat at a time, until absorbed into the dough, scraping down the sides of the bowl and the dough hook as needed. Continue until all the butter is added, 5 to

Hydration
The hydration percentage for this recipe may seem very low (43%), but it doesn't account for the large portion of liquid (milk) in the tangzhong.

8 minutes. Increase the speed to medium and mix for 1 to 2 minutes more, until the dough smooths out and clings to the dough hook once again. The dough will be silky smooth, elastic, and a little shiny. Transfer to a container for bulk fermentation.

● **MEASURE THE TEMPERATURE OF THE DOUGH:** Compare it to the DDT and record it as the final dough temperature. Cover the dough.

4. Bulk fermentation

▪ **Duration:** About 3 hours 30 minutes at warm room temperature: 74°–76°F (23°–24°C)

▪ **Folds:** 3 sets of stretches and folds at 30-minute intervals

● **SET TIMER AND MAKE A NOTE:** Write down the current time as the start of bulk fermentation, set a timer for 30 minutes, and let the dough rest in a warm place.

● **STRETCH AND FOLD:** When your timer goes off, give the dough one set of stretches and folds. Using wet hands, grab one side of the dough and lift it up and over to the other side. Rotate the bowl 180 degrees and repeat. Then rotate the bowl a quarter turn and stretch and fold that side. Rotate the bowl 180 degrees again and finish with a stretch and fold on the last side. The dough should be folded up neatly. Cover and repeat these folds every 30 minutes for a total of 3 sets of stretches and folds.

● **LET THE DOUGH REST:** After the last set, cover the bowl and let the dough rest for the remainder of bulk fermentation, about 2 hours.

5. Chill the dough

● **CHECK THE DOUGH:** At the end of bulk fermentation, the dough will have risen significantly; it may have bubbles on top and at the sides, it should look smoother and less shaggy, and at the edge of the dough where it meets the container, it should dome downward. If you wet a hand and gently tug on the surface of the dough, it will feel elastic and cohesive, resisting your pull. If you don't see dough that's airy, strong, and "alive," leave it for another 15 minutes in bulk fermentation and check again.

● **FIRM THE DOUGH:** Uncover your bulk fermentation container and place the container in your refrigerator for 15 to 25 minutes. This time will firm and slightly chill the dough to make shaping easier.

6. Divide and shape

● **PREPARE THE BAKING PAN:** Liberally butter a 9-inch square baking pan with butter (even if your pan has a nonstick liner).

● **DIVIDE AND SHAPE THE DOUGH:** Using a bowl scraper, gently scrape the dough onto a floured work surface. Dust the top of the dough with flour. Using a bench knife in one hand, and the other hand dusted with flour, divide the dough into

Shaping small rounds, soft dough, bench knife method

RECIPE CONTINUES →

BUNS, ROLLS & MORE

16 pieces of 70g each (you might have a small bit of scrap dough left over). Using your bench knife in your dominant hand, and with your other hand lightly floured, shape each piece of dough into a tight ball. Place the balls in the prepared baking pan. (See Soft Dough: Use a Bench Knife, page 109, for more detail.) Place the pan inside an airtight reusable plastic bag and seal.

Overnight Proofing Option
Once the dough is shaped and in the baking pan, you can retard the rolls (proof overnight at cold temperature) until the next morning. Place the covered pan in the refrigerator overnight. The next morning, continue with the remaining steps of the recipe, adding 30 minutes to 1 hour to the final room temperature proof since the dough will need to warm to room temperature and then finish proofing.

7. Proof

▪ **Duration:** 2 to 3 hours at warm room temperature: 74°–76°F (23°–24°C)

● **LET THE DOUGH PROOF:** Put the pan in a warm place to proof for 2 to 3 hours. The rolls are ready when they are well risen and are very soft to the touch. If you gently poke their surface, you shouldn't feel any dense spots or tight areas; if you do, let proof 15 minutes more and check again.

8. Bake

▪ **Duration:** 40 minutes in the oven

● **PREPARE THE OVEN:** Place an oven rack in the middle position and preheat the oven to 425°F (220°C).

● **TOP THE DOUGH:** Make the egg wash by whisking together the egg and 1 tablespoon milk. Using a pastry brush, brush the wash evenly on top of the dough. If desired, lightly sprinkle coarse sea salt over the rolls.

● **BAKE THE DOUGH:** Slide the baking pan into the oven and bake for 20 minutes. Rotate the pan 180 degrees and reduce the temperature to 350°F (175°C). Bake for 20 minutes more, or until the internal temperature reaches 204°F (95°C) and the crust is golden and shiny.

● **FINISH AND COOL:** Transfer the baking pan to a wire rack and let cool for 10 minutes. Remove the rolls from the pan, place on a wire rack, and let cool for at least 30 minutes before eating. These rolls are best the day they're made but are great the next day with a quick reheat in a warm oven.

HOW TO TINKER

HOT DOG BUNS

This dough makes amazing hot dog buns. Divide the dough into 9 pieces of 130g each, shape into 4-inch-long bâtards (see page 102), and line them up side by side in a long rectangular baking pan. Before baking, brush the dough with the egg wash. If desired, sprinkle with white sesame seeds.

MAKE THESE VEGAN

To make these rolls vegan, substitute the dairy milk in the tangzhong with water, a full-fat nut milk, or a full-fat oat milk. For the butter in the dough, use a butter substitute such as Earth Balance vegan butter.

MINI HERB ROLLS

Slightly buttery, herby rolls
with a thin and crunchy crust

THESE SMALL, buttery rolls are equally great for lunch, dinner, or appetizers. In contrast to my Soft Dinner Rolls (page 333), these are a little chewier and sturdier, thanks to the added durum flour and fewer enrichments. Fresh rosemary imbues these with an intense aroma and woodsy flavor that brightens and adds savoriness. To switch up the flavor, use thyme, dill, herbes de Provence, or chives, adding them at the same time as you would the rosemary. If you don't have extra-fine durum flour, use whole wheat, spelt, or even Khorasan in its place. *(See photograph on page 331.)*

BAKING TIMELINE

1 Levain

    12 hours (overnight)

2 Mix

3 Bulk Fermentation

    4 hours

4 Divide and Shape

5 Proof

    2 hours

6 Bake

    25 minutes in the oven

TOTAL

18 hours 25 minutes

VITALS

Total dough weight	930g
Pre-fermented flour	14.5%
Levain	35.6%
Hydration	53.0%
Yield	Twenty-four 35g mini rolls in a 9 × 13-inch baking pan

TOTAL FORMULA

INGREDIENT	BAKER'S %	WEIGHT
White flour (~11.5% protein)	70.0%	342g
Durum flour, "extra fancy" (or whole wheat)	30.0%	147g
Whole milk	17.0%	83g
Unsalted butter	11.0%	54g
Honey	5.0%	24g
Fresh rosemary, finely chopped	1.0%	5g
Water	53.0%	259g
Fine sea salt	1.8%	9g
Ripe sourdough starter, 100% hydration	1.4%	7g

ADDITIONAL INGREDIENTS

Egg wash: 1 egg and 1 tablespoon of whole milk or heavy cream (optional)

White flour (optional) and flaky sea salt, such as Maldon, for topping

INGREDIENT	BAKER'S %	WEIGHT
White flour (~11.5% protein)	100.0%	71g
Water	100.0%	71g
Ripe sourdough starter, 100% hydration	10.0%	7g

INGREDIENT	WEIGHT
White flour (~11.5% protein)	271g
Durum flour	147g
Whole milk	83g
Unsalted butter	54g
Honey	24g
Fresh rosemary, finely chopped	5g
Water	188g
Fine sea salt	9g
Levain	149g

Butter

Make sure the butter is softened just enough before you use it: Gently press a butter pat with your finger. It should easily show an indentation, but not be wet or melted. If the butter is too warm, place it in the freezer for 5 minutes and test again. Conversely, if the butter is too firm, microwave it for 10 seconds and check again.

1. Levain

- **Duration:** 12 hours (overnight) at warm room temperature: 74°–76°F (23°–24°C)

- **MIX THE LEVAIN:** Warm or cool the water to about 78°F (25°C). In a medium jar, mix the levain ingredients until well incorporated (this liquid levain will feel quite loose) and loosely cover. Store in a warm place for 12 hours.

2. Mix

- **Desired dough temperature (DDT):** 78°F (25°C)

- **CHECK THE LEVAIN:** It should show signs of readiness: well aerated, risen, bubbly on top and at the sides, loose, and with a sour aroma. If the levain is not showing these signs, let it ferment 1 hour more and check again.

- **PREPARE THE BUTTER:** Cut the butter into ½-inch-thick pats. Place the pats on a plate on the counter to warm to room temperature.

- **MIX THE DOUGH:** Warm or cool the water (see page 138 on how to calculate) so the temperature of the mixed dough meets the DDT of this recipe. To the bowl of a stand mixer fitted with the dough hook, add the flour, milk, honey, water, salt, and ripe levain. Mix on low speed for 1 to 2 minutes until combined. Increase the speed to medium and mix for 3 to 4 minutes until the dough begins to cling to the dough hook. This dough is on the stiff side, so it should cling to the hook after just a few minutes of mixing. Let the dough rest in the bowl, covered, for 10 minutes.

- **INCORPORATE THE BUTTER AND ROSEMARY:** With the mixer on low speed, add the butter, one pat at a time, until absorbed into the dough, scraping down the sides of the bowl and the dough hook as needed. Continue until all the butter is added, about 5 minutes. Mix for 1 to 2 minutes more until the dough smooths out and clings to the dough hook once again. Add the rosemary. Mix for 1 minute until incorporated. The dough will be silky smooth and elastic, but will feel slightly tacky due to the milk and butter additions. Transfer to a container for bulk fermentation.

- **MEASURE THE TEMPERATURE OF THE DOUGH:** Compare it to the DDT and record it as the final dough temperature. Cover the dough.

3. Bulk fermentation

- **Duration:** About 4 hours at warm room temperature: 74°–76°F (23°–24°C)
- **Folds:** 1 set of stretches and folds after 1 hour of bulk fermentation

- **SET TIMER AND MAKE A NOTE:** Write down the current time as the start of bulk fermentation, set a timer for 1 hour, and let the dough rest in a warm place.

- **STRETCH AND FOLD:** When your timer goes off, give the dough one set of stretches and folds. Using wet hands, grab one side of the dough and lift it up and over to the other side. Rotate the bowl 180 degrees and repeat. Then rotate the bowl a quarter turn and stretch and fold that side. Rotate the bowl 180 degrees again and finish with a stretch and fold on the last side. The dough should be folded up neatly.

- **LET THE DOUGH REST:** Cover the bowl and let the dough rest for the remainder of bulk fermentation, about 3 hours.

4. Divide and shape

- **CHECK THE DOUGH:** At the end of bulk fermentation, the dough will have risen in the bulk container; it may have bubbles on top and at the sides, it should look smoother and less shaggy, and at the edge of the dough where it meets the container, it should dome downward. If you wet a hand and gently tug on the surface of the dough, it will feel elastic and cohesive, resisting your pull. If you don't see dough that's airy, strong, and "alive," leave it for another 15 minutes in bulk fermentation and check again.

- **PREPARE THE BAKING PAN:** Lightly grease a 9 × 13-inch baking pan with butter.

- **DIVIDE AND SHAPE THE DOUGH:** Using a bowl scraper, gently scrape the dough onto a work surface and use your bench knife to divide it into 24 pieces of 35g each. Using both hands, shape each piece of dough into a very small, tight round. (See Stiff Dough: Pinch It, page 109, for more detail.) Place the rounds in the prepared pan in four rows of six with about ½ inch or so in between. Place the pan inside a reusable plastic bag and seal.

Shaping small rounds, stiff dough, pinching method

5. Proof

Duration: About 2 hours at warm room temperature: 74°–76°F (23°–24°C)

- **LET THE DOUGH PROOF:** Put the pan in a warm place to proof for about 2 hours. The dough is ready when the rounds have relaxed outward and are puffy to the touch. If they still look or feel dense when gently poked, let them proof 15 minutes more and check again.

6. Bake

Duration: 25 minutes in the oven

- **PREPARE THE OVEN:** Place an oven rack in the middle position and preheat the oven to 400°F (200°C).

- **TOP THE DOUGH:** Make the egg wash by whisking together the egg and 1 tablespoon milk. Use a pastry brush to brush a very light layer of the egg wash onto each roll. If desired, put some white flour in a small fine-mesh sieve and dust a small amount of the flour on the tops of the rolls. Sprinkle some coarse sea salt on the top of each roll.

- **BAKE THE DOUGH:** Slide the pan into the oven and bake for 15 minutes. Rotate the pan 180 degrees and bake for about 10 minutes more, or until the internal temperature reaches 204°F (95°C) and the tops are golden.

- **FINISH AND COOL:** Remove the pan from the oven and let cool for 5 minutes. Transfer the rolls to a wire rack to cool. These are fantastic warm right from the oven, or they will keep in an airtight container for 3 to 4 days.

CIABATTA ROLLS

Extremely open and light with a soft interior and thin crust

CIABATTA IS a relatively new style of bread to come out of Italy, as it was invented in the early 1980s. It's characterized by loaves with an elongated "slipper" shape, a striking flour-marked crust, and an open, light interior. Typically, ciabatta is a highly hydrated dough made entirely of white flour, however, I like to work in some whole wheat for a little more flavor and crust color.

Ciabatta is traditionally mixed in a stand mixer due to the high hydration and level of development needed; for this home baker's version, I opt to mix by hand and use an increased number of stretches and folds to strengthen the dough. The cold bulk fermentation not only brings additional flavor through longer fermentation but also helps make handling a high hydration dough much easier.

BAKING TIMELINE

1. Levain

   12 hours (overnight)

2. Autolyse

   1 hour

3. Mix

4. Warm Bulk Fermentation

   3 hours 30 minutes

5. Cold Bulk Fermentation

   20 hours (overnight)

6. Divide

7. Proof

   1 hour

8. Bake

   40 minutes in the oven

TOTAL

37 hours 10 minutes

VITALS

Total dough weight	1,000g
Pre-fermented flour	10.1%
Levain	23.4%
Hydration	77.0%
Yield	Six small ciabatta rolls

TOTAL FORMULA

INGREDIENT	BAKER'S %	WEIGHT
High-protein white flour (~12.7%-14% protein)	85.0%	473g
Whole wheat flour	15.0%	84g
Water 1 (levain and autolyse)	72.0%	401g
Water 2 (mix)	5.0%	28g
Fine sea salt	1.8%	10g
Ripe sourdough starter, 100% hydration	0.9%	5g

INGREDIENT	BAKER'S %	WEIGHT
High-protein white flour (~12.7%–14% protein)	70.0%	39g
Whole wheat flour	30.0%	17g
Water 1	100.0%	56g
Ripe sourdough starter, 100% hydration	10.0%	5g

INGREDIENT	WEIGHT
High-protein white flour (~12.7%–14% protein)	434g
Whole wheat flour	67g
Water 1	345g

INGREDIENT	WEIGHT
Water 2	28g
Fine sea salt	10g
Levain	117g

Container

I like to make rectangular rolls with this dough, so I use a rectangular bulk fermentation container. This way, after bulk fermentation, I can simply dump the dough right onto my work surface to reveal a rectangular slab that can be quickly divided into 6 rectangular pieces with minimal handling. A round container is perfectly fine to use; you'll just have to stretch the dough to coax it into a rectangular shape.

1. Levain

- **Duration:** 12 hours (overnight) at warm room temperature: 74°–76°F (23°–24°C)

● **MIX THE LEVAIN:** Warm or cool the water to about 78°F (25°C). In a medium jar, mix the levain ingredients until well incorporated (this liquid levain will feel quite loose) and loosely cover. Store in a warm place for 12 hours.

2. Autolyse

- **Duration:** 1 hour at warm room temperature: 74°–76°F (23°–24°C)
- **Desired dough temperature (DDT):** 78°F (25°C)

● **MIX THE AUTOLYSE:** About 1 hour before the levain is ready, warm or cool the autolyse water (see page 138 on how to calculate) so the temperature of the mixed dough meets the DDT for this recipe. Place the flour and water in a large bowl and use wet hands to mix until no dry bits remain. Use a bowl scraper to scrape down the sides of the bowl to keep all the dough in one area at the bottom. Cover the bowl and let it rest for 1 hour.

3. Mix

- **Desired dough temperature (DDT):** 78°F (25°C)

● **CHECK THE LEVAIN:** It should show signs of readiness: well aerated, risen, bubbly on top and at the sides, loose, and an assertive sour aroma. If the levain is not showing these signs, let it ferment 1 hour more and check again.

● **ADJUST THE WATER TEMPERATURE:** Take the temperature of the dough and compare it to the DDT for this recipe: If it's higher, use cold water for the remaining water; if it's lower, use warm water.

● **MIX THE DOUGH:** To the autolyse, add the water, salt, and ripe levain. Using wet hands, mix the ingredients until well incorporated. Continue to mix and fold the dough over itself until it forms a cohesive mass, 2 to 4 minutes. (If your dough is very wet and slack at the beginning, that's perfect. This recipe includes lots of dough strengthening steps that will get it in shape.) Transfer to a container for bulk fermentation.

● **MEASURE THE TEMPERATURE OF THE DOUGH:** Compare it to the DDT and record it as the final dough temperature. Cover the dough.

4. Warm bulk fermentation

- **Duration:** About 3 hours 30 minutes at warm room temperature: 74°–76°F (23°–24°C)
- **Folds:** 6 sets of stretches and folds, the first 4 vigorous sets at 15-minute intervals, and the last 2 gentle sets at 30-minute intervals

- **SET TIMER AND MAKE A NOTE:** Write down the current time as the start of bulk fermentation, set a timer for 15 minutes, and let the dough rest in a warm place.

- **STRETCH AND FOLD:** When your timer goes off, give the dough one set of stretches and folds. Using wet hands, grab one side of the dough and lift it high up and over to the other side. Rotate the bowl 180 degrees and repeat. Then rotate the bowl a quarter turn and stretch and fold that side. Rotate the bowl 180 degrees again and finish with a stretch and fold on the last side. The dough should be folded up neatly. Cover the bowl and repeat the next 3 sets every 15 minutes. After the fourth set, perform 2 more sets at 30-minute intervals.

- **LET THE DOUGH REST:** After the last set, cover the bowl and let the dough rest for the remainder of the warm bulk fermentation, about 1 hour 30 minutes.

5. Cold bulk fermentation

- **Duration:** About 20 hours (overnight) in a home refrigerator: 39°F (4°C)

- **MOVE THE DOUGH TO THE REFRIGERATOR:** After the warm bulk fermentation, place the covered bulk fermentation container in the refrigerator overnight.

6. Divide

- **PREPARE THE PROOFING PAN:** Line an 18 × 26-inch full sheet pan or two 13 × 18-inch half-sheet pans with parchment paper.

- **DIVIDE THE DOUGH:** Liberally flour your work surface. Uncover the bulk fermentation container and liberally dust the top of the dough with flour. Using a bowl scraper, scrape down into your bulk fermentation container at the sides to loosen the dough. Then quickly invert the container centered over your floured work surface. Using a bench knife, divide the dough directly in half. Then divide each long half into 3 equal pieces, for a total of 6 pieces. There is no shaping for this dough; gently transfer the pieces to the prepared proofing pan, leaving space between them. Cover the pan with a large airtight reusable bag and seal.

A Light Touch

The key to open and light ciabatta is to avoid pressing into the dough with blunt fingertips. Instead, use your hands like spatulas to pick up and move the dough. The fewer interactions you have with the dough, the more open-textured the resulting ciabatta will be.

RECIPE CONTINUES →

7. Proof

▢ **Duration:** About 1 hour at warm room temperature: 74°–76°F (23°–24°C)

● **LET THE DOUGH PROOF:** Put the pan in a warm place to proof for about 1 hour. Check on the pieces periodically toward the end of this period; they are ready when they are very puffy and have some large visible bubbles forming beneath the surface.

8. Bake

▢ **Duration:** 35 to 40 minutes in the oven

● **PREPARE THE OVEN:** Place an oven rack in the bottom third of the oven with no rack above it. Place a baking stone/steel on the rack and set a roasting pan with lava rocks on the bottom of the oven. (See Baking Directly on a Surface, page 124, for more detail). Preheat the oven to 475°F (245°C) for at least 1 hour.

● **BAKE THE DOUGH:** Slide the sheet pan of dough onto the baking surface. Steam the oven by pouring a cup of ice into the steaming pan with lava rocks and quickly close the oven door. Bake for 20 minutes. Vent the oven of steam by removing the steaming pan. Reduce the oven temperature to 450°F (230°C) and bake for 15 to 20 minutes more, or until the internal temperature reaches 206°F (96°C), the crust is golden and crisp, and the loaves feel very light in hand.

● **FINISH AND COOL:** Let the loaves cool on a wire rack for at least 1 hour before slicing.

TROUBLESHOOTING

THE DOUGH WAS INCREDIBLY STICKY AND SLACK.

Be sure to use strong, high-protein flour for this recipe and hold back water during mixing, only adding it if the dough feels like it can handle it. Additionally, give it another set or two of stretches and folds during bulk fermentation if necessary. It's very important to sufficiently strengthen this dough both during mixing and through stretches and folds, which will make it easier to handle.

I HAVE HUGE HOLES IN MY CIABATTA!

If your baked ciabatta has a dense crumb on the bottom of each loaf with large holes on top, this could be a sign of overhydration. Omit the reserved water entirely.

CRUNCHY BREADSTICKS

(Grissini)

Olive oil–flavored, crispy, and perfect for dipping

GRISSINI ARE essentially very long and spindly breadsticks. They're mild flavored, crunchy, and irresistible. The dough is easy to mix, shape, and stretch, and they stay fresh for days stored in a paper bag on the counter. While I like to prepare these plain, they can also be topped with seeds, spices, or herb-infused olive oil (see How to Tinker, page 348). These are fun to make with kids; they're naturals at stretching the dough in a single, confident motion—and even if they shape a little wildy, their creative endeavors sometimes make the best grissini.

If your sourdough starter is refreshed regularly and at 100% hydration, you can swap out the levain in this recipe for your starter. See page 302 for more information.

BAKING TIMELINE

1 Levain

> 12 hours (overnight)

2 Mix

3 Shape

4 Proof

> 3 hours

5 Cut and Bake

> 25 minutes in the oven

TOTAL

15 hours 25 minutes

VITALS

Total dough weight	500g
Pre-fermented flour	12.6%
Levain	30.5%
Hydration	58.0%
Yield	About 24 grissini

TOTAL FORMULA

INGREDIENT	BAKER'S %	WEIGHT
White flour (~11.5% protein)	100.0%	285g
Extra-virgin olive oil	12.0%	34g
Superfine sugar	2.0%	6g
Water	58.0%	165g
Fine sea salt	2.0%	6g
Ripe sourdough starter, 100% hydration	1.4%	4g

ADDITIONAL INGREDIENT

Extra-virgin olive oil, for brushing

INGREDIENT	BAKER'S %	WEIGHT
White flour (~11.5% protein)	100.0%	36g
Water	100.0%	36g
Ripe sourdough starter, 100% hydration	10.0%	4g

INGREDIENT	WEIGHT
White flour (~11.5% protein)	249g
Extra-virgin olive oil	34g
Superfine sugar	6g
Water	129g
Fine sea salt	6g
Levain	76g

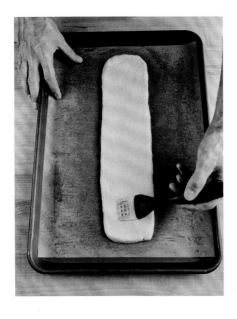

1. Levain

■ **Duration:** 12 hours (overnight) at warm room temperature: 74°–76°F (23°–24°C)

● **MIX THE LEVAIN:** Warm or cool the water to about 78°F (25°C). In a medium jar, mix the levain ingredients until well incorporated (this liquid levain will feel quite loose) and loosely cover. Store in a warm place for 12 hours.

2. Mix

■ **Desired dough temperature (DDT):** 78°F (25°C)

● **CHECK THE LEVAIN:** It should show signs of readiness: well aerated, bubbly on top and at the sides, loose, and with a sour aroma. If the levain is not showing these signs, let it ferment 1 hour more and check again.

● **MIX THE DOUGH:** To the bowl of a stand mixer fitted with the paddle, add the flour, olive oil, sugar, water, salt, and ripe levain. Mix on low speed for 1 minute until combined. Increase the speed to medium and mix for 3 minutes until the dough clings to the paddle. Let the dough rest for 5 minutes in the bowl.

● **CONTINUE MIXING:** Mix on medium speed for 2 minutes or until the dough once again clings to the paddle. The dough will be very smooth and soft.

3. Shape

● **PREPARE THE PROOFING PAN:** Line a 13 × 18-inch half-sheet pan with parchment paper and, using a pastry brush and olive oil, lightly grease a center strip about 3 inches wide and 14 inches long.

● **SHAPE THE DOUGH:** Using a bowl scraper, scrape the dough onto the center of the prepared sheet pan on top of the greased center strip. Using your hands, pat, stretch, and straighten the dough into a rectangle about 3 × 14 inches. Using a pastry brush, very lightly brush the dough with olive oil. Place the pan inside a reusable plastic bag and seal.

4. Proof

■ **Duration:** About 3 hours at warm room temperature: 74°–76°F (23°–24°C)

● **LET THE DOUGH PROOF:** Put the pan in a warm place to proof for about 3 hours. The dough is ready when it is lightly puffed up and soft to the touch. If the dough feels dense and tight, let it proof 30 minutes more and check again.

RECIPE CONTINUES →

5. Cut, stretch, and bake

> ■ **Duration:** About 25 minutes in the oven

● **PREPARE THE OVEN:** Place an oven rack in the middle position and preheat the oven to 350°F (175°C).

● **PREPARE THE BAKING PAN:** Line a half-sheet pan (13 × 18 inches) with parchment paper.

● **CUT THE DOUGH:** Uncover the dough. Using a bench knife, cut the dough crosswise into a strip ½ inch wide and 3 inches long. Using both hands, pick up the strip by the ends and, in one confident motion, stretch the piece of dough out to about 12 inches and place it in the prepared pan. Repeat with the remaining pieces, spacing them about ½ inch apart. (I find it easier to cut and shape one piece at a time, but if you'd prefer, cut the entire rectangle into pieces and then shape them.)

● **BAKE THE DOUGH:** Slide the pan into the oven and bake for about 25 minutes or until the grissini just start to turn golden and are crunchy.

● **FINISH AND COOL:** Remove the pan from the oven and let the grissini cool for 10 minutes on the pan. They are great the day they are made, and they also keep incredibly well in a paper bag at room temperature for 2 to 3 days.

TROUBLESHOOTING

SOME OF MY GRISSINI BURNED!

Be sure that when you divide and stretch the dough that the sticks are as uniform as possible. If some of the sticks are very thin and others very fat, you'll have uneven baking.

HOW TO TINKER

TOP WITH SEEDS AND SPICES

After the dough is fully proofed but before cutting, sprinkle on sesame seeds, crushed fennel seeds, za'atar, ground chile powder, or herbes de Provence. Gently tap the dough with your hand to ensure any seeds stay in place, then proceed with cutting the dough.

TOP WITH HERB-INFUSED OLIVE OIL

In step 3, when you shape the dough, instead of brushing it with plain olive oil, use one that's herb-infused.

POTATO BUNS

The softest and sturdiest
burger buns

THESE ARE without a doubt my favorite burger bun, and while you won't notice a distinct potato flavor in them, you *will* notice how very soft they are. Adding a large percentage of cooked potato ("gelatinized starches," if we're being science-y) brings profuse softness to the crust and crumb. Yet they still have great strength: These are soft and airy enough to impart that satisfying squish when bitten, but still rigid and sturdy enough to support a thick hamburger with towering condiments. In finding this balance, they completely avoid the dreaded soggy bun syndrome that's unfortunately so common in many buns.

My favorite way to serve these is to slice them in half, smear on a thin coat of butter, and toast them for a few minutes right on a hot grill. As they sear, a thin crust forms while the interior remains soft and supple. Then layer on the condiments, veggies, and protein without fear; the buns will support them all.

BAKING TIMELINE

1. Levain

   } 3 hours

2. Mix

3. Bulk Fermentation

   } 3 hours 30 minutes

4. Divide and Shape

5. Proof

   } 2 hours 30 minutes

6. Bake

   } 30 minutes in the oven

TOTAL

9 hours 30 minutes

VITALS

Total dough weight	1,250g
Pre-fermented flour	12.0%
Levain	40.9%
Hydration	12.0%
Yield	Ten 120g buns

TOTAL FORMULA

INGREDIENT	BAKER'S %	WEIGHT
White flour (~11.5% protein)	100.0%	508g
Whole milk	35.0%	178g
Egg, beaten	18.0%	91g (about 2 medium)
Unsalted butter	22.0%	112g
Superfine sugar	5.0%	25g
Russet potato, baked, peeled, riced, and cooled (see note on page 351)	40.0%	203g (about 2 medium)
Water	12.0%	61g
Fine sea salt	2.1%	11g
Ripe sourdough starter, 100% hydration	12.0%	61g

ADDITIONAL INGREDIENTS

Egg wash: 1 egg and 1 tablespoon whole milk or heavy cream

Sesame seeds (black, white, or both) or poppy seeds, or a mixture of both, for topping (optional)

1. Levain

- **Duration:** 3 hours at warm room temperature: 74°–76°F (23°–24°C)

- **MIX THE LEVAIN:** Warm or cool the water to about 78°F (25°C). In a medium jar, mix the levain ingredients until well incorporated (this liquid levain will feel quite loose) and loosely cover. Store in a warm place for 3 hours.

INGREDIENT	BAKER'S %	WEIGHT
White flour (~11.5% protein)	100.0%	61g
Water	100.0%	61g
Ripe sourdough starter, 100% hydration	100.0%	61g

2. Mix

- **Desired dough temperature (DDT):** 73°–75°F (22°–23°C)

- **CHECK THE LEVAIN:** It should show signs of readiness but not be overly ripe: moderate bubbles on the surface and a slight sour smell. If the levain is not showing these signs, let it ferment 30 minutes more and check again.

- **PREPARE THE BUTTER:** Cut the butter into ½-inch-thick pats. Place the pats on a plate on the counter to warm to room temperature.

- **MIX THE DOUGH:** To the bowl of a stand mixer fitted with the dough hook, add the flour, milk, eggs, sugar, salt, and ripe levain. Mix on low speed until combined. Scrape the sides of the bowl and the dough hook with a scraper. Increase the speed to medium and mix for 3 to 5 minutes until the dough begins to cling to the dough hook and remove from the sides of the bowl. Let the dough rest for 10 minutes.

- **CONTINUE MIXING:** Mix on medium speed for 2 to 3 minutes more until the dough again begins to cling to the hook and look smoother. If you were to do a Windowpane Test (page 83) at this point, it would not pass, but it would start to show a thin membrane forming.

- **TEST THE BUTTER:** Gently press a butter pat with your finger: It should easily show an indentation but not be wet or melted. If the butter is too warm, place it in the freezer for 5 minutes and test again. Conversely, if the butter is too firm, microwave for 10 seconds to warm it, then check again.

- **ADD THE BUTTER:** With the mixer running on low speed, add the butter, one pat at a time, until absorbed into the dough, scraping down the sides of the bowl and the paddle as needed. Continue until all the butter is added, about 5 minutes. Then, mix on medium speed for 1 to 2 minutes more until the dough clings to the dough hook once again. The dough will be silky smooth, elastic, and a little shiny.

- **ADD THE RICED POTATO:** Add half of the riced potato and mix on low speed until incorporated, about 1 minute. Add the remaining riced potato and mix until the potato is mostly incorporated, about 1 minute more. The dough will feel smooth and elastic, but a little tacky because of the enrichments and added potato. Transfer to a bulk fermentation container.

- **MEASURE THE TEMPERATURE OF THE DOUGH:** Compare it to the DDT and record it as the final dough temperature. Cover the dough.

INGREDIENT	WEIGHT
White flour (~11.5% protein)	447g
Whole milk, cold	178g
Egg, beaten	91g (about 2 medium)
Unsalted butter	112g
Superfine sugar	25g
Russet potato, baked, peeled, riced, and cooled	203g (about 2 medium)
Fine sea salt	11g
Levain	183g

Baked Potatoes

Baking the whole potatoes (instead of boiling or microwaving them) prevents them from absorbing excessive water, which would adversely affect the dough. To bake potatoes, prick washed potatoes all over with a fork. Bake on a parchment-lined sheet pan at 425°F (220°C) for 45 to 60 minutes, flipping halfway, until tender and the internal temperature reaches 208°–211°F (98°–99°C). Let cool, peel, then rice or mash until smooth. Cool completely before using.

RECIPE CONTINUES →

3. Bulk fermentation

- **Duration:** About 3 hours 30 minutes at warm room temperature: 74°–76°F (23°–24°C)
- **Folds:** 3 sets of stretches and folds at 30-minute intervals

● **SET TIMER AND MAKE A NOTE:** Write down the current time as the start of bulk fermentation, set a timer for 30 minutes, and let the dough rest in a warm place.

● **STRETCH AND FOLD:** When your timer goes off, give the dough one set of stretches and folds. Using wet hands, grab one side of the dough and lift it up and over to the other side. Rotate the bowl 180 degrees and repeat. Then rotate the bowl a quarter turn and stretch and fold that side. Rotate the bowl 180 degrees again and finish with a stretch and fold on the last side. The dough should be folded up neatly. Cover and repeat these folds every 30 minutes for a total of 3 sets of stretches and folds.

● **LET THE DOUGH REST:** After the last set, cover the bowl and let the dough rest for the remainder of bulk fermentation, about 2 hours.

4. Divide and shape

Chill the Dough for Easier Shaping

This dough is very, very soft. An optional step to make shaping easier is to place the bulk fermentation container in the refrigerator for 20 to 30 minutes until the dough cools and is slightly firm to the touch.

Shaping small rounds, soft dough, bench knife method

● **PREPARE THE BAKING PANS:** Line two 13 × 18-inch half-sheet pans with parchment paper.

● **DIVIDE THE DOUGH:** Using a bowl scraper, gently scrape the dough onto a liberally floured work surface. Lightly flour the top of the dough and your hands, then use your bench knife to divide the dough into 10 pieces of 120g each.

● **SHAPE THE DOUGH:** Lightly flour the top of the dough pieces. Using floured hands and a bench scraper, shape each piece into a tight ball (see Soft Dough: Use a Bench Knife, page 109, for more detail). Place the balls on the prepared pans with 3 inches between them. Place each pan inside a reusable plastic bag and seal.

5. Proof

- **Duration:** About 2 hours 30 minutes at warm room temperature: 74°–76°F (23°–24°C)

● **LET THE DOUGH PROOF:** Put the pans in a warm place to proof for about 2 hours 30 minutes. Check on the dough periodically after the first 2 hours, using the Poke Test (page 116) to assess its proof level. The dough is ready when it feels very puffy and delicate.

6. Bake

- **Duration:** 25 to 30 minutes in the oven

● **PREPARE THE OVEN:** Place one rack in the top third and one rack in the bottom third of the oven. Preheat the oven to 450°F (230°C).

● **TOP THE DOUGH:** Make the egg wash by whisking together the egg and 1 table-spoon milk. Uncover the pans and, using a pastry brush, brush an even layer of the egg wash on the tops of the dough (avoid using too much, since the wash will just pool at the base and burn in the oven). If desired, liberally sprinkle the rolls with seeds of your choice.

● **BAKE THE DOUGH:** Slide the sheet pans into the oven and bake for 15 minutes. Rotate the pans back to front, switch their racks, and bake for 10 to 15 minutes more, or until the internal temperature reaches 204°F (95°C) and the tops are shiny and a deep golden brown.

● **FINISH AND COOL:** Let the buns cool for 5 minutes on the pans. Then transfer to a wire rack to cool for at least 30 minutes. If you cut the buns too early (or eat one straight off the sheet pan), they may be excessively soft. These will keep well for 2 to 3 days covered and on the counter.

HOW TO TINKER

SWEET POTATO BUNS

Substitute all the russet potato in the recipe with sweet potato. Regular orange sweet potatoes will work, but I love satsuma-imo (Japanese sweet potatoes). They're easily mashed or riced into a creamy pulp, making for smoother incorporation into the dough, and impart a subtle, chestnut flavor. Regardless of the variety, prepare the sweet potatoes in the same way the white potatoes are prepared in the recipe, but pay attention to the consistency of the dough, adding more flour if it feels excessively slack or weak.

POTATO PULL-APART ROLLS

Instead of dividing these buns into 120g pieces, scale out twelve 75g pieces and shape them into tight balls. Place the balls side by side in a 9 × 13-inch baking pan (you'll have 4 rows of 3). Proof the dough as described in the recipe. Brush with egg wash and top with chunky sea salt. Bake at 425°F (218°C) for 10 minutes. Then reduce the oven temperature to 350°F (176°C) and bake for 15 minutes more, or until the internal temperature reaches 204°F (95°C) and the tops are golden brown and shiny.

HEARTY SANDWICH BUNS

A wholesome and soft bun perfect for sandwiches or burgers

WHOLESOME AND FILLING, these buns are perfect for supporting ingredients that are on the wet side (BBQ brisket, sloppy joes), though my favorite way to use them is for egg sandwiches. I like using whole white wheat for the whole grain portion of this recipe because it has a gentler flavor. I also make these the day before eating them as they benefit from a longer rest time after baking.

There is sometimes confusion between *whole white wheat flour* and *white flour*. White wheat is a special variety of wheat that differs from red wheat (which is most often used to make common "whole wheat" flour). The white wheat berry is lighter in color and lacks the more strongly flavored phenolic compounds of red wheat. Because of this, it has a gentler, less robust "wheaty" flavor. If you can't find white wheat flour, simply use whole wheat flour.

BAKING TIMELINE

1 Levain

> 3 hours

2 Mix

3 Bulk Fermentation

> 3 hours 30 minutes

4 Divide and Shape

5 Proof

> 3 hours 30 minutes

6 Bake

| 25 minutes in the oven

TOTAL

10 hours 25 minutes

VITALS

Total dough weight	1,250g
Pre-fermented flour	12.1%
Levain	41.3%
Hydration	16.0%
Yield	Ten 120g buns

TOTAL FORMULA

INGREDIENT	BAKER'S %	WEIGHT
White flour (~11.5% protein)	60.0%	313g
Whole white wheat flour (see headnote)	40.0%	208g
Whole milk	35.0%	182g
Egg, beaten	35.0%	182g (3 to 4 medium)
Unsalted butter	35.0%	182g
Superfine sugar	5.0%	26g
Water	16.0%	84g
Fine sea salt	2.0%	10g
Ripe sourdough starter, 100% hydration	12.0%	63g

ADDITIONAL INGREDIENTS

Egg wash: 1 egg and 1 tablespoon whole milk or heavy cream

Sesame seeds (black, white, or both), poppy seeds, or a mixture, for topping (optional)

1. Levain

■ **Duration:** 3 hours at warm room temperature: 74°–76°F (23°–24°C)

● **MIX THE LEVAIN:** Warm or cool the water to about 78°F (25°C). In a medium bowl, mix the levain ingredients until well incorporated (this liquid levain will feel quite loose) and loosely cover. Store in a warm place for 3 hours.

INGREDIENT	BAKER'S %	WEIGHT
White flour (~11.5% protein)	100.0%	63g
Water	100.0%	63g
Ripe sourdough starter, 100% hydration	100.0%	63g

2. Mix

■ **Desired dough temperature (DDT):** 75°F (24°C)

● **CHECK THE LEVAIN:** It should show signs of readiness but not be overly ripe: moderate bubbles on the surface and a mild sour aroma. If the levain is not showing these signs, let it ferment 30 minutes more and check again.

● **PREPARE THE BUTTER:** Cut the butter into ½-inch-thick pats. Place the pats on a plate on the counter to warm to room temperature.

● **MIX THE DOUGH:** To the bowl of a stand mixer fitted with the dough hook, add the flour, milk, egg, sugar, water, salt, and ripe levain. Mix on low speed until combined. Scrape the sides of the bowl and dough hook with a scraper. Increase the mixer to medium speed and mix for 3 to 5 minutes until the dough begins to cling to the dough hook and remove from the sides of the bowl. Let the dough rest, covered, for 10 minutes.

● **CONTINUE MIXING:** Mix on medium speed for 4 to 6 minutes until the dough again begins to cling to the hook and look smoother. If you were to do a Windowpane Test (page 83) at this point, it would not pass, but it would start to show a thin membrane forming.

● **TEST THE BUTTER:** Gently press a butter pat with your finger: It should easily show an indentation but not be wet or melted. If the butter is too warm, place it in the freezer for 5 minutes and test again. Conversely, if the butter is too firm, microwave it for 10 seconds to warm it, then check again.

● **ADD THE BUTTER:** With the mixer running on low speed, add the butter, one pat at a time. Wait a few seconds between additions to let it incorporate into the dough. Stop the mixer and scrape down the sides of the bowl and the dough hook as necessary. Continue until all the butter is added, about 5 minutes. Increase the mixer speed to medium and mix for 2 to 3 minutes more until the dough smooths out and clings to the dough hook once again. The dough will be silky smooth, elastic, and a little shiny. If it is still excessively shaggy, wet, and loose, mix for a few more minutes on medium speed. If the dough never comes together and remains wet and loose, add a sprinkle of flour and mix for a few more minutes until incorporated. Transfer to a container for bulk fermentation.

● **MEASURE THE TEMPERATURE OF THE DOUGH:** Compare it to the DDT and record it as the final dough temperature. Cover the dough.

RECIPE CONTINUES →

INGREDIENT	WEIGHT
White flour (~11.5% protein)	250g
Whole white wheat flour (see headnote)	208g
Whole milk	182g
Egg, beaten	182g (3 to 4 medium)
Unsalted butter	182g
Superfine sugar	26g
Water	21g
Fine sea salt	10g
Levain	189g

3. Bulk fermentation

- **Duration:** About 3 hours 30 minutes at warm room temperature: 74°–76°F (23°–24°C)
- **Folds:** 3 sets of stretches and folds at 30-minute intervals

● **SET TIMER AND MAKE A NOTE:** Write down the current time as the start of bulk fermentation, set a timer for 30 minutes, and let the dough rest in a warm place.

● **STRETCH AND FOLD:** When your timer goes off, give the dough one set of stretches and folds. Using wet hands, grab one side of the dough and lift it up and over to the other side. Rotate the bowl 180 degrees and repeat. Then rotate the bowl a quarter turn and stretch and fold that side. Rotate the bowl 180 degrees again and finish with a stretch and fold on the last side. The dough should be folded up neatly. Cover and repeat these folds every 30 minutes for a total of 3 sets of stretches and folds.

- **LET THE DOUGH REST:** After the last set, cover the bowl and let the dough rest for the remainder of bulk fermentation, about 2 hours.

4. Divide and shape

- **PREPARE THE SHEET PANS:** Line two 13 × 18-inch half-sheet pans with parchment paper.

- **DIVIDE THE DOUGH:** Using a bowl scraper, gently scrape the dough onto a liberally floured work surface. Lightly flour the tops of the dough and your hands, then use your bench knife to divide the dough into 10 pieces of 120g each.

- **SHAPE THE DOUGH:** Lightly flour the tops of the dough pieces. Using floured hands and a bench scraper, shape the portions into tight balls (see Soft Dough: Use a Bench Knife, page 109, for more detail). Place the balls on the prepared pans, 5 per pan, with 3 inches in between them. Place each pan inside a reusable plastic bag and seal.

Shaping small rounds, soft dough, bench knife method

5. Proof

- Duration: About 3 hours 30 minutes at warm room temperature: 74°–76°F (23°–24°C)

- **LET THE DOUGH PROOF:** Put the pan in a warm place to proof for about 3 hours 30 minutes. Check on the dough periodically after the first 2½ hours, using the Poke Test (page 116) to assess its proof level. The dough is ready when it feels very puffy and delicate with no tight spots.

6. Bake

- Duration: 20 to 25 minutes in the oven

- **PREPARE THE OVEN:** Place one oven rack in the bottom third and one in the top third of the oven. Preheat the oven to 425°F (220°C).

- **TOP THE DOUGH:** Make the egg wash by whisking together the egg and 1 tablespoon milk. Uncover the pans and, using a pastry brush, brush an even layer of the egg wash on the tops of the dough (avoid using too much, since the wash will just pool at the base and burn in the oven). If desired, liberally sprinkle on the seeds of your choice.

- **BAKE THE DOUGH:** Slide the sheet pans into the oven and bake for 10 minutes. Rotate the pans front to back, switch their racks, and bake for 10 to 15 minutes more, or until the internal temperature reaches 204°F (95°C), and the tops are shiny and a deep mahogany color.

- **FINISH AND COOL:** Let the buns cool for 5 minutes on the sheet pans. Then transfer to a wire rack to cool for 1 hour. If you cut the buns too early (or eat one straight off the sheet pan), they may be excessively soft. These will keep well for 3 to 4 days covered and on the counter.

TROUBLESHOOTING

MY BUNS BURST IN THE OVEN!

This issue is usually due to the dough being underproofed. Next time, try proofing them for a longer time before baking, which will help temper that dramatic rise in the oven. Additionally, be sure to evenly coat the top of each bun with the egg wash to ensure the surface remains moist during baking.

ENGLISH MUFFINS

Classically light muffins with soft sides, deeply browned tops and bottoms, and gentle fermentation flavors

THIS SOURDOUGH English muffin is a regular part of our breakfast repertoire. To me, a successful English muffin is one that's soft, light, a little chewy, and when torn apart with a fork has an interior that's open with craters scattered about like the surface of a distant meteor. This irregular landscape is a jagged field of crunch when properly toasted, best served with a thick pat of butter left to melt into delicious golden pools.

I often find myself making a double batch to ensure everyone gets seconds, plus these English muffins freeze exceptionally well. After they have fully cooled, stack them in a freezer bag (like stacking coins) and place in the freezer. To thaw, take the bag out and leave in the refrigerator overnight. The next morning, toast them on a hot griddle or in a toaster.

BAKING TIMELINE

1 Levain

12 hours (overnight)

2 Mix

3 Bulk Fermentation

3 hours 30 minutes

4 Divide and Shape

5 Cold Proof

20 hours (overnight)

6 Warm Proof

3 hours

7 Cook

30 minutes on the stove, 15 minutes in the oven

TOTAL

39 hours 15 minutes

VITALS

Total dough weight	1,000g
Pre-fermented flour	10.2%
Levain	24.0%
Hydration	62.0%
Yield	Twelve 80g English muffins

TOTAL FORMULA

INGREDIENT	BAKER'S %	WEIGHT
High-protein white flour (~12.7%-14% protein)	90.0%	493g
Whole spelt flour	10.0%	55g
Whole milk	10.0%	55g
Unsalted butter	6.0%	33g
Superfine sugar	1.6%	9g
Water	62.0%	339g
Fine sea salt	1.8%	10g
Ripe sourdough starter, 100% hydration	1.1%	6g

ADDITIONAL INGREDIENTS

Semolina flour (preferred), cornmeal, or white flour, for dusting

Clarified butter, for cooking

1. Levain

▪ **Duration:** 12 hours (overnight) at warm room temperature: 74°–76°F (23°–24°C)

● **MIX THE LEVAIN:** Warm or cool the water to about 78°F (25°C). In a medium jar, mix the levain ingredients until well incorporated (this liquid levain will feel quite loose) and loosely cover. Store in a warm place for 12 hours.

INGREDIENT	BAKER'S %	WEIGHT
High-protein white flour (~12.7%-14% protein)	100.0%	56g
Water	100.0%	56g
Ripe sourdough starter, 100% hydration	10.0%	6g

2. Mix

▪ **Desired dough temperature (DDT):** 78°F (25°C)

● **CHECK THE LEVAIN:** It should show signs of readiness: well aerated, risen, bubbly on top and at the sides, and with a sour aroma. If the levain is not showing these signs, let it ferment 1 hour more and check again.

● **PREPARE THE BUTTER:** Cut the butter into ½-inch-thick pats. Place the pats on a plate on the counter to warm to room temperature.

● **MIX THE DOUGH:** Warm or cool the water (see page 138 on how to calculate) so the temperature of the mixed dough meets the DDT of this recipe. To the bowl of a stand mixer fitted with the dough hook, add the flour, milk, sugar, water, salt, and ripe levain. Mix on low speed for 1 to 2 minutes until combined. Increase the speed to medium and mix for 3 minutes until the dough begins to cling to the dough hook. Let the dough rest in the bowl for 10 minutes.

● **TEST THE BUTTER:** Gently press a butter pat with your finger: It should easily show an indentation but not be wet or melted. If the butter is too warm, place it in the freezer for 5 minutes and test again. Conversely, if the butter is too firm, microwave it for 10 seconds to warm it, then check again.

● **ADD THE BUTTER:** With the mixer running on low speed, add the butter, one pat at a time, until absorbed into the dough, scraping down the sides of the bowl and the paddle as needed. Continue until all the butter is added, 2 to 3 minutes. Increase the speed to medium and mix for 1 to 2 minutes more until the dough smooths out and clings to the dough hook once again. The dough will be smooth and shiny. Transfer to a container for bulk fermentation.

● **MEASURE THE TEMPERATURE OF THE DOUGH:** Compare it to the DDT and record it as the final dough temperature. Cover the dough.

INGREDIENT	WEIGHT
High-protein white flour (~12.7%-14% protein)	437g
Whole spelt flour	55g
Whole milk	55g
Unsalted butter	33g
Superfine sugar	9g
Water	283g
Fine sea salt	10g
Levain	118g

Mix by Hand

The dough can also be mixed by hand using a strengthening technique like slap and fold (see page 83).

3. Bulk fermentation

▪ **Duration:** 3 hours 30 minutes at warm room temperature: 74°–76°F (23°–24°C)
▪ **Folds:** 3 sets of stretches and folds at 30-minute intervals

● **SET TIMER AND MAKE A NOTE:** Write down the current time as the start of bulk fermentation, set a timer for 30 minutes, and let the dough rest in a warm place.

RECIPE CONTINUES ›

- **STRETCH AND FOLD:** When your timer goes off, give the dough one set of stretches and folds. Using wet hands, grab one side of the dough and lift it up and over to the other side. Rotate the bowl 180 degrees and repeat. Then rotate the bowl a quarter turn and stretch and fold that side. Rotate the bowl 180 degrees again and finish with a stretch and fold on the last side. The dough should be folded up neatly. Cover and repeat these folds every 30 minutes for a total of 3 sets of stretches and folds.

- **LET THE DOUGH REST:** After the last set, cover the bowl and let the dough rest for the remainder of bulk fermentation, about 2 hours.

4. Divide and shape

- **PREPARE THE PROOFING PAN:** Liberally dust a 13 × 18-inch half-sheet pan with semolina flour (or cornmeal or white flour) and set aside.

- **DIVIDE THE DOUGH:** Uncover the container and lightly dust the top of the dough and a work surface with flour. Gently scrape the dough onto the floured work surface and use your bench knife to divide it into 12 pieces of 80g each.

- **SHAPE THE DOUGH:** Using a lightly floured hand and your bench scraper, shape each piece into a taut ball and place it on the sheet pan; you should be able to comfortably fit all 12 pieces with space in between. Place the sheet pan inside a reusable plastic bag and seal.

5. Cold proof

- **Duration:** About 20 hours (overnight) in a home refrigerator: 39°F (4°C)

- **LET THE DOUGH COLD PROOF:** Place the sheet pan in the refrigerator overnight.

6. Warm proof

- **Duration:** About 3 hours at warm room temperature: 74°–76°F (23°–24°C)

- **LET THE DOUGH WARM PROOF:** The next day, uncover the sheet pan and let the rounds proof at warm room temperature. The dough is ready when it is very, very soft and puffed up; it should feel extremely delicate. (For the lightest and most tender muffins, it's essential to give this dough plenty of time to finish proofing.) If it feels dense or tight, let it proof 30 minutes more and check again.

7. Cook

- **Duration:** 30 minutes on the stove, 15 minutes in the oven

- **PREPARE THE OVEN AND SHEET PAN:** Place an oven rack in the middle position and preheat the oven to 350°F (175°C). Line a 13 × 18-inch half-sheet pan with parchment paper and set it next to the stove.

TROUBLESHOOTING

THE MUFFIN DOUGH WAS VERY SOFT AND HARD TO SHAPE.

Try mixing the dough a little longer in the stand mixer next time. Additionally, you could place the bulk fermentation container, uncovered, in the refrigerator for 30 minutes to firm up the dough and make shaping a little easier.

MY MUFFINS BULGED EXCESSIVELY WHEN COOKING IN THE SKILLET.

Such bulging can be a sign that the dough was not strengthened sufficiently during mixing and/or it was underproofed. Next time, try giving the dough another set of stretches and folds during bulk fermentation and extending the final proof time by 30 minutes.

COOK THE MUFFINS: Place a heavy cast-iron skillet over medium-low heat (or preheat a griddle). Lightly grease the skillet with clarified butter. Using a flat spatula, gently transfer 2 or 3 dough rounds to the skillet to cook until the bottoms are a deep brown, about 3 minutes. Flip the muffins and cook until the second sides are very dark brown, 2 to 3 minutes. Transfer the muffins to the prepared sheet pan and repeat with the remaining dough rounds, greasing the pan again with clarified butter between each batch.

BAKE THE MUFFINS: Transfer the pan to the oven and bake for 15 minutes. When done, the muffins will have colored a little more at the edges, but they won't be completely browned.

FINISH AND COOL: Let the muffins cool on a wire rack for at least 30 minutes. These will keep for 3 to 4 days on the counter, covered. For longer storage, transfer to a zip-top plastic freezer bag once completely cool, and freeze for up to 3 months.

CHEESE AND CHIVE-STUFFED ROLLS

A flaky and tender dough stuffed with a cheesy-chive filling

THESE ROLLS make for a cheerful midday snack and an even better weekend brunch addition. The combination of cheeses has a harmonious effect: Whereas the melted Gouda becomes silky smooth, creamy, and mild, the cheddar—a pungent aged variety would be a fine choice—brings savory, sharp, and tangy flavors. This dough can also serve as a base for any combination of savory cheeses and herbs; see How to Tinker, page 366, for another delicious option.

BAKING TIMELINE

1 Levain

    12 hours (overnight)

2 Mix

3 Bulk Fermentation

    3 hours 30 minutes

4 Chill

    1 hour

5 Roll and Divide

6 Proof

    2 hours 30 minutes

7 Bake

    35 minutes in the oven

TOTAL
19 hours 35 minutes

VITALS

Total dough weight	1,000g
Pre-fermented flour	15.1%
Levain	37.3%
Hydration	15.0%
Yield	Nine rolls in a 9-inch square baking pan

TOTAL FORMULA

INGREDIENT	BAKER'S %	WEIGHT
White flour (~11.5% protein)	100.0%	537g
Whole milk	36.0%	193g
Egg, beaten	17.0%	91g (about 2 medium)
Unsalted butter	15.1%	81g
Water	15.1%	81g
Fine sea salt	1.9%	10g
Ripe sourdough starter, 100% hydration	1.5%	8g

CHEESE AND CHIVE FILLING

125g (1 cup) shredded Gouda cheese

100g (¾ cup) shredded yellow or white cheddar cheese

6g (2 tablespoons) fresh chives, chopped

ADDITIONAL INGREDIENTS

Egg wash: 1 egg and 1 tablespoon whole milk or heavy cream

20g (¼ cup) finely grated cheddar or parmesan cheese, for topping

INGREDIENT	BAKER'S %	WEIGHT
White flour (~11.5% protein)	100.0%	81g
Water	100.0%	81g
Ripe sourdough starter, 100% hydration	10.0%	8g

INGREDIENT	WEIGHT
White flour (~11.5% protein)	456g
Whole milk	193g
Egg, beaten	91g (about 2 medium)
Unsalted butter	81g
Fine sea salt	10g
Levain	170g

1. Levain

■ **Duration:** 12 hours (overnight) at warm room temperature: 74°–76°F (23°–24°C)

● **MIX THE LEVAIN:** Warm or cool the water to about 78°F (25°C). In a medium jar, mix the levain ingredients until well incorporated (this liquid levain will feel quite loose) and loosely cover. Store in a warm place for 12 hours.

2. Mix

■ **Desired dough temperature (DDT):** 76°F (24°C)

● **CHECK THE LEVAIN:** It should show signs of readiness: well aerated, risen, bubbly on top and at the sides, loose, and with a sour aroma. If the levain is not showing these signs, let it ferment 1 hour more and check again.

● **PREPARE THE BUTTER:** Cut the butter into ½-inch-thick pats or cubes. Place the butter on a plate on the counter to warm to room temperature.

● **MIX THE DOUGH:** To the bowl of a stand mixer fitted with the dough hook, add the flour, milk, egg, salt, and ripe levain. Mix on low speed 1 to 2 minutes until combined. Increase the speed to medium and mix for 3 to 5 minutes until the dough begins to cling to the dough hook and clear the sides of the mixing bowl. This is a lower-hydration dough so it should come together rather easily and feel strong at this point, but remember, adding butter will soon slacken and soften the dough. (If the dough doesn't come together during mixing, add a splash of milk to help.) Let the dough rest in the bowl for 10 minutes.

● **TEST THE BUTTER:** Gently press a butter pat with your finger: It should easily show an indentation but not be wet or melted. If the butter is too warm, place it in the freezer for 5 minutes and test again. Conversely, if the butter is too firm, microwave it for 10 seconds to warm it, then check again.

● **ADD THE BUTTER:** With the mixer running on low speed, add the butter, one pat at a time, until absorbed into the dough, scraping down the sides of the bowl and the dough hook as needed. Continue until all the butter is added, about 5 minutes. Increase the mixer speed to medium and mix for 3 to 5 minutes more until the dough smooths out and clings to the dough hook once again. The dough will be silky smooth, elastic, and a little shiny. It still may not completely pass the Windowpane Test (page 83), but that's fine. Transfer to a container for bulk fermentation.

● **MEASURE THE TEMPERATURE OF THE DOUGH:** Compare it to the DDT and record it as the final dough temperature. Cover the dough.

3. Bulk fermentation

▧ **Duration:** 3 hours 30 minutes at warm room temperature: 74°–76°F (23°–24°C)

▧ **Folds:** 3 sets of stretches and folds at 30-minute intervals

● **SET TIMER AND MAKE A NOTE:** Write down the current time as the start of bulk fermentation, set a timer for 30 minutes, and let the dough rest in a warm place.

● **STRETCH AND FOLD:** When your timer goes off, give the dough one set of stretches and folds. Using wet hands, grab one side of the dough and lift it up and over to the other side. Rotate the bowl 180 degrees and repeat. Then rotate the bowl a quarter turn and stretch and fold that side. Rotate the bowl 180 degrees again and finish with a stretch and fold on the last side. The dough should be folded up neatly. Cover and repeat these folds every 30 minutes for a total of 3 sets of stretches and folds.

● **LET THE DOUGH REST:** After the last set, cover the bowl and let the dough rest for the remainder of bulk fermentation, about 2 hours.

4. Chill the dough

▧ **Duration:** 1 hour in a home refrigerator: 39°F (4°C)

● **CHILL THE DOUGH:** Place the bulk fermentation container in the refrigerator for 1 hour.

5. Roll and divide

● **PREPARE THE BAKING PAN:** Liberally butter the bottom and sides of a 9-inch square baking pan.

● **PREPARE THE CHEESE AND CHIVE FILLING:** In a medium bowl, mix the 125g Gouda, 100g cheddar, and 6g chives with your hands. Set aside.

● **ROLL OUT THE DOUGH:** Using a bowl scraper, gently scrape the dough onto a floured work surface. Flour the top of the dough and, using a rolling pin, roll it out into a rectangle about 16 × 15 inches, where the shorter sides are at the east and west on your work surface. Evenly spread the cheese filling over the top, leaving a small 1-inch margin on the very top edge. Starting at the southeast corner of the dough, start rolling up by folding up a small portion of the dough and then continuing to fold, working your way across the long side until you reach the southwest corner to create a small, tight roll. It's important to roll the dough up tightly to ensure it doesn't fall apart while proofing. Continue rolling until all the dough is rolled up, gently pressing to seal the end. With each roll, grab the just-rolled portion and pull it toward yourself to create a little extra tension and tightness in the cylinder. Using a sharp knife, cut the cylinder every 1½ inches to create 9 rolls. Place the cut pieces in the prepared baking pan with a little room in between them. Place the baking pan inside a reusable plastic bag and seal.

Overnight Option

To bake the rolls any time the next day, leave the dough in the refrigerator overnight instead of for just 1 hour. The next day, take the container out and proceed with the remaining steps. (Let stand at room temperature for 30 minutes before rolling out.)

RECIPE CONTINUES >

BUNS, ROLLS & MORE

6. Proof

▪ **Duration:** About 2 hours 30 minutes at warm room temperature: 74°–76°F (23°–24°C)

● **LET THE DOUGH PROOF:** Put the pan in a warm place to proof for about 2 hours 30 minutes. The rolls are ready when they have relaxed out and have puffed up.

7. Bake

▪ **Duration:** 35 minutes in the oven

● **PREPARE THE OVEN:** Place an oven rack in the middle position and preheat the oven to 400°F (200°C).

● **BAKE THE ROLLS:** Make the egg wash by whisking together the egg and 1 tablespoon milk. Uncover the baking pan and use a pastry brush to evenly brush on the egg wash. Slide the baking pan into the oven and bake for 20 minutes. Rotate the pan back to front and reduce the oven temperature to 350°F (175°C). Bake for 15 minutes more, or until the internal temperature reaches 200°F (93°C) and the tops are golden.

● **FINISH, COOL, AND TOP:** Let the rolls cool for 5 to 10 minutes in the pan. While still warm, top with a sprinkling of cheddar or parmesan cheese and enjoy. These are best the day they're made, but they will keep in an airtight container in the fridge for up to 7 days. Reheat in a warm oven.

HOW TO TINKER

MAKE IT ITALIAN-ISH

Replace the cheese and chive filling with the following: Whisk together 125g (1 cup) ricotta cheese, 100g (1 cup) finely grated parmesan cheese, 3g (1 tablespoon) chopped fresh thyme, and scant ½ teaspoon fine sea salt.

BAGELS

Fluffy, chewy, and slightly crisp with complex flavors from natural fermentation

MY DAD'S restaurant had a back alley that connected all the other small businesses occupying the same commercial corner; one was a small dry-cleaning shop and the other was a bagel shop aptly named NY Bagels. Spending the summers at the restaurant meant my brother and I would explore every square foot of that commercial area, sneaking into one business after the next with a few goals in mind. The first, and most important, was never to be seen, ever. The second, to go from the restaurant to the bagel shop and get a fresh everything bagel topped high with cream cheese. Our hearts raced as we scampered through the dry-cleaning shop under scores of hanging clothes, dodging carts next to strange mechanical ironing devices, waiting for just the right moment to sprint across the open area, out the front door, and into the adjacent bagel shop.

To this day, when I eat one, I'm reminded of our shenanigans during those summers. While I'm sure those bagels weren't sourdough, this recipe is my version that attempts to replicate—and dare I say improve upon—them. These are rightfully chewy with a slightly crisp exterior crust pocked with tiny blisters; they're irresistible and, thankfully, don't require any sneaking about.

BAKING TIMELINE

1 Levain

    12 hours (overnight)

2 Mix

3 Bulk Fermentation

    3 hours

4 Divide and Shape

5 Warm Proof

    2 hours

6 Cold Proof

    17 hours (overnight)

7 Boil

    5 minutes

8 Bake

    50 minutes in the oven

TOTAL

34 hours 55 minutes

VITALS

Total dough weight	1,600g
Pre-fermented flour	12.0%
Levain	23.2%
Hydration	55.0%
Yield	Twelve 125g bagels

TOTAL FORMULA

INGREDIENT	BAKER'S %	WEIGHT
High-protein white flour (~12.7%-14% protein)	100.0%	964g
Superfine sugar	3.0%	29g
Barley malt syrup or honey	3.0%	29g
Water	55.0%	530g
Diastatic malt powder	0.7%	7g
Fine sea salt	1.9%	18g
Ripe sourdough starter, 100% hydration	2.4%	23g

ADDITIONAL INGREDIENTS

Cornmeal, for the sheet pans

Everything bagel mix, sesame seeds, poppy seeds, or rolled oats, for topping (optional)

INGREDIENT	BAKER'S %	WEIGHT
High-protein white flour (~12.7%–14% protein)	100.0%	116g
Water	50.0%	58g
Ripe sourdough starter, 100% hydration	20.0%	23g

INGREDIENT	WEIGHT
High-protein white flour (~12.7%–14% protein)	848g
Superfine sugar	29g
Barley malt syrup	29g
Water	472g
Diastatic malt powder	7g
Fine sea salt	18g
Levain	197g

Hydration Adjustments

This recipe is very sensitive to hydration changes, which might be necessary depending on the flour you're using. In addition to using Central Milling High Mountain flour, I've tested it with King Arthur Bread Flour and the results are great. If you use King Arthur flour, I'd suggest holding back about 25g water during mixing, adding it in slowly if it feels like the dough can handle the addition. When mixing, this dough should feel very stiff and strong; if it's wet and slack, it might end up being overhydrated.

1. Levain

■ **Duration:** 12 hours (overnight) at warm room temperature: 74°–76°F (23°–24°C)

● **MIX THE LEVAIN:** Warm or cool the water to about 78°F (25°C). In a medium bowl, mix the levain ingredients until well incorporated. Use your hands to knead the mixture until all dry bits of flour are incorporated (this stiff levain will feel strong and dry). Transfer to a jar and loosely cover. Store in a warm place for 12 hours.

2. Mix

■ **Desired dough temperature (DDT):** 78°F (25°C)

● **CHECK THE LEVAIN:** It should show signs of readiness: well aerated, risen, soft, sticky, and with an assertive sour aroma. If the levain is not showing these signs, let it ferment 1 hour more and check again.

● **ADJUST THE WATER TEMPERATURE:** Warm or cool the water (see page 138 on how to calculate) so the temperature of the mixed dough meets the DDT of this recipe.

● **MAKE THE BARLEY MALT SYRUP SLURRY:** To help ensure the sticky barley malt syrup is easily incorporated into the dough, make a slurry. In a small bowl, add the barley malt syrup, a little of the water, the sugar, diastatic malt powder, and salt. Stir until mostly dissolved. Set aside.

● **MIX THE DOUGH:** You have two mixing options. (For both, be sure to break up the ripe levain into little bits and scatter into the stand mixer or mixing bowl to help it incorporate during mixing.)

■ With a mixer: To the bowl of a stand mixer fitted with the dough hook, add all the ingredients, including the slurry. Mix on low speed for 5 to 6 minutes until the dough smooths out and gains elasticity. The dough should be quite strong at the end of mixing. If using a KitchenAid or similar mixer, be cautious not to stress the mixer: If the dough quickly clumps around the hook or the mixer sounds like it's straining, stop and proceed with the rest of the recipe. Transfer the dough to a bulk fermentation container.

■ By hand: Treat this dough like a pasta dough. To a large bowl, add all the ingredients, including the slurry. Mix by hand, squeezing and pinching until everything comes together in a cohesive mass. Turn the dough out onto a clean work surface and knead it like pasta: Fold it over in half and push with the palm of your hand away from you. Rotate the dough a quarter turn and repeat. Continue to knead in this way for 8 to 10 minutes until the dough smooths, gains elasticity, and becomes hard to fold over and knead any longer. Transfer the dough to a bulk fermentation container.

● **MEASURE THE TEMPERATURE OF THE DOUGH:** Compare it to the DDT and record it as the final dough temperature. Cover the dough.

RECIPE CONTINUES →

RECIPE CONTINUES →

Strengthening
Due to the low hydration, strong flour, and level of gluten development, this dough does not need additional strengthening during bulk fermentation.

3. Bulk fermentation

- **Duration:** 3 hours at warm room temperature: 74°–76°F (23°–24°C)
- **Folds:** None.

● **SET TIMER AND MAKE A NOTE:** Write down the current time as the start of bulk fermentation, set a timer for 3 hours, and let the dough rest in a warm place. The dough is ready when it has risen significantly and it will likely have a few large bulges on the surface.

4. Divide and shape

● **PREPARE THE PROOFING PAN:** Scatter a thin layer of cornmeal on a 13 × 18-inch half-sheet pan.

● **DIVIDE THE DOUGH:** Using a bowl scraper, gently scrape the dough onto a clean work surface and use your bench knife to divide it into 12 pieces of 125g each (you might have some scrap dough left over). Try to divide the dough so that each piece ends up in a thin, rectangular shape.

● **SHAPE THE DOUGH:** Taking the first piece, degas it by gently tapping it from the top to the bottom. Then cinch (roll) down the dough from the top, so the dough ends up in a little cylinder. This cinching doesn't have to be forceful, but it helps to get the dough into a rough shape to facilitate shaping. Next, use your hand to roll the center of the cylinder a few times to create a bulb at each end. Then switch to two hands and roll the dough outward to about 12 inches, forming a cylinder that's mostly the same diameter from end to end (A). If you prefer a bagel with a large hole, roll out the cylinder so it's longer. Pick up the two ends, one in each hand, and wrap them around the backside of one of your hands between your knuckles and wrist. Overlap the two ends in the palm of your hand and press together (B). Next, press your palm down on the work surface and roll the dough forward and backward repeatedly to seal where the dough overlaps (C). Transfer the ring to the prepared sheet pan (D). Repeat with the remaining pieces, ending up with 4 rows of 3 rings each. Place the pan inside a reusable plastic bag and seal.

Shaping bagels

5. Warm proof

- **Duration:** About 2 hours at warm room temperature: 74°–76°F (23°–24°C)

● **LET THE DOUGH WARM PROOF:** Put the pan in a warm place to proof for about 2 hours. The dough is ready when it has puffed up slightly. If it still feels dense and tight, let it proof 30 minutes more and check again.

6. Cold proof

- **Duration:** About 17 hours (overnight) in a home refrigerator: 39°F (4°C)

● **LET THE DOUGH COLD PROOF:** Place the sheet pan in the refrigerator to proof overnight.

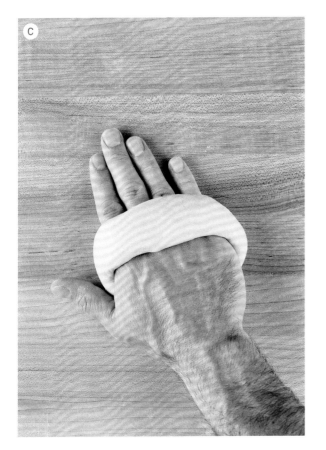

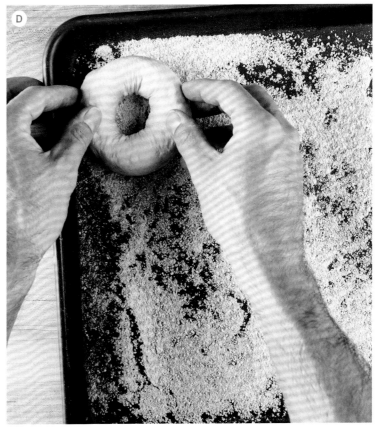

371

7. Boil

▪ **Duration:** 1 to 2 minutes

● **PREPARE THE SHEET PANS:** Line two 13 × 18-inch half-sheet pans with parchment paper.

● **PREPARE THE OVEN:** Place an oven rack in the bottom third of the oven. Place a baking stone/steel on the rack to preheat along with the oven. Set a roasting pan with lava rocks at the bottom of the oven (see Baking Directly on a Surface, page 124, for more detail). Preheat the oven to 450°F (230°C) with convection or 475°F (245°C) without convection.

● **PREPARE THE BOIL:** Wait until the oven and baking surface are fully preheated before boiling the dough pieces. Fill a large (6- to 7-quart) Dutch oven or pot three-quarters full with water (it should be deep enough so the bagels can boil without coming close to the bottom). Bring the water to a low boil. Set a spider strainer next to the stove and place a wire rack over a large sheet pan or towel.

● **BOIL THE DOUGH:** Take the sheet pan of dough rings out of the fridge. Place 3 pieces of dough into the water and boil for 40 seconds. Flip the dough and boil for 40 seconds more. Using the spider, transfer the bagels to the wire rack to drain. Quickly repeat with 3 more dough pieces.

● **TOP THE BOILED DOUGH (OPTIONAL):** If you want to top the bagels, pour out a thin layer of toppings in a wide bowl and dunk the tops of the moist, just-boiled dough rings into the toppings, then put them on a prepared sheet pan with about 2 inches between the pieces. You can also flip the dough to coat the bottoms if more toppings are desired.

8. Bake

▪ **Duration:** 20 to 25 minutes in the oven

● **BAKE THE BAGELS:** Slide the sheet pan onto the baking surface. Steam the oven by pouring a cup of ice into the steaming pan with lava rocks and quickly close the oven door. Bake for 10 minutes. Vent the oven of steam by removing the steaming pan. Rotate the sheet pan back to front and bake for 5 minutes longer. Reduce the oven temperature to 425°F (220°C) convection or 450°F (230°C) without convection and bake for 5 to 10 minutes more, or until the bagels have a golden-brown color and are slightly crispy. Avoid overbaking these as they will become hard and dense.

● **FINISH AND COOL:** Transfer the bagels to a wire rack to cool for at least 15 to 20 minutes before slicing. Repeat the boiling and baking process with the remaining dough rings. These are best the first day they're baked, but they will keep in a bread box for 5 days. They can also be frozen: Let cool completely, slice in half, and freeze in a freezer bag. Reheat in a toaster straight from the freezer.

Boiling

Bagels are unique because you boil the dough before baking it. This boiling gelatinizes the starches in the flour, giving the resulting bagel more chew and a noticeable, but thin, crust, and it also helps the crust shine. The longer you boil bagels, the thicker their crust and the chewier they will become. However, there is a limit to the boil duration, as they will degrade in the water if left to boil for too long. I have found boiling the dough 40 seconds on each side, for a total of 1 minute 20 seconds, to be just right.

HOW TO TINKER

MAKE THEM A TOUCH SWEETER

If you're looking to get closer to Montreal-style bagels, try adding 2 to 4 tablespoons of barley malt syrup to your boiling liquid and stir to dissolve. Then boil the bagels as directed.

TROUBLESHOOTING

MY BAGEL DOUGH WAS WET/TACKY/STICKY WHEN SHAPING!

The hydration of this recipe might need to be adjusted based on the flour you're using. For your next attempt, reduce the hydration of this dough by 5% and see if that improves shaping and handling. If the dough is still wet, continue to drop the hydration until you find what works best for your flour.

MY BAGELS SANK WHEN I PUT THEM INTO THE BOILING WATER!

It's okay if they sink initially, but they should pop up after 10 to 20 seconds in the boiling water. If they never float, it's likely the dough overproofed. Next time, reduce the warm proof period from 2 hours to 1½ hours.

MY BAGEL HAS DARK SPOTS ALL OVER!

This could be due to oven and/or altitude differences. Reduce the baking temperature by 25°F (20°C) next time.

GERMAN-STYLE
SOFT PRETZELS

Large, soft, and chewy with
a deeply colored crust

THESE GERMAN-STYLE pretzels are lofty, tender, and chewy, and perfect for tearing and dunking in mustard or cheese. The shiny, deeply colored crust comes from taking the traditional path of dipping the proofed and chilled pretzel dough into a 3% to 4% lye bath prior to baking. Lye is sodium hydroxide (aka caustic soda), an alkaline compound that's used in many other forms of food preparation and processing. The food-grade lye dissipates completely when the dough is baked in the oven but gives the pretzels their signature crust, thanks to the Maillard reaction. Lye also imparts that traditional "pretzel flavor" you've come to expect. For more on the use of lye in this recipe and how to use baking soda instead, if you prefer, see page 377.

BAKING TIMELINE

1 Levain

    12 hours (overnight)

2 Mix

3 Bulk Fermentation

    3 hours 30 minutes

4 Divide, Preshape,
    Bench Rest

    15 minutes

5 Shape

6 Proof

    1 hour 30 minutes

7 Lye Bath

8 Bake

    20 minutes in the oven

TOTAL

17 hours 35 minutes

VITALS

Total dough weight	1,420g
Pre-fermented flour	11.9%
Levain	28.3%
Hydration	55.0%
Yield	Twelve 115g pretzels

TOTAL FORMULA

INGREDIENT	BAKER'S %	WEIGHT
High-protein white flour (~12.7%-14% protein)	74.0%	635g
White flour (~11.5% protein)	20.0%	171g
Whole wheat flour	6.0%	51g
Unsalted butter	7.0%	60g
Water	55.0%	471g
Diastatic malt powder	0.4%	3g
Fine sea salt	2.0%	17g
Ripe sourdough starter, 100% hydration	1.2%	10g

ADDITIONAL INGREDIENTS

38g food-grade lye (sodium hydroxide; see Resources, page 424), for the lye bath

Pretzel salt or flaky salt, such as Maldon, for topping

INGREDIENT	BAKER'S %	WEIGHT
White flour (~11.5% protein)	50.0%	51g
Whole wheat flour	50.0%	51g
Water	100.0%	102g
Ripe sourdough starter, 100% hydration	10.0%	10g

INGREDIENT	WEIGHT
High-protein white flour (~12.7%-14% protein)	635g
White flour (~11.5% protein)	120g
Unsalted butter	60g
Water	369g
Diastatic malt powder	3g
Fine sea salt	17g
Levain	214g

Mixing

Due to the stiff nature of this dough, I do not recommend mixing it in a KitchenAid stand mixer. However, if you have a professional bread dough mixer (like a Häussler Alpha, Famag, or other), use it: To the bowl of the mixer, add all the ingredients. Mix on speed 1 for 2 to 3 minutes until combined. Let the dough rest for 5 minutes. Mix on speed 2 for 4 to 6 minutes until the dough becomes smooth and elastic.

1. Levain

- **Duration:** 12 hours (overnight) at warm room temperature: 74°–76°F (23°–24°C)

- **MIX THE LEVAIN:** Warm or cool the water to about 78°F (25°C). In a medium jar, mix the levain ingredients until well incorporated (this liquid levain will feel quite loose) and loosely cover. Store in a warm place for 12 hours.

2. Mix

- **Desired dough temperature (DDT):** 76°F (24°C)

- **CHECK THE LEVAIN:** It should show signs of readiness: well aerated, risen, bubbly at the top and at the sides, loose, and with a sour aroma. If the levain is not showing these signs, let it ferment 1 hour more and check again.

- **PREPARE THE BUTTER:** Cut the butter into small cubes. Place them on a plate and let them come to room temperature.

- **ADJUST THE WATER TEMPERATURE:** Warm or cool the water (see page 138 on how to calculate) so the temperature of the mixed dough meets the DDT of this recipe.

- **MIX THE DOUGH:** Treat the dough like a pasta dough. To a large bowl, add all the ingredients. Mix by hand, squeezing and pinching until everything comes together in a cohesive mass. Turn the dough out onto a clean work surface and knead it like pasta: Fold it in half and push with the palm of your hand away from you. Rotate the dough 180 degrees and repeat. Continue to knead in this way for 8 to 10 minutes until the dough smooths, gains elasticity, and becomes hard to fold over and knead any longer. Transfer to a container for bulk fermentation.

- **MEASURE THE TEMPERATURE OF THE DOUGH:** Compare it to the DDT and record it as the final dough temperature. Cover the dough.

3. Bulk fermentation

- **Duration:** About 3 hours 30 minutes at warm room temperature: 74°–76°F (23°–24°C)
- **Folds:** 1 set of stretches and folds after 1 hour of bulk fermentation

- **SET TIMER AND MAKE A NOTE:** Write down the current time as the start of bulk fermentation, set a timer for 1 hour, and let the dough rest in a warm place.

- **STRETCH AND FOLD:** When your timer goes off, scrape the dough out to a clean work surface. Traditional stretches and folds won't be effective with this dough because it's extremely strong and stiff. Instead, stretch one side of the dough out, up, and over to the other side. Rotate the dough 180 degrees and repeat. Return the dough to the bowl.

- **LET THE DOUGH REST:** Cover the bowl and let the dough rest for the remainder of bulk fermentation, about 2 hours 30 minutes.

4. Divide and preshape

- **CHECK THE DOUGH:** At the end of bulk fermentation, the dough will have risen significantly and be puffy and smooth. If you don't see dough that's puffed up, strong, and "alive," leave it for another 15 minutes in bulk fermentation and check again.

- **DIVIDE AND PRESHAPE THE DOUGH:** Using a bowl scraper, gently scrape the dough onto a clean work surface and use your bench knife to divide it into 12 rectangular pieces of 115g each. For each piece, degas heavily with a flat hand (really be assertive with the dough) and gently stretch it into a small rectangle with the shorter sides at east and west. The fewer the seams, pits, and uneven sides, the cleaner and more uniform the resulting pretzel will be. Using your fingertips, fold down a small piece of the long, north side of the rectangle and gently press it down into the dough with your fingers to begin rolling a cylinder. Continue to roll the dough down, gently sealing as you go, until the dough is rolled up into a long cylinder (about 5 inches). Seal the bottom seam well. Cover the cylinders with a large piece of plastic and let rest for 15 minutes.

RECIPE CONTINUES

Keep It Covered

This dough can quickly dry out and become unworkable. When I'm not handling the dough (both the large mass I'm dividing and the preshaped pieces), I like to keep it covered with a large piece of plastic (a reusable plastic proofing bag also works well).

LYE

While some might be worried about using lye, with the proper precautions it's not a danger. Though lye is caustic, meaning it can burn your skin if left in contact for too long, a good pair of rubber gloves (preferably those that extend up to the elbows) and a pair of safety glasses (if desired) will cover all the bases. After dipping your pretzels, slowly pour the lye bath liquid down the drain and flush with cool water. If by chance some of the lye solution does get on your skin, just quickly wash it off in the sink. As with all household chemicals, it's best to keep lye out of curious reach. Food-grade lye can be found at various online retailers (see Resources, page 424).

If you'd prefer not to use lye when making these pretzels, you can use regular baking soda in its place, though the flavor will be slightly different (less "pretzel" flavor) and the pretzels will not have as deep a color. In a large pot, combine 2 tablespoons baking soda and 6 cups water and bring to a boil. Follow the recipe and instead of placing the pretzel dough in the lye bath, dunk it in the boiling baking soda bath using a spider for 1 minute. Remove from the bath and let cool on a wire rack for a few minutes, then continue with the recipe.

5. Shape

● **PREPARE SHEET PANS:** Line two 13 × 18-inch half-sheet pans with parchment paper or silicone baking mats.

Shaping pretzels

● **SHAPE THE DOUGH:** Starting with the piece you first preshaped, place the cylinder in front of you so the ends are at east and west. Begin with your hands slightly overlapping in the middle, press down and roll the dough back and forth, away and then toward your body. As you are rolling, begin moving your hands outward to encourage the cylinder to elongate and taper as you move from the center out to the ends (aim for 18 inches long). If the dough becomes too elastic and resists rolling outward, let it rest for a few minutes, covered, before continuing. You want to keep an exaggerated bulge in the very center of this rope—this will be the large part of the pretzel you score to encourage rise in the oven. Finally, classic technique suggests leaving small bulbs at the extremes of the rope, but that is up to your preference.

● Grab the ends of the dough and arrange the dough so it loops away from you Ⓐ. Holding the ends, make two twists about 3 inches from the ends Ⓑ. Fold the ends up over the knot in the middle, and place each end on its corresponding side inside the loop. It looks nice to have a little overlap with each tip. Then gently press down the ends into the sides to seal Ⓒ. Transfer the pretzel to a prepared sheet pan and loosely cover while shaping the remaining dough. When finished shaping all the dough, place each pan in a reusable plastic bag and seal.

6. Proof

▪ **Duration:** About 30 minutes at warm room temperature (74°–76°F/23°–24°C) and then 45 minutes to 1 hour in a home refrigerator (39°F/4°C)

● **LET THE DOUGH PROOF:** Put the sheet pans in a warm place to proof for about 30 minutes. Uncover the pans and transfer them to the refrigerator for 45 minutes to 1 hour. (Chilling the dough in the refrigerator, uncovered and exposed to the air, serves two purposes: First, it makes the dough firmer, which will make the lye bath to come much easier; second, the dough develops a thin, dry skin on the outside, resulting in a chewy crust on the pretzels.)

7. Lye bath

- **PREPARE THE OVEN:** Place one oven rack in the bottom third of the oven and one in the top third. Preheat the oven to 450°F (230°C).

- **SET UP A LYE BATH:** Take out the sheet pans of fully proofed pretzel dough. Gather your pretzel salt, a razor blade for scoring, a 13 × 18-inch half-sheet pan lined with parchment paper with a wire cooling rack inside, a stainless steel bowl for the lye bath, and a pair of latex or rubber gloves. The goal is to set up an assembly line where you can work quickly.

- While wearing the gloves, add 940g cool water to a stainless steel bowl (make sure the bowl is not aluminum, which will cause a reaction to occur). To the water, add 38g food-grade lye while gently mixing with a stainless steel whisk or large spoon. The mixture will initially be cloudy; keep stirring until all the powder/pellets are dissolved.

- While still wearing the gloves, pick up one shaped pretzel and transfer it to the lye bath. Let it sit in the bath for 15 to 20 seconds and then transfer it to the wire rack to drain. Repeat with 5 more pretzels. Then transfer the pretzels back to the original sheet pan (make sure it still has parchment paper or a silicone mat on top) and set aside. Repeat with the remaining dough. Carefully pour the remaining lye solution down the drain and flush with cool water.

8. Bake

Duration: 16 to 20 minutes in the oven

- **SCORE THE DOUGH:** Carefully score each pretzel using a razor blade to make a single straight cut across the top of the bulge. Sprinkle the bulge (or the whole pretzel, if you prefer) with pretzel salt.

- **BAKE THE PRETZELS:** Slide the sheet pans into the oven and bake for 10 minutes. Rotate the pans back to front and switch racks. Reduce the oven temperature to 425°F (220°C). Bake for 6 to 10 minutes more, or until the pretzels are a deep brown color and shiny. Keep an eye on the pretzels; if they are browning too quickly, turn the oven down to 400°F (200°C).

- **FINISH AND COOL:** Let the pretzels cool on the pans for 10 to 15 minutes. These are best the day they are baked—especially when still warm from the oven—but they will keep in an airtight container at room temperature for 2 days. Enjoy warm with butter, mustard, and a pint of beer, of course.

HOW TO TINKER

A DIFFERENT SHAPE

Instead of shaping the dough into cylinders and knotting, divide it into 100g balls and shape as small rounds to make pretzel rolls. Proceed as directed in the recipe and when scoring, make a little X shape on top and sprinkle with pretzel salt.

GRAIN SWAP

Substitute the whole wheat flour in the recipe with whole rye flour for a slightly different flavor.

SKILLET CORN BREAD

Rich corn flavor with subtle sour notes from the sourdough starter and buttermilk

THE WELL-FERMENTED sourdough starter and buttermilk bring a noticeable tang to this easy-to-mix corn bread, but they also contribute to its tenderness. This is one of those back-pocket recipes that can be thrown together with little notice, provided you have a bottle of buttermilk and some good-quality cornmeal on hand.

I like to make this corn bread in my trusty 10-inch cast-iron skillet. If you don't have the right size skillet, you can also use a 9-inch square baking pan. Enjoy it warm on its own, topped with a pat of butter, or made a little sweeter with a drizzle of honey.

Makes one 10-inch corn bread

INGREDIENT	WEIGHT
Unsalted butter	69g (about 5 tablespoons)
Cornmeal (fine to medium grind)	230g
Buttermilk	311g
Eggs	108g (2 medium)
Pure maple syrup	23g
Fine sea salt	3g (½ teaspoon)
Baking soda	6g (1 teaspoon)
Ripe sourdough starter, 100% hydration (may use discard)	196g

● In a small saucepan, melt the butter over medium-low heat. Let cool.

● Preheat the oven to 375°F (190°C). Place about 14g (1 tablespoon) of the melted butter in a 10-inch cast-iron skillet and place the skillet in the preheating oven.

● In a large bowl, mix together the remaining cooled melted butter, the cornmeal, buttermilk, eggs, maple syrup, salt, baking soda, and sourdough starter. The mixture will be rather loose and frothy.

● Carefully remove the heated skillet from the oven and tilt it to coat the bottom with the melted butter. Pour the batter into the pan.

● Bake for 25 to 30 minutes, or until the internal temperature reaches 194°F (90°C) and the top is a deep golden yellow with the edges a deep chestnut color. Remove the skillet from the oven, let cool slightly, and serve the corn bread directly from the skillet.

TROUBLESHOOTING

BATTER IS TOO THICK OR TOO RUNNY

This is a loose batter and should have a consistency somewhat like pancake batter. If it feels too loose (more like water), add a little extra cornmeal, 1 tablespoon at a time, until the batter thickens slightly. Conversely, if the batter is too thick, thin with additional buttermilk.

HOW TO TINKER

MAKE CORN BREAD MUFFINS

The batter can be divided equally among the 12 cups of a standard muffin tin lined with paper liners or liberally buttered. Skip preheating the pan inside the oven and preheat the oven to 425°F (220°C). Bake the muffins for 5 minutes. Decrease the oven temperature to 375°F (190°C) and bake for 20 to 25 minutes more, or until a wooden pick inserted in the center comes out clean.

MAKE IT SPICY

To make jalapeño corn bread, add 1 seeded and finely chopped jalapeño to the batter.

FLAKY DROP BISCUITS

An easy path to tender and flaky biscuits

Makes 8 biscuits

INGREDIENT	WEIGHT
Unsalted butter	113g (1 stick)
Pastry flour or all-purpose flour	227g
Baking powder	20g (1 tablespoon)
Fine sea salt	5g (¾ teaspoon)
Buttermilk	140g, plus more as needed
Ripe sourdough starter, 100% hydration (may use discard)	75g

DROP BISCUITS are kind of the ultimate shortcut. Like a cross between a pie crust and a cut biscuit, these give you all the flaky, buttery, and comfort-evoking feelings that each of those elicits, without having to fuss too much with the dough. Mix up the flour, drop in some buttermilk and your ripe sourdough starter, and you're just a few minutes away from delicious biscuits that can be eaten solo, with butter and jam, or used as a rustic cobbler topping (see How to Tinker, below).

- Slice the butter into ½-inch pats and place in the freezer.

- Place an oven rack in the middle of the oven and preheat the oven to 425°F (220°C). Line a sheet pan with parchment paper.

- In a large bowl, whisk together the flour, baking powder, and salt. Add the chilled butter and toss to coat. Using a pastry cutter or your fingers, cut the butter into the flour, stopping occasionally to coat the butter with flour, until the butter is the size of small peas. (Alternatively, freeze the stick of butter and then use a box grater to grate it into the flour, or pulse the butter and flour in a food processor.)

- In a small bowl, stir together the buttermilk and sourdough starter. Pour the buttermilk mixture into the flour mixture and stir with a spatula until just combined (avoid overmixing). Add a little buttermilk if needed to get the dough to come together, but be conservative; the dough should *just* come together when squished with your hands.

- Using a 2-ounce cookie scoop or ¼-cup measuring cup, make 8 mounds of dough on the prepared sheet pan.

- Bake for 20 to 25 minutes, or until the tops are golden brown and a toothpick inserted comes out with just a few moist crumbles. Transfer the biscuits to a plate and cover with a clean kitchen towel to keep them soft and moist as they cool. Serve warm.

HOW TO TINKER

DROP BISCUIT COBBLER

Place an oven rack in the middle of the oven and preheat the oven to 375°F (190°C).

Follow the recipe for the biscuit dough up to scooping out the mounds of dough.

In a medium bowl, combine 700g fresh blueberries (or a mix of blueberries and a stone fruit, chopped), 38g granulated sugar, 1 tablespoon cornstarch, 1 teaspoon vanilla extract, 1 tablespoon fresh lemon juice, ¼ teaspoon fine sea salt, and ¼ teaspoon ground cinnamon. Gently stir, then pour into a 10-inch round skillet or 8-inch square baking pan.

Gather the drop biscuit dough into a mound and roll out to about a ½-inch thickness. Using a small biscuit cutter, cut out rounds. Gather up and reroll the scraps and cut out more rounds. Place the rounds over the top of the berry mixture so the pieces are just touching. Optionally, brush a light layer of heavy cream or whole milk on top and sprinkle turbinado sugar onto each round.

Bake for 35 to 40 minutes, or until the top is golden and the juices are bubbling. Let cool for 15 to 30 minutes. Serve warm with a dollop of whipped cream or a scoop of vanilla ice cream.

SOURDOUGH
STARTER
CRACKERS

Crispy, a little salty,
and deliciously irresistible

THESE CRACKERS come together easily and are a fantastic way to use your sourdough starter discard. Because the starter is not responsible for leavening, it's there simply for flavor. This means you can store your daily discard in your cache (see Saving and Using Discard, page 37) through the week, then use it to make these crackers in one large batch on the weekend for the coming week. The recipe is very flexible, so you can use any flour combination (my favorites being wheat and spelt, and wheat and rye), mix any seeds or dried herbs into the dough that sound good to you, and top them with just about anything (see How to Tinker, opposite, for ideas). If you take the optional time to let the dough ferment further, the extra fermentation will help bring increased sour flavor and nutrition to the crackers.

Makes about 36 crackers

INGREDIENT	WEIGHT
White flour (~11.5% protein)	50g
Whole spelt flour	50g
Extra-virgin olive oil	25g
Fine sea salt	2g (scant ½ teaspoon)
Ripe sourdough starter, 100% hydration (may use discard)	172g
Coarse sea salt, for sprinkling	

● In a medium bowl, mix the white flour, spelt flour, oil, fine sea salt, and sourdough starter until combined. (Alternatively, mix in a stand mixer fitted with the paddle.)

● The dough can be rolled and baked immediately after mixing, or you can cover the dough and let it proof for 1 to 2 hours at warm room temperature: 74°–76°F (23°–24°C) or overnight in the refrigerator.

● Place one oven rack in the top third and one in the bottom third of the oven. Preheat the oven to 350°F/175°C (or 325°F/160°C convection). Line two 13 × 18-inch half-sheet pans with parchment paper, then move the parchment paper to your work surface (the dough will be rolled out directly on the parchment paper and then transferred to the pans for baking).

● Lightly flour a work surface and the top of the dough in the bowl, then turn the dough out onto the work surface. Lightly flour the new top and divide the dough directly in half. Place one half on each piece of parchment and, using a rolling pin, roll the dough out very thinly, about ¼ inch thick. Be sure to roll the cracker dough out to an even thickness—if any parts of the dough are left thick, they will require a longer bake time. (You can also use a pasta machine set on the thinnest setting to roll out the dough.)

● Using a fluted or straight-edge pastry wheel (a pizza wheel or chef's knife will also work), cut the dough into 1½-inch squares. Use a handheld water sprayer to lightly spritz the cracker dough with water (or brush it on with a pastry brush) and sprinkle with coarse sea salt. The crackers will puff during baking, which I like, but if you prefer them thin and crispy, dock them by punching a single time in the center of each square with the tines of a fork. Transfer each piece of parchment to a sheet pan.

● Slide the pans into the oven and bake for 10 minutes. Rotate the pans back to front, switch racks, and bake for 10 minutes more, or until the crackers are golden brown and very crispy.

● Let the crackers cool completely on the pans. They will keep in airtight containers at room temperature for 1 week.

HOW TO TINKER

CHANGE UP THE FLOUR

You can use any single flour or blend of flours to make these crackers. Try 75% whole rye and 25% all-purpose for a rye-crisp-style cracker, or 100% whole wheat flour for a super-healthy slant. This recipe is a great place to use up little odds and ends of flour in the pantry.

CHANGE UP THE TOPPINGS

Here are a few of my favorites:

- Before baking, add a heavy dusting of za'atar or top with seeds (sesame, poppy, crushed fennel, or any combination).

- If you buy beans from Rancho Gordo, pick up a bottle of their Stardust Dipping Powder (a mixture of lime, oregano, brown sugar, and chile) and dust on a light layer as soon as you pull the crackers from the oven.

- After baking, lightly brush the crackers with olive oil and toss them in a bowl with nutritional yeast for a cheesy (and vegan) cracker.

SWEETS

D *All of these recipes can be made using the discard from your sourdough starter, as they rely on the starter primarily for flavor rather than leavening.*

Cinnamon Babka

HOT CROSS BUNS

Soft and sweet buns with cinnamon, nutmeg, and allspice

HOT CROSS buns are enriched buns laden with mixed fruit, usually a mélange of raisins, candied peel, and other dried fruit. These buns are an Easter-time tradition in the UK, but I think they're just as welcome during the fall and winter. The flavor is almost equally sweet and spiced, though the sticky simple syrup glaze gives sweet the win. As for texture, these buns are airy, delicate, and fluffed up thanks to the aggressive yeast activity from the sweet levain (see page 76) and the added egg, butter, and milk—all enrichments contributing to a supple interior. I love the bright punch of lemon and orange zest here, too. A mix of Thompson raisins, currants, and dried cranberries is also a favorite, but feel free to try a mix of other dried fruit and candied peel.

BAKING TIMELINE

1 Levain

} 12 hours (overnight)

2 Mix

3 Bulk Fermentation

} 4 hours

4 Divide and Shape

5 Proof

} 3 hours

6 Bake

| 30 minutes in the oven

TOTAL

19 hours 30 minutes

VITALS

Total dough weight	1,150g
Pre-fermented flour	12.5%
Levain	37.2%
Hydration	33.0%
Yield	Nine 115g hot cross buns

TOTAL FORMULA

INGREDIENT	BAKER'S %	WEIGHT
High-protein white flour (~12.7%-14% protein)	100.0%	513g
Whole milk	30.0%	154g
Egg, beaten	10.0%	51g (about 1 medium)
Unsalted butter	10.0%	51g
Superfine sugar	8.0%	41g
Thompson raisins (soaker)	15.0%	77g
Currants (soaker)	10.0%	51g
Ground cinnamon	0.6%	3g (1½ teaspoons)
Ground allspice	0.2%	1g (½ teaspoon)
Freshly ground nutmeg	0.2%	1g (½ teaspoon)
Zest of 1 lemon		
Zest of 1 orange		
Water	33.0%	169g
Fine sea salt	1.9%	10g
Ripe sourdough starter, 100% hydration	5.1%	26g

ADDITIONAL INGREDIENT

Egg wash: 1 egg and 1 tablespoon whole milk or heavy cream

SIMPLE SYRUP GLAZE

52g granulated sugar

52g water

CROSS

50g white flour (~11.5% protein)

40g water

15g vegetable oil (or other neutral oil)

Pinch of fine sea salt

INGREDIENT	BAKER'S %	WEIGHT
High-protein white flour (~12.7%-14% protein)	100.0%	64g
Superfine sugar	20.0%	13g
Water	100.0%	64g
Ripe sourdough starter, 100% hydration	40.0%	26g

INGREDIENT	WEIGHT
High-protein white flour (~12.7%-14% protein)	449g
Whole milk	154g
Egg, beaten	51g (about 1 medium)
Unsalted butter	51g
Superfine sugar	28g
Ground cinnamon	3g (1½ teaspoons)
Ground allspice	1g (½ teaspoon)
Freshly ground nutmeg	1g (½ teaspoon)
Zest of 1 lemon	
Zest of 1 orange	
Water	105g
Fine sea salt	10g
Levain	167g

1. Prepare the levain and fruit soaker

■ **Duration:** 12 hours (overnight) at warm room temperature: 74°–76°F (23°–24°C)

● **MIX THE LEVAIN:** Warm or cool the water to about 78°F (25°C). In a large bowl, mix the levain ingredients until well incorporated (this sweet levain, page 76, will expand and rise considerably, so be sure to use a container that has plenty of room). Loosely cover and store in a warm place for 12 hours.

● **PREPARE THE SOAKER:** Put the 77g raisins and 51g currants in a medium bowl. Pour in some water to just cover the dried fruit (the excess will be drained before it's added to the dough). Cover the bowl and let soak until bulk fermentation.

2. Mix

■ **Desired dough temperature (DDT):** 78°F (25°C)

● **CHECK THE LEVAIN:** It should show signs of readiness: well aerated, risen very high, very bubbly, and frothy. If the levain is not showing these signs, let it ferment 1 hour more and check again.

● **PREPARE THE BUTTER:** Cut the butter into ½-inch-thick pats. Place in a bowl on the counter to warm to room temperature until mixing.

● **WARM THE INGREDIENTS:** Given the fact that many of the ingredients are from the refrigerator, warm the water and the milk to about 75°-76°F (23°-24°C) to ensure you hit the DDT of 78°F (25°C).

● **MIX THE DOUGH:** Due to the lengthy mixing time and soft nature of this dough, I highly recommend mixing in a stand mixer. To the bowl of a stand mixer fitted with the dough hook, add the flour, milk, egg, half of the sugar, water, salt, and ripe levain. Mix on low speed for 1 to 2 minutes until combined. Increase the speed to medium and mix for 5 minutes until the dough begins to tighten and cling to the dough hook and pull from the sides. Let the dough rest for 10 minutes in the bowl.

● **MAKE THE SPICE MIXTURE:** In a small bowl, combine the cinnamon, allspice, nutmeg, and lemon and orange zests.

● **CONTINUE MIXING:** Add the spice mixture and the remaining sugar to the bowl and mix on low speed for 1 to 2 minutes until the additions are absorbed and the dough comes back together. Increase the speed to medium and mix for 3 to 6 minutes until the dough is smooth and strong; it should cling to the dough hook but may not completely remove from the sides of the bowl. Use the Windowpane Test (page 83) to see if the dough is intensively developed. If the dough does not spread clearly or tear cleanly, mix on medium speed for 2 minutes more and test again.

● **ADD THE BUTTER:** With the mixer running on low speed, add the butter, one pat at a time. Wait until each pat is mostly absorbed before adding the next pat. Scrape down the sides of the bowl and the dough hook as needed. Continue mixing on medium speed for 1 to 2 minutes more until the dough smooths out and clings to the dough hook. The dough will be silky smooth, elastic, and shiny. Transfer to a container for bulk fermentation.

- **MEASURE THE TEMPERATURE OF THE DOUGH:** Compare it to the DDT and record it as the final dough temperature. Cover the dough.

3. Bulk fermentation

- **Duration:** About 4 hours at warm room temperature: 74°–76°F (23°–24°C)
- **Folds:** 3 sets of stretches and folds at 30-minute intervals

- **SET TIMER AND MAKE A NOTE:** Write down the current time as the start of bulk fermentation, set a timer for 30 minutes, and let the dough rest in a warm place.

- **ADD THE INCLUSIONS AND STRETCH AND FOLD:** When your timer goes off, drain the fruit soaker of any excess water. Spread about one-quarter of the soaker evenly over the dough. Using wet hands, pick up one side of the dough and stretch it up and fold it over. Spread another one-quarter of the fruit over the top. Rotate the bowl 180 degrees and perform another stretch and fold. Evenly spread on another one-quarter of the fruit. Rotate the bowl a quarter turn, perform a stretch and fold, and spread on the remaining fruit. Rotate the bowl 180 degrees and perform the last stretch and fold. The dough should be folded up neatly. Cover the bowl and repeat these folds every 30 minutes for a total of 3 sets of stretches and folds.

- **LET THE DOUGH REST:** After the last set, cover the bowl and let the dough rest for the remainder of bulk fermentation, about 2 hours 30 minutes.

4. Divide and shape

- **PREPARE THE BAKING PAN:** Liberally butter a 9-inch square baking pan. If your pan is not nonstick, consider lining the pan with parchment paper and skip buttering.

- **CHECK THE DOUGH:** At the end of bulk fermentation, the dough will have risen significantly; it should look smooth and airy, and at the edge of the dough where it meets the container, it should dome downward. If you wet a hand and gently tug on the surface of the dough, it will feel elastic and cohesive, resisting your pull. If you don't see dough that's airy, strong, and "alive," leave it for another 15 minutes in bulk fermentation and check again. It's important your dough rises and becomes lofty at this point; don't rush it.

- **DIVIDE AND SHAPE THE DOUGH:** Using a bowl scraper, gently scrape the dough onto a clean work surface and use your bench knife to divide it into 9 pieces of 115g each. Using your bench knife in your dominant hand and with your other hand wet to reduce sticking, shape each piece of dough into a tight round. (See Soft Dough: Use a Bench Knife, page 109, for more detail.) Place the rounds in the prepared baking pan in 3 rows of 3. Place the pan inside a reusable plastic bag and seal.

Change Up the Pan

I bake these in my 9-inch square nonstick baking pan for buns that are super soft, but you could also bake them right on a sheet pan with a little space in between if you want buns that have a well-colored and firmer crust all around.

Shaping small rounds, soft dough, bench knife method

RECIPE CONTINUES ➔

SWEETS

5. Proof

▪ **Duration:** About 3 hours, or longer, if needed, at warm room temperature: 74°–76°F (23°–24°C)

● **LET THE DOUGH PROOF:** Put the pans in a warm place to proof for 3 hours. This is a slow-moving dough due to all the enrichments; it might take longer if your kitchen is cooler. The bun dough is ready when it is very soft to the touch with no dense spots and well risen. If using the 9-inch pan, the dough should have risen to the rim or a little higher. If the dough isn't puffy and soft to the touch, proof 30 minutes more and check again.

6. Prepare the glaze and cross mixture and bake

▪ **Duration:** 25 to 30 minutes in the oven

● **PREPARE THE OVEN:** Place an oven rack in the middle position and preheat the oven to 400°F (200°C).

● **PREPARE THE GLAZE:** Combine the 52g water and 52g sugar in a small saucepan over medium heat and bring to a boil. Let it simmer, stirring occasionally, until the mixture turns clear, 2 to 4 minutes. Let cool to room temperature. The simple syrup can be stored in an airtight container in the refrigerator indefinitely.

● **PREPARE THE CROSS:** In a small bowl, combine the 50g white flour, 40g water, 15g oil, and pinch of salt until a thick paste forms. It's important that the paste not be too thick or too thin; it should just barely flow off the edge of a spoon (similar to a thick cream). If the mixture is too dry or thick, add a small splash of water as needed to loosen. Transfer to a pastry bag or a plastic bag with a small cut made at the corner to pipe out the mixture. Set aside.

● **BAKE THE BUNS:** Make the egg wash by whisking together the egg and 1 tablespoon milk. Uncover the pan and brush a light layer of the egg wash on the buns. Pipe a thin, vertical line of the cross mixture down the center of each column of buns. Rotate the pan a quarter turn and pipe another line down the center of each column, forming a cross on each bun. Bake for 15 minutes. Rotate the pan back to front, reduce the oven temperature to 350°F (175°C), and bake for 10 to 15 minutes more, or until the internal temperature reaches 195°F (90°C) and the buns are golden brown on top.

● **FINISH AND COOL:** Remove the pan from the oven and brush a light layer of the simple syrup on the buns. Let cool for 5 minutes. Either serve warm straight from the pan or let them cool on a wire rack. They're best the day they are baked but can be stored in an airtight container for 1 day. Reheat in the oven, cut in half with a spread of butter on each half.

HOW TO TINKER

CHOCOLATE AND CRANBERRY

Swap out the raisins for semisweet chocolate chips, and the currants for dried, sweetened cranberries. The semisweet chocolate pairs incredibly well with the tart cranberries and spices in the dough.

WEEKEND CINNAMON ROLLS

Swirls of soft dough and warm cinnamon topped with a sweet icing

THESE CINNAMON rolls can be baked as a same-day recipe, or spread over two days. I like to prepare the dough Saturday morning, let it bulk ferment during the day, then place it in the fridge overnight. Sunday morning, I get up a little early to roll out the dough, cut it, and let it finish proofing while the oven heats and the house stirs. When the rolls go into the oven, they sing like Odysseus's Sirens, drawing out sleeping kids, adults—even my dog comes running—in a way that no alarm clock can compete with.

This cinnamon roll recipe is slightly different than the one I've had on my website for many years. It has fewer enrichments, which you might think means a less-tender cinnamon roll, but I've found this adaptation to be better overall—and it's an easier dough to handle. The results are cinnamon rolls with a wonderfully tender texture, and they stop short of being overly rich or sweet—right in balance.

1 Levain

> 3 hours

2 Mix

3 Bulk Fermentation

> 4 hours

4 Chill

> 2 hours or overnight

5 Roll and Divide

6 Proof

> 2 hours 30 minutes

7 Bake

| 25 minutes in the oven

TOTAL

11 hours 55 minutes

VITALS

Total dough weight	1,260g
Pre-fermented flour	12.3%
Levain	41.9%
Hydration	12.3%
Yield	Nine cinnamon rolls

TOTAL FORMULA

INGREDIENT	BAKER'S %	WEIGHT
White flour (~11.5% protein)	100.0%	579g
Whole milk (cold)	34.0%	197g
Egg (cold), beaten	25.0%	145g (about 3 medium)
Unsalted butter	24.0%	139g
Superfine sugar	8.0%	46g
Water (levain)	12.3%	71g
Fine sea salt	2.1%	12g
Ripe sourdough starter, 100% hydration	12.3%	71g

BROWN SUGAR CINNAMON FILLING

175g dark brown sugar

28g (2 tablespoons) unsalted butter, melted

12g all-purpose flour

6g (2¼ teaspoons) ground cinnamon

Small pinch (¼ teaspoon) fine sea salt

SUGAR ICING

175g powdered sugar

28g (2 tablespoons) whole milk

14g (1 tablespoon) unsalted butter, melted

2g (½ teaspoon) vanilla extract (optional)

1. Levain

⊘ **Duration:** 3 hours at warm room temperature: 74°–76°F (23°–24°C)

● **MIX THE LEVAIN:** Warm or cool the water to about 78°F (25°C). In a medium jar, mix the levain ingredients until well incorporated (this liquid levain will feel quite loose) and loosely cover. Store in a warm place for 3 hours.

INGREDIENT	BAKER'S %	WEIGHT
White flour (~11.5% protein)	100.0%	71g
Water	100.0%	71g
Ripe sourdough starter, 100% hydration	100.0%	71g

2. Mix

⊘ **Desired dough temperature (DDT):** 78°F (25°C)

● **PREPARE THE BUTTER:** Cut the butter into ½-inch-thick pats. Place the pats on a plate on the counter to warm to room temperature.

● **CHECK THE LEVAIN:** It should now show signs of ripeness but not be overly ripe, with moderate bubbles on the surface, and a slight sour smell. If the levain is not showing these signs, let it ferment 30 minutes more and check again.

● **MIX THE DOUGH:** To the bowl of a stand mixer fitted with the dough hook, add the flour, milk, egg, sugar, salt, and ripe levain. Mix on low speed for 1 to 2 minutes until combined. Increase the speed to medium and mix for 3 to 4 minutes. The dough should cling to the dough hook; if it doesn't, continue mixing for a few more minutes until it gains strength and clumps together. This dough will be rather stiff before adding in the butter. Let the dough rest for 10 minutes in the bowl.

● **TEST THE BUTTER:** Gently press a butter pat with your finger: It should easily show an indentation but not be wet or melted. If the butter is too warm and pressing with a finger offers no resistance, place it in the freezer for 5 minutes and test again. If the butter is too firm, microwave it for 10 seconds to briefly warm it, then check again.

● **INCORPORATE THE BUTTER:** With the mixer on low speed, add the butter, one pat at a time, until absorbed into the dough, scraping down the sides of the bowl and the dough hook as needed. Continue until all the butter is added, 5 to 8 minutes. Increase the mixer speed to medium and mix for 1 to 2 minutes more until the dough smooths out and clings to the dough hook once again. The dough will be silky smooth, elastic, and a little shiny. Transfer to a container for bulk fermentation.

● **MEASURE THE TEMPERATURE OF THE DOUGH:** Compare it to the DDT and record it as the final dough temperature. Cover the dough.

INGREDIENT	WEIGHT
White flour (~11.5% protein)	508g
Whole milk (cold)	197g
Egg (cold), beaten	145g (about 3 medium)
Unsalted butter	139g
Superfine sugar	46g
Fine sea salt	12g
Levain	213g

3. Bulk fermentation

⊘ **Duration:** 4 hours at warm room temperature: 74°–76°F (23°–24°C)
⊘ **Folds:** 1 set of gentle slaps and folds after 1 hour of bulk fermentation

● **SET TIMER AND MAKE A NOTE:** Write down the current time as the start of bulk fermentation, set a timer for 1 hour, and let the dough rest in a warm place.

Temperature

The milk and eggs for this recipe are used cold, straight from the refrigerator, which helps offset the heat generated by using a mechanical mixer. At the end of mixing, your dough should have a final dough temperature of 78°F (25°C). If it ends up cooler, keep the dough in a warm spot in your kitchen for the first part of bulk fermentation and expect that it might need more time before being placed in the refrigerator. Conversely, if the final dough temperature is higher, keep the dough in a cooler spot and expect that it might need to be placed in the refrigerator sooner.

RECIPE CONTINUES →

● **GENTLE SLAP AND FOLD:** When your timer goes off, give the dough one set of slaps and folds (see page 83 for more detail). Scrape the dough onto a clean work surface and give it two to four gentle slaps and folds. The dough should be very smooth and taut. Round the dough a bit on the counter to gather it into a tight ball, then transfer it back to the bulk fermentation container.

● **LET THE DOUGH REST:** If the dough looked smooth and felt strong, let it rest for the remainder of bulk fermentation, about 3 hours. If the dough felt weak (it was still shaggy and easily broke apart), set a timer for 30 minutes and give it another set of slaps and folds.

4. Chill the dough

▪ **Duration:** At least 2 hours or overnight in a home refrigerator: 39°F (4°C)

● **CHECK THE DOUGH:** It should have risen 20 to 30 percent. If it still looks dense, leave it for another 30 minutes in bulk fermentation and check again.

● **CHOOSE WHEN YOU WANT TO BAKE THE ROLLS:**

▪ Same-day bake: Place the bulk fermentation container in the refrigerator for 2 hours until the dough is cold and firm to the touch, which will make it much easier to roll out. If the dough still feels sticky or warm, refrigerate it for 30 minutes more and check again.

▪ Next-day bake: Put the bulk fermentation container in the refrigerator overnight.

5. Roll and divide

● **PREPARE THE BAKING PAN:** Liberally butter the bottom and sides of a 9-inch square baking pan. If your pan is not nonstick, line the pan with parchment paper.

● **PREPARE THE BROWN SUGAR CINNAMON FILLING:** In a medium bowl, whisk together the 175g dark brown sugar, 28g melted butter, 12g flour, 6g cinnamon, and small pinch of salt. Cover and set aside.

● **ROLL OUT THE DOUGH:** Scoop the dough out onto a floured work surface. Flour the top of the dough and roll it out into a square, about 15 × 15 inches. Spread the filling evenly over the dough leaving a 1-inch border along the edge farthest from you. Starting at the southeast corner, start rolling up the dough by folding up a small portion and then continuing to fold up the dough, working your way across that side until you reach the southwest corner to create a small, tight roll. Continue rolling until the dough is completely rolled, pressing to seal at the very end. The cylinder should measure 15 inches in length. Using a chef's knife, cut the cylinder every 1½ inches to make 9 pieces. I like to trim the rounded ends just barely to keep everything neat. Transfer the rolls to the prepared baking pan with equal spacing between them. Place the pan inside a reusable plastic bag and seal.

6. Proof

- **Duration:** About 2 hours 30 minutes at warm room temperature: 74°–76°F (23°–24°C)

- **LET THE DOUGH PROOF:** Put the pan in a warm place to proof for about 2 hours 30 minutes.

7. Bake

- **Duration:** 20 to 25 minutes in the oven

- **PREPARE THE OVEN:** Place an oven rack in the middle position and preheat the oven to 400°F (200°C).

- **CHECK THE ROLLS:** The rolls should have puffed and feel very soft to the touch. Uncover the dough and use a finger to poke it in a few places; if it doesn't feel puffy and soft, cover the pan again and let it proof 15 minutes more and check again.

- **BAKE THE ROLLS:** Place the uncovered pan in the oven. Bake for 20 to 25 minutes, or until the internal temperature reaches 192°F (89°C) and the tops have just started to turn a darker shade of brown.

- **PREPARE THE ICING:** In a medium bowl, whisk together 175g powdered sugar, 28g milk, 14g melted butter, and 2g vanilla until creamy and soft.

- **FINISH AND COOL:** Let the rolls cool in the pan for 5 to 10 minutes. I like to ice only the rolls I'm serving or eating right then; this way any uneaten rolls (if there are any!) can be saved in an airtight container for the next day. These are best still warm the day they're made, but they keep well in an airtight container for 1 to 2 days. You can also freeze the baked rolls (without icing), thaw in the refrigerator, and then reheat in the oven. Spread on the icing before serving.

HOW TO TINKER

CREAM CHEESE ICING

You can also top these with a cream cheese icing. In a stand mixer fitted with the whisk, beat together 114g (4 ounces) room-temperature cream cheese, 62g powdered sugar, 37g whole milk, and 2g (1 teaspoon) vanilla extract (optional) until creamy and soft.

COLD PROOF IN SHAPE

Another convenient way to prepare these rolls is to cover the pan of rolled and cut dough and place it in the fridge (again) to proof overnight. In the morning, take out the covered pan, let it proof as necessary until the dough is extremely soft to the touch, 2 to 2½ hours (temperature depending), then bake.

ITALIAN DOUGHNUTS
(Bomboloni)

Light, airy, and naturally leavened

THESE BOMBOLONI carry special significance for me, since they will forever remind me of the summertime trips my family made to southern Italy to visit relatives. We were fortunate enough to stay for weeks at a time, settling into a routine of late-night hide-and-seek with cousins, and even later meals around long dinner tables with plates of pasta, meat, and gelato in plastic cups. We spent the mornings scurrying from one bakery to the next, where I would order a bombolone with *crema pasticcera* (pastry cream) inside, still warm from the fryer.

These bomboloni (which means "bombs") are so soft and airy I imagine it must be what holding a cloud is like. The texture is light with a slight crispness when you bite through the briefly fried exterior. This recipe is a bit of a process, so I like to stretch it out over 3 days so the bomboloni are ready for eating warm in the morning on day three, but don't worry, most of the time is hands-off with the dough left to ferment.

BAKING TIMELINE

1. Levain

    12 hours (overnight)

2. Mix

3. Warm Bulk Fermentation

    7 hours

4. Cold Bulk Fermentation

    17 hours (overnight)

5. Divide and Shape

6. Warm Proof

    9 hours

7. Cold Proof

    15 hours (overnight)

8. Fry

    30 minutes

TOTAL

60 hours 30 minutes

VITALS

Total dough weight	1,100g
Pre-fermented flour	14.0%
Levain	40.8%
Hydration	20.0%
Yield	Sixteen 65g bomboloni

TOTAL FORMULA

INGREDIENT	BAKER'S %	WEIGHT
High-protein white flour (~12.7%-14% protein)	50.0%	271g
White flour (~11.5% protein)	50.0%	271g
Egg, beaten	37.0%	200g (about 4 medium)
Unsalted butter	20.0%	108g
Superfine sugar	20.0%	108g
Water	20.0%	108g
Fine sea salt	2.0%	11g
Ripe sourdough starter, 100% hydration	4.2%	23g

ADDITIONAL INGREDIENTS

Refined coconut oil (my preference), vegetable, or other high-heat frying oil, for deep-frying

200g granulated sugar and 2g (1 teaspoon) ground cinnamon, for rolling

Crema Pasticcera (page 403), for filling (optional)

INGREDIENT	BAKER'S %	WEIGHT
White flour (~11.5% protein)	100.0%	76g
Superfine sugar	20.0%	15g
Water	100.0%	76g
Ripe sourdough starter, 100% hydration	30.0%	23g

INGREDIENT	WEIGHT
High-protein white flour (~12.7%-14% protein)	271g
White flour (~11.5% protein)	195g
Egg, beaten	200g (about 4 medium)
Unsalted butter	108g
Superfine sugar	93g
Water	32g
Fine sea salt	11g
Levain	190g

Mixing

Due to the lengthy mixing time required to develop this dough, I highly recommend mixing in a spiral or stand mixer. Also, because this dough is very soft, instead of using the dough hook, use the paddle for more effective gluten development.

1. Levain

■ **Duration:** 12 hours (overnight) at warm room temperature: 74°–76°F (23°–24°C)

● **MIX THE LEVAIN:** Warm or cool the water to about 78°F (25°C). In a large bowl, mix the levain ingredients until well incorporated. This sweet levain (see page 76) will expand and rise considerably, so be sure to use a container that has plenty of room. Loosely cover and store in a warm place for 12 hours.

2. Mix

■ **Desired dough temperature (DDT):** 78°F (25°C)

● **CHECK THE LEVAIN:** It should show signs of readiness: It should have risen very high, be very bubbly, and be frothy. If your starter is not showing these signs, let it ferment 15 minutes more and check again.

● **PREPARE THE BUTTER:** Cut the butter into ½-inch-thick pats. Place the pats on a plate on the counter to warm to room temperature.

● **MIX THE DOUGH:** To the bowl of a stand mixer fitted with the paddle, add the flour, eggs, half of the sugar, the water, salt, and ripe levain. Mix on low speed for 1 to 2 minutes until combined. Increase the speed to medium and mix for 5 minutes until the dough begins to tighten, cling to the paddle, and pull from the sides. Let the dough rest for 10 minutes in the bowl.

● **ADD THE REMAINING SUGAR:** Add the remaining sugar and mix on low speed for 1 to 2 minutes until it is absorbed and the dough comes back together. Increase the speed to medium and mix for 3 to 6 minutes until the dough is smooth and strong. Use the Windowpane Test (page 83) to see if the dough is fully developed. If the dough does not spread clearly or tear cleanly, mix on medium speed for 2 to 4 minutes more and test again.

● **INCORPORATE THE BUTTER:** With the mixer running on low speed, add the butter, one pat at a time. Wait a few seconds between additions to let it incorporate into the dough. Scrape down the sides of the bowl and the paddle with a bowl scraper as needed. Continue until all the butter is added, about 6 minutes (be patient with this step and avoid adding too much butter too fast, which will cause the dough to break apart). Mix on medium speed for 2 minutes more until the dough smooths out and clings to the paddle. The dough will be silky smooth, elastic, and shiny, but will feel slightly tacky due to the enrichments. Transfer to a container for bulk fermentation.

● **MEASURE THE TEMPERATURE OF THE DOUGH:** Compare it to the DDT and record it as the final dough temperature. Cover the dough.

3. Warm bulk fermentation

- Duration: About 7 hours at warm room temperature: 74°–76°F (23°–24°C)
- Folds: 1 set of gentle slaps and folds after 1 hour of bulk fermentation

● **SET TIMER AND MAKE A NOTE:** Write down the current time as the start of bulk fermentation, set a timer for 1 hour, and let the dough rest in a warm place.

● **GENTLE SLAPS AND FOLDS:** When the timer goes off, scrape the dough onto a clean work surface and give it two to four gentle slaps and folds (see page 83 for more detail). The dough should be very smooth and taut. Round the dough a bit on the counter to gather it into a tight ball, then transfer it back to the bulk fermentation container.

● **LET THE DOUGH REST:** If the dough looked smooth and felt strong, let it rest for the remainder of bulk fermentation, about 6 hours. If the dough felt weak (it was still shaggy and easily broke apart), set a timer for 30 minutes and give it another set of slaps and folds as above.

4. Cold bulk fermentation

- Duration: About 17 hours (overnight) in a home refrigerator: 39°F (4°C)

● **MOVE THE DOUGH TO THE REFRIGERATOR:** After the warm bulk fermentation, place the covered bulk fermentation container in the refrigerator overnight.

5. Divide and shape

● **PREPARE THE PROOFING PANS:** Prepare two 13 × 18-inch half-sheet pans by dusting them with an even, thin layer of white flour.

● **DIVIDE THE DOUGH:** Take the bulk fermentation container out of the refrigerator and let it warm for 15 minutes. Uncover and use a bowl scraper to scrape the dough onto a clean work surface. The dough will feel cold and firm but still be pliable (if it's still very firm, let it warm for another 10 minutes and check again), which will make shaping it much easier. Divide the dough into 16 pieces of 65g each.

● **SHAPE THE DOUGH:** Using your hands, or one hand and your bench knife, shape each piece of dough into a smooth and very tight round. It's very important there be no visible seam at the bottom of each round; when you finish shaping a taut ball, flip it over and pinch closed any seam that may have formed. (See Soft Dough: Use a Bench Knife, page 109, for more detail.) Place the rounds on the prepared proofing pans, 8 per pan in 4 rows of 2, with even spacing between them. Place each pan inside a reusable plastic bag and seal.

6. Warm proof

- Duration: About 9 hours at warm room temperature: 74°–76°F (23°–24°C)

● **LET THE DOUGH PROOF:** Put the pans in a warm place to proof for about 9 hours. The dough is ready when it is puffed up and light. If you poke a piece with

RECIPE CONTINUES ⇢

Timing

Due to the high percentage of enrichments in this dough, the warm bulk fermentation is significantly longer to ensure sufficient fermentation before the dough is transferred to the refrigerator.

Shaping small rounds, soft dough, bench knife method

your finger, the indentation should slowly spring back. If the dough is still dense, tight, and the indentation doesn't stay depressed, let it proof 1 hour more and check again.

7. Cold proof

- ▪ **Duration:** About 15 hours (overnight) in a home refrigerator: 39°F (4°C)

- ● **LET THE DOUGH COLD PROOF:** Place the pans in the refrigerator overnight.

8. Fry

- ▪ **Duration:** 30 minutes

- ● **LET THE DOUGH WARM:** In the morning, remove the pans from the refrigerator and leave them to warm while you prepare your sugar mixture and frying oil.

- ● **PREPARE THE SUGAR COATING:** In a medium bowl, combine the 200g granulated sugar and 2g cinnamon.

- ● **CHECK THE DOUGH:** At this point, the dough should be very puffy and, if poked, feel light like a marshmallow. If it is dense, let it warm for 15 minutes more and check again.

- ● **HEAT THE OIL FOR FRYING:** Place a deep 3.2-quart or larger Dutch oven on the stove and fill it with frying oil just shy of two-thirds full. If you have one,

place a frying thermometer in the oil. Set the pot over medium heat and heat the oil until it reaches 360°-370°F (180°-185°C). For the best results, try to keep the temperature of the oil within this range.

- ● **PREPARE THE FRYING STATION:** Next to the Dutch oven, place a slotted spoon (or spider) for flipping and transferring the bomboloni, a timer, and a wire cooling rack set inside a sheet pan lined with several layers of paper towels.

- ● **FRY THE BOMBOLONI:** Use a thin spatula to *gently* transfer 3 pieces of dough to the oil. Flip each round over so the smooth, top side is facing down first in the oil—this will help the bomboloni rise evenly. Start your timer for 1½ minutes and let the dough balls fry until they are golden brown on the bottom Ⓐ. Then use your slotted spoon (or a chopstick) to flip them over Ⓑ. Fry the other side for another timed 1½ minutes until golden brown. Transfer the bomboloni to the wire rack. Bring the temperature of the oil back up to 360°-370°F (180°-185°C) and repeat with the remaining dough.

- ● **ROLL THE BOMBOLONI IN SUGAR:** Once the bomboloni are cool enough to handle, roll them in the cinnamon and sugar mixture. At this point, you can fill the bomboloni with *crema pasticcera* (opposite) or leave them as they are Ⓒ. They're best the day they are made but will also keep in a sealed paper bag for 1 day.

TROUBLESHOOTING

MY BOMBOLONI HAD HUGE BUBBLES WHEN I WAS FRYING; THEY WOULDN'T STAY ON ONE SIDE.

It's likely your dough was underproofed. Give the dough more time in warm proof to ensure it's fully proofed. If the first few pieces of dough you fry in the morning do this, hold off from doing the rest of the batch. Let the dough proof, covered, at warm temperature for an hour and then try again.

MY BOMBOLONI HAD BLISTERS ON THE SURFACE WHEN FRYING.

I see this from time to time and have yet to determine the cause. My guess is it is like bread dough that's been retarded and blisters when baking. These little blisters don't really cause any issue and, in my opinion, don't compromise the eating experience!

MY BOMBOLONI PUFFED UP WHEN FRYING, BUT THE INTERIOR WAS A LITTLE DENSE.

You likely needed to proof the dough longer. Next time, give the dough an extra hour in bulk fermentation before refrigerating, and then, if necessary, an extra hour in the warm proof stage after shaping.

HOW TO TINKER

CHOOSE A FILLING

These bomboloni can be filled with many different creams, jams/jellies (apricot, cherry, strawberry, etc.), and even Nutella. Or try my favorite, *crema pasticcera*.

Crema Pasticcera (Pastry Cream)

This *crema* is like a bowl of pure sunshine. You might be tempted to omit the lemon zest, but I highly recommend the addition. It will take at least an hour for this cream to cool and firm in the fridge before it can be used. If using to fill the bomboloni, be sure to make it in advance. The following makes enough *crema* to fill about half of the bomboloni, depending on how much you pipe into them. Double the recipe if you'd like them all filled.

INGREDIENT	WEIGHT
Whole milk	365g
White flour (~11.5% protein)	30g
Superfine sugar	100g
Fine sea salt	1g
Egg yolks	72g (about 2 yolks)
Vanilla extract	4g
Lemon zest	Zest of 1 lemon

In a saucepan, warm the milk over medium heat until bubbles start to form on the sides, but do not boil, about 5 minutes.

In a medium bowl, combine the flour, sugar, and salt. Add the egg yolks and whisk until incorporated and a thick paste forms. Pour the warm milk into the egg mixture a little bit at a time, whisking to incorporate after each addition. Pour the mixture back into the saucepan, set over medium heat, and cook, whisking constantly, until it just begins to boil, 4 to 6 minutes.

Using a fine-mesh sieve, strain the mixture into another bowl. Stir in the vanilla and lemon zest. Let cool completely.

Cover the bowl with plastic wrap, pressing it to the surface of the cream to prevent a skin from forming. Refrigerate until set, about 1 hour.

To fill the bomboloni, fill a piping bag with some *crema*, cut the side of each bomboloni with a paring knife, insert the piping bag tip, and squeeze to fill.

The *crema* will keep in an airtight container in the fridge for 3 to 4 days.

CINNAMON BABKA

A moist and rich enriched dough twisted around a cinnamon-spiced filling

BABKA IS a Central and Eastern European dessert made of a filled and twisted dough baked in a pan. My naturally leavened version is a sticky, gooey, and sinfully delicious treat. The enriched dough is ultra tender with swirls of sweet filling. There are many ways to fill this dough: you can add finely chopped nuts or the zest of an orange to the filling here, or even a splash of orange juice in the simple syrup glaze. See How to Tinker, page 409, for more ideas.

VITALS

Total dough weight	800g
Pre-fermented flour	12.9%
Levain	44.4%
Hydration	13.0%
Yield	One babka

BAKING TIMELINE

1 Levain

    3 hours

2 Mix

3 Warm Bulk Fermentation

    4 hours

4 Cold Bulk Fermentation

    12 hours (overnight)

5 Roll and Shape

6 Proof

    5 hours

7 Bake

    45 minutes

TOTAL
24 hours 45 minutes

TOTAL FORMULA

INGREDIENT	BAKER'S %	WEIGHT
White flour (~11.5% protein)	100.0%	357g
Whole milk (cold)	30.0%	107g
Egg (cold), beaten	30.0%	107g (about 2 medium)
Unsalted butter	28.0%	100g
Superfine sugar	8.1%	29g
Water	12.9%	46g
Fine sea salt	2.2%	8g
Ripe sourdough starter, 100% hydration	12.9%	46g

ADDITIONAL INGREDIENTS

Egg wash: 1 egg and 1 tablespoon of whole milk or heavy cream

CINNAMON FILLING

175g dark brown sugar

42g (3 tablespoons) unsalted butter, melted

12g white flour (~11.5% protein)

6g (2¼ teaspoons) ground cinnamon

Small pinch (¼ teaspoon) fine sea salt

SIMPLE SYRUP GLAZE

52g granulated sugar

52g water

INGREDIENT	BAKER'S %	WEIGHT
White flour (~11.5% protein)	100.0%	46g
Water	100.0%	46g
Ripe sourdough starter, 100% hydration	100.0%	46g

INGREDIENT	WEIGHT
White flour (~11.5% protein)	311g
Whole milk (cold)	107g
Egg (cold), beaten	107g (about 2 medium)
Unsalted butter	100g
Superfine sugar	29g
Fine sea salt	8g
Levain	138g

Temperature

The milk and eggs for this recipe are used cold, straight from the refrigerator, which helps offset the heat generated by using a mechanical mixer. At the end of mixing, the dough should have a final dough temperature of 78°F (25°C). If it ends up cooler, keep it in a warm spot in your kitchen for the first part of bulk fermentation and expect that it may need more time before being placed in the refrigerator. Conversely, if the final dough temperature is higher, keep the dough in a cooler spot and expect it may need to be placed in the refrigerator sooner.

1. Levain

▦ **Duration:** 3 hours at warm room temperature: 74°–76°F (23°–24°C)

● **MIX THE LEVAIN:** Warm or cool the water to about 78°F (25°C). In a medium jar, mix the levain ingredients until well incorporated (this liquid levain will feel quite loose) and loosely cover. Store in a warm place for 3 hours.

2. Mix

▦ **Desired dough temperature (DDT):** 78°F (25°C)

● **PREPARE THE BUTTER:** Cut the butter into ½-inch-thick pats. Place the pats on a plate on the counter to warm to room temperature.

● **CHECK THE LEVAIN:** It should now show signs of ripeness but not be overly ripe (it should be at a young stage): moderate bubbles on the surface, and a slight sour smell. If the levain is not showing these signs, let it ferment 30 minutes more and check again.

● **MIX THE DOUGH:** To the bowl of a stand mixer fitted with the dough hook, add the flour, milk, egg, half of the sugar, the salt, and ripe levain. Mix on low speed for 1 to 2 minutes until combined. Increase the speed to medium and mix for 3 to 4 minutes until the dough clings to the dough hook. If it doesn't, continue mixing for a few more minutes until the dough gains strength and clumps together. Let the dough rest for 10 minutes in the bowl.

● **TEST THE BUTTER:** Gently press a butter pat with your finger: It should easily show an indentation but not be wet or melted. If the butter is too warm, place it in the freezer for 5 minutes and test again. Conversely, if the butter is too firm, microwave it for 10 seconds to warm it, then check again.

● **INCORPORATE THE BUTTER:** With the mixer on low speed, add the butter, one pat at a time, until absorbed into the dough, scraping down the sides of the bowl and the dough hook as needed. Continue until all the butter is added, 5 to 8 minutes. Increase the speed to medium and mix for 1 to 2 minutes more until the dough smooths out and clings to the dough hook once again. The dough will be silky smooth, elastic, and a little shiny. Transfer to a container for bulk fermentation.

● **MEASURE THE TEMPERATURE OF THE DOUGH:** Compare it to the DDT and record it as the final dough temperature. Cover the dough.

3. Warm bulk fermentation

▦ **Duration:** 4 hours at warm room temperature: 74°–76°F (23°–24°C)
▦ **Folds:** 1 set of gentle slaps and folds after 1 hour of bulk fermentation

● **SET TIMER AND MAKE A NOTE:** Write down the current time as the start of bulk fermentation, set a timer for 1 hour, and let the dough rest in a warm place.

- **GENTLE SLAPS AND FOLDS:** When your timer goes off, give the dough one set of slaps and folds (see page 83 for more detail). Scrape the dough onto a clean work surface and give it two to four gentle slaps and folds. The dough should be very smooth and taut. Round it a bit on the counter to gather it into a tight ball, then transfer it back to the bulk fermentation container.

- **LET THE DOUGH REST:** If the dough looked smooth and felt strong, let it rest for the remainder of bulk fermentation, about 3 hours. If the dough felt weak (it was still shaggy and easily broke apart), set a timer for 30 minutes and give it another set of slaps and folds as above.

4. Cold bulk fermentation

Duration: About 12 hours (overnight) in a home refrigerator: 39°F (4°C)

- **CHECK THE DOUGH:** It should have risen 20 to 30 percent during the warm bulk fermentation. If it looks dense and tight, leave it for another 30 minutes at warm temperature and check again. When it looks well risen, cover the bulk fermentation container and place it in the refrigerator overnight.

5. Roll and shape

- **PREPARE THE CINNAMON FILLING:** In a medium bowl, whisk together the 175g dark brown sugar, 42g melted butter, 12g flour, 6g cinnamon, and a small pinch of salt.

- **PREPARE THE PAN:** Grease a 9 × 4 × 4-inch Pullman pan (or a 9 × 5 × 2¾-inch standard loaf pan) with butter or oil and line it with a piece of parchment paper so the paper comes up and over the two long edges of the pan. You may need to fold or cut the parchment to act like a "sling" across the bottom, with the long sides to be used as handles to lift out the babka and help prevent it from sticking.

- **ROLL OUT THE DOUGH:** Scoop the dough out onto a floured work surface. Flour the top and work quickly to roll the dough out to a rectangle about 10 × 24 inches, with one of the short sides facing you (see Rolling, page 396). Spread the filling evenly over the dough, leaving a 1-inch border along the short edge farthest from you. Starting at one of the corners nearest you, fold up a small portion of the dough, then work your way across the entire long side creating a small, tight roll. Continue rolling until the dough is completely rolled up, pressing to seal at the very end. Place the cylinder on a 13 × 18-inch half-sheet pan and put it in the freezer for 10 minutes to firm up. This will make cutting and twisting the dough much easier.

RECIPE CONTINUES →

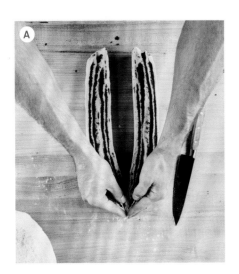

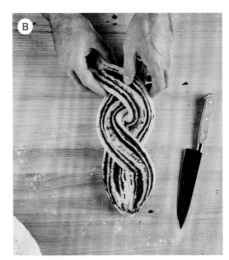

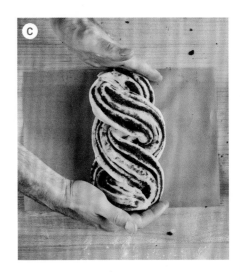

- **CUT AND TWIST THE DOUGH:** Remove the parchment paper from the Pullman pan and place it on the work surface; you will use it as a sling to lower the dough cleanly into the baking pan. Use a sharp knife to cut the cylinder in half down its length. Take the ends of the split cylinder at one side and pinch them together (A). Then twist the two halves of the cylinder over each other, working from top to bottom, then pinch the two ends together to seal (B). Place the twisted dough in the middle of the parchment paper, squishing the top and bottom, if necessary, to make it fit completely (C). Then pick up the two sides of the parchment sling and transfer the dough into the baking pan. Place the pan inside a reusable plastic bag and seal.

A Slow Dough

This can be a slow-moving dough due to the high percentage of enrichments, which interfere with natural fermentation. Be sure to give it sufficient time to proof.

6. Proof

- Duration: About 5 hours at warm room temperature: 74°–76°F (23°–24°C)

- **LET THE DOUGH PROOF:** Put the pan in a warm place to proof for about 5 hours. It is ready when it has risen to about 1 inch below the rim of the pan and feels very soft to the touch. If not, let proof 30 minutes more and check again.

7. Bake

- Duration: 40 to 45 minutes in the oven

- **PREPARE THE OVEN:** Place an oven rack in the middle position and preheat the oven to 350°F (175°C).

- **BAKE THE BABKA:** Make the egg wash by whisking together the egg and 1 tablespoon milk. Uncover the pan, use a pastry brush to gently brush on a thin layer of the egg wash, and slide the pan into the oven. Bake for 40 to 45 minutes, or until the internal temperature reaches 204°F (95°C), the top is deeply colored from the sugar in the filling, and the dough is shiny from the egg wash. If the top of the babka begins to color too rapidly, reduce the oven temperature to 325°F (160°C) and continue to bake until the internal temperature reaches the target.

- **PREPARE THE SIMPLE SYRUP GLAZE:** In a small saucepan, combine the 52g granulated sugar and 52g water and bring to a boil over medium heat. Let simmer, stirring occasionally, until the mixture turns clear, 2 to 4 minutes. Let cool to room temperature. The simple syrup can be stored in an airtight container in the refrigerator indefinitely.

- **FINISH AND COOL:** Transfer the pan to a wire rack. Using a plastic spatula, loosen the short sides of the babka (the sides without parchment) from the sides and bottom of the pan. Using a pastry brush, brush on a thin layer of the simple syrup—the more you add, the sweeter the crust will become. Let the babka rest for 10 minutes in the pan. Do not let it rest for longer than 10 minutes or it'll be hard to remove from the pan.

- **COOL THE BABKA:** Lift the babka out of the pan using the parchment paper sling. Remove the parchment paper and let the babka cool on a wire rack for about 20 minutes. It's even better if it sits for 1 hour to let the crust fully harden. The babka is best the day it's baked, but it keeps for several days in an airtight container at room temperature.

TROUBLESHOOTING

I DIDN'T END UP WITH A LOT OF SUGARY LAYERS INSIDE THE BABKA.

If you want more layers inside the center of the babka, after you slice the cylinder in half, turn one (or both) of the pieces on its side instead of having both with their cut sides facing up. Then twist the two pieces as indicated in the recipe.

MY BABKA DIDN'T RISE AND IS A LITTLE SQUAT!

Be sure you use a ripe starter to create the levain. Then keep the levain warm while it's ripening—at 78°F (25°C), if possible—and use it when it's ripe. Finally, give the dough the time it needs in warm bulk fermentation and in the final proof, even if that means more time than indicated in each step. If the dough was placed in the fridge for the cold bulk fermentation a little early, the final proof will take longer—let it proof until it rises to ½ inch, or less, below the rim of the pan.

HOW TO TINKER

CHOCOLATE BABKA FILLING

- 75g unsalted butter
- 110g granulated sugar
- 70g bittersweet chocolate, chopped
- 25g unsweetened Dutch process cocoa powder

In a medium saucepan, melt the butter over medium-low heat. Remove the pan from the heat and add the sugar and chocolate. Stir until the chocolate melts and the mixture is smooth. Add the cocoa powder and stir well. Set aside to cool until ready to use.

HAZELNUT BABKA FILLING

- 70g hazelnuts, toasted and skinned
- 30g unsalted butter, melted
- 140g granulated sugar
- ¼ teaspoon fine sea salt

In a food processor, process the hazelnuts until only very small bits remain (avoid overprocessing them). Transfer to a small bowl and add the melted butter, sugar, and salt. Mix and cover until ready to use.

CINNAMON-PECAN BABKA FILLING

- 140g granulated sugar
- 70g pecan meal or finely chopped toasted pecans
- 30g unsalted butter, melted
- 4g (2 teaspoons) ground cinnamon
- ¼ teaspoon fine sea salt

In a small bowl, combine all of the ingredients and mix well. Cover the filling until ready to use.

SUNDAY MORNING PANCAKES

Classic fluffy pancakes with increased flavor and tenderness

Makes 10 to 12 pancakes

INGREDIENT	WEIGHT
Eggs	108g (2 medium)
Whole milk	245g
Whole-milk yogurt, Greek or regular (optional)	60g
Ripe sourdough starter, 100% hydration (may use discard)	250g
Vanilla extract (optional)	4g (1 teaspoon)
All-purpose, einkorn, or a mix of all-purpose and whole wheat flour	180g
Baking soda	6g (1 teaspoon)
Baking powder	4g (1 teaspoon)
Fine sea salt	5g (1 teaspoon)
Granulated sugar	50g
Unsalted butter, melted and cooled	56g (½ stick), plus more for greasing

SOMEWHERE IN adulthood I transformed from a staunch waffle eater to an avid connoisseur of all things pancakes. When I was younger, I almost always passed on soft, pillowy pancakes, opting instead for crunchy waffles, with their deep pockets of maple syrup. This pancake recipe likely forced my conversion, and these days they grace our table just as often as my Buttermilk Waffles (page 412).

I've provided two options here. The first is a make-right-away version that's perfect anytime. The other calls for the batter to ferment overnight, which results in a little extra tang, a deeper flavor, and an extra-tender interior. Pancakes often require adjustment at the end of mixing to achieve the right consistency, and these are no different. You want the batter to just start to run off a spoon when tilted. If too thick, add a little milk to thin; if too thin, add a little more flour to thicken.

Morning-of Pancakes

- Separate the eggs into two medium bowls, one for the yolks and one for the whites. Lightly beat the yolks and add the milk, yogurt (if using), sourdough starter, and vanilla (if using). Stir to incorporate.

- In another medium bowl, whisk together the flour, baking soda, baking powder, salt, and sugar. Add the yolk mixture to the dry ingredients, stirring to incorporate. Stir in the melted butter.

- Whisk the egg whites to stiff peaks. Fold the egg whites into the batter (avoid overmixing).

- Melt a small pat of butter on a hot griddle or large skillet. For each pancake, drop about ¼ cup of batter onto the griddle and cook until bubbles start to form and remain open, 3 to 4 minutes. Flip the pancakes and cook until lightly browned, 4 more minutes. Transfer to a wire rack set inside an oven set to very low heat to keep warm.

Overnight Pancakes

- The night before, in a medium bowl, combine the milk, yogurt (if using), sourdough starter, flour, and sugar. Leave out on the counter to ferment overnight.

- In the morning, add the vanilla (if using), baking soda, baking powder, salt, and melted butter.

- Separate the eggs into two medium bowls, one for the yolks and one for the whites. Whisk the whites to stiff peaks. Lightly beat the yolks. Fold the yolks and beaten egg whites into the batter just before cooking the pancakes as directed above.

HOW TO TINKER

CORNMEAL PANCAKES

Substitute 100g of the flour with cornmeal. To make these savory, omit the sugar and in the morning fold in a chopped and seeded jalapeño, diced scallions, and ½ cup shredded cheddar cheese. Top with more shredded cheese and sour cream or Greek yogurt.

BUTTERMILK WAFFLES

Crispy, golden, and
gently sour

LIKE THE PANCAKES, this recipe can be made two ways: with an over-night fermentation or start-to-finish in the morning. As you probably guessed, the version with the overnight fermentation leads to a tangier waffle (in the best way possible) and breakfast that's halfway prepared. But if spontaneity is your thing—and let's be honest, some weekends are best left to a no-plan plan—this recipe still makes for the best breakfast. Speaking of, if you don't have butter-milk, substitute with half whole milk and half yogurt (Greek or regular).

I usually double this recipe to make extra waffles, which freeze and reheat in a toaster incredibly well. To freeze, let them cool completely on a wire rack and then stack them in a freezer-safe bag, seal, and put in the freezer. During the week, take out one or two waffles and reheat them directly in a toaster (preferably one with a "frozen" mode).

Makes 10 to 12 waffles

INGREDIENT	WEIGHT
All-purpose flour	250g
Granulated sugar	14g
Fine sea salt	5g (1 teaspoon)
Baking soda	3g (½ teaspoon)
Buttermilk	460g, plus 50g to thin the batter if needed
Unsalted butter, melted and cooled	85g (6 tablespoons)
Ripe sourdough starter, 100% hydration (may use discard)	100g
Eggs, at room temperature	108g (2 medium)

Morning-of Waffles

● Preheat a waffle iron according to the manufacturer's instructions.

● In a large bowl, whisk together the flour, sugar, salt, and baking soda. In a separate medium bowl, whisk together 460g of the buttermilk, the melted butter, sourdough starter, and eggs.

● Pour the buttermilk mixture into the flour mixture and whisk until only a few small clumps remain (it's okay if the mixture isn't completely smooth). If necessary, use some of the remaining 50g of buttermilk to loosen the batter until it can slowly pour from a spoon.

● Cook in the hot waffle iron until done to your liking.

Overnight Waffles

● The night before, in a large bowl, combine the 460g buttermilk and the melted butter. Add the sourdough starter and mix thoroughly (use a whisk if needed). Sprinkle the sugar over the top and add the flour, a little at a time, while whisking to incorporate. If necessary, use some of the remaining 50g of buttermilk to loosen the batter until it can slowly pour from a spoon. Cover and let sit at room temperature overnight (however, if your kitchen is warmer than 72°F/22°C, place the covered bowl in the refrigerator overnight).

● In the morning, the batter will have risen in the bowl and show signs of strong fermentation: bubbles on top and a smell not unlike that of yogurt. Preheat a waffle iron according to the manufacturer's instructions.

● Sprinkle the salt and baking soda on top of the batter. Lightly beat the eggs, pour into the fermented batter, and gently stir until incorporated.

● Cook in the hot waffle iron until done to your liking.

HOW TO TINKER

PLAYING WITH THE FLOUR

Tinkering with the flour in this recipe is always fun; I've used just about every type of flour that's found its way through my pantry over the years and the following are my favorites:

- Buckwheat waffles: Substitute 100g of the flour with buckwheat flour.

- Healthyish wheat waffles: Substitute 75g of the flour with raw wheat germ.

- Cornmeal waffles: Substitute 75g of the flour with cornmeal.

SAVORY WAFFLES

Omit the sugar in the recipe and proceed as directed. These are great with sunny-side up eggs, bacon, feta cheese, scallions, fried chicken, sausage and gravy, and so much more. One favorite of mine: Fold grated parmesan cheese and thinly sliced scallions into the batter.

SOURDOUGH SCONES

Subtle sweetness paired with a flaky and moist texture

I MIGHT have started by saying these scones are simply an easy way to use up your daily (or weekly) sourdough starter discard (see Saving and Using Discard, page 37), but the truth is, they are much more than that. They're a wonderful morning or brunch snack that's flexible enough to work with almost any dried fruit in the pantry or fresh seasonal fruit. These scones are not the dry and brittle variety; rather, they're soft, flaky, and have a touch of sweetness. If you don't stock buttermilk, you can use heavy cream (preferred) or whole milk instead.

Makes 8 triangular scones

INGREDIENT	WEIGHT
All-purpose flour	300g
Granulated sugar	78g
Fine sea salt	Small pinch (⅛ teaspoon)
Baking powder	15g (3 teaspoons)
Cold unsalted butter, cut into ½-inch pats	186g (1½ sticks plus 1 tablespoon)
Dried cherries	75g
Egg	54g (1 medium)
Ripe sourdough starter, 100% hydration (may use discard)	87g
Buttermilk	75g
Turbinado sugar, for sprinkling	12g to 24g (1 to 2 tablespoons)

● Preheat the oven to 400°F (200°C). Line a sheet pan with parchment paper.

● In a large bowl, whisk together the flour, sugar, salt, and baking powder. Add the butter pieces and toss to coat. Using a pastry blender or your fingers, cut the butter into the flour until the butter is the size of small peas. Mix in the dried cherries.

● In a medium bowl, whisk together the egg, sourdough starter, and buttermilk. Add the egg mixture to the flour mixture and stir to combine. Use your hands to form the dough into a large ball and then turn it out onto a lightly floured work surface. Shape the dough into a round about 1 inch thick. Using a knife or bench scraper, cut the round into 8 triangles like you would slice a pizza (cut in half, then quarters, then eighths). Transfer the triangles to the prepared sheet pan with space in between, alternating the direction of each triangle. Sprinkle the turbinado sugar on top of the triangles and place the sheet pan in the refrigerator for 15 minutes.

● Bake the scones 25 to 30 minutes, or until golden. These are best the day they're made (especially when warm from the oven).

HOW TO TINKER

WHOLE-GRAIN SPELT BLUEBERRY SCONES

Substitute half of the all-purpose flour with whole-grain spelt. Swap out the dried cherries for fresh blueberries and add the zest of 1 lemon. Hold back 1 tablespoon of the flour and toss the blueberries in this flour before adding them to help prevent the berries from sinking to the bottom during baking.

CRÊPES

Thin and light with a luxurious butter, egg, and vanilla aroma

THESE SOURDOUGH crêpes are ethereal and lacy like sheets of translucent paper. When I was a kid, sleepy weekend mornings usually meant I'd find my mom in the kitchen swirling her wide pan to create a tall stack of warm, French-style crêpes. The aroma in the kitchen was rich with egg and a tinge of browned butter, a fragrance capable of summoning even devoted weekend sleepers. We'd often enjoy them first with a thin layer of butter, then a thicker slather of her homemade peach or apricot preserves. After adding the filling, we would roll them up and arrange them side by side, sometimes with a final dusting of powdered sugar. These days I find myself rising early on the weekends to swirl the pan, but I still enjoy these simply with butter and homemade preserves. They're also quite wonderful with a thick spread of ricotta and a mixture of chopped fresh fruit, a little sugar, and a dash of lemon juice.

Makes 10 crêpes

INGREDIENT	WEIGHT
Pastry flour or all-purpose flour	120g
Fine sea salt	3g (½ teaspoon)
Granulated or superfine sugar	13g
Eggs	108g (2 medium)
Whole milk	160g
Ripe sourdough starter, 100% hydration (may use discard)	75g
Unsalted butter, melted and slightly cooled	70g (½ stick plus 1 tablespoon)
Vanilla extract	4g (1 teaspoon)
Clarified butter (or ghee) or unsalted butter, for greasing	28g (about 2 tablespoons)
Powdered sugar, for serving (optional)	

● In a medium bowl, combine the flour, salt, and sugar. Add the eggs and about half of the milk, and whisk well. Add the rest of the milk, the sourdough starter, melted butter, and vanilla and whisk until smooth. The batter should be fluid (it should run off a spoon like oil) and without lumps. Cover and refrigerate for about 30 minutes (or overnight).

● Place an 8-inch seasoned steel crêpe pan or a well-seasoned 8-inch skillet over medium heat for a few minutes. When it's ready, a small drop of clarified butter (or ghee) put into the pan will just start to show whisps of smoke.

Tilt the pan or use a paper towel to coat the bottom with clarified butter. Pour about ⅓ cup of batter into the center of the pan with one hand while you immediately lift and swirl the pan with the other hand to form a thin layer of batter on the bottom. Set the pan over the heat and cook until the top begins to look dry, 1½ to 2 minutes. Using a thin spatula, gently flip the crêpe and cook for 1 minute more. Crêpes should be very thin, lightly browned, and soft with a lacy texture. Serve immediately, dusted with powdered sugar if desired.

TROUBLESHOOTING

WHEN COOKED, MY CRÊPES LOOK UNIFORM IN COLOR, AND I'M NOT GETTING THAT LACY LOOK!

Usually, you'll get this result when the pan is not hot enough and/or there isn't enough butter in it when the crêpes are first cooked. Often, one side has this look and the other does not, so fill the crêpes so the lacy side faces out.

HOW TO TINKER

ALTERNATE FILLINGS

Try any of the following for your sweet crêpes:

▪ Mascarpone with any chopped, fresh fruit

▪ Nutella and sliced strawberries or bananas

▪ Whipped cream and peaches

417

BANANA BREAD 2.0

Rich and moist with subtle
notes of caramel and spice

I DEVELOPED a sourdough banana bread recipe years ago to find a use for my sourdough starter discard. This version is 2.0 because it's an evolution of the first recipe I published on my blog many years ago. This iteration is moister, richer, and has completely supplanted any other quick bread in my kitchen. One of the ingredients that helps amp up the flavor is dark brown sugar, which has great richness due to the amount of molasses in it. In a pinch, you can use granulated sugar.

This banana bread is also an excellent way to use up flour stragglers from the pantry: I usually blend a majority of all-purpose flour with whatever little bits of flour are hanging around. Whole spelt, whole wheat, durum, and einkorn are excellent choices.

Makes 1 loaf

INGREDIENT	WEIGHT
Butter, for greasing	
Walnuts (or pecans), coarsely chopped	125g
Dark brown sugar	125g
Very ripe bananas	365g (about 4)
Ripe sourdough starter, 100% hydration (may use discard)	100g
Honey	40g
Extra-virgin olive oil	125g
Vanilla extract	2g (1 teaspoon)
Eggs	108g (2 medium)
All-purpose flour, whole spelt flour, whole wheat flour, or a mix	225g
Baking soda	3g (½ teaspoon)
Fine sea salt	3g (½ teaspoon)
Ground cinnamon	3g (1 teaspoon)
Ground cloves (optional)	Small pinch (⅛ teaspoon)

● Preheat the oven to 350°F (175°C). Grease a 9 × 4 × 4-inch Pullman pan or 9 × 5 × 2¾-inch loaf pan with butter (unless it has a nonstick liner).

● In a small bowl, combine 30 grams of the walnuts with a few large pinches of the brown sugar. Set the topping mixture aside.

● In a medium bowl, combine the bananas and sourdough starter and use an immersion blender to blend until smooth. (Alternatively, use a potato masher or the back of a fork to mash everything to a smooth puree.)

● In a large bowl, whisk together the honey, oil, vanilla, remaining brown sugar, and the eggs. Stir in the banana puree.

● In a medium bowl, whisk together the flour, baking soda, salt, cinnamon, and cloves (if using). Fold the flour mixture into the banana mixture and then stir in the remaining walnuts. Pour the batter into the prepared pan and smooth the top with a spatula. Sprinkle on the reserved walnut/brown sugar topping.

● Bake for 55 to 65 minutes, or until the internal temperature reaches 200°–205°F (93°–96°C). Let the loaf cool in the pan for 10 minutes. Remove the loaf from the pan and gently transfer it to a wire rack to thoroughly cool before slicing.

HOW TO TINKER

ZUCCHINI AND CHOCOLATE CHIP

Substitute the banana for 300g shredded zucchini and swap out the walnuts for 55g semisweet chocolate chips. Instead of blending the sourdough starter with the banana, add the starter to the egg mixture and stir to combine. Add the zucchini to the egg mixture just before folding in the flour.

MAKE INTO MUFFINS

Divide the dough into the 12 cups of a standard muffin tin lined with paper liners and bake for 25 minutes, or until the tops are golden. If you want, top the muffins with a quick streusel instead: Combine 50g all-purpose flour, 50g room-temperature unsalted butter, 25g brown sugar, and ⅛ teaspoon salt and mix well. Sprinkle over the muffins just before baking.

PEACH AND BLUEBERRY CROSTATA

A buttery and flaky crust for sweet and savory fillings

A CROSTATA is a casual dessert that comes together quickly and easily. If you're familiar with galettes and pies, you'll be right at home here. The addition of a sourdough starter isn't intended to ferment this dough in any way; it adds a very subtle sourness and significant tenderness. Once you make this crust, you might find returning to crusts without sourdough a thing of the past. Plus, this dough can be used for pie, too: The recipe makes enough for a single-crust pie; just double the ingredients for a double-crust pie.

Here, I've provided my favorite summertime crostata: peach and blueberry. But this crust works well with lots of different fillings, both sweet and savory.

Makes 1 crostata

INGREDIENT	WEIGHT
CRUST	
All-purpose flour	175g
Granulated sugar	7g (1½ teaspoons)
Fine sea salt	3g (½ teaspoon)
Unsalted butter, cold	113g (1 stick)
Ripe sourdough starter, 100% hydration (may use discard)	115g
Cold water	37g (3 tablespoons)
FILLING	
Peaches, sliced	450g (3 to 4 medium)
Fresh blueberries	150g
Fresh lemon juice	14g (1 tablespoon)
Granulated sugar	50g
Cornstarch	5g (2 teaspoons)
Fine sea salt	3g (½ teaspoon)
TO FINISH	
Egg wash: 1 egg and 1 tablespoon of whole milk or heavy cream	
Coarse sugar, for sprinkling	

● **MAKE THE CRUST:** In a large bowl, whisk together the flour, sugar, and salt. Cut the butter into small cubes. Add the butter and lightly toss to coat with flour. Using a pastry blender or your fingers, cut the butter into the flour until the butter is the size of small peas. Add the sourdough starter and water. Stir with a spatula until well combined. The dough should just come together, but if it's still very dry, add more water, 1 tablespoon at a time, as needed.

● Scrape the dough onto a clean work surface and gather and gently knead it into a disc shape. Tightly wrap the disc in plastic wrap and refrigerate for 2 hours (or overnight) before rolling out.

● **MAKE THE FILLING:** In a large bowl, combine the peaches, blueberries, lemon juice, sugar, cornstarch, and salt.

● Preheat the oven to 400°F (200°C). Line a 13 × 18-inch half-sheet pan with parchment paper.

● Unwrap the dough and place it on a lightly floured work surface. Using a rolling pin, roll the dough out into a round about 12 inches in diameter. Transfer to the lined sheet pan. Scoop the filling into the center of the crust, leaving a 2-inch border all around. Then fold the border of the crust up over the filling in a series of pleats as you make your way around the crostata. Refrigerate for 30 minutes.

● **TO FINISH:** In a small bowl, whisk together the egg and milk. Remove the crostata from the refrigerator and brush the egg wash onto the crust. Sprinkle the coarse sugar over the crust and on top of the fruit.

● Bake for 40 minutes, or until the juices are bubbling and the crust is golden brown. Let cool for 25 to 30 minutes and serve warm.

CHERRY-ALMOND BISCOTTI

Crunchy, flaky, and sweet twice-baked cookies, perfect for your morning cappuccino

I REMEMBER complaining to my Italian grandmother once that the biscotti she made were so hard I had to soak them in coffee before I could eat them. With her huge '70s-style glasses and red, white, and green apron (not kidding), she looked over as she easily crunched right through a biscotti, smugly replying, "They're not good if they don't threaten to break a tooth." While it was hard to argue with her when it came to food—especially Italian food, and especially food she made from scratch—I've made my sourdough version less likely to send you on a visit to the dentist. Self-restraint seems to melt away with these biscotti, and if you venture to add inclusions like dried cherries, you're in even more trouble.

This recipe calls for 75g of almond flour (preferably made from raw almonds with skins on, not blanched), which adds a flaky consistency to the biscotti and a small measure of almond flavor. If you don't have almond flour, feel free to substitute with all-purpose flour.

Makes about 25 biscotti

INGREDIENT	WEIGHT
Whole almonds, raw	100g
All-purpose flour	300g
Almond flour, preferably with skins	75g
Baking powder	7g (1½ teaspoons)
Whole anise seed	2g (1 teaspoon)
Fine sea salt	Small pinch (¼ teaspoon)
Unsalted butter, at room temperature	113g (1 stick)
Granulated sugar	150g
Eggs	162g (3 medium)
Ripe sourdough starter, 100% hydration (may use discard)	50g
Anise extract	2g (1 teaspoon)
Sweetened dried sour cherries (or cranberries)	75g
Whole milk, for egg wash	A splash

● Preheat the oven to 350°F (175°C). Line a 13 × 18-inch half-sheet pan with parchment paper.

● Spread the whole almonds out on a separate sheet pan. Toast for 8 to 10 minutes, until fragrant. Let cool and then coarsely chop and set aside.

● In a medium bowl, whisk together the all-purpose flour, almond flour, baking powder, anise seed, and salt.

● In a stand mixer fitted with the paddle, combine the butter and sugar. Beat on medium speed until light and fluffy, about 2 minutes. Add 2 of the eggs, one at a time, and beat on low speed until incorporated. Add the sourdough starter and anise extract. Beat on low speed until combined. Add the flour mixture and beat on low speed until just combined (be careful not to overmix). Use a spatula to stir in the cherries and reserved toasted almonds.

● Scoop the dough onto a lightly floured surface. Lightly flour the top and then divide the dough in half. Shape each half into a flat rectangle about 9 × 4½ inches and ½ inch thick. Put the rectangles on the prepared sheet pan parallel to the short sides of the pan, with a few inches between them.

● In a small bowl, whisk the remaining egg and a splash of whole milk and brush the egg wash in a thin layer on the top of each rectangle. Then gently flip the rectangles over and brush egg wash on the bottom. Flip them back over.

● Bake for 15 minutes. Remove the pan from the oven and gently flip the rectangles over. Bake for 15 minutes more, or until they're a deep golden yellow.

● Remove the pan from the oven and let cool for 5 minutes. (Leave the oven on.) Transfer the rectangles to a cutting board and cut into ¾-inch-thick slices. Set the slices back on the sheet pan cut-side down. Bake for 5 minutes. Flip each cookie over. Bake 5 minutes more, until the biscotti are a light golden brown with hazelnut-colored edges. Transfer the biscotti to a wire rack to cool.

RESOURCES

Flour

Barton Springs
bartonspringsmill.com

Cairnspring Mills
cairnspring.com

Carolina Ground
carolinaground.com

Central Milling
centralmilling.com
Type 00 flour used in Sourdough Pizza Dough, page 294

Giusto's Vita-Grain
giustos.com

Grist and Toll
gristandtoll.com

Hayden Flour Mills
haydenflourmills.com

King Arthur Baking Company
kingarthurbaking.com
Rye chops used in Roggenvollkornbrot, page 288, diastatic malt powder, flour, and many other ingredients and tools

Maine Grains
mainegrains.com

Other Ingredients and Tools

Amazon.com
Food-grade lye, culinary-grade lava rocks, seeds, and other tools

Equipment

Brød & Taylor
brodandtaylor.com
Folding proofer and other tools

Challenger Breadware
challengerbreadware.com
High-quality baking pans for trapping steam and other baking tools

Lloyd Pans
lloydpans.com
Excellent pans for pizza and rolls

Pleasant Hill Grain
pleasanthillgrain.com
KoMo grain mill, mechanical mixers, ovens, and more

San Francisco Baking Institute
sfbi.com
Proofing baskets, including 12-inch baskets for larger loaves like a miche, and many other breadmaking tools

Thermoworks
thermoworks.com
Excellent thermometers (Thermapen), timers, and more

USA Pan
usapan.com
Pullman loaf pan, focaccia pan, and other baking pans

Additional Baking Information

The Bread Bakers Guild of America
bbga.org
Formulas and technical articles about every facet of baking, plus a lively baking community

The Perfect Loaf
theperfectloaf.com
On my website you'll find a whole suite of baking tools, including a downloadable baking notes template, a mixing water temperature calculator, my baker's math spreadsheets, and more.

References and Further Reading

Calvel, Raymond. *The Taste of Bread.* Aspen Publishers, 2001.

Faber, Abram, Craig Ponsford, and Jeffrey Yankellow. "Formatting Guild Formulas," *Bread Lines.* The Bread Bakers Guild of America. https://www.bbga.org /files/2009FormulaFormattingSINGLES.pdf

Gänzle, Michael G., Jussi Loponen, and Marco Gobbetti. "Proteolysis in Sourdough Fermentations: Mechanisms and Potential for Improved Bread Quality," *Trends in Food Science & Technology* 19 (2008):513–21. DOI: https://doi.org/10.1016/j.tifs.2008.04.002

Gänzle, Michael, Michaela Ehmann, and Walter Hammes. "Modeling of Growth of Lactobacillus sanfranciscensis and Candida milleri in Response to Process Parameters of Sourdough Fermentation," *Applied and Environmental Microbiology* 64 (1998):2616–23. DOI: https://doi.org/10.1128 /AEM.64.7.2616-2623.1998

Gianotti, A., L. Vannini et al. "Modelling of the Activity of Selected Starters During Sourdough Fermentation," *Food Microbiology* 14 (1997):327–37. DOI: https://doi .org/10.1006/fmic.1997.0099

Gobetti, Marco. "The Sourdough Microflora: Interactions of Lactic Acid Bacteria and Yeasts," *Trends in Food Science & Technology* 9 (1998): 267–74. DOI: https://doi.org/10.1016/S0924-2244 (98)00053-3

Gobbetti, Marco, Maria De Angelis, and Maria Calasso. "Novel Insights on the Functional/Nutritional Features of the Sourdough Fermentation," *International Journal of Food Microbiology* 302 (2018):1–11. DOI: https://doi.org/10.1016/j.ijfoodmicro.2018.05.018

Gobbetti, Marco., A. Corsetti, and J. Rossi. "The Sourdough Microflora. Interactions Between Lactic Acid Bacteria and Yeasts: Metabolism of Amino Acids," *World Journal of Microbiology & Biotechnology* 10 (1994):275–79. DOI: 10.1007/BF00414862

Gobbetti, Marco, and Michael Gänzle. *Handbook on Sourdough Biotechnology.* Springer, 2013.

Gobbetti, Marco, M. S. Simonetti, et al. "Volatile Compound and Organic Acid Productions by Mixed Wheat Sour Dough Starters: Influence of Fermentation Parameters and Dynamics During Baking," *Food Microbiology* 12 (1995):497–507. DOI: https://doi .org/10.1016/S0740-0020(95)80134-0

Hamelman, Jeffrey. *Bread.* John Wiley, 2013.

Landis, Elizabeth A. "The Diversity and Function of Sourdough Starter Microbiomes," *eLife* (January 26, 2021). Accessed March 25, 2021. https://elifesciences .org/articles/61644.DOI: 10.7554/eLife.61644

Miller, R. A., and R. C. Hoseney. "Role of Salt in Baking," *Cereal Foods World* 53, no. 1 (2008):4–6. DOI: 10.1094 /CFW-53-1-0004

Salovaara, H., and T. Valijakka. "The Effect of Fermentation Temperature, Flour Type, and Starter on the Properties of Sour Wheat Bread," *International Journal of Food Science and Technology* 22 (1987):592.

Spicher, Gottfried, and Werner Nierle. "Proteolytic Activity of Sourdough Bacteria," *Applied Microbiology and Biotechnology* 28 (1988):487–92. DOI: https://doi .org/10.1007/BF00268220

Venturi, F., A. G. Sanmartin, and A. Zinnia. "The Kinetics of Fermentations in Sourdough Bread Stored at Different Temperature and Influence on Bread Quality," *Bioprocessing & Techniques* 3 (2013):1–5. DOI: http://dx.doi.org/10.4172/2155-9821.1000134

Wink, Debra. "Fermentations in Sourdough," *The Fresh Loaf* (August 2021).

ACKNOWLEDGMENTS

This book is the result of more than ten years of my constant obsession with all things natural fermentation. And while this book has my name on the cover, it's the result of endless help from many others. It's hard to thank everyone who has contributed, but here's a start:

My parents, grandparents, and all my family back in Italy for inspiring me from a young age to cherish and appreciate good food and, ultimately, to return to food in earnest. My wife, Pooja, and our two sons, Luca and Avi, for your patience while I spent countless hours writing, testing, photographing, and baking for this book. Luca and Avi—I hope this book inspires you to follow your passions just as I have. And if it's bread, even better.

Margie Laughlin for helping to review the manuscript and test many recipes, and for our conversations about the mysteries of sourdough through the years. Your words of advice, constant encouragement, and willingness to help with anything have always been appreciated.

Ian Pope for checking the manuscript and my endless spreadsheets, and for our conversations through the years about anything and everything sourdough.

Ian Lowe for reviewing the manuscript and for inspiring bakers with your enthusiasm, dedication, and depth of knowledge in breadmaking.

Debbie Wink for your keen review of this manuscript, reminding me to focus on the mission for the book and helping me to keep all the science in check—as you often say, *It's never that simple with living things.*

My editor, Jenn Sit, for helping me shape a large manuscript into a tidy, very bakeable result. Jenn, you went the distance making your own starter and your very first loaves from this book. Thank you (and Rich!) for that. Ashley Meyer, your sharp edits to the recipes helped keep them consistent and much more readable.

The entire team at Clarkson Potter for making this beautifully designed book a reality: Jen Wang for turning endless tables and my writing into something beautiful, production editor Christine Tanigawa for your attention to the smallest details, production manager Kelli Tokos, marketer Allison Renzulli, and publicist Erica Gelbard.

Aubrie Pick for making some of the most wonderful images for this book while I was busy mixing, mixing, mixing. There's an espresso here for you anytime you stop by. And Claire Mack for sending boxes (and boxes) of beautiful props.

My test bakers Karen Bachrach, Margie Laughlin, Kyle Renalds, and Robert Woerne, thank you for your time and your help ironing out the kinks in many of the recipes throughout this book.

All my fellow bakers on Instagram, thanks for creating a community of like-minded bakers who are supportive and inclusive, who never fail to keep baking exciting, and who keep us all pushing the craft forward.

All the bakers mentioned in this book, and those unmentioned, for inspiring this engineer to return to food, engage my hands, and bake bread that's nourishing, delicious, and fulfilling.

And finally, to all the visitors who've stopped by *The Perfect Loaf* over the past ten-plus years, thank you for trusting my recipes and letting me into your kitchens.

INDEX

Note: Page references in *italics* indicate recipe photographs. Page references in **boldface** indicate QR code tutorials.

Published in the United States by Clarkson
Potter/Publishers, an imprint of Random
House, a division of Penguin Random House
LLC, New York.
ClarksonPotter.com
RandomHouseBooks.com

CLARKSON POTTER is a trademark and
POTTER with colophon is a registered
trademark of Penguin Random House LLC.

Photographs on pages 16, 30, 31, 33, 35,
45–48, 51, 53, 55, 61, 69, 70, 76, 82, 83,
90, 94, 97, 103, 104, 106, 107, 109, 111, 112,
125, 134, 141, 245, 255, 261, 286, 297, 317,
348, 371, 378, 402, and 417 are courtesy of
the author.

Library of Congress Cataloging-in-
Publication Data is available upon request.

ISBN 978-0-593-13841-0
Ebook ISBN 978-0-593-13842-7

Printed in China

Book Credits
Food stylist: Maurizio Leo
Prop stylist: Claire Mack
Editor: Jennifer Sit
Editorial assistant: Bianca Cruz
Cover and interior designer: Jen Wang
Production editor: Christine Tanigawa
Production manager: Kelli Tokos
Compositor: Merri Ann Morrell
Copy editor: Kate Slate
Indexer: Elizabeth Parson
Marketer: Allison Renzulli
Publicist: Erica Gelbard

Cover photographs by Aubrie Pick

10 9 8 7 6 5 4 3 2 1

First Edition